Foreword

It has not been common for educational planners, administrators, and school officials to view teachers as significant agents in the process of educational reform. On the contrary, the dominant approach has been to "train" teachers to be efficient implementers of policies and practices developed by others who are removed from the classroom. From this perspective, there has been little interest in developing the capabilities of teachers to exercise their judgment about educational matters in or outside of the classroom. Teachers are not taught to acquire the dispositions and self-monitoring skills that will enable them to learn from their practice and become better teachers throughout their teaching careers.

This top-down approach to educational reform has not been very successful in influencing what goes on in classrooms. Announcing changes in schooling—even demanding these—will not change what happens in schools and classrooms if teachers resist and subvert these changes. If one conclusion can be drawn from educational reform efforts over the last 30 years, it is that qualitative changes in classroom practice will occur only when teachers understand them and accept them as their own. During the last decade, a movement has been underway throughout the world to prepare teachers to be reflective practitioners who play a much more significant role in determining what goes on in schools (e.g., the purposes and end of their work, the curriculum) and in the process of educational reform. This concept of the teacher as reflective practitioner means that the process of understanding and improving one's teaching must start from reflection on one's own experience. Furthermore, the process of learning to teach continues throughout a teacher's career. The implication of this view is that teacher education programs need to prepare teachers from the very beginning to aim for this new, more expanded role and to help them acquire the dispositions and skills that will enable them to learn from their practice.

This book focuses on preparing teachers to be the kind of reflective practitioner that has increasingly become the goal in teacher education programs throughout the world. It rejects the limited role of "teacher as technician" who only implements in a passive way what others decide. It argues that teachers also have an important role to play in designing and interpreting curricular and instructional guidelines and educational reforms. An important theme throughout this book is the goal of working for a high quality of education for all children, something that we have not been able to achieve to date in any society in the world. The achievement of an educational system in which the quality of education received is not dependent on one's ethnic background, race, gender, social class, or religion is necessary for the realization of a democratic and just society.

This book recognizes that the teacher's role is not limited to the classroom and includes attention to such important issues as the broader context of the school and relations with parents and the community. One of the strengths of this book is that its structure and organization are consistent with its message.

The various activities for prospective teachers that have been built into each chapter encourage a very active and reflective role for those who use them. This consistency between the message and the method is often lacking in teacher education programs, which serves to undermine the achievement of one's goals. The wealth of material in this book will assist prospective teachers to become the kind of educational leaders that are necessary for the 21st century.

Ken Zeichner
Madison, Wisconsin

371.
102

371.102

£22.99
4 24398

AB

St...hing

SECOND EDITION

A Proce...Practice

Rose A. Howard
Bellarmine University

Marie M. Sanders
Bellarmine University

Foreword by Ken Zeichner

PEARSON

Merrill
Prentice Hall

Upper Saddle River, New Jersey
Columbus, Ohio

Library of Congress Cataloging-in-Publication Data

Goethals, M. Serra
    Student teaching: a process approach to reflective practice/M. Serra Goethals, Rose A.
Howard, Marie M. Sanders.- 2nd ed.
    p. cm.
    ISBN 0-13-098744-1 (pbk.)
    1. Student teaching-Handbooks, manuals, etc. 2. Teachers-Training of—Handbooks,
manuals, etc. I. Howard, Rose A. II. Sanders, Marie M. III. Title.
LB2157.A3G57 2004
370'.71-dc21   2002044480

Vice President and Executive Publisher: Jeffrey W. Johnston
Executive Editor: Debra A. Stollenwerk
Associate Editor: Ben Stephen
Editorial Assistant: Mary Morrill
Production Editor: Kris Robinson
Production Coordination: Carlisle Publishers Services
Design Coordinator: Diane C. Lorenzo
Cover Designer: Jeff Vanik
Cover image: SuperStock
Production Manager: Pamela D. Bennett
Director of Marketing: Ann Castel Davis
Marketing Manager: Darcy Betts Prybella
Marketing Coordinator: Tyra Poole

This book was set in Palatino by Carlise Communications, Ltd. It was printed and bound by Banta Book Group.
The cover was printed by Phoenix Color Corp.

Pearson Education Ltd.   Pearson Education Australia Pty. Limited
Pearson Education Singapore Pte. Ltd.   Pearson Education North Asia Ltd.
Pearson Education Canada, Ltd.   Pearson Educación de Mexico, S.A. de C.V.
Pearson Education—Japan   Pearson Education Malaysia Pte. Ltd.

10 9 8 7 6 5 4 3 2 1
ISBN: 0-13-098744-1

Preface

CONCEPTUAL FRAMEWORK

Welcome to the second edition of *Student Teaching: A Process Approach to Reflective Practice.* For more than a dozen years while directing or facilitating seminars and field experiences for undergraduate and graduate student or intern teachers, we searched for meaningful activities and processes that engage and guide beginning teachers. Our search focused on strengthening the link between education courses and the field-based aspects of learning to teach. In addition, we wanted to provide student teachers with opportunities to reflect on their professional knowledge and personal growth—to integrate these understandings into their total experience of being a teacher.

Student Teaching: A Process Approach to Reflective Practice encourages student or intern teachers and those pursuing alternative teacher certification to engage in reflective thinking, reflective practice, and reflective writing—the doors that lead to effective teaching based on sound pedagogy. Authentic teacher tasks are designed to invite beginning teachers to recall learning acquired through courses in the arts and sciences, content from the teaching major, and educational research and best practice. These reflective activities are process oriented and challenge each student or intern teacher to take ownership of the journey by actively engaging in a thoughtful examination of what they do in the classroom and the rationales that fuel their performance.

Expected outcomes and activities in the text take the preservice or intern teacher through the *whys* and *hows* of reflective practices by actively involving the teacher in the application of these practices. Beginning teachers are challenged to contemplate current educational paradigms and practices, analyze them, effectuate them, and reflect on their learning experiences in a journal forum. Involving preservice and inservice teachers in the application of educational best practices promotes ownership and helps them build a professional life with reflective practice at its core.

A constructivist learning approach underwrites each chapter and invites beginning teachers to consciously relate all types of learning to new situations and to make meaning from this learning. Student or intern teachers are encouraged to combine their personal investments and experiences of teaching with recognized best practice. Throughout the student or intern teaching experience, the beginning teacher is urged to develop a positive attitude toward what is observed and practiced at the school level, to look for opportunities for learning, to raise questions, and to seek understanding through reflection. It is our goal that through reflective practice, beginning teachers will use their knowledge and experience of teaching to create an electronic or digital portfolio that documents their ability to impact student learning. It is our hope that beginning teachers will continue to engage in this process throughout their professional career.

Audience and Intended Uses

We offer a practical guide for reflective practice in day-to-day teaching and provide models of current best practice based on national standards. The book can be used in a variety of ways with beginning or experienced teachers.

- Undergraduate student teachers will find this process approach to learning helpful throughout their professional placement in the school setting and in the seminar or class accompanying the experience.
- Graduate interns or others interested in pursuing an alternate route in obtaining state licensure will find exemplary reflective teaching practices needed to facilitate learning.
- Beginning teachers trained by school system consultants will find the reflective process a strong support in bridging theory and practice.
- Experienced teachers desiring to refresh and refine their own reflective teaching practices may review the teaching strategies and application to the national standards.

Organization of the Text

Student Teaching: A Process Approach to Reflective Practice calls the student or intern teacher to develop a professional teaching identity through reflective practice. The text is organized around a double focus: personal experience and applying recognized best practices of the teaching-learning experience.

Focus One encourages beginning teachers to reflect on their own personal and professional development and the accompanying perceptions, attitudes, and feelings about assuming a new role, that of teacher. Specially designed activities offer student or intern teachers opportunities to tell their individual stories about life as a classroom teacher to explore their personal and professional development and gain insights from others as they move toward becoming a professional teacher. Cooperative learning groups are suggested for this portion of the seminar to encourage purposeful dialogue.

Focus Two engages student or intern teachers in reflection about the recognition and use of theories connected with effective teaching and learning. Beginning teachers review and apply their knowledge of learning theory and implement strategies recognized as educational best practice. **Focus Two** briefly reviews research that supports selected teaching strategies and connects them to national standards. Through meaningful application activities, teachers apply these best practices in classroom instruction and reflect on their impact on student learning. Follow-up questions prompt discussion and direct beginning teachers to clarify and analyze problems and decisions made in their classrooms, gain new insights into their practice through discussion, and initiate change necessary for more effective teaching.

Format

- The Introduction invites active engagement in the process of reflective learning and provides a road map for using subsequent chapters of the text. This section concludes with suggestions for active involvement in a cooperative learning group. It is intended as a model to enhance teachers' ability to establish and contribute to an atmosphere of professional responsibility within their classrooms and the school.
- Chapters 1 through 3 include observation techniques, designing and planning for instruction, and activities connected with the initial weeks of the beginning teaching experience.

- Chapter 4 reinforces the continued exploration and provision of appropriate instruction that values and addresses diversity among learners and promotes individual and collective academic achievement.
- Chapter 5 extends instruction through the use of technology to enhance and impact teaching and learning.
- Chapters 6, 7, and 8 refine lesson presentation, address the stimulation of critical thinking through questions, and highlight other key teaching strategies to support instruction for all learners.
- Chapters 9 and 10 are devoted to creating and maintaining the learning climate within the classroom. Included are suggested methods and models of discipline strategies designed to assist the beginning teacher in making connections with observation and practice in the classroom.
- Chapter 11 focuses on the use of multiple assessment instruments for assessing student learning and offers suggestions for communicating the results to students and parents or guardians.
- Chapter 12 emphasizes collaborative efforts with parents, colleagues, and community, and suggests activities for developing a collaborative spirit.
- Chapters 13 and 14 focus on refining student or intern teachers' reflection and assessment of their teaching experience and developing a commitment to professional growth.
- Chapter 15 provides suggestions and procedures for pursuing a teaching position. Suggestions for professional portfolios, including an electronic or digital portfolio, are given in this chapter.

SPECIAL FEATURES

A learner-centered, reflective, and participatory approach to instructional planning is presented. Beginning teachers are encouraged to adopt an inquiring mind with respect to their observations and experiences in schools.

- Organization is logical and motivational, so that beginning teachers can use this book as a framework to refine their teaching strategies and attitude toward teaching, and as a practical resource in a professional education career.
- Affective activities acknowledge and validate the importance of beginning teachers' personal involvement and ownership in building their professional lives as reflective educators.
- Cooperative learning groups are actively promoted, involving the beginning teacher in the group process.
- Probing discussion questions ask beginning teachers to observe, examine, explain, and discuss their field experiences with peers.
- Developing a professional portfolio is emphasized to help beginning teachers clarify and communicate their educational philosophy and growth as teachers. Portfolio Tasks based on INTASC Performance Standards are included in Chapters 3, 7, 9, 11, 12, and 13 to guide the design of such a portfolio to procure a teaching position.
- The summary at the end of each chapter captures major concepts.
- Chapter 4 is devoted to diversity among learners in the classroom. The idea of diversity is developed in subsequent chapters to reflect the changing demographics of today's classrooms and demonstrate the need for teachers to use strategies that work for all learners.
- The integration of technology into teaching and learning is a new feature of the text. Chapter 5 provides Web sites for student or intern teachers to use as resources.
- Journal Excerpts provide current views and experiences of student or intern teachers from secondary, middle, elementary, and special education placements.

- References and suggested readings at the end of each chapter give student or intern teachers ample materials to further their exploration or reinforce the concepts presented.

NEW TO THE SECOND EDITION

The second edition features much new content:

- A new chapter with a strong focus on integrating technology in teaching and learning accompanied by Web sites (Chapter 5).
- Up-to-date information on electronic or digital portfolios and multiple job-search Web sites (Chapter 15).
- Technology standards for teachers and students (Appendix C).
- A stronger emphasis on multicultural and special education.
- Facilitator tips for instructors with ideas for using the text (Appendix B).
- Expanded section on learning styles (Chapter 2).
- Up-to-date information about best practices.
- Additional examples of lesson plans based on national and state standards (Appendix E).
- A number of new student reflective journals.
- Updated references and suggested readings in all chapters.

A NOTE TO THE FACILITATOR, INSTRUCTOR, OR SUPERVISOR

The chapters and learning experiences described in the text are designed for you to reference, use, or revise to meet the specific needs of your student or intern teachers. Facilitator tips are provided in Appendix B to assist you with engaging student or intern teachers in reflective practice through individual and group learning activities. Although facilitators remark that the sequence of the text meets their student teachers' needs, you may reorder the sequence of the chapters as you wish. Each chapter stands alone, and you may present the material in the sequence that best connects with what your student or intern teachers are seeing and doing in the classroom.

ACKNOWLEDGMENTS

In preparing this second edition we have benefitted from the invaluable assistance of a number of creative and reflective colleagues, classroom teachers, school administrators, and friends. We would like to express the gratitude we have for the experience of working together within a community of learning. Coming together to create a second edition allowed us keener insights into the reciprocal nature of the teaching and learning process, and gave us time to critically reflect on the first edition of this text. Prior to making changes, we examined how the text was being used to facilitate the student or intern teaching experience. We obtained verbal and written feedback from students engaged in the process, and we visited classrooms to observe or assist preservice teachers as they bridged theory and practice in their everyday teaching and learning. We reflected on the needs of today's student or intern teachers as they sometimes struggled to meet the many demands of teaching, including the most challenging: meeting the needs of individual learners while maintaining the integrity of the content and use of best practices in education. We are indebted and grateful to these student teachers for their candor and openness, and their willingness to share through reflective journals and discussions their experiences of teaching, their questions, and their concerns about becoming teachers who indeed make a difference.

We are indebted to Ken Zeichner, Ph.D., a recognized scholar of reflective teaching, for his Foreword which warmly endorses the process approach to reflective practice.

We extend special appreciation to our editor, Debbie Stollenwerk, for her enthusiastic support throughout this revision process. We also want to recognize the helpful staff at Merrill/Prentice Hall. A special note of thanks to the reviewers who allowed us to engage in our own reflective practice throughout the revision and editing of this manuscript: Carolynn Akpan, Pace University; Sandra L. DiGiaimo, University of Scranton; Allan F. Cook, University of Illinois, Springfield; Manina Urgolo Dunn, Seton Hall University; and Randa Gick, Arizona State University.

Brief Contents

Contents

NOTE: Every effort has been made to provide accurate and current Internet information in this book. However, the Internet and information posted on it are constantly changing, so it is inevitable that some of the Internet addresses listed in this textbook will change.

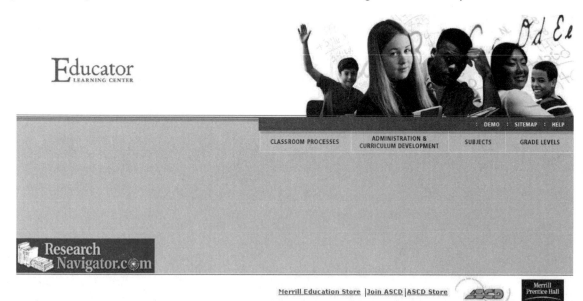

Introducing the Reflective Approach

> *" . . . When students and teachers make use of reflection as a tool for learning and assessment, they are creating an opening that allows them to enter into students' work, making sense of their endeavors and accomplishments, and learning how they judge their success. . . . "*
>
> R. Zessoules & H. Gardner

REFLECTIVE PRACTICES AND YOU

Congratulations! You are entering the most challenging, rewarding, and critical stage of your educational experience. As a practicing professional you are expected to apply all that you've learned thus far about the art and science of teaching. You have been in classrooms and taught lessons to large and small groups of students. You have had experiences with the diversity among the students in today's classrooms and have come to recognize and value those differences. You have worked with teachers and perhaps developed an Individualized Education Plan (IEP) for a student with special needs. This course will enable you to refine your methodologies and teaching techniques through practice, discussions, learning activities, and reflection. During this exciting period of reflective learning, your philosophy of education will become grounded in best practice—that is, a compilation of state-of-the-art practices based on national standards and recognized and outlined by learned societies. Zemelman, Daniels, and Hyde (1993) describe best practice as a "shorthand emblem of serious, thoughtful, informed, responsible, state-of-the-art teaching." This critical stage of your experience offers you a number of challenging opportunities for personal and professional growth as an educator.

You are invited to begin this journey of discovery learning by actively engaging in the processes of reflective learning as outlined in this text. This second edition of *Student Teaching: A Process Approach to Reflective Practice* acts as a unique guide to your student or intern teaching experience. Its interactive format allows you to identify, analyze, reflect, and act upon your personal insights about teaching. Your ideas, discoveries, and understanding of the teacher's role are validated through reflective practices and engaging, thoughtful activities.

Why Do We Say Reflective Practices?

We say *reflective practice* because reflection and the construction of new meaning from new situations, or constructivist learning, are two key factors associated with effective teaching. Reflection is a thoughtful response to either preplanned or spontaneous but conscious decisions and actions. The reflective process asks you to focus continuously on questions such as "What am I doing?" "Why?" "How well are my students learning?" "How do I know?" (Cruikshank, 1987; Fellows & Zimpher, 1988). You are asked to recall the learning acquired through courses in the arts and sciences, content from your teaching major, and the education courses that form your past experiences and understanding. Learning acquired through your previous work with children and adolescents, inside and outside a school setting, enables you to better understand and appreciate the connection between theory and practice. It is through reflective practice that this deeper level of learning occurs.

Constructivist learning asks you to consciously relate all types of learning to new situations and to make meaning from this learning. Your ongoing development depends on a gradual and systematic consideration of what is studied, observed, and discussed. How to integrate your learning into your repertoire of teaching practices becomes the challenge! The seminar format of this text allows you to share and gain from your own experiences and those of your peers. The seminar setting invites and nurtures open-mindedness, and the possibility of individual and collective growth, through meaningful and focused interactions with different group members to gain new and varying perspectives on the same topics or issues in education. You, as a beginning teacher, provide case studies from your own classroom and school experiences for discussion in the seminar. These examples of practical situations allow you to analyze what is happening in the classroom and make professional and ethical decisions. Follow-up discussions in the seminar provide you opportunities to act on your insights and your decisions.

How Do We Engage in the Reflective Process?

The chapter activities are designed for your use in collaborating with your supervising teacher, meeting with your college supervisor, and sharing with your colleagues in the seminar setting. We encourage you to become involved in a variety of tasks and to reflect on what you are learning. We have outlined a continuum of opportunities to involve you in activities and situations similar to those you plan for your students.

As manager and director, you are the designer and planner of instruction. Having experience and practice with activities similar to those you assign students better enables you to ask guiding questions of your students and direct them along the path of meaningful inquiry. Through directions and questions you assist your students in locating and using information and applying concepts to meaningful learning situations. You provide your students with instruction that connects the different disciplines and relates to real-life situations. Relying on your experience as a learner enhances the learning process for those you teach.

Subsequent chapters focus on such skills as planning, giving directions, questioning, lesson presentation, behavior management, and assessment. Each session you are asked to apply and reflect on one of these skills. Practicing these skills within your classroom helps you to analyze your strengths and note areas for improving your teaching performance.

Focus One

WHAT IS FOCUS ONE?

Each seminar session opens with a **Focus One** activity that allows you to engage in critical dialogue with your peers. This is an opportunity for thinking back about the pressing, exciting, and challenging situations you experience in your classroom. You share with others your insights, your questions, and your successes and tell how you want to grow; in other words, you tell your own story and you hear others' stories about learning to be a teacher. When personal stories and other narratives are shared with another person or group, a sense of belonging is created and stories take on deeper meaning. Stories attach us to others and to our own histories by providing a tapestry rich with threads of time, place, and character. They lead us to discover that which needs doing in our lives! Great teaching grows out of a clear sense of self and often leads to a reinvention of ourselves as teachers (Pang, 2001; Preskill, 1998; Whang & Waters, 2001; Witherell & Noddings, 1991). These narratives can help you connect your personal experiences with the ideals of best practices, while offering a forum to discuss ethical concerns you may have about teaching.

Focused Conversation and Teacher Discourse

In each session you are invited to participate in the activities of **Focus One.** These activities are designed to allow you time to clarify the meaning of the past session's events and reflect their impact on you during the days that followed. Sharing teaching and learning experiences with your peers helps you to see that what you experience in the classroom is typical at this stage of your development as a professional. This type of teacher discourse builds a sense of community, links teacher to teacher, and creates the setting in which rich and critical dialogue can occur. Simply reading about motivational ideas and good teaching practices does not magically transform you into a highly successful and competent teacher. The process of becoming competent is gained through steady, ongoing practice and a desire to overcome the initial trials associated with teaching. Gradual and steady growth coupled with analytical reflection will aid you in this experience. There are no incantations or magical chants to transform you into the teacher you desire; only in fairy tales is there instant transformation and triumph, and that is usually a result of hard work and challenges (Isenberg, 1994).

    Focus One topics are sequenced to coincide with the challenges met by many student/intern teachers, but may be rearranged by the facilitator to better match the experience encountered by beginning teachers in your particular seminar.

Facilitator Comments

In this second edition, you will find a special feature titled **Facilitator Comments.** The term *facilitator* is used to designate the person teaching the seminar and directing the activities. The comments are easily located and can assist the facilitator in preparing the seminar. The text provides a variety of options for achieving the intended purpose of **Focus One.** You may choose to use this portion as (a) a whole-group instructional strategy, (b) a whole-group instructional setting with small groups participating in the **discussion questions,** or as (c) a cooperative learning group process that includes all seminar members. Guidelines for using the cooperative learning group process appear in Appendix B of this textbook. In addition, you will find a diagram of the cooperative learning group process along with forms that can be copied and sample responses for modeling purposes. Facilitators will discover other resources that can be selected for specific chapters.

Discussion Questions for Focused Conversation

The discussion questions address significant issues and concerns that affect beginning teachers. The questions ask novice teachers to analyze and reflect on events experienced in their particular classrooms, and share the insights and new learning that result from the experiences. Other concerns and issues may arise during student teaching, and facilitators are encouraged to add to or modify the questions to better accommodate the situations and needs of their student or intern teachers.

Critical Outcomes

In each chapter **Focus One** enables you as a beginning professional teacher to:

1. identify your accomplishments
2. analyze your personal response to your successes
3. verbalize and plan actions in areas that need strengthening
4. engage in critical dialogue with your peers
5. discuss concerns about the school setting
6. raise questions about assumptions observed at the school level
7. build on insights gained from interactions with others
8. adopt actions to meet group goals successfully as stated on the action plan (under the cooperative group option)

Focus Two

WHAT IS FOCUS TWO?

Whereas **Focus One** invites you to reflect and discuss your personal experiences and insights about classroom life, **Focus Two** encourages you to look more deeply into the underlying structure of the teaching-learning situation. **Focus Two** introduces you to selected teaching behaviors and skills for best practice. In addition, **Focus Two** involves you in a variety of activities designed to organize your reflective learning and practice. At this time your mind is whirling with many basic questions about establishing yourself as a professional teacher:

- What is the schedule? How will block scheduling affect me?
- When do I start teaching? How will I know what to teach?
- In what ways do I accommodate for special learners in the class?
- Will the students recognize me as a teacher or another visitor?
- Who decorates the bulletin boards?

Through a reflective process you will not only be able to answer these questions but hundreds of others.

Focus Two challenges you to explore and put into practice:

- your knowledge of content
- your beliefs about teaching
- your understanding of best practice
- your vision of your own teaching

To make **Focus Two** user-friendly, an overview and explanation of the categories in each chapter follows.

Expected Performance

How do we measure performance of these best practices for beginning teachers? State and national standards provide specific criteria for new teacher performance standards. Criteria selected from these standards we label **Expected Performance;** these criteria are included in each chapter. Focusing on several criteria for meeting a new standard each session gives you the opportunity to improve with practice every day. In addition, portfolio tasks are suggested in specific chapters as a means to document what you consider to be best practice within the classroom during this time.

Overview: Connecting Focus One and Focus Two

A brief connection is made between **Focus One** and **Focus Two.** Reading the brief overview may add a different perspective to your group sharing and allow you to initiate additional ideas for best practice. Reflecting on **Focus One** and implementing **Focus Two** challenges you and your peers to come to each session charged and excited, eager to share your successes and your stories. Communicating your pride in each other's accomplishments with such expressions as "that's awesome!", "how did you ever?", "how imaginative, creative!" will build a community of learners. This kind of support system and networking is professionally invaluable, especially when you need a new teaching strategy, another way to handle a difficult student, or even affirmation that others have shared your "unique" experience.

Application: Instructional Best Practice

Each chapter focuses on a best practice or teacher behavior to be practiced during your experience. These teacher behaviors or instructional skills have been selected so that you specifically focus on them for a period of time. This does not mean you neglect others of equal importance. On the contrary, your reflection journal will continue to portray your progress in the areas that may need improvement and to document your successes.

Assigned Activities

Organizational skills are a must for effective teaching. Practicing organization and responding to questions and assigned tasks can help you plan, process, and reflect on classes you observe or teach. Even though you may be teaching prior to the actual presentation within the text, the emphasis and treatment of this best practice reinforces and develops it in greater depth. The assigned tasks keep you focused on the continuing development of effective teacher behaviors. Periodically you are asked to complete a specific task such as a focused conversation with your supervising teacher to discuss a teaching behavior and connect you to the experienced teacher to facilitate your own journey toward professionalism by using the experienced teachers' insights and direction.

SUMMARY

A brief summary is presented to recapture the main emphasis of the chapter. In addition, you can use the summary at your next session for reviewing the assigned best practice you implemented in the classroom, keeping in mind the impact on student learning.

FOLLOW–UP QUESTIONS AND SHARED INSIGHTS

These questions can be used as a follow-up to the assigned activities or as reflective questions in a seminar. They are provided to encourage sharing your application of the best practice. You may want to use your journal and assignment as referents. This may be done with a partner, a small group, or the entire group. Whether you are in a Professional Development School (PDS) or public or private school, each group of learners challenges the beginning teacher in a different way. Sharing with your colleagues contributes to a deeper perspective and understanding of the teacher's role, the students, and the school environment.

JOURNAL OF EXPERIENCE

The journal or log of experience is written documentation of your observations and/or reflective response to the teaching methods, classroom organization, and student response to the learning environment relative to your classroom. Journaling or keeping a daily log of your student or intern teaching experiences is an important means of becoming more perceptive about yourself as teacher.

The journal is a valuable instrument toward becoming a more effective teacher. You begin to develop your own style of teaching when observing, reflecting, and documenting your use of best practices. As you plan and implement your own instructional strategies, keep in mind what worked for the supervising teacher and yourself. Journaling about your strengths and planning for improvement after each lesson allows you to reflect on the specific teaching behaviors you wish to implement in your teaching for the next lesson. Honest self-reflection can lead you toward new understanding of how your beliefs influence your present choices and actions (Eby & Martin, 2001). Your journal is an important opportunity to become a reflective teacher.

The format for this student or intern experience is a series of selected, weekly topics for written comments and/or analysis of your observations and experiences. Identifying theories in practice and teaching strategies challenges you to reflect on how you might introduce or plan to incorporate these into your own teaching. Likewise, identifying teacher dispositions to record in your journal permits you a glimpse of the ways in which personal characteristics, beliefs, and attitudes about teaching and learning play out in the classroom. As you gain new perspectives from observing the experienced supervising teacher and reflecting on your own teaching, you are building your own philosophy of education.

In your journal, be sure to keep your observations clear and concise. Your preservice observations equip you with specific skills to analyze and label classroom behavior. Daily practice in identifying and labeling specific teaching skills helps you to become aware of your own classroom behavior and improve your teaching skills. Write about the critical happenings in the classroom that help you learn to be an effective teacher, and avoid listings of the daily routines and sweeping generalizations about the profession in general. This journal reflects your personal journey toward becoming a professional educator. Write about the "big questions" (Why? How? Who? When? What? What if?) and issues surrounding your daily interactions with learners and others at the school level. Raise questions about the planning process, talk about conversations with and suggestions from your supervising teacher, analyze your interactions with students, and record your observations about the system in general.

Your personal response to classroom life will fuel your ability to change that which you find unacceptable as you continue to learn and understand how specific experiences affect you on any number of levels. Focus your reflections by attending to the **Expected Performance** tasks for **Focus One** and **Focus Two** listed in each chapter and the **Assigned Activities,** along with your group's **action plan.** This may seem like a tall order, but each piece is integrated purposefully so you may get the most from this exercise in self-reflection and self-understanding.

Journal Excerpts from high school, middle, elementary, and special education student or intern teachers are included. They are selected because they relate to the best practice emphasized in each chapter. These beginning-teacher journal entries are intended to serve as "jump-starts" for your own journal writing.

LOG OF HOURS

To assist you in recording time you spend in observing, participating, and teaching during this experience, a **log of hours** chart is located in Appendix D. Documentation is required in many states as evidence of the specific number of supervised student teaching hours completed. Keeping a careful log and making sure the supervising teacher signs it upon completion of your experience enables you to provide the evidence you may need for your portfolio.

PORTFOLIO TASKS

Portfolios are increasingly becoming the means of demonstrating the skills, experiences, and accomplishments of the beginning teacher. Portfolio entries are an excellent means for assessing your teaching ability. Standards established by national and state groups are guidelines to assist you in the development of your portfolio. This collection of information may be ongoing throughout your teacher education program. We are providing you with what we call **Portfolio Tasks** based on national and state new teacher standards that you may complete during your student or intern teaching experience. As you design and perform each portfolio task, you are documenting what you and your students accomplish as a result of your planning and teaching. In addition, you engage in reflection about the decisions you made as the teacher. This is a major purpose for developing a teaching portfolio, reflecting and documenting your professional growth and competence as a student or intern teacher. Recommendations and resources for developing and designing an electronic portfolio are presented in Chapter 15.

Integrating technology into teaching and learning is no longer an option, as indicated by teacher standards. The authors recognize the critical role technology plays in compiling a portfolio that provides the reader evidence of your teaching, implementation, and understanding of best classroom practice. Teachers have multiple opportunities to use technology daily, from Internet searches to word processing to teaching students how to discern information and use technology in their everyday lives. The purpose of teaching is to impact student learning. The use of technology allows you to demonstrate your ability to positively affect student learning—deepening student learning to prepare them for their roles as contributing members of society.

In addition to the teacher education program requirements, many school systems require portfolios for initial teacher candidate interviews based on state and national standards. Three national professional education organizations have developed standards connected to teacher education goals. The National Council for the Accreditation of Teacher Educators (NCATE) accredits teacher education programs based on specific standards. The Interstate New Teacher Assessment and Support Consortium (INTASC) develop standards for beginning teachers, whereas the National Board for Professional Teaching Standards (NBPTS) employs portfolios in the certification of outstanding experienced teachers. Many states have produced their own standards and require that teacher education programs be written according to these standards.

Earlier in your teacher education program you may have developed portfolio entries. Significant additions to your portfolio may be made during your student or intern teaching experience. To assist you with this development, the text presents Portfolio Tasks that are based on INTASC standards. Appendix C contains a copy of both the INTASC standards and standards from one of the states, Kentucky New Teacher Standards for Preparation and Certification. You will find suggested Portfolio Tasks in chapters under **Focus Two.** A briefcase symbol is used to alert you to the task. Beginning with Chapter 3, we provide you with opportunities to perform and reflect on your progress under the guidance of supervising teachers and college supervisors.

REFERENCES AND SUGGESTED READINGS

References provide current research and sources of information. Other sources are suggested for purposes of content review and further understanding of teaching strategies found in the chapter.

APPENDICES

Appendices are located at the end of the text. You will be alerted when forms, checklists, and other materials appear in the Appendix.

REFERENCES AND SUGGESTED READINGS

Ambach, G. (1996). Standards for teachers: Potential for improving practice. *Phi Delta Kappan, 78*(3), 207–210.

Brink, B., Laguardia, A., Grisham, D., Granby, C., & Peck, C. (2001). Who needs student teachers? *Action in Teacher Education, 23*(3), 33–45.

Brubacher, J. W., Case, C. W., & Reagan, T. G. (1994). *Becoming a reflective educator: How to build a culture of inquiry in the schools.* Thousand Oaks, CA: Corwin Press.

Burn, K., Hagger, H., Mutton, T., & Everton, T. (2000). Beyond the concerns with self: The sophisticated thinking of beginning student teachers. *Journal of Education for Teaching, 26*(3), 259–278.

Clark, C. M., & Peterson, P. L. (1986). Teachers' thought processes. In M. Wittrock (Ed.), *Handbook of research on teaching* (pp. 255–296). New York: Macmillan.

Clift, R. T., Houston, W. R., & Pugach, M. C. (1990). *Encouraging reflective practice in education: An analysis of issues and programs.* New York: Teachers College Press.

Cruikshank, D. R. (1987). *Reflective teaching: The preparation of students of teaching.* Reston, VA: Association of Teacher Education.

Darling-Hammond, L., & Falk, B. (1997). Using standards and assessments to support student learning. *Phi Delta Kappan, 79*(3), 190–199.

Dewey, J. (1904). The relation of theory to practice in education. In C. A. McMurray (Ed.), *The third yearbook of the National Society for the Study of Education.* Chicago: University of Chicago Press.

Eby, J. W., & Martin, D. B. (2001). *Reflective planning, teaching, and evaluation for the elementary school* (3rd ed.). Upper Saddle River, NJ: Merrill/Prentice Hall.

Ethell, R. G., & McMeniman, M. M. (2000). Unlocking the knowledge in action of an expert practitioner. *Journal of Teacher Education, 51*(2), 87–101.

Fellows, K., & Zimpher, N. L. (1988). Reflectivity and the instructional process: A definitional comparison between theory and practice. In H. Waxman &

J. Freiberg (Eds.), *Images of reflection in teacher education.* Reston, VA: Association of Teacher Educators.

Gandal, M., & Vranek, J. (2001). Standards here today, here tomorrow. *Educational Leadership, 59*(1), 7–13.

Glickman, C. D. (2002). *Leadership for learning: How to help teachers succeed.* Alexandria, VA: Association for Supervision and Curriculum Development.

Grossman, S., & Williston, J. (2001). Strategies for teaching early childhood students to connect reflective thinking to practice. *Childhood Education, 77*(4), 236–240.

Guskey, T. R. (2001). Helping standards make the grade. *Educational Leadership, 59*(1), 20–37.

Henderson, J. (2001). *Reflective teaching* (3rd ed.). Upper Saddle River, NJ: Merrill/Prentice Hall.

Isenberg, J. (1994). *Going by the book: The role of popular classroom chronicles in the professional development of teachers.* Westport, CT: Bergin and Garvey.

Kluth, P., & Straut, D. (2001). Standards for diverse learners. *Educational Leadership, 59*(1), 43–46.

Loughran, J. J. (2002). Effective reflective practice: In search of meaning in learning about teaching. *Journal of Teacher Education, 53*(1), 33–43.

Odell, S. J., & Huling, L. (Eds.). (2000). *Quality mentoring for novice teachers.* Washington, DC: Association of Teacher Educators.

Pang, V. O. (2001). *Multicultural education: A caring-centered reflective approach.* Boston: McGraw-Hill.

Preskill, S. (1998). Narratives of teaching and the quest for the second self. *Journal of Teacher Education, 49*(5), 344–357.

Schön, D. A. (1983). *The reflective practitioner: How professionals think in action.* New York: Basic Books.

Slavin, R. L. (1989-1990). Research on cooperative learning: Consensus and controversy. *Educational Leadership 47*(4), 42–54.

Sumsion, J. (2000). Caring and empowerment: A teacher educator's reflection on an ethical dilemma. *Teaching in Higher Education, 5*(2), 167–180.

Valli, L. (Ed.). (1992). *Reflective teacher: Education cases and critiques.* Albany: State University of New York Press.

Valverde, L. (1982). The self-evolving supervisor. In T. Sergiovanni (Ed.), *Supervision of teaching* (p. 86). Alexandria, VA: Association for Supervision and Curriculum Development.

Wallace, D. K. (Ed.). (1996). *Journey to school reform: Moving from reflection to action through story telling.* Washington, DC: National Education Association.

Whang, P. A., & Waters, G. A. (2001). Transformational spaces in teacher education. *Journal of Teacher Education, 52*(3), 197–210.

Witherell, C., & Noddings, N. (1991). *Stories lives tell: Narrative and dialogue in education.* New York: Teachers College Press.

Zeichner, K., & Liston, D. (1987). Teaching student teachers to reflect. *Harvard Educational Review, 57*(1), 23–48.

Zemelman, S., Daniels, H., & Hyde, A. (1993). *Best practice: New standards for teaching and learning in America's schools.* Portsmouth, NH: Heinemann.

Zessoules, R., & Gardner, H. (1991). Authentic assessment: Beyond the buzzword and into the classroom. In V. Perrone (Ed.), *Expanding student assessment* (p. 58). Alexandria, VA: Association for Supervision and Curriculum Development.

chapter

1

Observing and Analyzing the Teaching-Learning Process

" A process of looking inside, of doing some soul searching, and then using this learning to refocus your vision is purposeful. "

Goethals & Howard (2000)

FIRST OBSERVATIONS

Your head and heart both affect what you say and do in the classroom. **Focus One** provides an opportunity to reflect on your growing perceptions about teaching. The process presented here allows you to identify and analyze your feelings and insights about the role of the professional teacher, and invites you to look inside and do some soul searching. Self-reflection is a powerful means of learning. Such powerful learning helps you to refocus your vision of yourself as an educator.

The experiences of your peers are another powerful source for learning. Sharing with one person or within a group allows you to hear your peers describe similar feelings and thoughts about their new experiences and further validates your own experience. As you offer one another support and encouragement, you create a type of bonding that over time strengthens and augments your insights about teaching.

Getting ready for your first teaching assignment brings with it many different thoughts and emotions. Prior to student teaching, earlier portions of your teacher education program provided research-based knowledge on effective teaching. Student and intern teaching offers you extended periods of time for working collaboratively with experienced teachers in applying this knowledge. Schön (1987) calls this practice of the professionals a "core of artistry . . . an exercise of intelligence, a kind of knowing . . . we learn about it by carefully studying the performance of unusually competent performers" (p. 13). Working with an experienced professional in a school setting enables you to reflect on the performance of your supervising teacher and analyze your own ideas of professionalism in terms of your personal performance, background, experience, and understanding of the teacher's role in the classroom.

Being in touch with yourself enables you to better perceive where you are now and contributes to your awareness of what is happening around you. If teachers are to understand and empathize with their students' individual situations, they must have a keen understanding of themselves. During this initial period of student or intern teaching, a variety of activities offer you the opportunity to engage in introspection as you observe what is happening around you. Throughout your journey in becoming and being a teacher, you are encouraged to (1) reflect deeply, (2) self-assess, and (3) seek feedback from others.

All of these experiences help you learn more about yourself as teacher and directly influence the type of teacher you become (Carter & Doyle, 1996; Cooper, 1999; Jersild, 1955; Zeichner & Liston, 1987).

Activities within this chapter invite you to address self-development and professional growth opportunities as you engage in teaching tasks and interact with others in various situations. This initial stage of teaching offers rich opportunities for you to observe, pose questions, and write about your learning. As you observe experienced teachers planning curriculum, preparing for a school year, and interacting with administrators and other staff members, you hear teachers voice their plans and concerns. Through your own filters of knowledge, attitudes, beliefs, and values, you process these experiences and reconstruct your own image of the teacher role. In doing so, you are infusing your "personal practical knowledge"—that is, you come to know teaching at the practical level of everyday events. To these immediate and local situations you integrate the formal knowledge you gained from general core- and content-specific courses and teacher education courses with your personal aspirations and cumulative experiences (Clandinin, 1989). Your teaching is an integral part of you and is shaped by what you know, practice, and learn.

The discussion questions below ask you to identify some insights and feelings you have about yourself as a beginning teacher. Write your personal response to these three questions. Be spontaneous with your writing and rest assured that your thoughts are the "right answers." You need not show others what you write. Begin with the question that is easiest to answer, then move to another. Leave some space for adding to an earlier response. To save time, write only the number of the question and then your response.

Questions

Teacher Role

1. Recalling your personal goals and knowledge gained from teacher preparation, make a list of teacher characteristics that you believe are most important for you to practice as a teacher.
2. Circle the characteristics that are the most difficult to integrate into your everyday thinking and living as a teacher. Why do you think these are difficult?
3. For some time becoming a teacher has been your goal. As you begin working within this school with these students and teachers, what will you contribute to the students, school, and other teachers?

Task for You

Place your written response in an envelope. Seal the envelope and write your name on the outside. The seminar facilitator collects the sealed envelopes and at a later session returns them to you unopened.

Discussion Questions

1. In answering questions about the teacher role, examine the responses you made. Discuss the reasons some were easier for you to write.
2. Discuss the characteristics you deemed most difficult to incorporate into your daily teaching experiences. Why are these so challenging to you?
3. What difference do you think your presence in the classroom and your team or department membership will make during the coming weeks?

Focus Two

Expected Performance

- Communicate results from using the observation components.
- Focus on learning goals/standards and outcomes.
- Analyze learning experiences that are developmentally appropriate for learners.
- Analyze learning experiences that challenge, motivate, and actively involve the learner.

In **Focus One** you shared personal experience to identify your insights and feelings about becoming a teacher. As a beginning teacher you bring your special talents and knowledge to the instructional setting. **Focus Two** gives you the opportunity to review, apply, practice, and reflect on selected instructional best practices. Reflective teaching requires the development of a variety of abilities, dispositions, and knowledge. The best way to gain knowledge about reflective teaching is to observe what is happening within the classroom and talk with teachers about their teaching experiences.

Developing skills for conceptualizing what teachers are doing comes with practice. If you can become aware of what happens in the classroom and can monitor accurately both your own intentions and the behaviors of your students, you are on your way to becoming an effective teacher. As a student or intern teacher, you are about to step into the peak experience of your teacher education program.

Student or intern teaching provides you the experience of working with professionals in the educational setting. You apply the knowledge, skills, dispositions, and values formed throughout your teacher education program to the actual teaching experience. Throughout your entire student or intern teacher experience, self-reflections are made and documented. This reflective process embraces an explanation of reflection by Yost, Sentner, and Forlenza-Bailey (2000), in which value-laden questions are asked and responses to stored selected data, or memory, are made. Various activities provide opportunities for reflecting on teaching: scheduled seminars, journal writing, actual daily practice in teaching, and video and audio recording of teaching. These reflective activities are significant opportunities for integrating all of your teacher education components into the teaching role and creating a portfolio that documents your effectiveness as a teacher. All of these processes point to the teacher as reflective learner.

APPLICATION: OBSERVING THE TEACHING–LEARNING PROCESS

Doyle (1986) characterized six key dimensions that frame teaching and learning in classrooms. Observing and anticipating how these affect your cooperating or supervising teacher may help to prepare you for your own teaching. Understanding how these dimensions affect teaching and learning calls you to critically examine how each plays out in the classroom, and the professional teacher's ability to work within them or in spite of them. These underlying dimensions help create the culture of the classroom and can impact learning in positive or negative ways. The teacher who is aware of their presence and limits their negative imprint on learning is well on the way toward using instructional time optimally. Review the six dimensions of teaching and learning to reflect on how they may have impacted your education as well as the teaching and learning that occurs in your classroom today. How does your cooperating teacher handle these more subtle demands of teaching and learning?

1. **Multidimensionality:** Many tasks and events are happening on a variety of difficulty levels that you as a beginning teacher must prepare and plan for the students, yet remain flexible to change.
2. **Simultaneity:** Many things happen at the same time and the beginning teacher must be patient, flexible, and calm while handling the time factor.
3. **Immediacy:** Responding to the fast pace of events takes quick decision making by the beginning teacher.
4. **Unpredictability:** Each day provides an unanticipated classroom climate—depending on students, events, or activities—that calls for calm handling of the situation.
5. **Publicity:** Classrooms are public places. Events are witnessed by students who can see how all others are treated by the teacher.
6. **Historicity:** Events happening earlier in the year may influence how classrooms function.

Systematic observations provide detailed and verifiable information that proves to be highly accurate and allows you to see and experience the multiple dimensions of teaching and learning. Becoming a perceptive observer assists you in the development of flexibility and accommodation of instruction and behavior management. Understanding how multidimensionality, simultaneity, immediacy, unpredictability, publicity, and historicity help structure teaching and learning is a first step toward working within those dimensions to plan student learning.

A LOOK AT CRITICAL OBSERVATION

To be a critical observer, one who uses data to inform teaching and learning, you must learn the skills professionals in other fields such as psychology, sociology, and other sciences employ to record, on a regular basis, data taken from observations.

- **Objectivity:** Objectivity is the most basic and most difficult skill to master. Is the learner doing something for a reason? The keen observer separates the observed event or behavior from speculation and interpretation.
- **Speculation:** Although some speculation may be necessary, it is important to use language that calls for deeper investigation such as, "it appears that the learner," "it is my belief," "in my estimation," and so forth. This attention to language allows the observer to more deeply attend to the observed behavior and prevents teachers and other professionals from labeling learners without enough data.
- **Context:** The setting or context within which the observation takes place is critical to generating a clearer picture of the learner and what is observed. For example, "The overhead lighting appeared bright enough to allow J. to read the notes with some assistance from the aide."
- **Writing:** Use concrete and concise words to describe what you see. Avoid using trigger words such as *shy, hostile, insecure, hyper,* and so on. The point is to "deliver the facts" as you witness them, not to analyze the learner, environment, or other factors.
- **Analysis:** You may be asked to analyze the data and facts you collect while in the classroom. If your notes are clear and free from bias, they can be used to guide instruction or to intervene to help a learner become more successful in learning content or working with others.

- **Reflection:** When asked to reflect on the experience, you want to connect what you see in the classroom with course work and other knowledge you have through personal experience. Don't be surprised if your reflection proposes new questions for you to investigate and answer about classroom life, teachers, and learners. It should!

ASSIGNED ACTIVITIES

The following topics serve as guides for your observations. Recording your observations in clear and precise language allows you to reflect upon your understanding of the teaching-learning environment, and gives you a clearer idea of the reciprocal nature of teaching and learning. Include your analysis of the data you collect and your reflection about its impact on you as a learner and new questions you may have to research.

1. Examine the physical features of the classroom, including: chalkboard space, bulletin board, desk arrangement, lighting, displays, technology, and instructional materials.
   - In what ways are they used to enhance learning in the classroom?
   - How will you plan to use or change the arrangement as you assume the teacher role?
2. Note the arrangements made for learners with special needs: equipment, special meetings, classroom seating and floor plan, schedules, and events.
   - In what ways are students' special needs met?
   - What questions do you have concerning these learners?
3. Describe the supervising or team teacher's approach and manner with students: personal characteristics, appearance, communication skill, voice, eye contact, facial expression.
   - To what extent do the teacher's characteristics and communication skills make a difference in the learning that takes place in the classroom?
4. Observe the classroom management and discipline approach: management strategies, student response to discipline, stated teacher expectations, and classroom rules and consequences for breaking posted rules.
   - How often and in what way does the teacher state expectations?
   - How are teacher expectations met in your classroom setting?
5. Focus on organizational strategies: daily routines, organization of teaching materials, and grouping for instruction techniques.
   - To what degree are organization and routine conducive to student learning?
6. Analyze instructional strategies: learner objectives, motivating techniques, questioning techniques, evaluation of learning, and closure.
   - Identify instructional strategies in which students are actively engaged in learning.
7. Discuss the learner in terms of interaction with the teacher and peers, individual learning styles, motivation, and following directions (written and verbal).
   - How are the students interacting with the teacher and with one another?
   - Compare and contrast engaged students with disengaged or unmotivated students. Summarize your observations.

SUMMARY

Various activities provide you opportunities for reflecting on teaching: weekly seminar, classroom observations, journal writing, daily practice in teaching, and video and audio recording of teaching. These reflective activities are significant opportunities for integrating all of your teacher education components into the teaching role. The events during this special professional experience focus on the significance of reflection in this integrative process.

You have spent considerable time observing all aspects of the teaching-learning process with your classes. Given any teaching-learning environment, a wide range of observations is possible. Your collection of data has significant insights into the instructional and behavioral management of the learners, as well as the culture of the classroom and the school.

FOLLOW-UP QUESTIONS AND SHARED INSIGHTS

Use your observation data, reflections, and journal entries to recall events since the last class meeting and share your response to the following questions:

1. In what ways do the outstanding physical features of the school, classroom, and other areas add to the learning environment?
2. How do the teacher's communication skills, voice, appearance, and personality affect the learning climate in the classroom?
3. What expectations of learner behavior are evident? How are these communicated to the learners?
4. What different instructional strategies modeled by the teacher will you want to incorporate and practice within your own teaching?
5. How were you introduced to the class or classes? What was the reaction of the students?
6. What were some of the ways you initiated assisting your partner-teacher?
7. Describe activities you directed, and any activities in which you interacted with students. How did the learners respond to you? For instance, did the learners refer any questions they had to you? Did they call you by name?

Additional questions may surface. It will be evident from your participation in the discussion the degree to which your observation skills are becoming more critical.

Journal Excerpts

High School

"Mr. S. introduced me to everyone and they all are so friendly and helpful. I just hope I can remember all of their names! I received my official parking pass and my *Faculty Handbook*. I read the *Handbook* and it helped me a great deal. All rules and policies are clearly explained and it is a great quick reference guide. I put paper clips on pages which were particularly important such as schedules, dress codes, school maps, and such. . . . We also had a department meeting. I met all of the teachers as well as the chair of the department. We discussed the curriculum for the upcoming year and Mr. S. gave me all the textbooks we are going to be using. It was great to learn about what we are going to be teaching this semester! Native American writings, Cotton Mather, and Edgar Allan Poe to name a few."

"Today I observed various arrangements made for special learners. The most obvious arrangements are made for students with serious skill deficiencies or learning differences. It provides highly individualized instruction in required subject areas. Specialized counseling services are also provided to assist the student in developing interests and abilities, setting goals, making career choices, and solving personal and social problems. . . . Some of the equipment made available are laptop computers and audiotapes of texts in the library. In order to assist with keeping students organized in their schedules, assignments, etc. they use an assignment notebook as a mandatory aspect of the program. A timer is often used to help keep students focused on their tasks. Upon request, weekly "Progress Reports" are issued to the student and the parents."

Middle School

"I am so tired! This is a lot of excitement for one day. Today I felt old. Every now and then I am reminded that I am responsible for a lot of stuff. Today was definitely one of those days. I spent the day helping students find classrooms, collecting strays, passing out forms, and making copies. I sound like I'm complaining, but I'm really not. I loved every minute of the day. I don't have the energy that they do, though! I found out that the more time I spent with them, the more peppy I seemed to be."

"Ms. I. gave the students a review of the rules, partly for my benefit. As she's talking, she says a name and continues on. She doesn't even have to wait. Those people off-task know it's time to pay attention. She introduced me much differently than Ms. P. and stressed that I will get respect from all of them. Ms. P. did this as well, but Ms. I. explained my situation and discussed it with them. Ms. P. did not want them to know I was a student."

Elementary

"This week has been a whirlwind of information and activity as I prepared to student teach. I have attended a number of faculty meetings to prepare for the coming semester. The first meeting I attended took place on Monday. . . . This meeting was aimed specifically at new teachers. I learned so much at this meeting! I immediately felt very welcome and a little overwhelmed."

"Ms. W., Ms. K., and I got together to discuss the day and plan a schedule for the next day. There are several special needs students in the class, but there was one who caused us concern. We discussed what worked with him, what didn't, and that we would have to watch him carefully and decide on interventions as needed. He was continually off-task and seemed to be on another planet most of the time."

"Today was another first for me in this assignment. I was feeling very badly and I realized today just how much energy teaching requires. It was an eye opener. I was exhausted being here just half a day."

Special Education

"Today was my first day and I spent the day getting to know the students, familiarizing myself with the point system, observing some of Mr. D.'s teaching techniques, and easing myself into the classroom. When the students came in the room they had a writing assignment on the board and got right to work. I was impressed by this. Some of the things I got to be involved in today were working with individual students, playing UNO during their free time, and monitoring their behavior for short periods of time."

"I am continuing to get more involved. The more the students see me do, the more they respect me as a teacher. Although I do not feel completely comfortable with the teacher's style, I am catching on to the way she does things, and trying to do similar things."

"I find that Ms. G. is extremely talented in her planning of interesting lessons for her students. Today the students worked on completing their self-portraits that will be hung around the room for open house. She tied the self-portraits into the "Art of the Month" and also with a social studies lesson talking about how people are different. The self-portraits were just great. I wrote the name of each student on the front of their portraits and then placed the date on the back. I think these works of art will be kept around their homes for a long time."

REFERENCES AND SUGGESTED READINGS

Beattie, M. (2001). *The art of learning to teach: Preservice teacher narratives.* Upper Saddle River, NJ: Merrill/Prentice Hall.

Borich, G. D. (1999). *Observation skills for effective teaching* (3rd ed.). Upper Saddle River, NJ: Merrill/Prentice Hall.

Carter, K., & Doyle, W. (1996). Personal narrative and life history in learning to teach. In J. Sikula (Ed.), *Handbook of research on teacher education* (2nd ed., pp. 120–142). New York: Macmillan.

Clandinin, D. J. (1989). Developing rhythm in teaching: The narrative study of a beginning teacher's personal practical knowledge of classrooms. *Curriculum Inquiry, 19*(2), 121–141.

Collier, S. (1999). Characteristics of reflective thought during the student teaching experience. *Journal of Teacher Education, 50*(3), 173–181.

Cooper, J. M. (Ed.). (1999). *Classroom teaching skills.* Boston: Houghton Mifflin.

Danielson, C. (1996). *Enhancing professional practice: A framework for teaching.* Alexandria, VA: Association for Supervision and Curriculum Development.

Doyle, W. (1986). Classroom organization and management. In M. Wittrock (Ed.), *Handbook of research on teaching* (3rd ed.). New York: Macmillan.

Goethals, S., & Howard, R. (2000). *Student teaching: A process approach to reflective practice.* Upper Saddle River, NJ: Merrill/Prentice Hall.

Hamilton, M. L., & Pinnegar, S. (2000). On the threshold of a new century: Trustworthiness, integrity, and self-study in teacher education. *Journal of Teacher Education, 51*(3), 234–240.

Haycock, K. (1998). Good teaching matters. . . a lot: Thinking K–16. *The Education Trust, 3*(2), 3–14.

Jersild, A. T. (1955). *When teachers face themselves.* New York: Teachers College Press.

Kronowitz, E. L. (1999). *Your first year of teaching and beyond* (3rd ed.). New York: Longman.

MacDonald, R. E., & Healy, S. D. (1999). *A handbook for beginning teachers* (2nd ed.). New York: Longman.

McIntyre, D. J., & Byrd, D. M. (Eds.). (1996). *Preparing tomorrow's teachers: The field experience.* Thousand Oaks, CA: Corwin Press.

Palmer, P. J. (1998). *The courage to teach: Exploring the inner landscape of a teacher's life.* San Francisco: Jossey-Bass.

Posner, G. J. (2001). *Field experience: A guide to reflective teaching* (5th ed.). New York: Longman.

Pultorak, E. G. (1996). Following the development process of reflection in novice teachers: Three years of investigation. *Journal of Teacher Education, 47*(3), 283–291.

Reed, A. J. S., Bergemann, V. E., & Olson, M. W. (1998). *A guide to observation and participation in the classroom* (3rd ed.). Boston: McGraw-Hill.

Roe, B. D., & Ross, E. P. (2002). *Student teaching and field experiences handbook* (5th ed.). Upper Saddle River, NJ: Merrill/Prentice Hall.

Ross, D. D., Bondy, E., & Kyle, D. W. (1993). *Reflective teaching for student empowerment.* New York: Macmillan.

Rust, F. O. (2001). Professional conversations: New teachers explore teaching through conversation, story, and narrative. *Teaching and Teacher Education, 15*(4), 367–380.

Schön, D. A. (1987). *Educating the reflective practitioner.* San Francisco: Jossey-Bass.

Valverde, L. (1982). The self-evolving supervisor. In T. Sergiovanni (Ed.), *Supervision of teaching* (pp. 81–89). Alexandria, VA: Association for Supervision and Curriculum Development.

Wallace, D. K. (Ed.). (1996). *Journey to school reform: Moving from reflection to action through story telling.* Washington, DC: National Education Association.

Wentz, P. (2001). *Student teaching casebook for supervising teachers and teaching interns.* Upper Saddle River, NJ: Merrill/Prentice Hall.

Yost, D. S., Sentner, S. M., & Forlenza-Bailey, A. (2000). An examination of the construct of critical reflection: Implications for teacher education programming in the 21st century. *Journal of Teacher Education, 51*(1), 39–49.

Zeichner, K., & Liston, D. (1987). Teaching student teachers to reflect. *Harvard Educational Review, 57*(1), 23–48.

chapter

2

Examining the Planning Process

> " *Becoming a professional teacher engages you in change and experimentation on many different levels and challenges you to initiate action.* "
>
> Goethals & Howard (below)

Focus One

Expected Performance

- Recall examples and talk with peers about student comments that demonstrate they view you as teacher.
- Examine and describe prior goals that you established for yourself as teacher and describe your current performance toward realizing these goals.

"A teacher's understanding of others can be only as deep as the wisdom he possesses when he looks inward upon himself."
A.T. Jersild

AM I INITIATING OR AM I HIDING BEHIND THE BOOKCASE?

Change calls for adaptive learning on the part of individuals meeting emerging needs and new situations. Waldron, Collie, and Davies (1999) define adaptive learning as the ability to respond flexibly and proactively to stressful situations and to initiate tasks that challenge these abilities. Being able to adapt provides greater self-control, which in turn allows you to confront or cope by modifying the task or yourself.

Choosing to teach is inevitably accompanied by change and opportunities for adaptive learning. The challenge of teaching is deciding what you want to be as teacher, what you care about, what you value, and how you will conduct yourself with students and others in the school (Ayers, 2001; Eby & Martin, 2001). Day by day you are transforming a self-established goal into a reality. In accomplishing this goal you continuously confront new and challenging situations and learn to cope by modifying tasks or your understanding of complex situations. For example, you support educational reform, but you may have to deal with conflicting viewpoints and levels of dedication at the school level. You recognize the need for knowledge and identify the skills necessary to work collaboratively to improve the conditions in the school, and you are willing to share your insights with others. Interacting with children and adolescents and collaborating with an experienced teacher provide you many opportunities for adaptive learning. Just as you are a unique individual, so are the situations and tasks confronting you and toward which you respond as teacher. Becoming a professional teacher engages you in change and experimentation on many different levels and challenges you to initiate action and "take charge" as the situation demands.

Focus One invites you to assess one aspect of becoming a professional teacher. You are asked to reflect on the levels of your ability to take charge and demonstrate initiative in the classroom. During this seminar session, candidly

19

recall and share examples of when and how you practice the taking-charge aspects of teaching.

As you enter the teaching profession, self-assessment takes on new meaning. In reflecting on your performance, compare your teacher behaviors with your philosophy of teaching. Are they compatible? Self-assessment on the part of the teacher begins early in the preparation period and is ongoing. Learning to be **teacher** is a process that extends over months and even years. Immediately after arriving in the classroom and meeting your students, the taking-charge stage of teaching begins. Your first experiences are short activities that may include handing out papers, reading aloud, or locating materials. After working with your supervising teacher and getting to know the students and the school, you will be invited to assume greater responsibilities for student learning. For now, enjoy the process of learning as you prepare to initiate activities.

How do you see yourself as a professional taking charge? Picture yourself within the classroom and recall the verbal and nonverbal exchanges taking place between yourself and the students. The following questions can guide you as you recall your recent classroom experiences.

- Where are you standing or sitting in the classroom?
- Do you take over and direct an activity when the supervising teacher is interrupted or called from the room?
- Are you working with one student or a group of students?
- What are you saying and/or demonstrating to the students?
- Are you enthusiastic? Knowledgeable?
- What does your tone of voice and facial expression convey about your feelings toward the activity?
- Do students ask you to help them?
- How do students view your role in the classroom?
- How initiating are you?

Discussion Questions

1. How do students describe your presence in their class? Share any comments about yourself that you have heard students make. From these comments, tell how you think students view you as **teacher.**
2. Describe some change you think is needed to expand your role from observer to participator or initiator in the classroom. What risks will be involved in making the change?
3. Recall some beliefs you hold about teaching. What tasks have you assumed that indicate you are experimenting with ways for making these beliefs become a part of you as **teacher?**

Focus Two

Ah, to be initiating, to take charge of the students—terrific! This seems like an easy task until you begin. Early on in your student or intern teaching, you may be asked to direct a small-group learning activity or teach the whole group a new skill. You may find something that appears simple, such as giving directions to students, turns out to be quite difficult. You may struggle with learners who ask for clarification or forget the order in which to proceed to complete a task. Providing clear directions for instructional and other purposes is critical to

Expected Performance

- Examine and reflect upon the relationships between learning expectations and daily lesson plans.
- Plan instruction based upon knowledge of subject matter, students, the community, and curriculum goals.
- Provide learning opportunities that support students' intellectual, social, and personal development.
- Incorporate strategies that address physical, social, and cultural diversity and show sensitivity to differences.

the teaching and learning process; it communicates expectations for learners and contributes to positive classroom management, whereas unclear directions may lead to learner confusion and a chaotic classroom.

Have you recognized how essential it is to clearly articulate directions and outline step by step with the learners what you or your supervising teacher expect them to do? Incorporating the following four strategies into your teaching repertoire may very well save you time in the classroom; time that can be better spent on instruction and learning. Plan to give directions just once by using the following techniques:

1. Use "group alert" to gain all students' attention prior to speaking. This saves you from repeating directions (Emmer, Evertson, & Worsham, 2000).
2. Modulate your voice to gain and retain student attention. Use a strong, clear voice when giving directions to better meet the needs of auditory learners.
3. Write the directions on the board or an overhead to better meet the needs of visual learners.
4. Check students' understanding of directions by asking a student to repeat the directions you give. This is often beneficial to you, as teacher, and provides clarity for other students.

Planning effective lessons for a specific group of learners requires you to engage in the planning process to hone your ability to state academic expectations for learners and plan lessons tied to those instructional goals. You are closely observing your cooperating and team teachers and focusing on the objectives and expectations they hold for the learners. Through your observation and recording of learner outcomes, you are developing deeper insights concerning lesson planning and learner achievement.

APPLICATION: DEVELOPING INSTRUCTIONAL PLANS

Preplanning

Writing a well-developed plan for teaching usually begins with a reflection on the needs of the individual learners within your class. Assessing what the learner knows and has demonstrated in previous lessons usually precedes the development of the plan. Using national or state guidelines to plan content-specific lessons and curriculum guides to pace instruction ensures that what you plan for students to learn is content appropriate and cognitively and socioemotionally appropriate to the grade level you teach.

In addition, formal and informal inventories provide important information about the learners and can serve to guide your instruction. These may be prepared activity sheets on which students check their interests or write a short piece describing their favorite academic subject, sport, hobby, music, travel experience, and book. This allows you a peek into students' interests and abilities, and perhaps gives you background information regarding students' cultural, religious, familial, and socioeconomic backgrounds. Using these tools to better know the population of learners you teach enables you to design lessons they can connect with. You may need to build background to develop concepts you wish to teach, and this should be part of the planning process.

Students learn in many different ways and come to class with background knowledge about many different areas of interest. Taking into account the learning styles of students, and capitalizing on the multiple intelligences and the wide range of diversity among your students enables you, as teacher, to develop lesson plans with a broader perspective and deeper connection to the learners.

"Learning styles are the preferred ways that different individuals have for processing and organizing information and for responding to environmental stimuli."
T. Shuell

Capitalizing on Students' Learning Styles

The learning styles approach to teaching and learning recognizes that all students can learn; however, each student has a specific mode or combination of modes for learning. Some students may be more visual and gain from written instruction on the chalkboard or overhead, flashcards, pictures, charts, posters, or computer programs. Others may prefer tape recordings, educational songs and rhymes, recitation, oral reading and reporting, and oral presentations using varied voice inflection, accent, pause, and tone. Still other students may prefer the kinesthetic approach with hands-on types of activities such as keyboarding, drama, dance, lab experiments, and manipulatives. Some students learn better in a more structured approach, whereas others prefer varied instructional strategies. Some students will learn quickly; others, more slowly. Some students are social learners who learn best by interacting with others, discussing, and participating in groups. Although some students learn more easily as independent learners, other students need additional teacher assistance. Silver, Strong, and Perini (2001) identify four basic ways students absorb and think about information:

1. **Mastery style** learners absorb information concretely, process information sequentially, and judge the value of learning in terms of clarity and practicality.
2. **Understanding style** learners focus on ideas and abstractions, learn through a process of questioning, reasoning, and testing, and evaluate learning by standards of logic and the use of evidence.
3. **Self-expressive style** learners look for images, use feelings and emotions to construct new ideas and products, and evaluate the learning process according to originality, aesthetics, and the capacity to surprise.
4. **Interpersonal style** learners focus on concrete information, preferring to learn socially, and assess learning in terms of whether it is helpful to others.

Students have preferred ways of learning, yet each individual student may need to learn how to vary his or her preferred learning style to fit the task or activity. You will be able to perceive the varied learning styles of your students by observing them as they interact within groups and as they explain in writing and speaking what they learned.

An instrument used to determine students' learning styles with high reliability and validity is the Dunn, Dunn, and Price Learning Style Inventory (LSI) for grades 3–12. The LSI provides information on how students prefer to learn and their perceptual strengths, outlines group arrangements most likely to affect student learning, tells which students are independent learners and which students need more structure, suggests how each student studies and does homework best, explains methods through which individuals are most likely to achieve, and discusses other assessment analysis.

As teacher and observer, you can begin to accommodate the different learning styles by being flexible and using a variety of instructional and assessment strategies to reach each student. In this way, you demonstrate the value you place on diversity and the respect you have for language differences and cultural traditions.

Incorporating Multiple Intelligences

Howard Gardner is the chief proponent of the **multiple intelligences** concept. His research portrays eight intelligences possessed by every person to some degree, but traditionally, schools tend to develop the first two intelligences to any extent. Gardner (1995) identifies these intelligences:

linguistic	interpersonal
bodily-kinesthetic	musical
spatial (visual)	intrapersonal
logical-mathematical	naturalist

The goal of the reflective teacher is to provide instruction that will include many of the above eight intelligences, and allow students to express their knowledge of subject matter using their preferred or dominant intelligence. Examples include writing journal entries in the **linguistic** category; role-playing in the **bodily-kinesthetic;** using the **spatial intelligence** by creating maps or graphs; creating simulations and completing puzzles in the **logical-mathematical;** participating in cooperative group activities **(interpersonal);** performing in a class musical **(musical);** using the **KWL** method (what I *know,* what I *want* to know, and what I *learned* from this instruction) in the **intrapersonal** category; or classifying plants, minerals, and animals in the Beta **naturalist** category. The diversity of intelligences found in any student population serves to enhance the learning among all students and bring content to life in the classroom.

Effective planning requires that teachers identify the varied learning styles and multiple intelligences of their students and adapt instruction to meet their needs. We encourage you to be sensitive in making judgments about students whose learning styles and cultural backgrounds are different from your own. Differences among students are to be understood, respected, and accepted, yet it is your responsibility as beginning teacher to nudge and guide students to learn to work outside their preferred ways of learning or cultural ways of knowing to become a more holistic learner (Gay, 2002). The important point is that you become aware of your students' varying needs and respond accordingly in the classroom. Trying to vary your instruction to include the different learning styles and multiple intelligences cannot be done in one lesson. It will take practice and experience to find what benefits your students and helps each to be a successful learner.

Meeting the Academic Needs of All Learners

You may find it easy to envision your students engaged in learning because of your capacity to capitalize on their strengths by keeping their learning styles and multiple intelligences in mind while planning lessons and learning activities that encourage their growth. What about learners who struggle more than others to understand a concept or use a skill consistently? What about the students who are gifted and talented who move at the speed of light in their capacity to learn? How do you meet the needs of all learners with regard to their abilities and disabilities when the range of ability is varied and the success of all your students reflects you as teacher?

Learning to scaffold learning or differentiate instruction among learners is a key to successful planning and teaching. Differentiating instruction, scaffolding instruction, and individualized instruction have one major goal—to create a bridge or ladder to learning that enables the student to learn and be a contributing member of the class regardless of ability or disability. This calls for you, as teacher, to outline the steps a learner with special needs may need to take to complete a task, provide materials that are adapted to the specific needs of the learner, and make sure the lesson is inclusive. A lesson that is inclusive engages all learners in specific activities such as reading, writing, speaking, and so on, but is tailored to the diverse needs of the learners including cultural, ethnic, gender ability, and disability. The outcome of the lesson should be such that each learner has performed to his or her level best and is able to complement or add to the learning of the other members of the class. Sapon-Shevin (2001) maintains that teachers who are committed to inclusive practices and use culturally inclusive instruction may erase the "artificial barriers" among regular, special, and gifted education. A detailed example of an inclusive lesson plan is provided in Appendix E.

Designing and Planning the Lesson

Developing lesson plans for teaching the learners in your class gives you direction and focus. You may have been given a particular format or outline for planning your lessons in your methods classes or from an instructor in your orientation for the student teacher or intern experience. Using district, state, or national curriculum standards in designing your plans provides the rationale for your choice of instructional strategies. In addition, the use of state and national standards will more likely guarantee that you are including what is important for learners to know and achieve at a particular level.

Writing Instructional Objectives

Essential to good planning for instruction is the demonstrated ability to write instructional objectives. If you are working toward becoming an effective teacher, it is essential that you know what you want your students to know, accomplish, or demonstrate prior to, during, and following your lesson. Stating your objectives in clear, observable language helps you assist learners to achieve the goals and objectives you have set for them. In other words, when you as teacher have clearly defined goals and objectives or outcomes, learners will know what is expected of them, and gradually, with reinforcement, students will become more self-evaluative and set high expectations for themselves. This is the ultimate goal of education!

You have planned lessons prior to student or intern teaching, but the focus has now shifted from creating one or two lesson plans for a particular group of students to creating lessons or units of study for learners to whom you are more accountable in terms of learning outcomes. Writing objectives that are clear and tied to assessment becomes a less daunting task if you take your cue from experts in the area of writing instructional objectives, and keep in mind the developmental levels of the students you teach.

Bloom, Engelhart, Furst, Hill, and Krathwohl (1956) developed a taxonomy for classifying objectives, and later in 1964 with Krathwohl and Masia, identified three domains for learning: cognitive, affective, and psychomotor. You may be more familiar with the cognitive domain of learning and have perhaps used the levels outlined by Bloom to write instructional objectives. Although each domain for learning is classified separately, they are essentially interrelated and important. When used thoughtfully, the three domains help students better grasp the concepts and knowledge embedded in the curriculum you teach. The three domains include the following dimensions of learning:

- **Cognitive**—"the recall or recognition of knowledge and the development of intellectual abilities and skills"
- **Affective**—"interests, attitudes, and values"
- **Psychomotor**—"manipulative and motor skills" (Krathwohl, Bloom, & Masia, 1964)

As an example, the learner may develop a piece of writing, recalling information and giving much thought to the topic (cognitive), type the piece of writing on the computer (psychomotor), and become enraptured in the unfolding of the writing piece (affective). Knowledge of Bloom's taxonomy will be helpful in formulating the best objectives for your lesson planning. For those of you who want to review the taxonomy of the three domains, the chart below, adapted from Bloom et al. (1956) and Krathwohl et al. (1964), may assist you.

Domain and Level Definition

Cognitive Domain

- *Knowledge:* recalls or recognizes information
- *Comprehension:* understands or knows what is being communicated
- *Application:* transfers learning from one context to another independently
- *Analysis:* breaks down a problem into parts and forms
- *Synthesis:* puts together elements to form a creative whole
- *Evaluation:* makes value judgments using specific criteria

Affective Domain

- *Receiving:* directs attention to the stimuli
- *Responding:* enjoys an activity or experience
- *Valuing:* commits to a belief, view, or idea and can defend or act on behalf of it
- *Organizing:* develops a system of values and lives by it

Psychomotor Domain

- *Imitation:* carries out basic directions for a skill
- *Manipulation:* performs a skill independently
- *Precision:* performs a skill accurately, efficiently, and meticulously

You may also want to review the components for writing instructional objectives. The following points are adapted from TenBrink (1999):

1. **Emphasize the instructional objective is learner oriented.**
   - ex. The *students* will select the main idea from a paragraph provided by the teacher.
   - ex. Students will compute solutions to a system of equations using the substitution, addition, and graphing methods.
2. **Determine what the learner will accomplish, that is, learner outcome** (which should be stated clearly and in observable terms).
   - ex. Given a list of organisms found in a particular tropical ecosystem (old lake, inland lake, beach, coral reef) *place the organisms in the order in which they would occur over time, from the pioneer community to the climax community.*
   - ex. After practice with first and second tenors, with baritone, and with bass parts, freshmen boys *will sing "Vive L'amour" with accuracy of pitch.*
3. **Set the acceptable criteria for assessing the level of performance.**
   - ex. Given five examples students will multiply two-digit numbers by one-digit numbers with *80% accuracy.*
   - ex. Using their original drawings, students will: (a) write a description of how the drawing was made, (b) use the proper sequence that would allow another to reproduce the drawing, and (c) complete a rough draft of a descriptive piece of writing *according to the rubric provided by the teacher.*

You may formulate good instructional objectives or outcomes at this time without any additional practice. Some texts and teacher guides include objectives appropriate for a particular grade level, and these may be helpful to you in formulating objectives for your students.

With practice in writing clear, complete, and observable instructional objectives, beginning teachers observing cooperating teachers can recognize what objectives have been selected to teach a specific lesson. Later in this text you will be directed to match the assessment of the lesson with your stated objectives. One of this chapter's assigned activities will give you practice in observing and writing instructional objectives for the learners within your classes.

Designing a solid lesson plan takes work and the ability to think things through! The following outline of a lesson plan (for three different levels—high school, middle school, and elementary) includes all the components you need to draw upon to assist you in your teaching. More examples of lesson plans for these levels and special education can be found in Appendix E.

Lesson Plan Guide

Course Level: English 210; eighth-grade Social Studies; third-grade Math
Period of Day: First—7:50 A.M.; Sixth—1:40 P.M.; 10:15–11:00 A.M.
Type of Lesson: Introductory; Reinforcement of concept; Direct instruction
Reflective Questions: Questions you will ask yourself as you reflect on the contents of your plan.

ex. Can students perform the tasks I have created for them in this lesson?
ex. Will the students work cooperatively with one another in carrying out the project?
ex. Does the content for this lesson flow from the lesson previously taught?

Objectives: What is it you hope your students will achieve in this lesson?
Assessment: Do the assessment means match the objective(s) you have written? How will you determine at what level the student has achieved the objectives?
Materials/Strategies: What specific materials will you need? Will you be using small groups, teacher-directed learning, webbing, KWL charting, or other methods of content delivery?

Procedure: A Description

Teacher's Words/Actions Instructional Sequence	Expected Learner Response
A. **Lesson initiation:** (motivation, review, overview): What will you say, show, ask learners to do or say to create and stimulate interest, focus attention, and engage journal learners in the activity or content?	Write what students are expected to do (i.e., verbal response, listen, journal writing).
B. **Lesson development:** (demonstration, modeling, activities, questions)	
C. **Guided practice:** (examples, illustrations, demonstrations used to accommodate diversity of learner and learning styles)	
D. **Independent practice:** (application of skill/concept, assignment, project): Students demonstrate they can apply and carry out the task themselves.	
E. **Assignment:** Is there an activity sheet, text page, or project to complete to reinforce the concept, skill, or theme?	
F. **Assessment:** What means will you select to determine at what level the student has achieved the objectives?	

Performance Criteria/Rubric: You may have a set criteria or rubric that specifies the different levels you as teacher will use in assessing the completed task or project.

Reflective Comments (Self-Assessment): After teaching the lesson, evaluate your teaching. Highlight the strengths and describe areas you want to improve.

Optional: You might want to highlight the following: higher level questioning, real-life application, concrete experience, strategies/considerations for learners with special needs, and/or cross-discipline integration.

ASSIGNED ACTIVITIES

1. In your journal, list learner objectives you observe for at least one class each day. For the outcomes listed, what activities were planned to provide the teacher written or verbal evidence of meeting this outcome? Describe the techniques you observe or use this week to reach the desired learning outcome (i.e., direct teaching, cooperative learning groups, role-playing, problem solving).

Date of Lesson

Subject   Class   Number of Learners

Number of Learners with IEPs

Objectives or Learner Outcomes

Assessment or Evidence of Learning Outcome

Teaching Techniques

---

2. Select at least two of the above objectives. In conference with your supervising teacher, share your list of objectives and discuss the instructional activities that focused on the objectives.
3. Describe the varied learning styles of the learners in your class. What accommodations are made to include varied ways in which students learn?
4. Beginning teachers vary in ability to initiate and participate in instructional tasks within the classroom. Giving directions can be a first step in the process of building your confidence. Determine whether you can detect the difference between students having difficulty following directions and those learners with limited listening skills. Volunteer to

give directions for at least one class or activity. Respond to the following questions:
- What are the considerations for stating explicit directions?
- What were the difficulties you perceived in giving clear directions?
- What were the difficulties you observed students exhibiting in following directions?

SUMMARY

You are beginning to take a closer look at the ways in which your students learn. It takes practice to formulate plans for determining the teaching process and selecting materials to be used for the content being presented. Deciding the means you will use to assess instruction also takes practice. As you become more perceptive in determining the objectives of the lesson being taught, you begin to see the connection between the objectives of the plan and the appropriate assessment. The selected content and strategies reinforce what you intend learners to achieve from the lesson.

Your cooperating teachers may vary the teaching strategies to assist students who may be more visual or aural. Learners may need more hands-on materials, especially in the teaching of mathematics and science. Visuals, technology, dramatizations, illustrations, and other resources appeal more to some learners and thereby reinforce their learning. Careful observations help you make connections among the different disciplines in the lessons being taught and the ways in which your cooperating teacher teaches to the students' needs. You may choose to jot down some ideas for future lessons.

FOLLOW-UP QUESTIONS AND SHARED INSIGHTS

Using your journal with the information and insights you have gathered from your observations of the teaching-learning environment, respond to the following:

1. Select one objective or learner outcome you observed and recorded. Describe the strategies used to obtain the desired learner outcome and state whether the observable performance was written or verbal.
2. List the varied teaching techniques used for the different content areas to accommodate special learning styles.
3. Share an example of a cross-disciplinary or integrated lesson plan you have observed.
4. Describe one thinking process or skill presented during a class. Did the learners receive individual or group reinforcement? What instructional materials were used in the presentation?
5. Give an example of directions you stated for learners. What factors helped students in following your directions?
6. When you explained an idea to students and they were confused, how did your rewording of the explanation affect the outcome for the learners?
7. Share one incident that demonstrates your involvement as partner-teacher at this time.

Journal Excerpts

High School

"One objective from last week was: After listening to the James Thurber story, 'The Night the Bed Fell,' students will identify and use examples of the criteria belonging in an effective personal narrative (i.e., characters, dialogues, etc.). Students are preparing to write personal narratives of their own. They have some study guides to complete as Mr. S. read and explained to them the criteria. We will check student writing samples to make sure that they have included the criteria discussed in class."

"Mr. W.'s classes are based primarily on a student-centered, cooperative learning approach. He definitely has all the various learning styles in mind. His instructional strategies and activities incorporate work in the large group, in co-operative groups of three with designated roles, and also independent practice. He also encourages students to take responsibility for their personal education and growth. He told the students that 'We value that which we learn'. . . . "

"I immediately noticed a difference between this class and other English classes. These students need very explicit directions or they will become very confused. For example, the supervising teacher told the students to write their paragraphs on every other line of the paper, giving space for teacher comments. It took almost ten minutes of explaining and modeling examples before the students caught on. I feel that teaching this class will teach me so much and help me to be a better educator."

"I think my biggest problem in giving directions is having to state them so many times. Also, students want to ask questions about the directions before you are finished giving them. Oftentimes they just choose not to follow them. . . . It is not an exaggeration to state that I probably give the same information (directions) about 10 times in one class period. My supervising teacher says that this always gets better after the first grading period."

Middle School

"In our class there is a great variety of learning styles. Although there are students who readily learn through the direct teaching approach and take notes, many others are being "left in the dark" as their learning styles are not catered to in class. These students include those who are visual learners as well as active learners who need hands-on experiences. As I begin to prepare my lessons, I plan on doing my best to reach out to all of the varied learning styles."

"I have made an effort to really be clear in giving directions. There are several things that I take for granted will be done automatically. I am learning that single words are important to include in the directions like 'now' or 'independently.' I'm learning to be more specific with directions mainly through minor mistakes that I make."

"In first period, we had a short team meeting to discuss some dates: field trips, monitoring a basketball game, etc. We also talked about parent-teacher conference day and career testing. It was basically organization of schedules. I just listened, but I am rather impressed by the planning this team does together."

Elementary

"After reading the focus question about learning styles of students, I got real worried. I thought, 'Oh no, am I addressing the needs of my students?' Today I really paid close attention to that in the classroom. One thing I like to have the class do is to write down what they are thinking before sharing in a small group. Then a few students have the opportunity to share in the large group. Well, right there I have hit on intrapersonal, interpersonal, as well as verbal/linguistic. This makes me feel good because I have done this naturally—just think about how effective I will be when I consciously address my students' needs!"

"I am still learning about the students' learning styles, but it is obvious through work, words, and actions that they all differ greatly from one another. Many students are difficult to motivate, but we usually do well. Most students may take time, but eventually they get on-task. A few initiate the move toward work, sharing, and participating in class. Some students are followers and will join in while others need more encouragement."

"Today I arrived early to discuss the lesson that I will be teaching tomorrow on graphing. I wanted to make sure that my lesson was approved by Mrs. D. The graphing lesson is connected to our reading activities. As a class we will be graphing our favorite zoo animal. Mrs. D. and I discussed my objectives and the best way to present my lesson. I find this very helpful when planning a lesson. The input of Mrs. D. is wonderful and I appreciate all of her experience."

Special Education

"I have always been fairly detailed when giving directions to anyone, much less my students. In fact, oftentimes I may give too many details in my instructions, but I believe that it can actually help students. I have learned through this whole process that all children hear, see, and interpret things differently. I first attempt to get all of the students' attention, speaking loudly and clearly so all can hear, trying not to be too talkative, then I ask a student to repeat back to the class what they are to do. My students seldom ask me to repeat my directions."

"Over the past few days I have already noted several different learning styles and preferences. Most all of the students seem to assimilate information better if the teacher actually says it verbally and also writes it on the board or hands it out to them. This visual learning style has also been encouraged through videos and posters in the room. Some students also participate actively, while others do not join in class discussion."

"Clear and concise directions are key for both of my supervising teachers because they have so much going on in the classroom. One teacher uses student recapping, the students repeat the directions given, and the other usually writes the directions on the board. Both of them repeat directions several times, and that allows plenty of time for answering any questions and clarifying of any statements! Much emphasis is placed on the individual learning styles and needs of each student."

SAMPLE LESSON PLAN

The sample lesson plan serves as a model to demonstrate ways the teacher can incorporate the many components necessary to planning effective lessons.

Name: Steven Straub
Lesson Length: Block Scheduling (85 minutes)
Grade Level: 10
Number of Students: 22

Number with IEP: 2
Subject: Algebra I, Part II
Topic: Systems of Equations

Objectives

In this lesson, students will:

- Solve systems of equations using the graphing method
- Simplify expressions involving substitution
- Solve systems of equations using substitution

Connections

These objectives relate to the following Kentucky Learner Goals:

- **Goal 2.8**—Students understand various mathematical procedures and use them appropriately and accurately.
- **Goal 2.7**—Students understand various number concepts and use numbers appropriately and accurately.
- **Goal 2.10**—Students understand measurement concepts and use measurements appropriately and accurately.
- **Goal 2.11**—Students understand mathematical change concepts and use them appropriately and accurately.
- **Goal 4.1**—Students effectively use interpersonal skills.

This lesson plan allows students to use a concept learned in Algebra I, Part II and apply it in new situation. After reviewing how to use the process of substitution to simplify an algebraic expression, students will learn the mathematical process about how to solve a system of equations using substitution. Students also use procedures as they complete their warm-up word problem.

Number concepts will also be measured as students use the order of operations to simplify algebraic expressions. Students will use their knowledge of numbers to simplify these expressions as well as check their answers when solving a system of equations. Number concepts will also be utilized as the class completes a review word problem for warm-up that requires them to analyze a problem and find the appropriate solution.

In addition, students will use measurement concepts as they review solving a system of equations using the graphing method. Students must measure and draw a line correctly in order to solve the system using the graphing method. Students will also explore the mathematical concept of change as they solve systems. Using substitution to solve a system of equations requires students to manipulate their equations and change the form in which they appear.

Activities in this lesson strengthen students' interpersonal skills. The use of the scavenger hunt activity allows students to work together to simplify expressions. Students can also ask each other for help as they work together at the end of the class solving problems using the whiteboards.

Context

This lesson is part of a unit on Systems of Equations. Students will ultimately learn three different methods for solving systems: graphing, substitution, and elimination. The homework will ensure that students understand the graphing method. The day's lecture and activities teach the substitution method.

Materials/Technology

The following materials are needed to complete the lesson:

- Overhead for warm-up and notes
- Overhead for warm-up word problem
- Homework solutions
- Scavenger hunt stations
- Scavenger hunt key
- Guided notes
- Overhead for guided notes
- Whiteboards (wipeboards), markers, and erasers
- Whiteboard practice problems
- Homework worksheet

Procedures

The following procedures must be completed to complete the lesson:

- As soon as the bell rings, students will take their seats and I will review with them the agenda for the day.
- Students will complete a short warm-up word problem using a five-step procedure that they learned to solve word problems. This practice helps students at the academic level continue to use basic arithmetic and reasoning skills.
- After the warm-ups are finished, as a class we will discuss the answers so students can get immediate feedback.
- We will then check homework assignments. After answers are read aloud, students can ask questions and I will work problems as requested. Once this process is completed, I will collect the homework for a grade based on completion.
- Students will complete a scavenger hunt to review the concept of substitution. Students will start at a particular station, work a problem, and find the answer at another station, where they will begin work on another problem. At the end of the scavenger hunt, students will check their "map" with the instructor.
- Guided notes will be used to present new material on how to solve a system of equations using substitution. The specific learning objective will be restated.
- Students may practice the substitution method by working on practice problems on the whiteboards. Students enjoy working with the boards because they can erase them easily if they make a mistake. As students finish a particular problem, they will hold up their answers and the teacher will check their work for accuracy, thereby providing immediate feedback.
- At the end of the period, students will review what they have learned about the substitution method. As time permits, students may start working on their homework.

Student Assessment

Students will be assessed in a variety of ways.

- Completion of homework. Students receive 10 points if they have attempted to solve every problem and have shown their work. No partial credit is given.
- Warm-up word problem. Students can earn up to 10 points if they solve the warm-up word problem. Students receive credit for using the five-step procedure that they have learned in class.

- Quality of participation during calculator activity as well as station work.
- Grade on unit test.

Impact

Overall, this lesson went rather well. Both the grades on the warm-ups as well as the completion of the homework indicated that students grasped how to solve a system of equations using the graphing method. A future lesson will show students how to solve a system graphically using their calculator, thereby reinforcing the material.

Both the scavenger hunt and the whiteboard activity provided the teacher and the students with immediate feedback about how students mastered the new concepts. The whiteboards also allowed students to correct minor mistakes as well as to visualize their errors.

Refinement

I need to correct one error in the scavenger hunt—one answer was repeated twice. I think I would also generate overhead keys for the homework check as students need a visual aid to check their systems by graphing. Simply reading the ordered pairs that are the solutions to the various systems does not meet the needs of visual learners in the class.

REFERENCES AND SUGGESTED READINGS

Allen, R. H. (2002). *Impact teaching: Ideas and strategies for teachers to maximize student learning.* Boston: Allyn & Bacon.

Armstrong, T. (1998). *Awakening genius in the classroom.* Alexandria, VA: Association for Supervision and Curriculum Development.

Ayers, W. (2001). *To teach: The journey of a teacher.* New York: Teachers College Press.

Bloom, B., Engelhart, M., Furst, E., Hill, W., & Krathwohl, D. (1956). *Taxonomy of educational objectives: Cognitive domain.* New York: Longman.

Brophy, J. (1998). *Motivating students to learn.* Boston: McGraw-Hill.

Campbell, L. (1997). How teachers interpret MI theory. *Educational Leadership, 55*(1), 14–19.

Campbell, L., & Campbell, B. (1999). *Multiple intelligences and student achievement: Success stories from six schools.* Alexandria, VA: Association for Supervision and Curriculum Development.

Checkley, K. (1997). The first seven . . . and the eighth. *Educational Leadership, 55*(1), 8–13.

Danielson, C. (1996). *Enhancing professional practice: A framework for teaching.* Alexandria, VA: Association for Supervision and Curriculum Development.

Darling-Hammond, L., & Rustique-Forrester, E. (1997). Investing in quality teaching: State-level strategies. *Perspective.* Education Commission of the States.

Dunn, R., & Dunn, K. (1993). *Teaching secondary students through their individual learning styles: Practical approach for grades 7–12.* Boston: Allyn & Bacon.

Eby, J. W., & Martin, D. B. (2001). *Reflective planning, teaching, and evaluation for the elementary school* (3rd ed.). Upper Saddle River, NJ: Merrill/Prentice Hall.

Emmer, E. T., Evertson, C. M., & Worsham, M. E. (2000). *Classroom management for secondary teachers.* Boston: Allyn & Bacon.

Gardner, H. (1993). *Multiple intelligences: The theory in practice.* New York: Basic Books.

Gardner, H. (1995). Reflections on multiple intelligences: Myths and messages. *Phi Delta Kappan, 77*(3), 200–209.

Gardner, H., & DeNozzi, R. (2002). *MI millennium: Multiple intelligence for the new millennium.* Los Angeles: Into the Classroom Media.

Gay, G. (2002). Preparing for culturally responsive teaching. *Journal of Teacher Education, 53*(2), 106–116.

Good, T., & Brophy, J. (2001). *Looking in classrooms* (8th ed.). New York: Longman.

Gordon, S. P., & Maxey, S. (2000). How to help beginning teachers succeed (2nd ed.). Alexandria, VA: Association for Supervision and Curriculum Development.

Gronlund, N. E. (1990). *How to write instructional objectives.* New York: Free Press.

Jersild, A. T. (1955). *When teachers face themselves.* New York: Teachers College Press.

Kagan, S., & Kagan, M. (1998). *Multiple intelligences: The complete MI book.* San Clemente, CA: Kagan Cooperative Learning.

Krathwohl, D., Bloom, B., & Masia, B. (1964). *Taxonomy of educational objectives, handbook II: Affective domain.* New York: David McKay.

Mager, R. F. (1997). *Preparing instructional objectives* (3rd ed.). Atlanta, GA: The Center for Effective Performance.

Rust, F. O., & Freidus, H. (2001). *Guiding school change: The role and work of change agents.* New York: Teachers College Press.

Sapon-Shevin, M. (2001). Schools fit for all. *Educational Leadership, 58*(4), 34–39.

Shaughnessy, M. F. (1998). An interview with Rita Dunn about learning styles. *The Clearing House, 71*(3), 141–146.

Shuell, T. (1981). Dimensions of individual differences. In F. Farley & N. Gordon (Eds.), *Psychology and education: The state of the union.* Berkeley, CA: McCutchan.

Silver, H., Strong, R., & Perini, M. (2001). *So each may learn: Integrating learning styles and multiple intelligences.* Alexandria, VA: Association for Supervision and Curriculum Development.

TenBrink, T. D. (1999). Instructional objectives. In J. Cooper (Ed.), *Classroom teaching skills* (6th ed., pp. 53–75). Lexington, MA: D.C. Heath.

Tomlinson, C. A. (1999). The differentiated classroom: Responding to the needs of all learners. Alexandria, VA: Association for Supervision and Curriculum Development.

Waldron, P. W., Collie, T. R., & Davies, C. M. W. (1999). *Telling stories about school: An invitation.* Upper Saddle River, NJ: Merrill/Prentice Hall.

Wolfe, P. (2001). *Brain matters: Translating research into classroom practice.* Alexandria, VA: Association for Supervision and Curriculum Development.

chapter 3

Designing and Planning Instruction

" *. . . by the year 2006, America will provide all students with what should be their educational birthright: access to competent, caring, and qualified teachers.* "

What Matters Most:
Teaching for America's Future
National Commission on Teaching
and America's Future

Focus One

Expected Performance

- Recognize, analyze, and share your emotional response to becoming a "competent, caring, and qualified teacher."
- Critically listen to your peers' classroom experiences to gain deeper insights into the multifaceted role of teacher.
- Determine which actions or attitudes will strengthen your ability to demonstrate effectively some aspect of the teacher role.

ANALYZING YOUR EMOTIONAL RESPONSE TO BEGINNING TEACHING

Are you feeling a part of the classroom, the team, the school? You now know the routines, the location of supplies, and the names of many students. You are responsible for directing students and planning instruction. You are examining and assessing your performance in some aspects of the teacher role. Away from the classroom and dialoguing with peers who are experiencing similar adjustments and learning, you can now concentrate on your personal development as a teacher.

Many recognize that new teachers feel overwhelmed by the sheer number and seriousness of the decisions and choices they are asked to make. You may question your readiness for so many responsibilities (Eby & Martin, 2001; Hutchinson, 2000). During field experiences you became aware of the complex cultural and social dynamics of classrooms. Repeatedly you hear about the new ways of teaching and learning promoted by the learned societies and performance standards outlined by national and state reform movements. You are also aware of entering the teaching profession at a time when instruction has become more student centered and learning activities more developmentally appropriate. Teachers are expanding the variety of approaches needed to tailor classroom experiences to the needs of individual learners to validate their cultural roots and examine content in light of multiple contributions. In this current high-tech era, teachers establish classrooms of "high touch," that is, a warm and human-oriented place for students where learning occurs in a caring, creative environment that focuses on relationship building and the importance of cultural context (Alley & Jung, 1995; Pang, 2001).

Experiencing the multifaceted role of the teacher and engaging in the rapid pace of the classroom, your head may be whirling and your emotions bubbling on the surface. One of the many pieces of your expanding reality is your emotional response to what you are learning and doing. Acknowledging and analyzing your feelings is a critical step toward becoming a professional.

This activity invites you to recognize what you are feeling and understand those emotions as a valid response to certain aspects and demands of the teacher role. You may be saddened by the fact that a number of students appear to not value learning. You may be outraged to know the neglect and abuse some students experience. You may feel exasperated when a gifted student refuses to use his or her talents. Feelings are a part of you! They count—they force you to action.

What aspiring or experienced teacher does not respond with a rousing "Yes!" to the quotation at the beginning of this chapter? The words most likely parallel the vision you have of yourself as a "competent, caring, and qualified" teacher. As you engage in the process of becoming that teacher, you gain a better understanding of the many dimensions of the teacher's role.

Student teaching immerses you into new situations and unfamiliar surroundings. Although the classroom is neither new nor unfamiliar to you, being the "teacher" in charge of instruction is different. Through the day-in and day-out routine of teaching, you are meeting the demands of teaching—planning, collaborating, explaining, demonstrating, and managing learner activities. Some of the stardust you experienced earlier about being a teacher has settled, and teacher responsibilities seem to extend across the horizon. How many different areas there are to monitor and manage! There is much activity—walking, talking, remembering names, organizing materials, checking and changing schedules. Much energy and continuous effort is expended. The ideas that seemed logical and well organized in your head may not have played out in what you said or did. Perhaps a class activity did not proceed as you mentally pictured it even though you spent hours planning it. What feelings and emotions are churning inside you as you practice the role of teacher? How do you feel about what you are doing?

Pause to recall the teacher responsibilities you have been given. Recognize and analyze what you are feeling. Are you bewildered? Overwhelmed? Anxious? Take 3 or 4 minutes to identify in writing what you feel at this time about the role you are assuming. How have you adapted to this new role? Using affective words, describe your feelings and emotions.

_____

_____

_____

Discussion Questions

1. Using words that convey deep feelings and responses to critical student or teacher issues (e.g., *swamped, eager, enthusiastic, anxious, excited, overwhelmed, frustrated, self-conscious, scared,* etc.), describe a single incident that moved or challenged you, and analyze your feelings regarding your responsibility or your role in the incident.

2. Think about the different roles teachers assume, those engaging the heart and those demanding knowledge and refined teaching techniques. How do your current responsibilities provide you opportunities to integrate what you have learned into your performance as a competent, caring teacher?

3. Telling and listening to stories and others' insights helps you integrate numerous experiences and make sense of them in light of your own. Individuals are often catalysts for helping you recognize and understand your own emotions, while deepening your insights about teaching. What knowledge, attitude, belief, or value have you related to or recalled after hearing others' stories? Explain the effect that hearing these stories had on insights about your own experiences in the classroom.

4. How comfortable are you sharing your feelings with others? To what extent does deep dialogue with others enhance your understanding of how to balance the affective (empathy with students) with the cognitive (understanding of the teacher's role) components of teaching?

Focus Two

Expected Performance

- Identify and design instruction appropriate to learners' stages of development, learning styles, strengths, and needs.
- Incorporate strategies that address physical, social, and cultural diversity that show sensitivity to differences.
- Identify when and how to access appropriate services or resources to meet exceptional learning needs.
- Seek to understand students' families, cultures, and communities, and use this information as a basis for connecting instruction to students' experiences.
- Propose and include learning experiences that challenge, motivate, and actively involve learners, and encourage students to be adaptable, flexible, resourceful, and creative.

It is normal to feel overwhelmed. It's okay to be bewildered, feel anxious, tired, or frustrated. Your feelings are part of the process of becoming a competent, caring, qualified teacher. As you shared experiences with your **Focus One** group, it was reassuring to hear others having similar feelings. Gaining competence in planning lessons will help reduce your sense of being overwhelmed.

Planning for the individual needs of your students can be a difficult process. Coordinating activities that meet the lesson objectives and responding to varied learners within a specified time frame takes organization and planning. Gathering information concerning achievement levels, language abilities, and student interests helps you prepare for the variations and adjustments necessary in planning for individual differences among learners. You have observed a number of teachers who seemed to have the key to effective and efficient planning, and perhaps learned techniques from them to help you grasp the big picture along with many ways in which to deliver content in smaller chunks so students may build understanding over time.

Orlich, Harder, Callahan, and Gibson (2001) suggest four techniques that effective teachers use in their planning process:

1. Plan routines to expedite the daily flow of instruction to ensure that students know upfront what is expected of them and the arrangements made to regulate activities.
2. Talk to yourself or use reflective dialogue about best instructional practices or management techniques to adopt with your class.
3. Develop interdependent planning levels (long range, unit, and daily) to help you convert long-range goals into daily activities.
4. Collect a treasury of teaching materials that provide you resources and the ability to create a rich environment for learning.

APPLICATION: DESIGNING AND PLANNING INSTRUCTION

The task of planning for classroom instruction requires knowledge of the planning process and skill in decision making. Selecting a particular framework will aid you in this planning process. In your teacher preparation courses you may have been taught to follow Rosenshine's (1983) six basic teaching functions, Hunter's (1984) Instructional Theory into Practice, the Sandra Kaplan Matrix (1979), or the James Cooper (1999) planning model when developing your lesson plan format. In this section you will find a suggested framework for planning. Teachers use this framework as they plan for linking the curriculum with assessment. As teacher you are asked to make decisions about curriculum based on data gathered from observation and other assessment sources. As you plan for different grade levels, decisions are made based on reflective insights gained from questions such as those listed under the five categories below. The following questions will enable you to develop a broad perspective as you begin to take on the teacher role.

Diagnosis and assessment of learner needs

1. At what level of independence are students in this class able to read?
2. What problem-solving skills do they demonstrate?
3. What works best for this group of learners, given their diverse cultural backgrounds, socioeconomic levels, gender, and preferred styles of interaction?

Development of learner expectations

1. What is it that you intend your students to achieve during this class period?
2. What expectations do you have for learners with special needs?
3. What expectations do you have for learners of color?
4. What knowledge will your students demonstrate after completing this unit?

Organization of content, resources, and learners

1. What instructional strategies will you use to meet the needs of individual learners?
2. What technology and other materials will you use to actively engage students in the learning process?
3. How will you arrange the classroom furniture, technology, and other materials to support the learning environment?

Assessment to determine learner outcomes

1. What criteria or scoring guides do you need to prepare? Does the activity require that a rubric be used for assessing performance?
2. What will focus student attention on what is to be learned and promote student self-assessment?
3. Have you matched the objectives with the assessment instruments you chose?

Practice and follow-up instruction

1. How might you restate, review, and practice skills and content with learners with special needs? What additional resources, webs, charts, and so forth might you design to help learners grasp essential content?
2. Do you ask the students to make connections between today's content and skills with those taught yesterday, last week, or at some earlier time? This is critical to deep and meaningful learning.
3. Based on the results of the assessment, do you need to reteach, reinforce, or move into more challenging content with all students? Some students?

Mastery of Knowledge

Fundamental to lesson preparation is mastery of the content being taught. Reading a number of outside sources may be required for you to gain a firm understanding of the content. Taking notes and making outlines from the readings may assist you in both short- and long-range planning. These notes may assist you when organizing the concepts and topics to be included in your presentations. Examining texts, curriculum standards, school system guidelines, the Internet, and other supplementary materials available in the school's media center provides additional information needed for teaching. This may seem like an overwhelming task at first, but as you build your knowledge of content your confidence in your ability to teach will soar. You are beginning to get a clearer picture of all the responsibilities that accompany high-quality teaching and learning. The complexity associated with meeting the diverse and individual needs of your student population requires you to have a high level of knowledge about the content you teach and a supportive environment in which to teach (Moon, Callahan, & Tomlinson, 1999).

Collaborative Planning

Your cooperating teacher is the conductor of the environment in which you find yourself. If you haven't noticed by now, he or she sets the stage for learning through direct communication with students and setting high expectations for *all* learners. Communicating with your cooperating teacher concerning your plans and your new ideas is essential if you are to engage learners in the processes you require of them to reach the outcomes you expect them to meet or master. Coupling your knowledge and background with the expertise of your supervising or cooperating teacher will empower you to teach in ways that exemplify best practices. You can reflect on the obvious characteristics of the professional teacher with whom you have been placed such as how he or she manages the classroom and puts procedures in place to facilitate student learning. You can observe how lessons flow, how he or she interacts with students, and the way interruptions are handled. However, you cannot know the teacher's thought process—how he or she makes daily and minute-by-minute decisions and choices. Having the teacher explain what he or she does in the classroom to ensure learning for all students is what Tom (1997) terms "transparency of practice." It is similar to the way you use "think-alouds" with your students when you want them to witness your thought processes by actually thinking aloud in class to model how you think when solving problems, reading, or writing. Ask your cooperating teacher to "think through" a lesson with you.

Your ability to observe, ask critical questions, and "get into the mind" of your cooperating teacher is critical at this time (Ethell & McMeniman, 2000). He or she is there to act as your mentor, and expects you to ask critical questions that allow you keen insights into the decision-making process necessary to effect student learning and achievement. When you are unclear about a procedure or process or teaching strategy, remember to ask your cooperating teacher questions that will serve you well in the long run such as: "Why did you place M. and K. together to work on the project? What do you do to help J. learn the concepts you are teaching when his ability level is so low? How do you handle the call-outs, and why are some acceptable when others are not?" These types of questions allow you to hear what your cooperating teacher is thinking prior to making a decision. It allows you to make connections between theory and practice as it unfolds before you (Ethell & McMeniman). Engaging him or her in "self-talk" with you can serve as a model for your own thought processes as you work to plan lessons and learning activities that are meaningful and generate student learning.

You may want to review grouping patterns, methods for diagnosing learner strengths and weaknesses, and arrangements for learners with special needs within the classroom and school with your cooperating teacher. An inclusive lesson plan ensures that all learners participate in learning and contribute to the collective experience. Again, ask *why* students are placed in certain groups. Are the groups flexible, used to reinforce a skill or learning strategy? Are the groups intentionally planned to generate deeper learning of the material or skill? Using groups is an effective practice only if they are implemented purposefully, with an eye on cognitive as well as social outcomes, and if members are held accountable to one another and the specified outcomes for their learning. If you plan to use groups in your classroom, make sure the task fits the demands of the content and learning activity, and that you have planned roles and responsibilities for group members. This is a process that takes time to teach students; modeling is critical if they are to work together as you envision them.

Keeping All Learners in Mind

How often have you found yourself confounded by a philosophy, pedagogy, or concept taught in your education classes or other college course work? Experiencing distress may have caused you to tune out the instructor or momentarily give up on learning. When you finally understood what you were charged with learning, what methods or examples were used to help you learn? In planning your instruction, be sure to generate numerous and varied examples to help students grasp the content you are teaching. Plan engaging activities that allow students to experience as much as possible what you want them to learn or be able to do. Students who are engaged in authentic learning, learn more deeply and classroom management issues are virtually nonexistent (Good & Brophy, 2000). As you plan to teach a lesson, focus on what the students will do and why. Be sure to let them know this important part of the lesson if you want them to take ownership for their learning and participate more fully in the exchange.

You may have had more experience in designing lesson plans for whole- or small-group activities. In your student or intern teaching experience you are expected to "grow into" teaching on a more professional level. Today, that requires you to know the students you are teaching, their cultural and socioeconomic backgrounds, preferred learning styles, abilities and disabilities. As you delve more deeply and take on the role of teacher, your lesson planning may take on a more reflective dimension. Knowing your students' abilities and challenges nudges you to create lessons with them in mind. One way to meet individual needs within a typical classroom setting is to differentiate instruction and activities to meet the diverse needs of learners. This approach to teaching challenges even veteran teachers, but we suggest you use the concept in planning at least one class during your student teaching or intern experience.

Differentiated Instruction

Differentiating instruction appears daunting at first. With practice and foresight, however, using this method to enhance planning allows you to design instruction that impacts student learning. Differentiating instruction becomes almost second nature to the process of planning as you think about what and how you plan to teach a lesson or unit of study. You are already accommodating the learners in your class who have special needs by following the recommendations on their IEPs; learning to differentiate instruction is a natural step in the attainment of your goal to meet the needs of all of your students (Matlock, Fielder, & Walsh, 2001).

Differentiating instruction requires you to use a task analysis approach to determine what it is that students can do with no help, little assistance, or more major interventions. Just like you make notes for what you need to do to accommodate P.'s IEP, note on the lesson plan how you provided A. and S. partially completed outlines to help them follow along with the class as you begin to teach a new area of content. For the rest of the class, you may provide skeleton outlines to help them focus on the lesson or task at hand. R. may have demonstrated a high level of competence in the area you are teaching. Note that you sent him to the computer lab or library to gather additional research to present to the whole class, or a small group of learners. While D. and M. fly through the vocabulary activity you planned to increase their understanding of the major concepts presented in your unit, J., F., and P. can barely read the words. Note on your lesson plan the ways in which you allowed them to work with only the prefixes or suffixes of the words you selected. They will present a chart to add to the word wall that defines each prefix or suffix and thereby contribute to the class' understanding. This is just a sampling of ideas to help you begin to think about what it is you teach, why you are teaching it, how you plan to teach it so all members of the class learn in ways that are meaningful while contributing to the overall collaborative climate of the classroom.

Reflection on Your Plan

Reflecting on your lesson plans can give you a keener insight into how effective it may be in facilitating students' learning on many different levels. Make sure that the lesson objectives are in tune with the assessments you plan. After determining from your informal and formal assessment whether you have achieved what you set out to achieve, you may choose to reteach, reinforce the concept, or move on to the next lesson.

ASSIGNED ACTIVITIES

This assignment focuses on preliminary identification of learner ability and examination of instructional resources.

1. Examine the diagnostic and assessment procedures for determining the needs of learners you will teach in your class. Look at the following items. Which items can you immediately address? Which items are not clear at this time? Give examples of any information collected on individual differences of the learner including:
   - Learner interests
   - Problem-solving ability
   - Independent reading ability
   - Verbal and written language ability
2. Study the varied uses of technology, curriculum guidelines, texts, and other materials used with learners. Briefly describe the use of technology and other materials you and/or the supervising teacher use with students.
3. To what extent have you initiated taking roll, grading papers, designing a seating chart, tutoring, checking homework, or handling additional responsibilities? Describe your participation.
4. How are decisions made about the content taught in your class? The breadth, the depth, and the time frame in which concepts and skills are developed among learners?
5. What strategies are included in planning lessons to meet the needs of individual students in the class?
   - How is background built or learning scaffolded for novice or apprentice learners?
   - How is learning extended for gifted learners?
   - What accommodations are made for learners with IEPs?
   - How are learners' cultural or religious backgrounds, or gender issues reflected in lesson plans?

SUMMARY

Your application focused on a framework that helped you with organizing your planning. In reflecting, you may have proceeded through the following tasks:

- observing closely the needs of learners
- developing and/or observing the objectives for lessons taught—what you intended that students know and be able to do during a particular class period
- examining materials, including activities that provide students with a positive learning experience
- discussing with the supervising teacher the assessment used with your students
- reflecting on what was accomplished and the means of accomplishment
- planning for review, reinforcement, and/or reteaching the lesson

As you continue reinforcing this process and refining your planning skills, you will discover that there is more to planning for your class than the lesson plan. Even though it is challenging and time consuming, planning can be exciting and rewarding.

FOLLOW-UP QUESTIONS AND SHARED INSIGHTS

Think back to the very beginning of your experience. Name sources of information that you used to help accumulate information concerning learner needs or learner differences. Look at your journals and assignments and, with the person next to you, locate examples of reflective-type comments. Reflections written soon after observing or teaching are often more accurate and insightful. Decide why your comments were reflective. Now think back over teaching that you did or observed. What were your expectations or those of your supervising teacher? How did you plan for them? What was your rationale for the techniques you planned? List changes you would make and rationale for those changes. Ask yourself these types of questions as you plan day by day:

- What is the concept to be taught?
- What is my purpose for using this strategy?
- How do I approach this concept in a creative way to engage more students?
- What can I do with the results of the student assessment?
- Do my students need to spend more time on this specific concept?
- How will I handle Brittany, Troy, Juan, or Merilou's group?
- How will I differentiate instruction to better meet the needs of all the students in my class?

Journal excerpts cite specific teaching behaviors you tried and your successes or limitations. You may want to relate these experiences to observations or previous knowledge about effective teaching and learning. Finally, note what new ideas, insights, or feelings come as a result of your responding in this manner.

Keep in mind all aspects of the planning process as you share your response to the following questions:

1. In what ways do you assist or direct students throughout the school day (a) during homeroom activities, (b) as students come into the classroom, (c) in the hallway, (d) during assemblies or programs, and (e) in cooperative groups?

2. How is the school day organized to schedule time with students with special needs in your class? In a collaborating teaching situation, how is teacher time organized to provide additional assistance to learners with special needs?
3. How does the teacher handle on-task time when students are leaving during class time?
4. Think about the decisions you are making in planning the content for a lesson. How do you decide the amount of content for a selected lesson?
5. What are your strengths in the planning process? In what areas do you need to improve? You may wish to add a personal action plan for the coming week to reinforce your steps to improve.
6. Examine at least two classes and describe the performance expected of the students.
7. Having examined the curriculum, textbooks, technology, and other materials, what are your plans for using these materials in your teaching?
8. What access do teachers have to resources in your school library or media center? Is there a special system for request or checkout?

Portfolio Tasks

Portfolios are increasingly becoming the means of demonstrating the skills, experiences, and accomplishments of the beginning teacher. Portfolio entries are an excellent means for assessing your teaching ability. Teacher Standards established by national and state groups will assist you in developing your portfolio. This collection of information may be ongoing throughout your teacher education program. We are providing what we call **Portfolio Tasks** based on national and state teacher standards that you may complete during your student or intern teacher experience. We urge you to examine the standards and begin to plan your portfolio tasks. As you design and perform each portfolio task, you are documenting what you and your students accomplish as a result of your planning and teaching. In addition, you are engaging in reflection about the decisions made as the teacher. This is a major purpose for developing a teaching portfolio: reflecting and documenting your professional growth and competence as a student or intern teacher.

Earlier in your teacher education program you may have developed portfolio entries. Significant additions to your portfolio may be made during your student or intern teacher experience. Portfolio tasks are placed in this chapter, and others, to assist you in creating or enhancing your professional portfolio based on Interstate New Teacher Assessment and Support Consortium (INTASC) standards. You may also refer to the New Teacher Standards (State) and International Society for Techology in Education Standards (ISTE) which are locate in Appendix C. Chapter 15 covers in detail the professional portfolio, including the electronic or digital portfolio, giving a more complete picture of how the portfolio can benefit you. You will find suggested portfolio tasks in select chapters under **Focus Two.** A briefcase symbol is used to alert you to the task.

Designs and Plans Instruction

Performance Standards

Your first task is based on the following national standards:

Standard 1: The teacher understands the central concepts, tools of inquiry, and structures of the discipline(s) he or she teaches and can create learning experiences that make these aspects of subject matter meaningful for students.

Standard 2: The teacher understands how children learn and develop and can provide learning opportunities that support their intellectual, social, and personal development.

Standard 3: The teacher understands how students differ in their approaches to learning and creates instructional opportunities that are adapted to diverse learners.

Standard 7: The teacher plans instruction based upon knowledge of subject matter, students, the community, and curriculum goals.

Performance Guidelines

In this first portfolio task, exhibit samples of lesson plans you have designed and planned for the classes you teach. Select six of your best lesson plans for this task. In developing your lesson plans consider such information as learner needs, expectations for learners, the content being taught, integration of technology with content strategies to engage the learner, and the assessment to be applied. Using your selected lesson plan format, demonstrate to the portfolio reader that your plan was developed according to the criteria below. You may want to include student work (one or two samples), an assessment tool or reflection on the impact and refinement of the lesson taught, activity forms that you have developed, pictures of students in group activities, student work on bulletin boards, or other artifacts to accompany your plans.

Performance Criteria

The quality of your product will be assessed to the extent that evidence provided:

1. Develops the student's ability to apply knowledge, skills, and thinking processes.
2. Integrates skills, thinking processes, and content across disciplines.
3. Proposes learning experiences that challenge, motivate, and actively involve the learner.
4. Proposes learning experiences that are developmentally appropriate for learners.
5. Incorporates strategies that address physical, social, and cultural diversity and show sensitivity to differences.
6. Establishes physical classroom environments to support the type of teaching and learning that is to occur.
7. Includes creative and appropriate use of technology as a tool to enhance student learning.
8. Includes comprehensive and appropriate school and community resources that support learning.
9. Includes learning experiences that encourage students to be adaptable, flexible, resourceful, and creative.

Caution

As author of your portfolio, all materials in the portfolio should be your own work. When adding student papers, change or delete the names to acknowledge the confidentiality of the students' work. Sample lesson plans that you receive from advisors, supervising or other teachers, or Internet sources must be credited and not considered your work. You may adapt the strategies from these plans to suit the needs and abilities of your students, formatting them in your own words to reflect your teaching style.

Web Sites

The following Web sites provide valuable information concerning copyright and multimedia use:

http://www.clarinet.com/brad/copymyths.html—an attempt to answer common myths about copyright material on the Internet and cover issues related to copyright and USENET/Internet publication.
http://www.nlc-bnc.ca/index.html—guidelines on software and copyright.

Journal Excerpts

High School

"Thus far, I have taken full responsibility for one block, pre-algebra, and I take over two more blocks starting a week from today. I have taken roll several times and graded homework papers, but have not given tests or quizzes yet. Mr. M. wanted to grade the first one to see how they were doing. I have been assisting several students before, during, and after classes. This week the students have standardized testing, so I am doing a lot of extra planning. I feel pretty involved right now overall."

"In deciding what and how much content is to be presented in a class for a certain lesson involves a number of things. Ms. J. and I take into consideration which class we're dealing with. We expect the advanced students to go more in depth with material. They are treated as though they are college students who are expected to excel in their work. We consider the students who may struggle with the material. We always make an effort to have a handout for students to see, we go over it aloud, and then many times we give students many examples to help them understand the materials. We also look at how we assess the students and we try to vary the assessment so the students have the opportunity to show their abilities."

Middle School

"During the day, I look ahead to future content so that I can get a general idea of where we are going so that I can begin to formulate lesson ideas. Decisions made about what and how much content is to be covered during a particular lesson is largely based on the students' needs and abilities. We look at what is to be taught during a lesson and try to decide how much and how well the students will be able to process within the time frame. We use the textbook as our content guide, sometimes rearranging sections, or even jumping chapters."

"After school, I shared tomorrow's lesson plan with Ms. H. She'd seen it before. We've been chatting about it all week and sort of sharing ideas. She is really helpful and doesn't mind sharing her ideas and materials with me."

"Many of the students voiced their concerns that the story and study guide were too hard to read and understand. But I stayed with them and encouraged them, giving them ways to find the meaning of a story. I showed a lot of empathy, and made sure not to act disgusted with their persistence that it was too hard. I encouraged them and told them I would not have assigned it if I didn't think they could handle it!"

Elementary

"Today I learned a valuable lesson in designing and planning instruction. No matter how beautiful a plan may look and how much time you have put into it, there is no telling what will happen and how you may have to be flexible and change everything. So far, I have noticed that a strong point I have is that I tend to incorporate different techniques for presenting the information."

"A problem I have with planning instruction is that I do not have a firm grasp on what these students are capable of achieving. A lot of times I think, 'This will be great!' and the students are lost because I have gone way over their heads. I also look at students' work and think, 'I can't believe they got this wrong,' or 'Can't they write faster than that?' I guess *I* am learning."

"There are students in my class that learn better with a hands-on approach, or through movement (kinesthetic learners). My supervising teacher incorporates movement into her lessons. For example, they clap, snap, stomp, etc., when spelling vocabulary words. I plan to do this also when I teach my lesson tomorrow."

Special Education

"I looked at the materials that my supervising teacher uses for math and reading . . . observed where each student was, and worked with several individuals. It seems like we are always teaching two or three lessons at once because the students are on such different levels. . . . This was a shock to my system because I had been used to large-group instruction and then working with individuals during the time I gave for independent practice. . . . When they feel that they are learning and are doing well, their behavior improves."

"I've taken the initiative with a number of the students by noting weaknesses and providing special helps in the afternoon homework hustle time. Also, in my lessons I am modifying different activities as needed by the students."

"I actually feel better about myself after my meeting with Dr. M. We closely analyze my lesson and discuss strengths and areas for improvement. Mrs. T. and I had a good talk today after school. Feedback from my supervising teachers and professors really builds my confidence level."

REFERENCES AND SUGGESTED READINGS

Alley, R., & Jung, B. (1995). Preparing teachers for the 21st century. In M. J. O'Hair & S. J. Odell (Eds.), *Educating teachers for leadership and change* (pp. 285–301). Thousand Oaks, CA: Corwin Press.

Borko, H., Michalec, P., Timmons, M., & Siddle, J. (1997). Student teaching portfolios: A tool for promoting reflective practice. *Journal of Teacher Education, 48*(5), 345–357.

Callahan, J., Clark, L., & Kellough, R. (2002). *Teaching in the middle and secondary schools* (7th ed.). Upper Saddle River, NJ: Merrill/Prentice Hall.

Campbell, K., Cignetti, P., Melenyzer, B., Nettles, D., & Wyman, R., Jr. (2001). *How to develop a professional portfolio* (2nd ed.). Boston: Allyn & Bacon.

Constantino, P. M., & DeLorenzo, M. N. (2002). *Developing a professional teaching portfolio: A guide for success.* Boston: Allyn & Bacon.

Cooper, J. (Ed.). (1999). *Classroom teaching skills* (6th ed.). Lexington, MA: D.C. Heath.

Darling-Hammond, L. (1997). *Doing what matters most: Investing in quality teaching.* New York: National Commission on Teaching and America's Future.

Eby, J. W., & Martin, D. B. (2001). *Reflective planning, teaching, and evaluation for the elementary school* (3rd ed.). Upper Saddle River, NJ: Merrill/Prentice Hall.

Ethell, R. G., & McMeniman, M. M. (2000). Unlocking the knowledge in action of an expert practitioner. *Journal of Teacher Education, 51*(2), 87–101.

Good, T. L., & Brophy, J. E. (2000). *Looking in classrooms* (8th ed.). New York: Longman.

Gregory, G. H., & Chapman, C. (2002). *Differentiated instructional strategies.* Thousand Oaks, CA: Corwin Press.

Hunter, M. (1984). Knowing, teaching and supervision. In P. Hosford, (Ed.), *Using what we know about teaching.* Alexandria, VA: Association for Supervision and Curriculum Development.

Hutchinson, J. N. (2000). "But I don't know what to do!" *Multicultural Education, 8*(1), 41–46.

Interstate New Teacher Assessment and Support Consortium. (1992). *Model standards for beginning teacher licensing and development: A resource for state dialogue.* Washington, DC: Council of Chief State School Officers.

Jersild, A. (1955). *When teachers face themselves.* New York: Teachers College Press.

Kaplan, S. N. (1979). *Inservice training manual: Activities for development of curriculum for the gifted/talented.* Ventura, CA: Ventura County Schools.

Kentucky Education Professional Standards Board. (1994). *New teacher standards for preparation and certification* (Rev. ed.). Frankfort, KY: Department of Education.

Klenowski, V. (2000). Portfolios: Promoting teaching. *Assessment in Education, 7*(2), 215–236.

Lyons, N. (Ed.). (1998). *With portfolio in hand: Portfolios in teaching and teacher education.* New York: Teachers College Press.

Mabry, L. (1998). *Portfolio plus: A critical guide to alternative assessment.* Thousand Oaks, CA: Corwin Press.

Marzano, R. J., Pickering, D. J., & Pollock, J. E. (2001). *Classroom instruction that works.* Alexandria, VA: Association for Supervision and Curriculum Development.

Matlock, L., Fielder, K., & Walsh, D. (2001). Building the foundation for standards-based instruction for all students. *Teaching Exceptional Children, 33*(5), 68–72.

Meyer, D. K., & Tusin, L. F. (1999). Preservice teachers' perceptions of portfolios: Process versus product. *Journal of Teacher Education, 50*(2), 131–139.

Moon, T. R., Callahan, C. M., & Tomlinson, C. A. (1999). The effects of mentoring relationships on preservice teachers' attitudes toward academically diverse students. *Gifted Child Quarterly, 43*(2), 56–62.

National Commission on Teaching and America's Future. (1996). *What matters most: Teaching for America's future.* New York: Author.

Orlich, D., Harder, R., Callahan, R., & Gibson, H. (2001). *Teaching strategies: A guide to better instruction* (6th ed.). Boston: Houghton Mifflin.

Pang, V. O. (2001). *Multicultural education: A caring centered reflective approach.* Boston: McGraw-Hill.

Pitton, D. E. (1998). *Stories of student teaching: A case approach to the student teaching experience.* Upper Saddle River, NJ: Merrill/Prentice Hall.

Rosenshine, B. (1983). Teaching functions in instructional programs. *Elementary School Journal, 83,* 335–351.

Schmoker, M. (2000). The results we want. *Educational Leadership, 57*(5), 62–65.

Sprenger, M. B. (2002). *Becoming a "wiz" at brain-based teaching.* Thousand Oaks, CA: Corwin Press.

Tom, A. (1997). The deliberate relationship: A frame for talking about faculty-student relationships. *Alberta Journal of Educational Research, 43*(1), 3–21.

Wade, R., & Yarbrough, D. (1996). Portfolios: A tool for reflective thinking in teacher education? *Teacher and Teacher Education, 12,* 63–79.

Wolfe, P. (2001). *Brain matters: Translating research into classroom practice.* Alexandria, VA: Association for Supervision and Curriculum Development.

Wood, A. S. (2000). Teaching portfolios. In J. McIntyre & D. M. Byrd (Eds.), *Research on effective models for teacher education.* Thousand Oaks, CA: Corwin Press.

Zeichner, K., & Wray, S. (2001). The teaching portfolio in US teacher education programs: What we know and what we need to know. *Teaching and Teacher Education, 17*(5), 613–621.

Zubizarreta, J. (1994). Teaching portfolios and the beginning teacher. *Phi Delta Kappan, 76*(4), 323–326.

chapter

4

Accommodating Diversity in the Classroom

> " If there is anything that we wish to change in the child, we should first examine it and see whether it is not something that could be better changed in ourselves. "

C. G. Jung

Focus One

Expected Performance

- Examine your own background including racial, cultural, religious, and socioeconomic histories and discuss how your background has impacted you as a beginning teacher.
- Identify times when you felt different or isolated from a group.
- Discuss learning activities designed to generate understanding and acceptance of differences.
- Model inclusive behaviors.

ANALYZING THE AFFECTIVE DIMENSIONS OF INCLUSION

- Do your students look alike or speak alike?
- Do they like the same books, music, and movies?
- Do they hold the same work and family values as you?
- Are there cultural and socioeconomic differences among your students and between you and your students?

Multicultural education has played a significant role in helping teachers to teach learners about different cultures and practices, but today's educators are challenged to move beyond the study and celebration of different cultures to embrace and respond to diversity in its myriad forms. Many differences exist among the students in today's schools. Learners come to you from different ethnic and socioeconomic backgrounds, religions, life experiences, abilities and disabilities, and genders. *Diversity* is a term that is more inclusive and speaks to the numerous differences among the people that create the interesting tapestry of America and its schools. According to Hodgkinson (2001), the "richness of American education is its diversity." Failing to acknowledge the rich diversity among the teachers and learners that define today's schools could very well contribute to the decline of education, especially among minority learners who compose almost half of the student population in the major cities and inner cities throughout the United States (Banks, 2002; Banks & Banks, 2001; Gay, 2000).

As schools become more diverse and representative of American society, the teaching force continues to draw from a small number of men and women who wish "to make a difference" and teach. You may fit the profile of the American classroom teacher if you are White, middle class, and female and have limited experience outside your own cultural frame of reference (Banks & Banks, 2001; Tiedt & Tiedt, 2002).

Getting in Touch With Your Own Identity

Because of the many differences that exist among your students, as teacher you play a significant role in providing an environment that is tolerant and designed to meet the individual needs of the learners in your classroom. It is important that you have a broad knowledge about cultures, yours as well as others, before you can effectively navigate the emotional and academic needs of the students. Meaningful conversations and interactions with your students will teach you not only about their preferences and patterns of interaction with one another, but as a reflective teacher you will also gain insight into the ways in which you respond to those patterns, including speech, conversation, body language, and the use of physical space (Gay, 2000).

Experts in the field emphasize the importance of experiential learning in influencing your attitudes and motivating you to integrate a multicultural perspective into the content of the courses you teach (Banks & Banks, 2001; Gay, 2000; Moore, 1996). In your earlier teacher education you most likely took courses related to diversity such as an introduction to special education or multicultural education. Perhaps each textbook you read highlighted the topic in at least one chapter to prepare you for teaching in today's classroom. Perhaps you are certified to teach special education and have a strong background in this area. **Focus One** builds on your prior knowledge and experience and asks you to take advantage of your current classroom setting by learning to teach with a *multicultural mind-set*. Knowing your students' abilities and needs on a professional as well as a personal level is critical to developing this mind-set and will allow you to better meet the individual needs of your students. Knowing yourself is of even greater importance: your capabilities, areas of strength, and areas needing improvement. Getting in touch with your roots and background experiences prepares you to interact with learners on a deep level to understand the critical importance of educating all learners to their fullest capacity.

Knowing Your Students

As a student or intern teacher you can expect the life experiences of your students to differ greatly from your own. The quality of your relationship with students from different cultures, backgrounds, socioeconomic levels, abilities and disabilities offers you important learning experiences if you are willing to engage in honest dialogue to examine critical issues surrounding equity and education. According to statistical projections, students in the 21st century will be more diverse than ever before. Projected demographics indicate that a higher percentage of students will reflect a variety of cultures and races, represent social classes, claim religious affiliation, and come from family backgrounds that may differ from their teachers'. Because of these factors, life for students within your classroom may contrast sharply with the life they experience outside your classroom. It is critical that you recognize and respond to the chasm that may exist between the worldviews and life experiences held by your students and those held by you—their teacher. It is critical to identity formation that learners value the culture of home, while learning the rules and operations of the dominant culture if they are to succeed individually and collectively once they enter the workforce.

You may have had little exposure or interactions with diverse cultures and ethnic groups, and find yourself ill at ease as you encounter student speech patterns and actions that challenge you. As a beginning teacher you need to learn to "deconstruct assumptions" by interacting with children from diverse backgrounds to learn about cultural patterns of interaction, language variations, and dialects. In addition, examining learning styles of ethnic groups may help you to challenge cultural myths and stereotypical thinking about diverse children. "Dialect does influence teachers' expectations, assumptions about children and their capacities to learn . . . even though there is little evidence that speaking in another dialect form . . . negatively affects one's ability" (Delpit, 1995). Examining your assumptions about children who speak and act differently from you may be instrumental in helping you to later navigate the cultural waters with what Banks and Banks (2001) term "cultural diplomacy" and deep understanding. It is important that you as a beginning teacher gain insights into yourself as teacher and your intentions toward and your interactions with diverse populations, but it is critical that you not blame yourself for the complex social and institutional structures that are in place in today's world.

From your students' perspectives, the way you speak and interact with them may be foreign to their personal experience or conflict with their cultural values. Both you and your students may experience tense moments, especially if students do not feel accepted in the classroom or if fairness becomes an issue. As the teacher, you may even feel uneasy about the students as a group! Uncertainty and lack of experience may cause you to focus your attention on the outspoken or inappropriate behaviors of specific students. Does any of this sound familiar?

Setting the Stage for Meaningful Learning

Before meaningful learning can occur, students and teachers must explore diversity within the classroom and set the stage for tolerance where differences are appreciated and similarities are noted. Take time to examine, understand, and appreciate the differences individually and collectively among the students in your classroom. Get to know those students whose backgrounds, beliefs, and value systems may differ from yours or other students'. To accommodate the diversity of learners, initiate conversations and invite participation from all members of the class. Learning takes place within a social setting and is influenced by the culture and needs of both students and teachers.

Conversations with other teachers help you expand your view of students as unique individuals. You recognize the great potential these young people have for learning and teaching others as a result of their different backgrounds, life experiences, and cultures. Your deeper perspective regarding your students' potential challenges you to explore teaching methods and use strategies that help them make connections, find meaning, and demonstrate understanding as they engage in learning that is critical and relevant. You are aware that African American males are overrepresented in special education and pull-out programs, and that they spend more time in detention than their peers (Montgomery, 2001). To avoid this "no win" situation, you want to create a classroom culture along with your students where student voices are heard, individual and group values are honored, and rules, mores, and rituals are developed to provide stability and structure so learning can happen. High expectations are held for all learners, and each class member is responsible and accountable to the community for his or her contributions to the class (Gay, 2000; Ladson-Billings, 1994; Pang, 2001). The amount and frequency of praise, and other genuine interactions with students, are a direct result of a healthy classroom climate (Garibaldi, 1992; Rust & Freidus, 2001).

This **Focus One** activity encourages you to become personally involved with your students to gain a sense of what "walking in their shoes" would feel like for you. Begin the activity by recalling your own experiences and feelings about school. Think about a time when you felt different in school, when you felt separate from others because of a real or perceived difference. It may have been when you were in elementary, middle, or high school. It may have happened more recently, while you were working in schools during a teacher preparation course. Did feelings about being different arise from cultural, social, ethnic, or racial remarks or interactions? What happened? Did anyone say or do anything that made you feel different or feel alienated from the group? Did anyone respond to you, help you feel more comfortable? Is there anything someone could have said to you to bring you back into the group? What could someone have done to help you feel included? Analyze the specifics of the situation, taking time to reflect on what you know about diversity. Label the emotions you experienced during the time you felt isolated from the group. In the space below write words, phrases, or sentences describing your feelings.

_____

_____

_____

Using the questions that follow, discuss your experiences, and listen to those of your peers.

Discussion Questions

1. How did you respond to feeling isolated, different from others? If you are comfortable, share your experience and feelings with your peers. How did your reactions affect the way you spoke with your peers, the way you initiated or approached an activity?
2. Think about the students you teach and identify one student whose family background is different from others in the class. What do you notice about that student that sets her or him apart from others? How might you approach this student and learn about her or his experience of school?
3. What values do you hold that appear to be at odds with the values your students or their parents display? Why might these values clash? How can you help your students understand and take on the values that will help them be more successful in the mainstream culture?
4. How might you integrate multicultural issues and diversity education and training into your lessons or classes? Give examples of activities that would highlight the diversity in your class and invite discovery, conversation, and learning about cultural, gender, racial, ethnic, ability, disability, and socioeconomic differences among the students in your class.
5. How has your own racial, ethnic, cultural, and socioeconomic background impacted who you are as teacher?

Focus Two

In **Focus One** you explored the cultural, social, physical, gender, socioeconomic, and ability differences of your students. You have come face to face with the challenges that call for teaching with a multicultural mindset. When education about diversity is integrated throughout the school curricula, teachers and students begin to live, learn, and work together in this culturally diverse world. Teachers and students learn to value the diversity that exists in their community.

Becoming aware of and affirmed in our own cultural roots is an important first step toward valuing diversity. As we begin to learn about and interact with people from various backgrounds and experiences, we begin to glimpse similarities between ourselves and others, and appreciate the differences among us. In becoming more knowledgeable and more sensitive to other cultures, we are free to validate others' experiences, beliefs, values, and customs while affirming our own.

"The richness of American education is its diversity and I cannot imagine how we could fail to acknowledge that diversity."
H. Hodgkinson

APPLICATION: ACCOMMODATING THE DIVERSITY OF LEARNERS

Increasing your cultural knowledge and examining instructional strategies to prepare students for living in a pluralistic society not only enriches students' personal lives, but positively contributes to their school experiences. A wealth of diversity can be explored in literature, social studies, art, and music. Stories and poetry can be drawn upon depicting human experiences of poverty, discrimination, conflict, liberation, exploration, and justice. Social studies can be explored from numerous perspectives: the oppressor, the oppressed, the liberated, and so on. Art and music add depth and meaning when contextualized within a historical framework and set alongside literary works to not only capture the imagination of the students, but also to help them grasp the "big picture," a preference among many African American and other students (Ladson-Billings, 1994). As you attempt to enrich the multicultural education of your students, your own class can provide a rich opportunity for community building. Your students are from diverse backgrounds and experiences—a rich mine for exploration and a great place to start.

Seeing Diversity

Many student/intern teachers make the critical mistake of not acknowledging color, the most "salient feature" of one's personhood (Gay, 2000; Ladson-Billings, 1994; McAllister & Irvine, 2000). If you have had limited experience working with children of color, now is the time to really look at learners, to ask questions that show you are interested in them and want to learn more about them and their lives outside the classroom. Knowing your students is the first step toward believing that all students can learn and putting that belief into practice to better individualize instruction.

Understanding a Broad Range of Differences

Assessing your students' abilities, needs, and cultural ways of knowing and learning is a significant and very important part of the planning process (Gay, 2000). Thus far in your journals and assigned activities, you have identified and examined differences among students in your classes regarding:

- learning styles
- multiple intelligences
- interests
- background and life experience
- abilities
- disabilities

You probably recognize that there are more aspects to diversity than you originally thought and wonder how you might adapt the instruction to meet all students' needs. It can be an overwhelming task to plan for and respond to the ethnic, racial, physical, religious, language, gender, and academic differences of students in your classes each day. All students have background experiences that contribute to the unique perspectives they bring to the classroom. As teacher, you are asked to provide developmentally appropriate instruction designed to value diversity and promote student achievement. If we believe that there are not inherent intellectual differences among ethnic, class, and gender groups, then overall academic performance across groups should be similar. The fact that there are differences in academic achievement presents us with the challenge to overcome those differences (Gollnick & Chinn, 1998). The challenge facing you is to become knowledgeable, competent, and flexible in selecting and practicing the instructional practices that best suit each individual student. Does this require you to develop 30 to 150 lesson plans per week depending on which grade level you teach? No! But it does require you to think about different ways to deliver instruction and vary learning activities that challenge learners across the broad range of their differences, from the most advanced learner to the most academically challenged learner, if you truly believe in the maxim: all students can learn.

Connecting Standards to Diversity

The standards movement has placed you in the company of excellent teachers as they struggle to relate learning to individual students' learning styles, cultural patterns of interaction, and home and school values that may be opposing. It is a grave challenge, one in which you are not alone, as you go about the business of relating to each student in your class and ensure they receive an equitable education and opportunities to successfully demonstrate their abilities. Effective teachers share their struggles and successes, and adapt their plans and instruction to meet the needs of all their students with patience and diligence on a daily basis to ensure the academic progress of all learners.

One of the first steps is to develop and model good communication skills with learners from different backgrounds, experiences, and cultures. Being aware of your own verbal and nonverbal behavior increases the possibility of positive interaction with students and others. Another approach is to give step-by-step directions and explanations about how an activity is to be accomplished so that the learner is secure about beginning the task. The following activities provide opportunities to observe, reflect, initiate, communicate, and demonstrate your willingness to promote multicultural education and increase the success rate of all students as they engage in learning activities and performance tasks.

ASSIGNED ACTIVITIES

1. Observe and list the teacher behaviors and attributes that positively support multicultural education in your school this week. How have these behaviors affected the learning environment?
2. Conduct a survey to determine the ethnic, religious, gender, physical, racial, and language differences in your classes. How will you use this information? How might it help sensitize you to the diverse experiences of your students and impact your planning? What activities will you provide that may bring all learners to a better understanding of each other?
3. Choose five students at random from your classes each day. Make a special effort to interact with them positively, if only with a smile, nod of approval, or morning greeting. What was their response? Yours?
4. Take special notice of your directions and explanations in at least four classes this week. Have you become more explicit in your instructions, leaving students with fewer procedural questions?
5. Research ideas for teaching strategies that will provide your students with ways to interact effectively and work cooperatively with others who may be culturally, socially, or physically different from themselves. Select an instructional approach or teaching strategy that may accomplish the expected outcome you have chosen. Be prepared to share your selection with your colleagues.

SUMMARY

In American society, students come to school from many cultural, religious, and socioeconomic backgrounds. Diversity among your students is also represented in the ways they think, speak, and engage with others inside and outside the classroom. These differences can be a source of misunderstanding and conflict for you as a beginning teacher, even though you want to know, appreciate, and employ the cultural backgrounds of your students to facilitate their individual learning processes and success in school. Learning to teach with a multicultural mindset takes time, experience, and more education on your part if you want to make a real difference in the world, but you can begin to take steps now to meet the challenges of the present and the future. Teaching that is culturally responsive requires the following:

- Promote gender and racial unity by creating a positive learning environment where all learners experience a sense of belonging.
- Find ways for all students to participate in class and be contributing members to a real learning community.
- Know your students, their faces, their personal histories, and their areas of strength.
- Together, build bridges to learning to mark progress academically and socially.
- Provide content that is stimulating and help students learn to think by providing resources and activities designed to enhance, extend, or practice what is learned in class.
- Scaffold learning so that all students can learn the curriculum and participate in meaningful learning activities.
- Directly teach and model the attitudes and skills you want your students to learn.
- Let students in on the "secrets" to learning, and tell them "why" what they are learning is important to their success inside and outside school.

Their learning successes reflect your success in teaching; their failures are your failures. When you design meaningful learning experiences that accommodate the diversity of all learners, you create a learning environment where individual needs are met and students are empowered by learning. This type of learning environment capitalizes on individual, as well as collective, strengths of the teacher and students. This type of learning environment is built upon the foundation of diversity.

"[S]chools in particular have been the great instruments of assimilation and the great means of forming an American identity. What students are taught in schools affects the way they will thereafter see and treat other Americans, the way they will thereafter conceive the purposes of the republic. The debate about the curriculum is a debate about what it means to be an American."
Arthur Schlesinger

FOLLOW-UP QUESTIONS AND SHARED INSIGHTS

Using the reflections in your journals, the assigned activities, and your background experiences, share responses to the following questions:

1. How can you determine whether you are discriminating against learners based on their gender? What steps can be taken to eliminate gender bias in the classroom?
2. How do you become aware of your cultural and social biases?
3. In what ways does your classroom show evidence of the involvement of both teacher and students learning about various cultures?
4. Describe your own experience in which personal bias or misunderstanding of cultural values or gender or ethnic issues caused you to misrepresent a particular group?

- What was the result of this misrepresentation?
- How did the misrepresentation contribute to conflict?
- How could the situation have been handled more constructively?

5. Identify teacher behaviors that support and demonstrate commitment to diversity and multicultural education.

Journal Excerpts

High School

"As a white girl growing up in a low middle class, conservative Catholic family in an area of mainly conservative white people, it would seem as if my identity would be similar to that of my surroundings. One experience that I still remember is when I volunteered at an after school program for inner city children. As I was now the minority, I wondered how the children would accept me, especially when I had to discipline them. What I discovered is that they didn't care what color I was or where I came from, they only wanted my attention, respect, and love. These children remind me of my belief and allow me to move forward hanging onto that belief."

"Although many people say that a person is a product of her environment, I have learned and I solemnly believe that a person is a product of her own making and that others may need to be opened-up to this realization. Growing up in a small farm town in the Midwest, I didn't have much experience with different races or cultures. Most were middle-class and white with the exception of one African-American and a few Hispanics. After coming to a larger city to college, I would ask questions of people from different cultures and I learned a lot. I think my 'cultural identity' and even perhaps my lack of ethnic and racial experiences make me both a teacher and a learner."

"I spend time at the beginning of class teaching students the basic skills of organization. With freshmen, especially those who need extra help, I insist that they write the homework in their assignment book. I remind the sophomores about their assignment, but with the freshmen classes I spend more time teaching and modeling for them techniques for organizing the different tasks. I tell them when they need to write down notes. I also either write on the board or on the overhead the notes they need to copy. This works especially well for visual learners. At times they also work in groups and read to each other the notes they have taken. This seems to help them use their notes and to improve their thinking about the information given."

Middle School

"I have gained the students' respect by paying attention to what they are highly interested in. Most of them **love** basketball! So one day in the gym I shot around with them for a little bit and they were totally knocked off their feet. They were totally impressed that I could play ball. I'm sure it looked weird to some of them that I as a white female teacher could shoot with the best of them. Since then they have begun to do the 'sideways fives' with me, the fist-knocking, and the 'whazup' head jerk. I see the value of relating to the students because now, when I stand up to teach, they are more attentive and focused on what I have to say."

"Even though I feel this placement has been tougher than some of the other places I could have gone, I wouldn't change it. I think this is right where I needed to be in terms of students. There are so many of them and they are so different—so many different backgrounds. I was a little intimidated at first, but not anymore. I love it, and I think that I am really gaining a deeper level of understanding for these differences and I rejoice in them."

"As our world has become more diverse over the past several years, I feel like my life has become more diverse as well, which has helped me teach in an ever-increasingly diverse school system. For example, when I was younger our neighborhood was made up primarily of white, traditional families. Within the past several years, my neighborhood has grown to include African-American families, a family from Afghanistan, and a gay couple. Our neighbors from Afghanistan and our family have become wonderful friends. I have learned so much about their culture from speaking with and observing them (e.g., their manner of dress, food, etc.). This has helped me feel comfortable interacting with all my students, many of whom have backgrounds different from mine."

Elementary

"I am white, middle class, and female. The students in my classroom come from all different races, ethnicities, and financial backgrounds. I have always been very respectful and conscious of others, their religions, and their backgrounds. I am very careful about what I say because I don't want to hurt anyone's feelings or offend anyone. I can identify with the children that come from middle class families because that is how I grew up, and I see a lot of similarities between my education and theirs. Regardless of my race, religion, or gender, I try my hardest to treat all the students equally."

"During our examination of the Kindergarten newspaper, we encountered a section on differences. At this point I stated the question, 'How are we alike?' The learner who responded related the question to himself and one neighbor, but not the whole class. I had to clarify what I was asking and restate the question as, 'What is one thing that we all share in common that makes us all alike?' This new question helped the students understand that I was searching for a similarity among all of us, not just pairs."

"Something I've been pondering for a while is the 'self-fulfilling prophecy' item. I think it is so scary that you can shape someone's performance by developing preconceived notions about them. I have to be very careful about being judgmental both socially and academically with a number of students. Today two or three seemingly below-average students surprised me very pleasantly by catching on quickly to the pattern concept."

Special Education

"True multiculturalism emphasizes common humanity."
D. Elkind

"We have a very diverse group of learners in our classroom! The students come because of disabilities such as cerebral palsy, SLD, ADD, ADHD, MMD, or autism. It is important for me as a beginning teacher to vary my teaching techniques because of the variety of learning styles."

"C. receives services from an OT because he is tactile sensitive. I have noticed that when he writes with a pencil, it is very light. Ms. K. said that he has really improved because last year he didn't even like to feel the paper under his hand when he wrote. She took gardening gloves and cut out the fingers so he could hold his pencil. His OT came in today with a 'grip' for his pencil and he was more than happy to use it."

"I worked with two students at the same time which was a big mistake. The academic difference between these two is remarkable. They have similar behavior problems, but J. has a much easier time focusing on tasks—if he wants to! On the other hand, M. gets very frustrated and loses it behaviorally. It is all very interesting! The one thing I have learned with M. is that you have to be extremely patient with him."

References and Suggested Readings

Banks, J. A. (2002). *An introduction to multicultural education.* Boston: Allyn & Bacon.

Banks, J. A., & Banks, C. A. (Eds.). (2001). *Multicultural education: Issues & perspectives* (4th ed.). New York: Wiley.

Ben-Peretz, M. (2001). The impossible role of teacher educators in a changing world. *Journal of Teacher Education, 52*(1), 48–56.

Bennett, C. (2001). Genres of research in multicultural education. *Review of Educational Research, 71*(2), 171–217.

Beyer, L. (2001). The value of critical perspectives in teacher education. *Journal of Teacher Education, 52*(2), 151–163.

Bracey, G. W. (2002, January 23). International comparisons: An excuse to avoid meaningful educational reform. *Education Week,* 1–5.

Brown, S. C., & Kysilka, M. L. (2002). *Applying multicultural and global concepts in the classroom and beyond.* Boston: Allyn & Bacon.

Byrd, D., & McIntyre, D. J. (Eds.). (1997). *Research on the education of our nation's teachers: Teacher education yearbook V.* Thousand Oaks, CA: Corwin Press.

Cochran-Smith, M. (2001a). Multicultural education: Solution or problem for American schools? *Journal of Teacher Education, 52*(2), 91–93.

Cochran-Smith, M. (2001b). Higher standards for prospective teachers. *Journal of Teacher Education, 52*(3), 179–181.

Cook, D. W., & Van Cleaf, D. W. (2000). Multicultural perceptions of 1st-year elementary teachers' urban, suburban, and rural student teaching placements. *Urban Education, 35*(2), 165–174.

Darling-Hammond, L. (2000). How teacher education matters. *Journal of Teacher Education, 51*(3), 166–173.

Delpit, L. (1995). *Other people's children.* New York: The New Press.

Elkind, D. (2001). The cosmopolitan school. *Educational Leadership, 58*(4), 12–17.

Freire, P. (1995). *Pedagogy of the oppressed.* New York: Continuum.

Garabaldi, A. M. (1992). Preparing teachers for culturally diverse classrooms. In M. E. Dilworth (Ed.), *Diversity in teacher education: New expectations.* San Francisco: Jossey-Bass.

Gay, G. (2000). *Culturally responsive teaching: Theory, research, & practice.* New York: Teachers College Press.

Gay, G. (2002). Preparing for culturally responsive teaching. *Journal of Teacher Education, 53*(2), 106–116.

Gollnick, D. M., & Chinn, P. (1998). *Multicultural education in a pluralistic society* (5th ed.). Upper Saddle River, NJ: Merrill/Prentice Hall.

Gordon, J. A. (2002). The color of teaching. *Journal of Teacher Education, 53*(2), 123–126.

Gorski, P. C. (2001). *Multicultural education and the Internet: Intersections and integrations.* Boston: McGraw-Hill.

Groulx, J. G. (2001). Changing preservice teacher perceptions of minority schools. *Urban Education, 36*(1), 60–92.

Hodgkinson, H. (2001). Educational demographics: What teachers should know. *Educational Leadership, 58*(4), 7–11.

Hodgkinson, H. (2002). Demographics and teacher education—an overview. *Journal of Teacher Education, 53*(2), 102–105.

Hutchinson, J. N. (2000). "But I don't know what to do!" *Multicultural Education, 8*(1), 41–46.

Irvine, J. J., & Armento, B. J. (2001). *Culturally responsive teaching.* Boston: McGraw-Hill.

Irvine, J. J., & Foster, M. (Eds.). (1996). *Growing up African American in Catholic schools.* New York: Teachers College Press.

Johnson, L. (2002). "My eyes have been opened": White teachers and racial awareness. *Journal of Teacher Education, 53*(2), 153–167.

Jung, C. G. (1933). *Modern man in search of a soul.* London: Kegan Paul, Trench, Trubner.

Kirkwood, T. G. (2001). Preparing teachers to teach from a global perspective. *The Delta Kappa Gamma Bulletin, 67*(2), 5–12.

Kozol, J. (1991). *Savage inequalities: Children in America's schools.* New York: Crown.

Ladson-Billings, G. (1994). *The dreamkeepers: Successful teachers of African American Children.* San Francisco: Jossey-Bass.

Ladson-Billings, G. (2000). Fighting for our lives: Preparing teachers to teach African American students. *Journal of Teacher Education, 51*(3), 206–214.

McAllister, G., & Irvine, J. J. (2000). Crosscultural competency and multicultural teacher education. *Review of Educational Research, 70*(1), 3–24.

Montgomery, W. (2001). Creating culturally responsive, inclusive classrooms. *Teaching Exceptional Children, 33*(4), 4–9.

Moore, J. A. (1996). Empowering student teachers to teach from a multicultural perspective. Presentation at American Association of Colleges for Teacher Education. (Chicago, February 21–24,) (ERIC Document Reproduction Service No. ED394979)

Morriss, V. G., & Morriss, C. L. (2002). Caring—the missing c in teacher education: Lessons learned from a segregated African American school. *Journal of Teacher Education, 53*(2), 120–123.

Pang, V. O. (2001). *Multicultural education: A caring-centered, reflective approach.* Boston: McGraw-Hill.

Pettus, A. M., Allain, V. A. (1999). Using a questionnaire to assess prospective teachers' attitudes toward multicultural education issues. *Education, 119*(4), 651–657.

Rust, F. O., & Freidus, H. (2001). *Guiding school changes: The role and work of change agents.* New York: Teachers College Press.

Schlesinger, A. M., Jr. (1992). The disuniting of America: Reflections on a multicultural society. New York: Norton.

Sleeter, C. E. (2001). Preparing teachers for culturally diverse schools: Research and the overwhelming presence of whiteness. *Journal of Teacher Education, 52*(2), 94–106.

Spring, J. (2001). *Deculturalization and the struggle for equality* (3rd ed.). Boston: McGraw-Hill.

Tatum, B. D. (2000). Examining racial and cultural thinking. *Educational Leadership, 57*(8), 54–57.

Tiedt, P. L., & Tiedt, I. M. (2002). *Multicultural teaching* (6th ed.). Boston: Allyn & Bacon.

Villegas, A. M., & Lucas, T. (2002). Preparing culturally responsive teachers: Rethinking the curriculum. *Journal of Teacher Education, 53*(1), 20–32.

Wadsworth, D. (2001). Why new teachers choose to teach. *Educational Leadership, 58*(8), 24–28.

Weissglass, J. (2001, August 8). Racism and the achievement gap. *Education Week,* 1–6.

Whang, P. A., & Waters, G. A. (2001). Transformational spaces in teacher education. *Journal of Teacher Education, 52*(3), 197–210.

Wilder, M. (2000). Increasing African American teachers' presence in American schools: Voices of students who care. *Urban Education, 35*(2), 205–220.

Xu, H. (2000). Preservice teachers integrate understanding of diversity into literacy. *Journal of Teacher Education, 51*(2), 135–142.

chapter 5

Integrating Technology Into Teaching and Learning

> *"...Increasingly, technology is poised to revolutionize teaching, learning, and assessment...."*

National Council for Accreditation of
Teacher Education, Standards of Excellence
in Teacher Education

Focus One

Expected Performance

- Share your emotional reaction to the thought of integrating technology in your everyday teaching.
- Recall and share experiences using technology that you found to be delightful, frustrating, or enlightening.
- Share experiences using technology that captivated students' interests and motivated them.

READY FOR A HANDHELD—OR HOLDING ON TO THE TOOLS OF THE PAST?

To find out how prepared you are to use technology in the classroom, ask yourself these questions:

- What technologies are available for my use in the classroom?
- Which technologies are appropriate for instructional purposes?
- How will I teach students to use technology to enhance their learning?

Are you one of every three teachers reported by the U.S. Department of Education (1999) who feel well prepared to use computers and the Internet? Can you name examples of classroom life where technology may have provided the motivation and means to transform ordinary learning into extraordinary learning? As you observe and interact with students learning what life and culture is like in another part of the world via e-mail and the Internet, perhaps you marvel at their changing worldviews. These learners have been accustomed to communicating across the globe on economic, environmental, and humanitarian issues for a number of years. At this point you have determined the importance of the instructional environment in which you teach—an environment likely filled with Internet users who have grown up in a digital world, the world in which you find yourself a teacher and model for technology.

Who Uses Technology?

According to a report for the Pew Internet and American Life (2001), 73% of youth ages 12–17 use the Internet. In the same age group 94% of youth who have access to the Internet say they use the Internet for research and 78% say they believe the Internet helps them with their school work. "Within a few short years, the Internet and the World Wide Web have gone from mere curiosities to

60

foundations for communicating" (Thornburg, 2002). Knowing your students means you know where and how they acquire information, and as a teacher for the 21st century you want to be competent teaching in a highly technological environment.

Many schools across the United States access technology to track absentee students, lunch counts, morning school district messages, and newsletters. Teachers use technology to write lesson plans and units and to design assessment instruments. Computers allow teachers to record and track grades, assign percentages, and tally results. If you are not already doing so, investigate and begin using this technology to make your classroom run more efficiently. Increasingly, students have access to laptop computers and other technology to facilitate the "paperless" classroom, work through assignments, and download textbook information relevant to the curriculum.

Decisions: Technology, Teaching, and Learning

Integrating technology into teaching happens by design because teachers who do so have a proficient level of knowledge and expertise about using a variety of technologies in the classroom. Some teachers report that they are not comfortable using computers and other technology. Observing student or intern teachers in the classroom reveals that a few are reluctant to access readily available technology such as an overhead projector to model writing and thinking processes across the curriculum. Can you count yourself among the small percentage of educators who are distinguished in the area of instruction and technology? If technology, primarily computers, is made available to schools, then teachers, students, families, and the community benefit. The use of technology has the potential to revolutionize the quality and degree of teaching and learning among all students.

Using technology in the classroom remains a controversial issue, and research presents many well-developed arguments and perspectives on the subject. Teachers are not always prepared to integrate technology into teaching due to the ever-changing nature of the field. You may have questions about content and instruction and the best ways to team those with technology into your teaching without compromising the integrity of the curriculum. How much technology do you use; when do you use it; how do you use it? How do you determine the effectiveness of technology as a tool for teaching and learning?

Nearly all agree that what teachers cause to happen in the classroom with learners is a key point in the argument (Bennett, 2002). If learners are to benefit from the use of technology in the classroom, the teacher's knowledge and skill levels impact the degree and quality of learning among students. You may not yet be expected to model handheld computers for students, but you are charged with bringing students into the 21st century by using the technologies available to you. You may not be familiar with all of the latest technological advancements in tech tools for teaching, but open-mindedness toward the use of technology and a willingness to take risks by using technology is of primary importance to your development as a professional educator.

Choosing the appropriate technological tool is an ongoing decision in your instructional planning, and requires that you consider a number of factors. What are the background experiences of your students in the area of technology? If you discover that their experiences surpass or fall short of your expectations, technology can assist you in your instructional decision making. Experts contend that "Effectiveness is not a function of the technology, but rather of the learning environment and the capability to do things one cannot do otherwise.

Technology works in a school not because test scores increase, but because technology empowers new solutions" (Jones, Valdez, Nowakowski, & Rasmussen, 1995, p. 1). Examine the adaptive technology devices in your school that allow students with special needs to learn alongside their peers. Adaptive technologies such as highlighter pens that provide definitions for unknown words in texts, and voice-to-text print, maximize learning for all students.

Using video, the Internet, overhead calculators, and myriad other technologies to enhance instruction should be your goal. Technology can act as the great equalizer, providing sight, sound, and interaction unavailable inside and outside the school. Individuals can select materials based on specific interest and pacing needs. Likewise, it can be used to challenge learners. Technology, when used purposefully, makes the curriculum more accessible for all learners regardless of ability, disability, or socioeconomic level.

Technology Impacts Learning

As teacher, you are charged with knowing and assessing how technology impacts the learning of each of your students (Carlson, 2001). In order to meet this challenge, you need to know not only what technology is available for your use, but also how to operate it, and when it is appropriate to use it. Before you can use technology in the classroom effectively, you must consider your students' learning styles and have in-depth knowledge of the content you are responsible for teaching. You want to engage students in learning the content by solving problems and processing information relevant to today's world in all areas of the curriculum. These are integral to the planning and designing phase of authentic instruction. Reflecting on the tools and the strategies you select, and noting how you might use them differently in future lessons, will help you make technology an everyday part of your instruction.

Do you use the chalkboard, chart paper, or the overhead to introduce, teach, or reinforce new concepts? Does the concept call for Internet research to gather details or more examples than the text offers? Does learning the concept require experiential learning on the part of the students? Would a PowerPoint or simulation be more appropriate to student learning? There are numerous aspects to teaching, and integrating technology with instruction is critical because it gives students opportunities to learn and demonstrate their learning in meaningful ways. It allows them access to sources and geographic locations for the express purpose of gathering data and information that is current and connected to real-life learning. Integrating technology with teaching and learning has the potential to bring the outside world into the classroom socially, politically, geographically, and scientifically. Student presentations in the form of slide shows, exhibits, video clips, and so on engage and motivate students to learn at high levels and make connections across the curriculum with your guidance as a content specialist and teacher.

Technology: Challenges and You

As a beginning teacher, you may find yourself lacking in expertise in the area of technology and instruction. You may find it challenging to integrate technology smoothly into the lessons you teach, or even feel frustration when students fail to respond as you anticipated. Perhaps you used technology and upon reflection it was more a "show or gimmick" than a deep learning experience for the students. The ability to state the purpose or rationale used in selecting technology for teaching and learning purposes is critical.

Now is the time to ask questions, investigate, and seek assistance. You may find teachers, media specialists, computer literacy teachers, or other personnel at your school enthusiastic and eager to share with you their knowledge and skills in using technology in the classroom setting. Suggestions and strategies may come from your department chair, team leader, technology coordinator, or your cooperating teacher. Their teaching and learning experiences, combined with your knowledge of technology, can enhance your planning and impact your students' learning.

CAPITALIZING ON STUDENTS' LEARNING STYLES

Authentic and lasting change is a process and may not happen overnight; change takes time and is incremental by nature. It demands that teachers not hold on to the familiar tools of the past when today's technologies have been shown to yield effective results in student learning. The National Council for Accreditation of Teacher Education (NCATE) (2001) requires that new and beginning teachers develop an understanding of the uses of technology for the subjects they plan to teach prior to student or intern teaching. The National Educational Technology Standards (NETS) provides a Performance Profile to assess your level of proficiency in this final stage of your professional journey (see Appendix C). You may be competent and eager to use computers and other technology as part of your everyday research, planning, and presentation of learning materials. It may be that other teachers look to you, a new member of the teaching profession, to integrate technology into teaching and learning to impact the educational process. Whatever the case, technology offers limitless possibilities in terms of teaching and learning for learners and teachers in today's classrooms.

Discussion Questions

1. Identify your first experiences with learning to use technology such as the computer, a VCR, a camcorder, the overhead projector, and so forth. How did you learn to operate the equipment? Name the frustrations or fears you experienced.
2. Think about the students you teach. How do their levels of expertise vary among the differing forms of technology compared to your level of competence?
3. What is your response to students who have little or no access to computers at home?
4. Describe your dream technological environment where teachers and students are using technology to its fullest capacity.
5. After reviewing the NETS Performance Profile (Appendix C), select two areas and discuss how you might increase your level of proficiency. Be specific. You may want to include this in your professional growth plan.

Focus Two

Recognizing that computers are an expected component of instruction, you are excited about the prospect of integrating technology with your teaching. The big question for you may be, How do I go about learning to use technology effectively and integrating it with instruction? How might you rate yourself in your ability to integrate technology into your everyday teaching and across the

Expected Performance

- Identify personal levels of competence across a broad range of technologies.
- Investigate and report teacher employment of technologies within their classroom and the school.
- Explore and analyze Web sites that could assist with integrating technology to impact instruction and student learning.
- Review the Acceptable Use Policy for Internet use within the school and district.
- Deconstruct a lesson plan that integrates technology within the curriculum.
- Explore ways to implement and use technology to enhance student learning within classes currently taught.

curriculum? For example, have you used the technology that allows you to graphically design key points of information to focus student learning? Are you knowledgeable about the software used at your school or district that filters out inappropriate Web sites? Have you used presentation software such as Microsoft's PowerPoint to create a presentation, or taught your students to use it? How do you select software designed to reinforce previously taught concepts? Have you used simulation software or observed simulation hardware such as Probeware, Riverdeep, and other interactive CD-ROMs and the Internet to engage students in real-life situations that call for problem solving and higher order thinking skills? Clifford (2001) and Willis and Raines (2001) suggest these as important tools teachers might consider when designing instruction. Students are expected to word process, design spreadsheets, and create databases from elementary through high school to meet national standards (International Society for Technology in Education [ISTE], 2000). If you are not familiar with these tools and ideas, we recommend that you consult with the media services specialist at your school or a public library, or a teacher who uses high levels of technology with students in the classroom.

APPLICATION: DEMONSTRATING TECHNOLOGY KNOW-HOW

Some researchers distinguish between the technical and instructional knowledge that teachers need. You may feel confident in operating and troubleshooting communication and computer hardware and software available for use in your school. With whom have you discussed the location of instructional technology and its access in your school? You may observe teachers being colearners and coinvestigators alongside their students. As technology advances, it could happen that you are the learner and the students are your teachers (Jones et al., 1995). Whatever your source of knowledge, honing your technical skills is of paramount importance and will ultimately impact how you team technology with teaching and learning in the classroom.

A second kind of knowledge, instructional knowledge, refers to selecting appropriate pedagogies, applying instructional strategies, and implementing teaching methods. For example, teachers need to know where to click the mouse and which menu commands to select. They must also be knowledgeable about how technology can allow students to access data, process data, and communicate their findings. This knowledge must then be adapted and applied to specific learners and levels of the content being taught. Teachers are expected to possess or to develop a set of complex skills and reasoning processes in their interface with technologies. Some school systems offer opportunities for teachers to increase and update their technical and instructional knowledge (Jones et al., 1995). As a beginning teacher you are developing and expanding those teaching strategies that enable you to determine the skills and concepts your students need and to employ a learning-by-doing approach for meeting their needs.

Teachers Determine Technology's Impact

Experienced teachers say that using technology is highly motivating for many students and you are eager to learn how to teach using technology. Wiles and Bondi (2001) maintain that such positive attitudes determine the effectiveness of using technology in teaching as teachers are the final filters in the development of curriculum and choices about instructional delivery. Wiles and Bondi suggest three ways that teachers typically employ technologies in teaching. Which of these have you used or observed being used in schools?

1. **Enhancing and enriching the existing curriculum** —The teacher extends and designs content learning by having students use software applications and simulations, and try out other selected programs to enhance their learning.

2. **Extending the existing curriculum** —The teacher helps the learner to move beyond textbook information, beyond school and community resources to interact with numerous sources of information and publications to extend learning. Learners at the middle and high school levels can interact with online courses offered through "virtual school." Even the possibility of online testing exists to give students immediate feedback on their learning (Technology Counts, 2002).

3. **Transforming the curriculum through technology** — In the not-too-distant future, teachers may be asked to design an Individualized Education Plan (IEP) for each student in the classroom to make learning more personal, relevant, and accessible to each student. In some districts, students e-mail homework to their teachers, and even ask for clarification on assignments. Some teachers post homework assignments on the school's Web page. Others set up chat rooms and online book clubs to engage students' learning outside the classroom.

Are any of the above examples familiar to you? How comfortable are you in operating the hardware and software needed for extending the curriculum in ways suggested? How confident are you using the hardware and software available in your current teaching placement? As teacher, you not only need such knowledge of technology, you also must be able to decide what to teach and how to use technology to impact the students you teach. Integrating technology into a lesson or unit of study requires you to have a high level of expertise using technology plus a keen understanding of the content you teach, and a plethora of methodologies to ensure student success in learning.

Think about concepts you want students to recognize and deeply understand. For example, you might bring complex problems into the classroom and use graphics, video, or animation to capture students' interest. These multimedia formats provide sounds and moving images that can be replayed to make textbook learning come alive. Learners can interact with the technology-based problem environment and observe the results. With your guidance, students might identify and choose problem-solving approaches and make inferences and decisions that can be assessed to evaluate your teaching as well as the students' learning. This challenging type of instruction engages students and gives them more control over their own learning. By manipulating the equipment, they can explore a problem using different learning modes and interact with information and situations connected with the problem. By using technology, you engage students in problem solving, project-based learning—two teaching strategies proven to be effective across disciplines. Thus you have enhanced, extended, and enriched the curriculum and provided a more authentic learning experience for all students (Goldman, Williams, Sherwood, & Hasselbring, 1999).

Integrating Technology Into the Curriculum

Integrating technology and instruction presents a bonus for educators because it increases the likelihood of accommodating a wide-range of learning styles and academic needs. Technology presents a wide range of multisensory approaches that facilitate your intent to stimulate and motivate visual and auditory learners. Technology manipulated by individual learners allows them to determine time and order for listening, and/or interacting with high-interest topics. Pictures and sounds convey information to reluctant readers and non-readers. Students are encouraged to try their ideas and solutions in an easy-to-change mode, thus promoting confidence in trial-and-error problem solving across many content areas.

As exciting as the idea of having your students use technology is, careful planning of instructional activities is necessary to obtain the outcomes you desire for students. You want to choose learning tasks that lead to authentic and purposeful learning. To accomplish this end you must help learners tap their knowledge of the subject matter and apply it in ways that connect to their real-life situations. As a result, these connections enable learners to practice basic and advanced skills as a means for learning higher level concepts (Jones et al., 1995).

Standards and Best Practice Guide the Process

Experts who endorse technology and its impact on teaching today's youth have agreed on a set of standards connecting curriculum and technology. The National Educational Technology Standards, or NETS (ISTE, 2000) provide teachers with guidelines for planning technology-based activities for their students. A copy of these guidelines (Technology Foundation Standards for Students) is in Appendix C. In addition to creating standards for students, NETS provide student performance indicators describing the technology competencies students should exhibit at particular grade levels, and examples and scenarios are provided to help you to integrate technology and curriculum. NETS is a tremendous resource that can be searched for the different subject areas for grades pre-K–2, 3–5, 6–8, and 9–12 and for various concepts. In addition, the NETS suggest strategies that connect mathematics education with real-world applications. For example, some activities include using the Internet, and depending on the course content, more specialized tools such as graphing calculators, simulations and spreadsheet software, real-time videoconferencing, and virtual reality simulations. Along with examples and scenarios, some Web sites are cited to allow you to know to what extent your students are learning the curriculum in comparison to other students at the same grade level.

Teaching with technology needs to be rooted in recognized best practices in education, standards, and assessment with the ultimate goal of making the curriculum accessible to all students. Keep in mind best practices as you refer to standards in planning your instruction. Resources such as curriculum guides include these best practices, suggest ways to effectively integrate technology into the different content areas, and are aligned with local, state, and national standards. In addition, the guides and other resources oftentimes provide well-defined indicators of success and suggest modifications that give all students access to technology and meet student needs (Appalachia Educational Laboratory, 2001).

At the present there are several available Web sites offering examples of curriculum integration. Similar resources are found in current journals from the different professional education organizations. At the end of this chapter is a list of selected sites where ideas for integrating curriculum are available and free to you. There are other sites, not listed here, to which you may subscribe and, after paying a fee, access examples of integrated lessons and units along with many other areas of teacher interests.

A Final Note: Technology Limits and Limitless Opportunities

The Internet and the World Wide Web (Web) hold tremendous resources for you and your students. The Web brings a massive set of information resources regardless of your school's location (Provenzo & Gotthoffer, 2000). Having access to worldwide interactions and events allows you to guide students in safe and acceptable practices in Internet usage. So great is the interest in this topic that the U.S. Department of Education's Office of Educational Technology established an Internet Safety link on its Web site. At this site you will find reports published by national commissions and working groups and information for parents about child safety. One link, http://www.cybercrime.gov/rules/kidinternet. htm, connects you to several options including *cyberethics website.* You can then access the U.S. Department of Justice *Internet Do's and Don'ts* that provides a child's game to determine good Netzenship, the Rules of the Road, and the implications of hacking.

Ethics and Technology

Students now have greater access to the Internet and that ultimately implies that teachers need to be alert to the potential problem of cheating. Gardiner (2001), an English teacher, provides his method for investigating cybercheating by high school students. When he suspects a paper was not written by a particular student, he relies on one of the search engines, Dogpile (http://www.dogpile. com). Dogpile digs into more than a dozen search engines at the same time. Gardiner ignores the Real Names matches and looks for matches in any other search engines included in Dogpile. Looking for unique phrases of 6 to 10 words, he types these inside quotation marks within the search line at the top of Dogpile. When the results show up, he scrolls down through the search engines looking for matches and clicks on the link, and the designated search engine takes him directly to the site showing an identical paper.

Using preventive measures to discourage students from downloading papers for an assignment confirms that the Web is a wonderful, powerful resource for research. Directing students' appropriate use of the Internet while doing research allows you to model attitudes and teach techniques for their future schooling experiences with technology (Gardiner, 2001).

Copyright laws are in place for a purpose—to protect authors from intentional (and unintentional) theft, from those who would claim an author's original ideas and materials as their own. But copyright laws have not kept up with the explosion in technology—especially in the field of education. Your school may have a Web page loaded with information about the school, policies, the calendar, and even samples of student work. State departments of education maintain Web sites where information, programs of study, core content, and even teacher pay scales can be accessed by the public efficiently and quickly. Classroom activities, lesson plans, and units of study are available to teachers and student or intern teachers at the click of a button. What liabilities are associated with importing copyrighted materials into school-based Web sites? Are teachers required to credit authors with lesson plans they download from the Internet? The ethical response is "Yes," and copyright laws should extend to cyberspace. However, tracking original sources is virtually impossible given the expanse of cyberspace and quantity of information available today.

We recommend that student or intern teachers use the Internet as a resource—a huge resource—for teaching and learning ideas. We hope you will make good use of those sites included at the end of this chapter to guide your planning. However, you are charged with critically examining the resources for misinformation, biases, and even plagiarism! Ownership is critical—you decide what components or combinations of lessons you wish to incorporate into your units of study or lesson plans. Give credit where credit is due. You are not expected to design plans with original ideas for every lesson you teach. You are expected to discern what best suits your students' needs and the content necessary to arrive at objectives you have written.

Although there is great enthusiasm for technology among educators and the public alike, the mutual goals these groups hold for technology have yet to be realized. Not all students are computer and technology literate, not every school has a readily available supply of better educational resources, and classroom and schoolwide pedagogical revolutions have not occurred, say Peck, Cuban, and Kirkpatrick (2002). Their yearlong study in California high schools found that technology "has not made any dramatic inroads into the academic mainstream" (p. 479). How does this claim match your observations and experiences of technology used for general instruction of students? The researchers' statement should spark a discussion about the investigation into the impact technology may or may not have on student learning at your school. As a beginning teacher you will have opportunities to engage in this discussion and expand the use of technology in your instructional practices.

ASSIGNED ACTIVITIES

The activities that follow allow you to combine technical, instructional know-how with content knowledge to integrate technology into teaching and learning in your classroom.

1. Which of the following technological tools have you used. Rate yourself in the space provided below. (The section "Familiar Favorites and New High-Tech Devices" on page 73 defines some of the tools listed.)

   1 = Yes, frequently,   2 = Yes, rarely,   3 = Not at all

Technology Tools	My Rating
Cell phone	_____
Desktop publishing (e.g., PageMaker)	_____
Digital camera	_____
Electronic instruction (e.g., PowerPoint)	_____
Fax machine	_____
Graphing calculators	_____
Handheld computer (e.g., Compaq iPaq, Palm OS)	_____
Internet Web browser/Online service	_____
Laserdisc player or DVD player	_____
Modem	_____
Quick Time	_____
Scanner	_____
Spreadsheets or databases (e.g., Excel)	_____
Video camcorder	_____
VCR	_____
Word processors (e.g., Word, Works, ClarisWorks)	_____
Web page (e.g., FrontPage, HomePage)	_____
Motorized chair	_____

Assistive technology _____

Keyboard enhancements _____

Eye-gaze Response Interface Computer Aid (ERICA) system (allows users with disabilities a means to control Windows applications with their eyes) _____

Voice input devices _____

Other _____

2. How do my students use computers in the classes I teach? Check all that apply.

To collect data and perform measurements _____

To communicate information as the result of investigations _____

To compensate for a disability or limitation _____

To create graphics or visuals of non-data products (e.g., diagrams, pictures) _____

To create visual data displays (e.g., graphs, charts, maps) _____

To create visual presentations _____

To analyze or interpret data _____

To organize and store information _____

To perform calculations _____

To plan, draft, proofread, revise, and publish written material _____

3. Select a lesson plan integrating technology with content to use for the following activity. You may select an integrated lesson plan from the Web sites cited in this chapter, or obtain an integrated lesson plan from another source.
   - Examine the objectives listed for the lesson and state what content or concepts and skills are being taught in the lesson.
   - Name the content standard(s) addressed in this lesson.
   - Discuss the developmentally appropriateness of the lesson in terms of student learning (e.g., oral questions, observational checklists, anecdotal records, etc.).
   - What student learning is being assessed and what types of assessment are used to determine the impact of the lesson on student learning?
   - To what degree can all students participate in the lesson? Highlight the accommodations made to engage all learners in the lesson.
   - Name an activity in this lesson that allows the student to meet at least one of the National Educational Technology Standards for Students. (These standards can be found in Appendix C.)

4. Locate and review the Acceptable Use Policy for students using the Internet within your school. Does this document also include appropriate Internet etiquette? How are the students at your school taught to operate and care for the equipment they use in instructional activities?

5. Conference with your supervising teacher about using technology to enhance or supplement your lessons. For example, what is the best way to locate new equipment, check out software, and practice with the equipment prior to using it in the classroom with students? What tips has your supervising teacher shared with you for preparing students to experience technology in the classroom?

   Note procedural insights about integrating technology into teaching recommended by your cooperating teacher. Be prepared to share these ideas with your peers and give specific examples of how the use of technology impacted student learning.

SUMMARY

Computers and other technology are tools you use to enhance teaching and learning throughout your beginning teacher experience. In this chapter, and in preteaching courses, you examined the rationale for teaching and learning with technology, and you observed and discussed the possibilities of integrating technology with teaching across the curriculum. You are challenged to examine and use new technologies, and explore examples for implementing these in the classroom. Selecting and managing these tools offers you the opportunity to use technology while you are in an environment that allows you to experiment and assess the results of your teaching on a class-by-class basis to inform and enhance your performance. Frequent practice with technology on your part models for students the importance of technology in today's society and imparts the message of learning as a lifelong venture.

FOLLOW–UP QUESTIONS AND SHARED INSIGHTS

Using the materials you completed for the assigned activities, share your discoveries and insights about instructional technology and its place in your planning of content lessons.

1. After rating yourself on your use of technology tools, tell what you found most surprising on the list of technology devices and your rating. What are your strengths? Areas for growth?
2. Best practice says that you need to begin instruction at the level the students are at in their learning. Where will you begin with teaching and integrating technology into your classroom?
3. After analyzing the lesson plan, how would you change it to better meet the needs of all learners and integrate technology with the content in different ways? For example, would your students benefit from a virtual tour or other experience related to the content you are teaching? Perhaps a visit to the National Aeronautics and Space Administration or the National Museum of Fine Arts would enable your students to better experience the concepts you are teaching and build background knowledge.
4. Locate and read the Acceptable Usage Policy for your school. Discuss the implications the policy has for your students. How might Web-filtering software affect your students' research work and consequently their ability to complete assignments? Explain how you can assist students who may have difficulty.

Web Sites Integrating Technology Into Curriculum

- Association for Supervision and Curriculum Development allows you access to lesson plans from all curriculum areas as well as topics addressing current instructional practices and many other educational issues.
  http://www.ASCD.org
- Classroom Connect provides the Net-happenings mailing list upon request. A subscription is required for in-depth exploration.
  http://www.classroom.com/community/html

- Council for Exceptional Children provides journals, books, and media and makes these resources available online. *CEC Today Online* is the organization's most current publication, with topics addressing instructional practices and other issues.
  http://www.cec.sped.org
- ePALS Classroom Exchange allows communication with classrooms speaking seven languages. The site map makes options readily available to you and lists projects, resources, and documentations for teachers and students anywhere in the world who have access to a computer.
  http://www.epals.com
- Harvard Learning Center offers suggestions for improving teaching using new technologies and resources in the Web site.
  http://learnweb.harvard.edu/ent/library/recommended.cfm
- International Education and Resource Network (iEARN) enables students to use the Internet and other new technologies to engage in collaborative educational projects, and hosts a great diversity of languages among participants worldwide.
  http://www.iearn.org
- National Council of Teachers of English (NCTE) Special Resources lists literary selections from EXXonMobile Masterpiece Theatre's American Collection, African American Read-In, and others. Curriculum ideas for elementary, middle, and secondary instruction are also available.
  http://www.ncte.org
- National Education Association (NEA) updates *Resources You Can Use*, a site that provides educators with lesson planning ideas.
  http://www.nea.org/cet
- National Educational Technology Standards (NETS) Projects is a database of lessons or units and the site provides you with additional directions.
  http://cnets.iste.org/sitemap.html
- National Science Teachers Association (NSTA) and the U.S. Food and Drug Administration offer free curriculum materials to order online. The Web site links you to U.S. Food and Drug Center. The second Web site lists other science-related Web sources.
  http://www.nsta.org/fda
  http://www.foodsafety.gov/~fsg/teach.html
- *Search Lessons and Units* lists the subject, grade range, and keywords for locating learning units. In addition to describing activities, each provides the grade range, content area standards, and NETS Performance Indicators that the lesson or unit includes.
  http://cnets.iste.org/search/s_search.html
- *Teaching Resources* are categorized by the 10 themes of the curriculum standards for social studies. It is easy to navigate the site and locate ideas and examples suiting your instructional needs.
  http://www.ncss.org/resources

Other Selected Sites

The list of Web sites you can browse for teaching ideas continues to expand. Some sites provide online workshops and discussion groups about technology and other topics related to teaching. Those selected are free to access and are suggested sites; however, there are many other excellent sites you can browse using the Internet.

- Apple Learning Interchange offers American government, history, and civics teachers access to lists of classroom resources including lesson plans, historical materials, and documents.
  http://ali.apple.com

- *Congress for Kids* offers younger students the opportunity to register individually and take a virtual tour of the federal government. *CongressLink* features lesson plans, online historical materials, and other information to assist teachers.
  http://www.congresslink.org/classroomresources.htm
  http://www.congressforkids.net
- International Monetary Fund promotes economic growth and high levels of employment; the World Bank assists developing nations.
  http://www.imf.org
  http://www.worldbank.com
- International Society for Technology in Education (ISTE) Standards Projects provides lists of topics related to educational technology implementation.
  http://www.iste.org/standards
- Learning Resources database provides multiple ideas for expanding your lesson plans and viewing other teachers' Web pages.
  http://www.pedagonet.com
- National Aeronautics and Space Administration (NASA) and the National Oceanic and Atmospheric Administration (NOAA) Web sites feature a number of teaching-learning topics.
  http://www.nasa.gov
  http://www.noaa.gov
- North Central Regional Educational Laboratory features an array of examples for classroom use and curriculum- and standards-based content.
  http://www.ncrel.org
- Royal Observatory at Greenwich, England, Web site explores modern astronomy.
  http://www.rog.nmm.ac.uk
- Education World provides a site guide featuring special themes, teacher lessons, and other education topics.
  http://www.education-world.com/search.jhtml
- WEB WATCH lists Web sites offering global perspectives and is published in *Phi Delta Kappan*, February 2002.
  http://www.pdkintl.org/kappan/k0202web.htm
- World Meteorological Organization, a unit of the United Nations, monitors world climate.
  http://www.two.org

Technology Tips: Equipment and Use

When using any kind of technology, be prepared for Murphy's Law to prevail: anything that can go wrong, will. Thinking ahead, what other strategies will you use if your plan does not work? Including the supervising teacher in the planning provides you a wonderful source of support. Whatever technology you are using, you will want to assemble the hardware and access the software or Web site. An experienced teacher suggests that "a teacher who wants to integrate technology needs to be prepared to spend time finding out about new equipment, checking out software, and looking up suitable Internet sites that will enhance or supplement that lesson" (Bjorklund, 2000, p. 43).

1. Prior to the first class, carefully plan and organize the procedures necessary for student success.
2. As class begins, provide students with an overview of the activity.
3. Clearly state your learning outcome(s) to the students: Outline what students will know and be able to do at the end of the lesson or project.

4. Model and use direct instruction to teach students how to use and access equipment responsibly.
5. Assess and reflect on students' success and areas that may still need improvement in subsequent sessions (Goethals & Howard, 2000).

Familiar Favorites and New High-Tech Devices

New technology items continuously appear on the market and some are exciting and helpful instructional tools. The following list reflects a number of recently introduced technologies, as well as some that educators have come to rely on in their teaching. You may know of other technological tools that students and teachers use.

Computer and accompanying peripherals — Laptop model is provided to each student; desktop model in lab setting is used by individual student or shared by pairs of students.

Graphics calculator — Projection device that displays graphs, equations, and other mathematical expressions.

Laser disc player — Contains images controlled by the teacher in several ways, such as through use of bar code reader or computer driven.

Compact disc read only memory (CD-ROM) — Commercially prepared programs that contain images and text.

Video camera and videocassette player — Camera records activities that are played back and edited by students and groups of students; used for demonstrations by students or teacher recording in all content areas; commercially prepared recordings are available.

Digital video camera — Offers digital camera capability and provides still images for downloading to a PC.

Liquid crystal display (LCD) panels — Projection device that displays computer screen images and script.

Handheld technology and probes — Graph data gathered from chemistry and physics experiments.

Optical Character Recognition — Means a computer recognizes printed or written text characters that can then be sent, read, or reproduced for other purposes.

Scanners and presentation assistants — Materials are scanned and immediately converted into images with crisp, clear visual quality. In addition, presentation equipment is available that displays Web sites to the entire class via large-screen monitors, LCD panels, or classroom televisions connected to a computer.

Digital recorder with Voice to Print (VTP) software — A pocket dictation machine with Voice to Print software allows you to dictate text, connect the recorder to your PC via a USB cable, and then convert your voice to a text file that you can edit, print, or e-mail. With the software from Audible.com, you can purchase and download spoken books and transfer them from your computer to the digital recorder or player. According to Van Horn (2001), software is available only for PCs.

Journal Excerpts

High School

"We use many forms of technology within the classroom. First of all, most notes or presentations given in the classes are done so by the use of PowerPoint presentations which helps students who learn visually. Also, with this technology, we are able to provide pictures and additional definitions, which help us move outside the textbook. We also use other visuals such as a laser disc player, films, and overhead transparencies."

"My second and fourth-period classes went to the writing lab where they could use the Internet to get ideas for their casting projects. The use of the Internet was helpful to them because they were able to find things and get ideas easier than searching through magazines. The actors they were searching for were more accessible on the Internet than they would be anywhere else. Videos are another example of the technology we use. We used *First Knight* as a wrap up to *Beowulf* and an opening to *Canterbury Tales*. The opportunity for students to watch a movie or video that follows the literature we read is a great way to see the characters, hear their speeches, and really get a fuller understanding of what we have been discussing in class. In many cases they are learning without knowing it."

Middle School

"Technology is something that you really have to go out of your way to integrate into your classroom at our school. I personally have pulled lesson plans and information from the Internet to use with classes. Actually, this is a fairly routine procedure with me. As far as the students go, they take their Accelerated Reader test on the computer and a few weeks ago I reserved the computer lab for them to write their final drafts of their personal narratives. Ms. H. and I circulated around the room, helping them to edit. I really don't see why more teachers don't utilize this resource. It's probably just the time factor, but it also could be a case of computer phobia. If this is the case then it definitely needs to be overcome because the future of education is ever mingling with technology. For this reason, my hopes are also my plans. I can see a day coming when all students will need to bring to school is their disc. Textbooks have already become obsolete in some areas and many opportunities are on the Web and in hands-on application of computer skills."

"Yesterday in algebra I taught my first lesson that did not go so well. I taught both Algebra classes and the second one did not go as well as the first one. I was leading the student through a lesson on how to draw points on the TI-83 calculators, then trace from one point to the next, discovering rise/run = slope. It seemed that knowledge of how to use the calculator interfered with the objective. Some students knew exactly how to do everything and others couldn't keep up. They seemed unfamiliar with the calculator and couldn't find certain keys. Other students who knew how to use the calculator were trying to help by shouting out what to do. Those unfamiliar with the calculators, were getting frustrated. Students familiar with the calculator were frustrated with the students who couldn't keep up, and I was frustrated not knowing what to do with the different levels of knowledge. Mrs. K. had to jump in, and I suppose I was embarrassed. But every day cannot be a great day. I'm not sure how to bridge the gap between the different levels of knowledge. Maybe I could type out a paper with step-by-step instructions as a student hand-out."

Elementary

"Students participate in a very interesting program, READ 180, which uses technology. READ 180 has three stations that students can rotate from individual reading, listening to books-on-tape, or to a third station with computers. On the computers they take reading skills tests and the test results are recorded for each student. Then when the students log on to a computer with their individual number, the computer brings up a story based on that student's reading levels. The students interact with different reading skills in the areas that need strengthening. Before logging off the computer, the students complete tests to measure their degree of success in mastering the skills being worked on."

"I am struggling with incorporating technology. My teacher only uses the computers for word processing. I would love to do so much more. But again, I feel like I am in over-drive and I cannot function. I am also there for such a limited time; I think I need to rule out a lot of what I would love to do with these classes."

Special Education

"There is one student who has difficulty with fine motor skills. We have some special supplies we hand out to him, i.e., scissors that spring back after making a cut, a ruler with a raised part so he can easily hold the ruler while using it, etc. We also have electronic spelling machines that are easier than dictionaries because the student types in how she/he thinks a word is spelled, and it corrects the word for him/her."

REFERENCES AND SUGGESTED READINGS

Allen, R. (2001, Fall). Teachers and technology. *Curriculum Update.* Alexandria, VA: Association for Supervision and Curriculum Development.

Appalachia Educational Laboratory. (2001). Highlights: Good models of teaching with technology. *Links,* 20(4).

Bennett, F. (2002). Computer technology: The future of computer technology in K-12 education. *Phi Delta Kappan* 83(8), 621–626.

Bigham, V. S., & Bigham, G. (1998). *Online education resources.* Upper Saddle River, NJ: Merrill/Prentice Hall.

Bjorklund, A. L. (2000). One more tool for the toolbox. *English Journal, 90*(2), 42–46.

Buckleinter, W. (2002). Teaching with technology. *Early Childhood Today, 16* (4), 10.

Carlson, P. (2001). A grassroots approach to educational partnerships. *T.H.E. Journal, 29* (3), 83–87.

Clifford, W. (2001). For technology's sake. *Momentum, 32* (3), 30–32.

Daniel, K., Finley, R., Koehler, K., & Picard, K. (2001). Equal access: Integrating technology into the elementary and secondary curriculum. *View, 33* (2), 63–69.

DiChristina, M. (2000). On-the-go learning. *Popular Science, 257* (5), 78–81.

Eib, B. J. (2001). Beyond the bells and whistles: Evaluating technology use in the classroom. *National Association of Secondary School Principals, 1* (9), 16–23.

Gardiner, S. (2001). Cybercheating: A new twist on an old problem. *Phi Delta Kappan, 83* (2), 172–174.

Goethals, S. Howard, R. (2000). *Student teaching: A process approach to reflective practice.* Upper Saddle River, NJ: Merrill/Prentice Hall.

Goldman, S. R., Williams, S. M., Sherwood, R. D., & Hasselbring, T. S. (1999). Technology for teaching and learning with understanding. In J. M. Cooper (Ed.), *Classroom teaching skills* (6th ed.). Boston: Houghton Mifflin.

Goldsborough, R. (2000). Using the Net to learn about the Net. *Reading Today, 18* (2), 14–16.

Gordon, D. (2001). The new digital divide. *NEA Today, 19* (6), 10.

Gorski, P. C. (2001). *Multicultural education and the Internet: Intersections and integrations.* New York: McGraw-Hill.

Henson, K. T. (2001). *Curriculum planning: Integrating multiculturalism, constructivism and education reform* (2nd ed.). New York: McGraw-Hill.

Holland, H., Mazzoli, K. (2001). Where everybody knows your name. *Phi Delta Kappan, 83* (4), 294–303.

International Society for Technology in Education (ISTE). (2000). *National Educational Technology Standards for Students—Connecting curriculum and technology.* Eugene, OR: International Society for Technology in Education and U.S. Department of Education.

Jobs, S. (2001, October 29). The classroom of the future. *Newsweek.*

Jones, B. F., Valdez, G., Nowakowski, J., & Rasmussen, C. (1995). New times demand new ways of learning. In *Plugging in: Choosing and using educational technology.* Washington, DC: North Central Regional Educational Laboratory. Retrieved January 31, 2002, from http://www.ncrel.org/sdrs/edtalk/toc.htm

Means, B. (2000). Technology in America's schools: Before and after y2k. In R. S. Brandt (Ed.), *Education in a new era.* Alexandria, VA: Association for Supervision and Curriculum Development.

National Council for Accreditation of Teacher Education (NCATE), Technology Initiative. (2001). Technology and the new professional teacher: Preparing for the 21st century classroom. Retrieved from http://www.ncate.org/accred/projects/tech/ntechnology.htm

Owen, T., & Hern, H. (2001). Learning with technology. *English Journal, 91* (2), 100–103.

Peck, C., Cuban, L., & Kirkpatrick, H. (2002). Techno-promoter dreams, student realities. *Phi Delta Kappan, 83* (6), 472–471.

Petropoulous, H. (2001). Are we there yet? *Momentum, 32* (3), 12–14.

Pew Internet and American Life Project. (2001). *Main findings about the Internet and education.* Washington, DC: Author. Retrieved from http://www.pewinternet.org

Pierson, M. E. (2001). Technology integration practice as a function of pedagogical expertise. *Journal of Research on Computing in Education, 33* (4), 413–460.

Priest, R. H., & Sterling, D. R. (2001). Integrating technology. *The Science Teacher, 68* (3), 61–64.

Provenzo, E. R., & Gotthoffer, D. (2000). *Quick guide to the Internet for education.* Boston: Allyn & Bacon.

Reese, S. (2001). Tools for thinking in sound. *Music Educators Journal, 88* (1), 42–47.

Robyler, M. D., & Edwards, J. (2000). *Integrating educational technology into teaching.* Upper Saddle River, NJ: Merrill/Prentice Hall.

Technology counts 2002; E-defining education [executive summary]. (2002, May 9). *Education Week.*

Thornburg, D. (2002). *The new basics: Education and the future of work in the telematic age.* Alexandria, VA: Association for Supervision and Curriculum Development.

Tourtner, J. (2000). Best software. *Teacher Librarian, 28* (1), 1–3.

U.S. Department of Education, U.S. Office of Education Technology. (1999). Teaching, learning and computing: Study methodology. Retrieved January 31, 2002, from http://www.ed.gov/Technology/Focus/edfocus3.html

Van Horn, R. (2001). Great gadgets. *Phi Delta Kappan, 83* (4), 283–284.

Van Horn, R. (2002). Virtual libraries and valuable .pdf downloads. *Phi Delta Kappan, 83* (10), 732–734.

Wiedmer, T. L. (1998). Digital portfolios. *Phi Delta Kappan, 79* (8), 586–589.

Wiles, J., & Bondi, J. (2001). *The new American middle school* (3rd ed.). Upper Saddle River, NJ: Merrill/Prentice Hall.

Willis, E. M., & Raines, P. (2001). Technology in secondary teacher education. *T.H.E. Journal, 29* (2), 54–64.

chapter

6

Practicing Lesson Presentation Strategies

> 66 *Ultimately, being an effective communicator is about repackaging and delivering a message so that someone can receive, respond, adapt, and use the information successfully.* 99

J. H. Stronge

Expected Performance

- Participate in a drawing activity.
- Consider your personal preference for receiving verbal communication.
- Discuss how student discourse contributes to the communication process.
- Explore ways for strengthening your communication as a teacher.

WHAT AM I SAYING? WHAT AM I HEARING?

You are initiating more and assuming greater instructional responsibilities. Consequently, you decide what information students receive and choose the means you will use for sending information to students. How clear is your communication with students? With your supervising teacher? Are you discovering that the message sent is not always the message received? How do your verbal communication skills contribute to instructional practices?

In a study of classroom discourse, Cazden (1986) maintains that spoken language is the medium by which much teaching takes place and in which students demonstrate much of what they have learned. Whatever teaching approach you choose—whether direct teaching, problem-based instruction, or cooperative learning—you use verbal language in helping students acquire knowledge. For example, if you are teaching students to write a process essay or to find the longitude lines on a map, you give directions and present information for the purpose of acquiring a specific outcome. You refer to the textbook and supplement the content to facilitate students' comprehension and use of the information. You are the "vehicle of instruction" (Good & Brophy, 2000). In your role as teacher you communicate using spoken language to direct students' attention and engage them in discourse.

The thoroughness of your communication affects student participation and, consequently, student achievement. Once you send students a clear and unambiguous message, do you take for granted that they "get it"? Can you recall quickly moving through an explanation to the whole class and asking students to apply the newly learned information to a task? Can you recall being so excited about the learning activity and concept you taught that you failed to consider the task from the learner's perspective? Forgot to check students' understanding or clarify your expectations of them? This kind of one-way communication is often the basis for teacher and student frustration (Harris, Bessent, & McIntyre, 1969). Giving directions for an activity without checking to

CHAPTER 6

Facilitator Tasks

- Name one person to be the Sender.
- Provide the Sender copies of Communication diagram #1 and #2 located in Appendix B.
- Allow time for the Sender to prepare directions.
- Provide two sheets of paper per person.
- Record the time used for each drawing activity.
- Collect and score drawings and return them to participants (during or following the group activity).

You may choose to do this as a small-group activity. Procedures are the same.

see if students understand what you expect of them is only one part of the communication process. An initial step in direct instruction (Arends, 1999, 2001) or active learning (Good & Brophy, 2000) is gaining student attention, explaining, and giving directions. Checking for understanding and getting feedback from students is necessary to the communication process.

Effective teaching depends on accurate communication between teacher and student and between student and student. Inviting students to talk about their understanding allows you a window into their thinking and an opportunity to provide corrective feedback when you observe faulty, incomplete understanding (Arends, 2001). Lesson clarity depends on two-way communication (Borich, 1999; Good & Brophy, 2000; Harris et al., 1969). An interactive communication process invites dialogue and clarification and helps ensure the message sent is the message received. You understand the importance of two-way communication when you see quizzical looks, dejected faces, blank stares, and other signs of distress on your students' faces! Taking time to read and respond to these visible signs of miscommunication lessens discouragement and confusion for the students and the teacher. Engaging in a two-way communication process helps you become a more astute decision maker.

The **Focus One** activity for this seminar session emphasizes the importance of verbal communication in the teaching-learning process. You are asked to examine your personal experience with two different ways for sending and receiving verbal communication. One is an uninterrupted, step-by-step message, whereas the other offers an opportunity for questions and interaction as the communication progresses. As you participate in the activity, keep in mind the following three points about receiving verbal communication:

- your preferred style of communication
- your peers' preferred style of communication
- the communication style preferred by students in your classroom

Prior to beginning the activity, the Facilitator may invite someone from the group to be the Sender in a whole-group setting, and provide this person with the diagrams to be used in each exercise. The diagrams and directions needed by the Sender(s) are located in Appendix B of this text. The other participants become the Receivers of the Sender's message. The Facilitator may choose to have you work in pairs: in this case, one member takes the role of Receiver and the other takes the role of Sender. The process is the same for completing the activity and serves as a prelude to the small-group discussion session.

This activity consists of two parts. First, you are asked to complete individually an activity demonstrating one-way communication followed by a similar task demonstrating two-way communication. Each activity asks you to draw a diagram or give directions for drawing a diagram. During each activity, reflect on your personal experiences with different styles of communication.

After completing the drawing portion of each activity, you are invited to discuss with other seminar members your experiences with each style of communication. The Discussion Questions will focus your discourse and guide you to apply what you are learning toward improving the quality of communication in your classroom.

Directions for the One-Way Communication Process

As the Sender in a whole-group setting, you verbally direct the Receivers in drawing Communication Diagram #1 found in Appendix B of the text. Take a position where all participants can hear clearly but not see either you or the diagram. Perhaps you will stand behind the group or behind a screen. (If working with a partner, you will want to sit back-to-back.) Before beginning the activity, the Sender will want to study the diagram. Being unable to see the participants' drawings may cause you to feel uncomfortable. Give your best effort to the following tasks:

- state directions using specific, understandable terms
- repeat directions you think are needed
- emphasize parts of the exercise you judge helpful
- pace moderately your speaking of directions
- allow lag-time between diagrams
- decide when the activity is completed and ask for participants' papers

Directions for the Two-Way Communication Process

Before beginning the two-way communication process, the Sender (in a whole-group setting) may take any position in the room that appears conducive to communicating with all Receivers. (If working in pairs, you will want to sit face-to-face.) Receivers do not see Communication Diagram #2 (found in Appendix B at the back of this textbook) that they are asked to draw. The Sender speaks the directions and Receivers are to follow those directions for drawing the different figures. Throughout the time, Senders keep in mind the following:

- Answer Receivers' questions.
- Look at Receivers but not their diagrams.
- Repeat directions at any time.
- Interact verbally with Receivers.
- Refrain from pointing, tracing in the air, showing pictures, and all other nonverbal clues.
- Collect Receivers papers after checking to see that drawings are complete.

Discussion Questions

Discuss the following questions in a large- or small-group format:
1. With which type of directions were you more comfortable? With which type were you more accurate? How does your preference compare with that of your peers?
2. When would you use one-way communication in the classroom? For what reason?
3. Give examples of two-way communication in the classroom. Analyze what you learned from students talking and "thinking aloud," interacting with you and one another in the communication process.
4. After examining your use of communication, what are some ways you could strengthen your one-way and two-way communication in the classroom?

OPTIONAL ACTIVITY: WHOLE-GROUP DISCUSSION OF PROCESS

A discussion of the activity as experienced by different participants provides a variety of insights and perspectives. The Sender's insights and experiences vary from those of the Receivers, and the Facilitator provides another perspective.

Focus Two

Expected Performance

- Identify and design instruction appropriate to students' stages of development, learning styles, strengths, and needs.
- Create a learning community in which individual differences are respected.
- Model or demonstrate the skills, concepts, attributes, and thinking processes to be learned.
- Use teaching approaches that are sensitive to the multiple experiences of learners and that address different learning and performance modes.
- Include creative and appropriate use of technology as a tool to enhance student learning.

The Sender may be dissatisfied with the performance. You can support your peers' willingness to take a risk by applauding and encouraging such personal learning.

As Receivers you can compare your level of performance on the two drawings. Sharing the comfort level you experienced while making the drawings allows you to compare your experience with that of peers. Listening to others helps you recognize the variety of your strengths and limitations as a verbal learner and provides insight into the students' preferred communication styles. Such information further expands your understanding of the complexity inherent in verbal communication.

The Facilitator's comments about observations made during the demonstration can be informative. The Facilitator might describe the participants' nonverbal responses while drawing the diagrams and also note the time differences between the two styles of communication.

Specific teacher behaviors are critical to student achievement. You recognize that communication is essential. **Focus One** emphasizes the importance of two-way communication. You are aware of the significance of effective communication to the introduction and the flow of a lesson. It sets the stage for students' engagement in an activity whether you expect them to listen actively or take notes.

Perhaps you observed an effective teacher using multimedia, the chalkboard, or an overhead projector in an overview of the lesson content and for presenting factual information. How amazed you were that the students seemed to be attentive to the teacher! Observing how the motivation or initial activity engages the students and prepares them for the lesson content is stimulating. You decide to use a motivating activity to grab the attention of the students at the beginning of each lesson you plan. This is an important strategy—a first step for activating students' prior knowledge and piquing their interest about what they will learn in your class. Mastering a number of teaching strategies associated with an effective plan will ensure that your students are motivated to learn and engaged in the process, and allow you to orchestrate learning and mark progress among your students.

APPLICATION: PRACTICING LESSON PRESENTATION STRATEGIES

The instructional strategies you select to implement your lesson plans should vary to accommodate the diverse learning styles and preferred ways of learning among your students. As you continue to learn, practice, and reflect on the strategies you use to engage learners, you may discover that you excel in some areas and need to work on others. You know that it is critical to capture students' attention at the beginning of a lesson and work toward that end by connecting classroom learning to real life, and asking students to reflect on the importance of what they learn in the scheme of things. You may have begun class with a read-aloud, a bit of poetry, music, or an activity to set the stage for learning. Capturing students' attention is instrumental in involving them in their own learning, and most learning theorists and teachers develop their own variations of lesson presentation strategies to engage learners at the onset of instruction, during instruction, and after instruction.

Maintaining the flow of the lesson, helping students retain the material or find solutions to problems, and assessing the outcomes of student learning are essential teacher behaviors. Lesson presentation strategies help you navigate your way through the curriculum, goals, and outcomes you are charged with in your teaching, and help maintain the integrity of the lesson: the content, concepts, and learning activities you design to facilitate student learning and critical thinking. We urge you to "try on" a presentation strategy, reflect on its use-fulness, and adapt it to suit your needs and the needs of your students. The strategies suggested below are a mere sampling of effective ways to manage student learning and implement a lesson plan. You may have a number of lesson presentation strategies you want to use and practice during your student or intern teaching experience—those modeled by your cooperating teacher or in university course work. Whatever you decide, the important thing is to remember to include presentation strategies in your planning and delivery of lessons. You and your students will benefit!

Presentation Strategies

Introducing the Lesson

Four critical aspects of an effective presentation of a lesson include the introduction to the lesson, the explaining behaviors, the reinforcing techniques, and the closure of the lesson. The introduction of the lesson is sometimes referred to as an advance organizer (Ausubel, 1978), the anticipatory set (Hunter, 1982), or the motivation (DeCecco, 1968). These serve to set the stage for learning, give students a reason to learn, and focus their attention on learning by describing new content (in expository or narrative form) prior to presenting it to students, familiarizing students with content by skimming the key points to introduce a concept, or depicting what students will learn by creating graphic organizers or other illustrations to prepare students to learn new material (Stone, 1983).

Explaining Behaviors

You will no doubt find it necessary to build the background knowledge of students. Using anticipatory sets, graphic organizers, discussions webs, and other tools to visually represent the concepts you teach allows students to make connections between what they already know about a topic and the new information they are expected to learn. If no connections are made, it is your responsibility to find ways to link new knowledge to existing schemas or start at ground zero to lay the foundation for learning. This can be done through explaining behaviors such as demonstrations; graphic organizers, such as compare and contrast, flow charts, and task analysis; explorations; and inductive or deductive teaching methods. Direct instruction of vocabulary and activities purposefully designed to help students grasp the vocabulary necessary to conceptual development is another way to explain concepts, build background, and engage students in purposeful learning. Before learners can generalize concepts, skills, or new learning, it is often necessary to teach learning or reading strategies in contextualized ways; that is, the skills or strategies must be taught in such a way that students make connections between what they know and what they are learning in meaningful and concrete ways, and understand why they are learning these concepts, strategies, or skills.

Focusing and keeping the learners' attention on the lesson content takes creativity and planning. Providing an overview of what the lesson will include, perhaps a short movie clip or brief outline on the chalkboard during the introduction of the lesson, may strongly encourage students' willingness to engage in the lesson and recall what was emphasized initially. For example, before continuing to work with students on their narrative writing project, the teacher may begin the class using Barry Lane's (1993) technique "exploding the moment."

> Class, today you will use your vocabulary cards for lesson number three and review vocabulary words with a partner. I will provide the phonetic spelling to help you with syllables and pronunciation of the words. Next, with a group of three you will move to five different stations that emphasize the use of five senses as a means for expanding the

use of descriptions in your writing. After this, I will show you how to use this detail and description to create a real special moment in your narratives. I call this, "exploding the moment." Finally, you will have time to work on the story you are writing and to find an event in which you can "explode the moment."

Reinforcing the Lesson

Varying the presentation and maintaining a high level of learner participation requires knowledge of the content and skill in the use of various interaction techniques, especially during the reinforcement of the lesson. Interacting with students throughout the presentation, clarifying learner questions, providing time for students to think about and use new learning are crucial to deep learning. Handling any miscommunication and emphasizing main ideas are teacher behaviors that aid student engagement in their own learning. Practicing a new skill or strategy in class gives the learner the courage to ask questions, or enlist peer or teacher assistance. Practice using the new knowledge allows students ownership of learning and encourages application beyond the classroom. Varying the type of lessons by using think-pair-share and/or large-group response, group or individual research, Internet searches, paired debates, problem solving, case study, and games such as Jeopardy keep students excited and motivated as learners.

One particularly effective strategy to use during the reinforcement of a lesson is Reciprocal Teaching developed by Palincsar and Brown (1984). Teaching students how to use this strategy provides a deep level of understanding because of its tiered and circular structure, and includes four components: Summarizing, Questioning, Clarifying, and Predicting. After students read a passage or chapter, they verbally summarize what they read. For modeling purposes, you may want to record student responses on the board or chart paper. After recording student responses, you add any missing or critical details to the summary. This allows you to learn what students know and target areas that need clarification. Students then ask questions about specific pieces of information in the passage or chapter, and the class responds based on their recollection of information in the material read. You may clarify confusing points in the reading at this point, or ask students to reread sections of the material. After clarifying the material, students make predictions about the next section of material based on new information. This strategy helps all learners learn to use more analytical strategies in reading and sets a purpose for continued reading. Modeling is critical if you expect your students to transfer this reciprocal learning strategy to other areas of curriculum.

The explanation and reinforcement component of the lesson is designed to allow students to achieve and retain learning through practice, practical application, and extensions of the learning. This is accomplished through real-world applications and connections, and reflection.

Closing the Lesson

Closure techniques that emphasize major points in a lesson are the most frequently researched skills and are recognized as best practice (Shostak, 1999). Helping learners summarize the content presented takes careful planning and time management. You may find that you rush through a lesson with students or engage so deeply with the content that class is over before you can bring closure to the day's lesson. Consider the following examples as closure for your lessons:

- Students explain the key points they have learned during the class.
- The teacher or a student gives a wrap-up or brief summary during the last few minutes of the class period.

- In self-contained classrooms the teachers summarize the outcomes from the morning session or in the afternoon before dismissal.
- Students write a summary statement or steps to be taken to proceed with an individual assignment or group project. You may want to design a special form for this purpose.
- Students briefly explain the process they used for completing an assigned task.
- Students submit class entry or exit cards responding to prompts and probes you design that are related to the lesson and learning. (Index cards work well to document student participation in class).

Using a specific closure strategy can help you transition from one instructional activity or lesson to the next, and help students see purposes and connections in learning. For example:

1. A student summarizes ideas discovered from reading about a science experiment.
2. You give directions for performing the science experiment.
3. Upon completion of the experiment, you ask the students to give a verbal or written summary of the results.

As closure for this "lesson" and "application activity," let's review the presentation strategies you can practice this week:

Introductory—advance organizers, set induction, anticipatory set, motivating activity, overview.
Explaining behaviors—definitions, examples, nonexamples.
Reinforcing techniques—practice, repeating, emphasizing.
Closure activities—summary, culminating or concluding activity, wrap-up session.

ASSIGNED ACTIVITIES

The following assignment affords you the opportunity to observe and practice your presentation strategies. Respond to the following using your observations and experiences:

1. Each day, choose a class to observe and record an example of the following:

	Date	Class	Teacher
Introduction			
Explaining behaviors			
Reinforcement techniques			
Closure methods			

2. In what ways do you help students focus or engage their attention:
   - During a lesson overview?
   - During group activities or discussion?
   - During a lecture or presentation by teacher, visitor, student?
   - During classroom interruptions?
   - During transitions between learning activities or daily routines?

3. To what extent do you practice the following:
   - Circulating around the classroom and monitoring learner activities?
   - Reviewing and making connections with the major idea or concept being taught?
   - Providing variety and challenge in practice and drill?
   - Keeping learners alert and focused on the task at hand?
   - Maintaining a moderate pace in lesson presentations?
   - Reviewing major points during a teacher-directed lesson?
   - Leading students to extend knowledge gained from the lesson?
4. Observe your supervising or another teacher using cooperative learning. Perhaps you also plan and use this instructional strategy.
   - How were the students prepared for the tasks to be accomplished?
   - In what ways were the students held accountable for the completion of the task?
   - Write in your journal any questions or reservations you have about cooperative learning at this time.

SUMMARY

Once you engage the learners, you realize the importance of carrying through the instruction. Instruction may take the form of a mini-lecture, a discovery activity, a writing project, or a problem-solving activity for an individual or a cooperative group. You want to make sure your explanations are clear whether emphasizing key points in an outline, reviewing vocabulary, or asking students to demonstrate their understanding of a concept through verbal or written response. Reinforcing the ideas, skills, and concepts through group projects or individual practice helps students retain basic information. Perhaps the most difficult portion of instruction is concluding the activity or lesson. To include a summary at the end of the lesson or unit, ask students to verbalize or write in their journal reflections of what they have learned. Managing your time for using closure strategies takes practice. You will develop and practice these and other instructional behaviors throughout your teaching career.

FOLLOW-UP QUESTIONS AND SHARED INSIGHTS

Using the following questions, share your observations and successes or difficulties you faced in practicing the introduction, explanation, reinforcement, and closure techniques in your lessons.

1. Relate an introductory exercise you observed or used that motivated and involved students with the content being presented. Tell how voice, technology or instructional aids, thinking strategies, and lesson review or overview were used to capture the learners' attention.
2. In what way was the introductory activity used later in the lesson to: (a) elicit further information, (b) make applications, and (c) make comparisons?
3. What types of quick recall, reinforcement, review, and emphasis using voice or chalk/dryboard were used in a lesson? Which techniques did you consider effective in attaining the outcomes set forth for the activity?

4. Give one example you used in helping learners organize their ideas, themes, and activities this past week.
5. What explaining behaviors have you used in lessons taught? Were there times when you called on one of the students for an explanation or example or when you observed group members explaining a concept or making a connection for other members?
6. Share the different closure techniques you observed or used in lessons this week. Describe how closure helped the learner organize and retain learning.

Journal Excerpts

High School

"Before a lesson is planned, I meet with both of my supervising teachers to decide what needs to be taught, what kinds of accommodation are necessary to meet the academic levels and diversity of learners, the level and diversity of learners, and what prior knowledge these students have. For example, when I taught the 'Leads' lesson to sophomores, I knew that they had learned something about leads already and that this would be more of a review lesson. I also knew that I needed to incorporate movement into the lesson, because the students would have been sitting doing procedural kinds of things for the first 15–20 minutes of class. Along with this, I needed to cue my learners with special needs in the class—using lots of visuals and cooperative groups."

"With the freshman, we are beginning The Process Essay or 'How To' paper. After notes were completed, the students were paired up. Each pair was given two cups of milk and four Oreo cookies. The partners had loose leaf paper and a pen to take notes. Each person was to explain How to Best Eat an Oreo Cookie, while the partner took notes on the steps they used. These were collected and then the class (as a group) brainstormed for topics for a How To paper."

"I am learning not to immediately call on a student the minute he raises his hand. Today I had not gotten two words out of my mouth before a student raised his hand. Instead of immediately calling on him, I said '_____ please put your hand down and listen. If you are afraid you will forget your question, jot it down.' He put down his hand and after I finished explaining, he still asked his question."

Middle School

"Ms. H. used an advance organizer at the beginning of fifth period. 'Remember, these are the things that you have to have included with your final draft. . . .' She lists on the overhead: web, rough draft, list of new lead questions, web of snapshot, final draft—in ink. 'If you need help, raise your hand and either Ms. C. or I will come help you.'"

"An example of explaining skills I used this week is from a language arts class. I told the class that we were going to read a story this week as a class; but before we could do that, we needed to know some words and their meanings. I wrote the words on the board. Then, I separated the tables of students into Guessers and Checkers. The Guessers wrote down their guess as to the meaning of the word, while the Checkers actually looked up the word. Then we compared answers. The Guessers typically used context clues to gain meaning, but occasionally meanings were gained through root words. By having the meaning and pronunciation of words repeated, I reinforced the vocabulary for the story. For closure to this part of the lesson, I asked the class to explain what we were doing and why they needed to know the vocabulary words in a story."

Elementary

"In second and third periods, we read a story in play format. It was enjoyable but challenging because reading seemed difficult for them. They had no idea about using expression even after we explained it and gave examples."

"I did a reading lesson using the book, *Corduroy.* Then, I wanted to do a sequencing lesson to reinforce what we did last week. We finished the story map, but the students had to finish the sequencing activity sheet after lunch. Nearly every student did perfect work on this assignment. They placed all of the pictures in the correct order. It's so pleasing to watch them learn."

"Today students were to begin working on their world maps and flags. I saw some very creative maps but I found myself reexplaining the directions about drawing the lines of latitude and longitude on the maps. I was a bit confused about why they weren't following my instructions. We even discussed the directions together before we started. I asked about questions they had. I'm anxious to see how the maps turn out at the end of the activity and think it may have been better to give directions and model for students each part of the activity rather than giving them all of the directions at the beginning of class."

Special Education

"Today I noticed how easy it is to lose the students. If you let them sit for even two minutes, then you lose them for an additional five. Anytime that I'm walking to get a marker, I try at least to keep talking to the students so I can fill the space and keep them focused on the concept or skill they are learning."

"During centers Melissa became very upset and complained that she couldn't complete her 'I can' paper. I gave her different suggestions which she disliked. However, we finally settled on 'I can read.' I had to work with her step-by-step until she finally completed the project. The only thing that I regret is that she took all of my attention away from the other students."

"I noticed that Ms. M. used familiar sentences in her spelling test. I think this is a good modification. As I see it, she is dedicated to doing whatever it is that will help our students to learn better. After school, while the students are waiting for their buses, I have started the routine of working with all of the students on their multiplication facts. I love the teaching in the resource room. With two teachers working together, we can individualize instruction for other children who need it."

REFERENCES AND SUGGESTED READINGS

Arends, R. I. (1999). *Classroom instruction and management.* Boston: McGraw-Hill.
Arends, R. I. (2001). *Learning to teach.* Boston: McGraw-Hill.
Ausubel, D. P. (1978). In defense of advanced organizers: A reply to the critics. *Review of Educational Research, 48,* 251–257.
Borich, G. D. (1999). *Observation skills for effective teaching* (p. 26). Upper Saddle River, NJ: Merrill/Prentice Hall.
Cazden, C. B. (1986). Classroom discourse. In M. C. Wittrock (Ed.), *Handbook of research on teaching* (p. 432). New York: Macmillan.

Collis, B., & Remmers, E. (1997). The World Wide Web in education: Issues related to cross-cultural communication and interaction. In B. H. Khan (Ed.), *Web-based instruction.* Englewood Cliffs, NJ: Educational Technology.

Darling-Hammond, L. (1997). *The right to learn: A blueprint for reform.* San Francisco: Jossey-Bass.

DeCecco, J. P. (1968). The psychology of learning and instruction. In *Educational psychology.* Upper Saddle River, NJ: Prentice Hall.

Gage, N. L., & Berliner, D. C. (1998). *Educational psychology* (6th ed.). Boston: Houghton Mifflin.

Good, T. L., & Brophy, J. E. (2000). *Looking in classrooms* (8th ed., pp. 26–82, 373–410). White Plains, NY: Longman.

Harris, B. M., Bessent, W., & McIntyre, K. E. (1969). *In-service education: A guide to better practice* (pp. 202–204). Upper Saddle River, NJ: Prentice Hall.

Hunter, M. (1982). *Mastery teaching.* El Segundo, CA: TIP.

Joyce, B., Weil, M., & Calhoun, E. (2001). *Models of teaching* (6th ed.). Boston: Allyn & Bacon.

Lane, B. (1993). *After the end: Teaching and learning creative revision.* Portsmouth, NH: Heinemann.

Louisell, R. D., & Descamps, J. (2001). *Developing a teaching style: Methods for elementary school teachers* (2nd ed.). Prospect Heights, IL: Waveland Press.

McIntyre, D. J., & Byrd, D. M. (2000). *Research on effective models for teacher education.* Thousand Oaks, CA: Corwin Press.

Moore, K. D. (2001). *Classroom teaching skills* (5th ed.). Boston: McGraw-Hill.

Orlich, D. C., Harder, R. J., Callahan, R. C., & Gibson, H. W. (2001). *Teaching strategies: A guide to better instruction* (6th ed.). Boston: Houghton Mifflin.

Ornstein, A. C., & Lasely, T. J. (2000). *Strategies for effective teaching* (3rd ed.). Boston: McGraw-Hill.

Palincsar, A. S., & Brown, A. L. (1984). Reciprocal teaching of comprehension fostering and comprehension monitoring activities. *Cognition and Instruction, 1*(2), 117–175.

Shostak, R. (1999). Involving students in learning. In J. M. Cooper (Gen. Ed.), *Classroom teaching skills* (6th ed.). Boston.

Stone, C. L. (1983). A meta-analysis of advanced organizer studies. *Journal of Experimental Education, 51*(7), 194–199.

Stronge, J. H. (2002). *Qualities of effective teachers.* Alexandria, VA: Association for Supervision and Curriculum Development.

Tomlinson, C. A. (1999). *The differentiated classroom: Responding to the needs of all learners.* Alexandria, VA: Association for Supervision and Curriculum Development.

Wilen, W., Ishler, M., Hutchison, J., & Kinsvatter, R. (2000). *Dynamics of effective teaching* (4th ed.). White Plains, NY: Longman.

chapter 7

Stimulating Critical Thinking: Questioning Strategies

> " For student teachers, the opportunity to talk about their actions, their thinking, their beliefs, and their feelings, is part of the process of learning to be a reflective teacher. "

A. E. Richert

Focus One

Expected Performance

- Examine current experiences that celebrate your accomplishments.
- Identify and share feelings about your progress as a student or intern teacher.
- Explore the connection between personal and professional success and motivation.

THE TEACHER'S JOURNEY: BALANCING THE IDEAL WITH THE REAL

Think back to your initial teacher education courses. What mental picture did you have of the teacher you wanted to be? How has this image changed? Expanded? As you are working with students and your supervising teacher, observing and implementing best practices, your image of the ideal teacher becomes clearer. You better understand who that ideal teacher is, and you have a broader and more in-depth expectation of how that person performs as teacher. How does what you know about yourself match the image of the teacher you carry around in your head and cherish in your heart? Are your actions and speech what you want them to be? When you compare your real self with your ideal self, you may feel discouraged that you don't measure up. Recognizing and acknowledging the difference between the ideal and the real teacher is a significant accomplishment along the journey toward becoming a professional teacher. Allow yourself to consider your progress and accomplishments, and look forward to the image of the practicing professional you now envision.

You have completed the initial weeks as a beginning teacher. You have moved from being on "cloud nine" to thinking, "I'm so tired, I don't think I can put one foot in front of the other!" You have felt elated, anxious, eager, afraid, frustrated, sorry for yourself, worried, put upon, put out, let down, and a litany of other emotions. But how you have grown! You are organized. You know routines and student names. You observe, plan, and direct instruction. You give clear directions and model effective communication skills. You name classroom management practices you intend to improve. You use a firm voice when reminding students of expected behavior. Planning takes less time, even though you are now teaching more classes. You are learning much and feeling more and more like a teacher.

Your Values and the Ethic of Caring

Take another look at your ideal teacher and what you intend to be. Ayers (2001) describes teaching as intellectual and ethical work that, when done well, requires wide-awake inquiry and critical and caring people. Although there is always more to learn and know as teacher, at the heart of teaching is a passionate regard for students. The ideal teacher works to see each student as capable of learning and creates an environment that nurtures and challenges the wide range of students in the class.

For more than a dozen years you have observed teachers, and to some degree you may have internalized their values, beliefs, and practices. Only now as a student or intern teacher are the values inherent in teaching taking root. Your value system, rooted in personal values, may also be heavily influenced by the values of your supervising teacher, the school, and others within that school (O'Hair & O'Hair, 1996; Zeichner & Gore, 1990). Identifying and understanding your personal and professional values points you in the direction of becoming that ideal teacher you envision.

Wanting to help children and adolescents may have motivated you to choose teaching. Perhaps your interest in teaching a certain subject, coupled with a desire to work with youth and contribute to the betterment of society, motivated you to become a teacher. You may have elected to leave another line of work to enroll in teacher education courses to meet a personal goal. You now have the opportunity to incorporate what you learned in these courses into your current classroom experiences. Perhaps you take initiative in using different strategies to teach reading, or take time to prepare and introduce supplemental materials and activities into a unit you are teaching. Perhaps you engage the learners by helping them connect new learning to old concepts and generate active learning. How does what you practice in the classroom connect with the teacher you dreamed of becoming?

Trying to connect what we make of ourselves with what we strive to accomplish in the lives of students is risky business (Green, 1995). Sometimes when we see our students engaged in instructional activities, our level of caring is elevated. In turn, students often respond to us with a bit more trust. At other times we acknowledge the painful fact that things can go badly in the classroom. Your journey toward becoming that ideal teacher is indeed a growth process. During this student or intern teaching experience, you have moved beyond the fantasy of becoming a teacher and stepped into the role of teacher; your backpack is stuffed with experiences! Looking back helps you get your bearings in this journey, set goals, and define markers of progress along the way.

This activity invites you to identify and share at least one accomplishment you associate with becoming the ideal teacher you envision. The incident or example you choose to share is important because it is representative of you becoming a professional teacher. Sharing your experiences generates valuable insights for others having similar experiences. Sharing and having others listen to your accomplishments can energize you and other group members. It allows you to imagine many ways for becoming the ideal of a "competent, caring, effective teacher." Sharing our experiences invites us to examine and perhaps reveal our personal insights about the process necessary to becoming a teacher.

Before sharing with the group, take time to recall a successful teaching experience. Think about a specific teacher attitude or practice you demonstrated. For example, you remained calm while feeling pulled in 20 different directions, or you praised a student for suggesting another way to think about the character in a story. Maybe you clearly stated what you expected of students and they responded to what you asked them to do! You may have written in your journal about a number of successful situations. What insights into teaching do you have as you reflect on these experiences? Describe how you felt using specific feeling words. In the space below, name at least one success story, then write words, phrases, or sentences that capture the emotions and feelings embedded within the teaching experience.

_____

_____

_____

Analyze the experiences you named. Did you include a list of teacher characteristics and practices? Do you see a connection between this list and the image you have of the teacher you want to be? How does analyzing this list of descriptors give you insights about yourself as a practicing professional?

Discussion Questions

1. Analyze and describe for others your insights and feelings about yourself as teacher at this point in your journey.
2. Compare and contrast your teaching accomplishments with your image of the ideal teacher. Summarize and share your findings.
3. Select at least one teaching technique and compare the results of your using it with that of your cooperating or supervising teacher.
4. Now that you are teaching, your perception of teaching may have changed. What most surprises or challenges your current perception of the teacher's role? What do you still question or wonder about this profession?

Focus Two

Sharing your teaching experiences with peers during **Focus One** boosts your overall confidence and renews your energy for getting students to think on higher levels. As beginning teacher you are practicing skillful questioning and problem-solving techniques that require learners to perform at higher cognitive levels. Higher order thinking is complex and challenges you to develop creative and adaptable questions.

Elevating students' understanding requires more from you than just telling them about a new idea, concept, or problem. To get them to think about specific content you must guide students' thinking from one level to the next. Once you identify the variety of cognitive levels at which students are operating, you can better assist all learners in moving to higher levels of thinking.

The process of inquiry, discovery, and problem solving relies heavily on student involvement. The constructivist philosophy actively engages the learner in the problem-solving approach to learning. Writing and asking meaningful questions is crucial to student learning and challenges them to operate and think more critically.

APPLICATION: STIMULATING CRITICAL THINKING WITH QUESTIONING STRATEGIES

Skillful questioning techniques in classroom instruction increase opportunities for learning. Dewey (1910) considered the questioning process as the very art of teaching. Effective teachers are skillful in balancing factual and critical thinking

Expected Performance

- Elicit samples of student thinking and stimulate student reflection on their own ideas and those of others.

- Demonstrate appropriate questioning strategies to engage students' cognitive processes and stimulate critical thinking.

- Develop a variety of clear, accurate presentations and representations of concepts, using alternative explanations to assist students' understanding and presenting diverse perspectives to encourage critical thinking.

- Integrate skills, thinking processes, and content across disciplines.

- Guide students to express, examine, and explain alternative responses and their associated consequences relative to moral, ethical, or social issues.

"[T]he right question at the right time can move children to peaks in their thinking that result in significant steps forward and real intellectual excitement."
E. Duckworth

questions. Selecting just the right question to emphasize a major point or to stimulate lively discussion takes practice. The type of question to ask depends on the objectives of the lesson, student progress, and the needs of the students. Questions designed for a lesson should focus on what is important. Alexander, Kulikowich, and Schulze (1994) found that the more students knew about a topic, the more interested they became in the topic.

Questions serve different purposes and can be separated into specific categories:

1. To give instructions to your students
2. To review and remind students of classroom procedures
3. To gather information
4. To determine student understanding of the concept or material
5. To discover student interests or experiences
6. To guide student thinking and learning (adapted from Callahan, Clark, & Kellough, 2002)

The Art of Asking Questions

The art of questioning requires that you provide questions that are clear, purposeful, brief, natural, and adapted to the level of the class, sequenced, and thought-provoking (Good & Brophy, 2000). The level of difficulty should be adapted to the academic abilities of the students in the class. Formulating questions to stimulate thinking and appropriate responding demands an understanding of the cognitive levels of development. The taxonomy of Bloom, Engelhart, Furst, Hill, and Krathwohl (1956) provides a framework for developing the types of questions you will want to include as you plan and analyze your questions according to your instructional objectives. The levels of cognitive development and examples of questions in each level are presented for your review.

Levels of Cognitive Development and Examples of Questions

Level 1: Knowledge (recalls or recognizes information)
    Ex: What is closure?
    Using your text, list the major steps for solving a math problem.
Level 2: Comprehension (understands or knows what is being
    communicated)
    Ex: Discuss some differences between the cultures of India and the
        United States. (Materials have been read.)
    Compare the Republican and Democratic platforms.
Level 3: Application (transfers learning from one context to another
    independently)
    Ex: Study the picture on page ___. Indicate what you would do to
        determine in what country this picture was taken.
    Mrs. Bell is purchasing a new home. She needs linoleum for her
        $20' \times 20'$ kitchen. How much linoleum will she need to
        purchase? At \$12 per square foot, what is her total cost?
Level 4: Analysis (breaks down a problem into parts and forms)
    Ex: After completing the science experiment, what do you
        conclude is the name of the gas in the unlabeled test tube?
    What information can you use to support the statement: President
        Lincoln was a friend to the slaves?

Level 5: Synthesis (putting together elements to form a creative whole)
> Ex: Create a new instructional activity for a listening skill.
> How can we raise money for the Crusade for Exceptional Children?

Level 6: Evaluation (makes value judgments using specific criteria)
> Ex: Which of these pictures do you like best?
> Do you think the asteroid F 97 will touch the earth?

You may want to practice your understanding and recognition of the different levels of questions. Locating questions from teacher guides to determine the different levels is a good start. A number of researchers have found that a disproportionately high percentage of lower level (recall or knowledge level) questions are found in teacher guides and student activity books. It is therefore essential that you develop activities to raise student thinking to higher levels. Here are some suggestions as you design your plans for incorporating and encouraging critical thinking in your classroom:

- Ask higher cognitive level questions prior to textbook reading, during your review, or as a part of your advance organizer.
- Increase the number of higher level questions asked of your students as the school year progresses.
- Discuss the cognitive levels of questions with students.
- Ask students to develop questions from textbook reading or other material.

Highlighting higher level questions on your lesson plan at this time alerts you to their importance and ensures using these questions throughout the lesson.

Student Response

Allowing sufficient wait or think time after asking a question gives the students confidence to respond. Knowledge or recall questions may not require more than a few seconds, whereas analysis and synthesis questions require a more reflective time for students to be able to prepare a response. Your response to the student affects subsequent teacher-learner interaction during a class. Recognizing and asking a variety of students, even those who have not raised their hand, assures the students that you are interested in and fair to all. You might rephrase or amplify student responses. At other times you may correct, clarify, or redirect student responses by inviting other learner ideas to be given. You may nod approvingly to several different students' responses to a question and then assist the class in connecting all the information into a comprehensive response. By expanding on student responses or asking another question, you may lead students to begin thinking on a higher level.

You may find the following guidelines helpful in refining your skills of questioning and receiving increased response from your students:

- Ask questions that are clear.
- Ask questions that are stimulating.
- Ask questions that are relevant to learners.
- Vary the length and difficulty of questions.
- Allow sufficient time for thinking.
- Follow up on incorrect responses.
- Encourage learners to ask questions of each other and to make appropriate comments.
- Ask questions that are suitable to all learner ability levels.

- Give all students opportunities to respond to multilevel questions.
- Ask questions that match lesson expectations.
- Call on volunteers, nonvolunteers, and disruptive learners.
- Listen carefully to learner response. (adapted from Ornstein & Lasely, 2001)

Questioning Strategies

As a reflective teacher, you want to model and encourage critical thinking in your students. Students develop thinking skills at different rates and through a variety of approaches. You, as teacher, will sometimes use discovery learning and inquiry teaching strategies with your students. Posing problems and asking probing questions encourages students' growth in their thinking process. Problem solving engages students in a process that begins with identifying the problem and concludes with proposing solutions. Students are more actively involved in seeking and discovering knowledge with problems that are real and connect to their life experiences. Allowing them time to reflect on their cognitive processes gives students insights into the ways in which they approach problems and think through situations. This kind of self-knowledge is critical to individual growth. Students may openly share their strategic thinking processes and give peers ideas and insights into what it takes to be a thinker and problem solver.

At other times, students will need a more direct teaching approach. Teaching them to classify, compare, sequence, infer, and predict is challenging. These are, however, the baseline skills students need to apply, interpret, and use information to solve problems, discover new ideas, and respond to higher level questions. Modeling and using teacher think-alouds to demonstrate how to classify, compare, contrast, and so on helps students become "insiders," enabling them to see how these types of thinking can help solve problems and deliver explanations in specific ways. Myriad resources can help students become critical thinkers. You may want to try Twenty Questions (Orlich, Harder, Callahan, & Gibson, 2001), an activity in which participants ask questions to identify some problem or concept. Another resource that supports problem-based learning—an instructional method that uses a real-world problem as the context for an in-depth investigation of core content—is the PBL Network. You can ask questions, share methods and materials, and learn more about problem-based learning from other interested professionals through a mailing list server and an electronic interactive forum on the Association for Supervision and Curriculum Development Web site at http://www.ascd.org.

Encouraging your students to ask probing questions and solve difficult problems challenges them in developing critical thinking. How exciting for you as teacher when students ask higher level questions and explore creative solutions to real-life problems!

ASSIGNED ACTIVITIES

1. Journal the levels and the effectiveness of the questions asked in at least four classes you observed or taught this week:

Class	Teacher	Date
Question		
Level		
In what ways were the questions effective?		

2. Journal an analysis of the diverse levels of questions found in a teacher's guide you use.
3. Journal examples of teacher responses to learners that you observe and make while interacting with learners.
4. To what extent do you guide learners in their response? Journal three examples.
5. Relate how student responses to questions caused you to rephrase and clarify what was said.
6. In what ways do you encourage student questions?

SUMMARY

Formulating a variety of good questions, listening carefully to student responses, modeling, and responding in ways that will build student confidence takes daily reflective practice. The design and manner in which you phrase your questions and responses influences the quality of learning within the classroom. Students often transition to new and more complex ideas through teacher or peer responses. Using probing questions to help students expand on their initial response, allowing students enough wait time to make a response, and positively reinforcing them for creative and critical thinking builds student self-confidence.

This week you observed the types of questions used by your supervising teacher. You are aware of your questions and the effect questions and responses have on learning in the classroom. Becoming "question-conscious" may lead to improving your questioning skills. Just think, you may be instrumental in creating real critical thinkers among your students. Isn't this the heart of teaching, the very process of reflection—getting students to question, to probe, to investigate, to solve problems, to discover that thinking is essential to learning?

FOLLOW-UP QUESTIONS AND SHARED INSIGHTS

Reflecting on your observations and teaching, assigned activities, and journal entries, respond to the following questions:

1. What effect did the questions you prepared for your lesson plan have on student responses?
2. Describe an incident or situation wherein student response caused you to clarify or rephrase your questions.
3. How did your use of different cognitive level questions help expand your understanding of how students think?
4. What kinds of questions do students ask? Share examples of new insights you gained from student questions.
5. Share examples of oral and written questions observed or used in your classes. You may give the context in which the questions were asked. As others share examples of the questions asked of their students, you may use the chart in Figure 7.1 for keeping a record of the variety of examples given by your peers. After everyone has the opportunity to share, check to see if you categorized the questions the same as your peers. Discuss any differences.
6. Share an example of a time you modeled a questioning strategy or used think-aloud to instruct students in the art of asking questions. Discuss their responses and insights.

FIGURE 7.1 *Questions Chart*

Questions	Knowledge	Comprehension	Application	Analysis	Synthesis	Evaluation

Portfolio Tasks

In Chapter 3 you used INTASC Performance Standards 1, 2, 3, and 7 to guide your Portfolio Tasks documenting your understanding of planning in the teaching and learning process. Portfolio Tasks in this chapter ask you to address the ways you demonstrate INTASC Standards 4, 5, and 6 through implementing and managing your instruction. New Teacher Standard III (State) located in Appendix C may also assist you in your documentation.

Implementing and Managing Instruction

INTASC Performance Standards

Standard 4: The teacher understands and uses a variety of instructional strategies to encourage students' development of critical thinking, problem solving, and performance skills.

Standard 5: The teacher uses an understanding of individual and group motivation and behavior to create a learning environment that encourages positive social interaction, active engagement in learning, and self-motivation.

Standard 6: The teacher uses knowledge of effective verbal, nonverbal, and media communication techniques to foster active inquiry, collaboration, and supportive interaction in the classroom.

Performance Guidelines

You are to provide evidence of your ability to motivate, support, and encourage group and individual reflective inquiry in the specific content area you teach. How do you organize and manage the group process? Reflective inquiry means that students are actively involved in an in-depth investigation of questions related to the content being taught. Your evidence should include strategies that address physical, social, and cultural diversity and describe the experiences for multiple levels of complexity to accommodate students at different levels of performance. Evidence needs to show student work over an extended period and should include the following:

1. A brief narrative outlining:
   a. the ways in which inquiry is used with learners in your class
   b. how each piece of evidence promotes inquiry
   c. the specific academic expectations toward which the inquiry is directed
   d. the specific group management techniques used
   e. a description of the class, any students with special needs, and adaptations of the instructional task for this particular class
   f. the preventive disciplinary approaches used with the class
2. Samples of student inquiry-related work, either individual or small group, showing a variety of different media; for example:
   a. use of written sources
   b. student written work
   c. databases and computer simulations
   d. student-produced artwork, music, and projects
   e. videotapes of student activity

Performance Criteria

The quality of your work will be assessed to the extent that the evidence provided:

1. Demonstrates that communication with students is challenging, positive, and supporting.

2. Establishes and maintains a standard of mutually respectful classroom interactions.
3. Incorporates strategies that address physical, social, and cultural diversity and describes experiences for multiple levels of complexity to accommodate students at different levels of performance.
4. Selects content and organizes materials, equipment, and technology appropriately and accurately to create a media-rich environment.
5. Demonstrates ability to use and manage individual and group inquiry.

Journal Excerpts

High School

"I asked, 'What is the literal and figurative meaning of the story?' After I got blank stares, I realized that the students needed to review the meaning of figurative and literal. I had taken for granted that students would remember. After they heard the definition, students were able to answer the question."

"The interaction of student responses to questions and my rephrasing and clarification are quite evident to me. For example the nonverbal responses to my directions or instructions often result in my rephrasing. When students' responses contain the general idea that I wanted the students to explain, I probe the student for a fuller response and then rephrase the more specific answer in my own words. Several times I ask a student to give the class a general definition and then I will write the more technical one on the board by incorporating the student's answer with my own clarification of the term."

"Sometimes student responses alert me to the fact that my question was not quite clear. They might ask, 'Do you mean . . . ?' or 'What do you mean by . . . ?' This obvious confusion helps me to be more clear in rephrasing and then follow up to make sure I was successful."

"I have encouraged the sophomores to be aware of their thinking process through the writing of a persuasive paper. They are required to submit brainstorming, outline, bibliography, copies of sources, and a first draft. I provided numerous comments to encourage them to be aware of their planning, organization, etc. On Friday they will bring their drafts to a peer review session and then submit a final draft. This activity allows them to analyze a piece of writing and obtain an objective opinion about their own overall thinking, writing, and planning process."

Middle School

"Knowledge level questions are very good for verbally quizzing students. In teaching a poetry lesson, I used higher levels of questions. I selected a particular poem written by a child living in the projects because it is a very moving and quiet poem that uses lots of descriptive language. Many of my students can relate to this situation. One student responded, 'He doesn't like it.' I asked, 'Why don't you think he likes it?' Then the student started giving examples from the poem. I like this level of questioning because it leads the students in many different directions. The discussion took a unique form and shape based on one student's answer to this question."

"I try very hard not to give the class the answer. First I might restate the question. Sometimes I will give examples of what I'm looking for in the answer. Often, I will ask other students if they can explain the question. If everyone seems lost, I start giving hints."

"We have many ESL students on our team. Because of this, I find myself rephrasing often. I rephrase based on the look on their faces more often than their verbal responses. I can tell when they're puzzled. I might repeat or use hand gestures to help clarify a question."

"The hardest kinds of questions for this class to answer are the ones that ask them what they think. For example, 'Why do you think this author wrote this poem?' When they stated, 'I guess he likes poetry, I don't know.' I further probed by asking 'What was his purpose for writing it?' This question got a better response."

Elementary

"I asked several questions during reading/language arts lesson today. The questions I asked were clearly phrased and matched the learning expectations I had stated. Some children had difficulty answering them. If a student got two events out of order, I helped them by saying, 'Are you sure that happened next?' "

"Before the grandparents came, Mrs. H. did a chart with the students and had them generate questions that they would like to ask the grandparents. For example, 'What is one question that you would like to ask the grandparents?' This was a good way to assess their ability to think logically and ask questions. Most of the students thought of relevant questions."

"Mrs. P. had the students do a problem-solving activity. She gave each table some Cheez-its and told them to work cooperatively to divide the crackers evenly among each person at the table. After every table had finished, she had them discuss what strategies they used to solve the problem. They did extremely well with this activity and gave us insights into how each child processes problems and arrives at solutions."

Special Education

"Character Education curriculum involves the class in a values lesson each morning. I have enjoyed watching the responses the students have to such lessons as honesty. The new word for the month is honesty, so Mrs. C. led a class discussion on honesty. She webbed out what the students thought honesty meant. It was interesting to see how they defined honesty."

"This week when the students were asked what was the main idea of *Yertle the Turtle*, the response they gave was not what I was looking for. Thus, I worked with the students and rephrased my question incorporating a term that I thought they could better relate to."

"After breakfast we played a Jeopardy-type game with the children using questions about the senses. This was neat because the students could get a lot of points by working as a team with their partner, and by staying quiet while others were answering. Getting the correct answer also gave them points. They seemed to like this and they worked well together to answer lower level knowledge questions."

References and Suggested Readings

Alexander, P. A., Kulikowich, J. M., & Schulze, S. K. (1994). How subject-matter knowledge affects recall and interest. *American Educational Research Journal, 31*(2), 313–337.

Ayers, W. (2001). *To teach: The journey of a teacher.* New York: Teachers College Press.

Beyer, B. K. (1995). Critical thinking. *Fastback* (No. 385). Bloomington, IN: Phi Delta Kappa Educational Foundation.

Bloom, F., Engelhart, M., Furst, E., Hill, W., & Krathwohl, D. (1956). *Taxonomy of educational objectives: Cognitive domain.* White Plains, NY: Longman.

Callahan, J. F., Clark, L. H., & Kellough, R. D. (2002). *Teaching in the middle and secondary schools.* Upper Saddle River, NJ: Merrill/Prentice Hall.

Carroll, S., & Yarger-Kanem, G. (2000). Designing projects to promote student teacher inquiry: An evolutionary approach. *Action in Teacher Education, 22*(2), 90–99.

Checkley, K. (1997). Problem-based learning: The search for solutions to life's messy problems. *Curriculum Update.* Alexandria, VA: Association for Supervision and Curriculum Development.

Ciardiello, A. V. (1993). Training students to ask reflective questions. *The Clearing House, 66*(5), 312–314.

Commeyras, M. (1995). What can we learn from students' questions? *Theory into Practice, 34*(2), 101–106.

Dewey, J. (1910). *How we think.* Lexington, MA: D.C. Heath.

Dillon, J. (Ed.). (1990). *The practice of questioning.* New York: Routledge.

Duckworth, E. (1987). *The having of wonderful ideas and other essays on teaching and learning.* New York: Teachers College Press.

Eby, J. W., & Martin, D. B. (2001). *Reflective planning, teaching, and evaluation for the elementary school* (3rd ed.). Upper Saddle River, NJ: Merrill/Prentice Hall.

Flick, L. (1992). Where concepts meet percepts: Stimulating analogical thought in children. *Science and Education, 75*(2), 215–230.

Freedman, R. L. H. (1994). *Open-ended questioning: A handbook for educators.* Menlo Park, CA: Addison-Wesley.

Good, T. L., & Brophy, J. E. (2000). *Looking in classrooms* (8th ed.) White Plains, NY: Longman.

Goodlad, J. I. (1984). *A place called school.* New York: McGraw-Hill.

Green, M. (1995). Choosing a past and inventing a future: The becoming of a teacher. In W. Ayers (Ed.), *To become a teacher* (pp. 65–77). New York: Teachers College Press.

Hunkins, F. P. (1994). *Effective questions, effective teaching* (2nd ed.). Needham Heights, MA: Gordon.

Hyman, R. T. (1979). *Strategic questioning.* Englewood Cliffs, NJ: Prentice Hall.

Jacobsen, D., Eggen, P., & Kauchak, D. (1999). *Methods for teaching: Promoting student learning* (5th ed.). Upper Saddle River, NJ: Merrill/Prentice Hall.

Meyers, C. (1986). *Teaching students to think critically.* San Francisco: Jossey-Bass.

Nelson, G. D. (2001). Choosing content that's worth knowing. *Educational Leadership, 59*(2), 12–16.

O'Hair, D., & O'Hair, M. J. (1996). Communication: Reflections and implications. In D. J. McIntyre & D. M. Byrd (Eds.), *Preparing tomorrow's teachers: The field experience* (pp. 211–218). Thousand Oaks, CA: Corwin Press.

Orlich, D. C., Harder, R. J., Callahan, R. C., & Gibson, H. W. (2001). *Teaching strategies: A guide to better instruction* (6th ed.). Boston: Houghton Mifflin.

Ornstein, A. C., & Lasely, T. J. (2001). *Strategies for effective teaching* (3rd ed.). Boston: McGraw-Hill.

Raths, L., Wassermann, S., Jonas, A., & Rothstein, A. (1986). *Teaching for thinking.* New York: Teachers College Press.

Richert, A. E. (1992). Voice and power in teaching and learning to teach. In L. Valli (Ed.), *Reflective teacher education cases and critiques* (pp. 187–197). Albany: State University of New York Press.

Rowe, M. (1986). Wait time: Slowing down may be a way of speeding up! *Journal of Teacher Education, 37,* 43–50.

Sadker, D., & Sadker, M. (1999). Questioning skills. In J. M. Cooper, (Gen. Ed.), *Classroom teaching skills* (6th ed.). Boston: Houghton Mifflin D. C. Heath.

Sanders, N. M. (1966). *Classroom questions: What kinds?* New York: Harper and Row.

Wassermann, S. (1992). Asking the right question: The essence of teaching. *Fastback* (No. 343). Bloomington, IN: Phi Delta Kappa Educational Foundation.

Wilen, W. W. (1991). *Questioning skills for teachers* (3rd ed.). Washington, DC: National Education Association.

Wilen, W. W., Ishler, M., Hutchinson, J., and Kindsvatter, R. (2000). *Dynamics of effective teaching* (4th ed.). White Plains, NY: Longman.

Zeichner, K. M., & Gore, J. M. (1990). Teacher socialization. In W. R. Houston (Ed.), *Handbook of research on teacher education* (pp. 329–348). New York: Macmillan.

chapter
8
Varying Instructional Strategies

> *" There must be links, above all, between what we are trying to make of ourselves and what we are striving to make possible in the lives of those we teach. "*
>
> Maxine Green

THE POWER OF REFLECTION: WHAT DO I NOW SEE?

Thinking back to your first days of teaching makes you aware of the many ways your perceptions about teaching have changed. These changes are the result of your experiences in the school, your reflective practice, and the sharing of your insights with others. Student or intern teachers tell us they have never learned so much in such a short period of time! How does reflection contribute to and impact learning so deeply?

Reflection is an active process through which you critically examine what you do in the classroom: your thinking and acting patterns, your questions and emotions, and your teaching methods and philosophy of education. True reflection engages you in a process that encourages growth. Although reflection is an internal process, it is assisted by external processes such as journaling, exchanging stories, dialoguing, and interacting with others. To encourage your growth as a professional, you engage in these intellectual pursuits to develop your potential as a reflective learner, one who is able to act on new insights, also known as reflective praxis.

Opportunities for Reflection

The reflective process provides you opportunities to refine your educational beliefs continually and develop professional skills that demonstrate your heightened understanding of teaching and learning as reciprocal processes. You analyze your teaching strategies, the students' responses, and the educational climate you create. You assume increased responsibility for yourself as teacher and learner while expanding your influence with students and others in the school setting. Implementing a reflective process approach to teaching allows you to stand back and gain a new, deeper perspective on what you are doing in the classroom and how it affects teaching and learning—your own as well as that of your students (Calderhead, 1992; Schön, 1987; Zeichner, 1992). As Richert (1992) points out:

> Voice is a necessary part of reflective teaching as it is an instrument of self consciousness that allows teachers to examine their beliefs and experiences. By talking about what they do, believe, feel, or think teachers raise to a level of consciousness the complex matters of their work. (p. 190)

Through discussion you identify the affective characteristics associated with the role of teacher. Through journal writing, dialoguing with peers, and conferencing with supervisors, you assess your progress daily. Because of these reflective interchanges you redirect your actions and refocus your thinking week by week. You live the life of the teacher, and your diverse experiences transform your understanding into personal learning about the teacher role.

Conversations about past and present perceptions of the teacher role allow you to examine the purpose and consequences of that role from your own experiences of becoming a teacher. In the initial stage of student or intern teaching, you responded to questions about the teacher role. You are now performing many teaching tasks and your experiences during the past weeks affect how you think and feel about the teacher role today. Your reflections lead you to think about your work and question its purpose and the consequences of what you do. With your peers, supervising teacher, and college supervisor, you raise new questions and share insights about the profession of teaching. According to Richert (1992), you "come to know" in a way that enables you to enter and participate in the social and intellectual life of the professional teacher. This "coming to know" is your elevated awareness of the teacher role as you examine, analyze, and take on the numerous dimensions of teaching.

REFLECTION: DEEPENING YOUR CONNECTION TO TEACHING

When you read the words *teacher role,* what's the first thing that comes to mind? More than likely you have mastered the everyday activities associated with teaching. Lunch count, attendance, and homework concerns seem routine. You are more fully involved in the lives of your students and understand their individual needs. You collaborate and network with other teachers, and you reflect on your classroom experiences. This deeper connection to the role of teaching helps you to focus on different aspects of what being a teacher means for you.

We realize that your growth during student teaching is mammoth and occurs at an unbelievably rapid pace. One way of helping you become more conscious of your growth and understanding is by asking you to examine and compare your earlier reflections about teaching to your present considerations.

This **Focus One** activity asks you to look once more at your perceptions about the teacher role. You are asked to revisit the same questions you answered before you became fully involved in the lives of learners and with other teacher-related activities. As the result of your ongoing experiences, the previous responses are likely to differ from what you now name as the expectations and duties of a teacher. You may describe new and deeper elements associated with teaching, and your response may indicate a more critical understanding of what is expected of teachers.

Read the three questions about the teacher's role and write a response to each. When responding, it is not necessary to recall what you wrote earlier. In fact, we prefer that you be spontaneous and write what comes to mind! Unless you choose to share with others, you are the only reader of your responses. To save time, write only the number to each question and your initial thoughts.

Questions?

Teacher Role

1. Recalling your personal goals and knowledge gained from your teacher preparation, make a list of teacher characteristics that you believe are most important for you to practice as a teacher.
2. Circle the characteristics that are the most difficult to integrate into your everyday thinking and living as a teacher. Why do you think these are difficult?
3. For some time becoming a teacher has been your goal. As you begin working within this school, with these students and teachers, what will you contribute to the students, the school, and other teachers?

Facilitator Tasks

For this activity the following are suggested:
• Paper and pencils
• Envelopes collected from Chapter 1 Focus One activity

While student/intern teachers are writing, the Facilitator distributes the envelopes and asks students to respond to all questions before opening their envelope.

After you finish writing, open the envelope given you by the Facilitator. Beginning with the first question, carefully examine what you wrote earlier in the semester and what you just completed writing. Compare the first response with your current one.

• What is common to both responses? Circle similar words and phrases.
• How is today's response different from the one written earlier? Make rectangular boxes around different aspects of the teacher role that you just wrote.
• Which responses express a deeper understanding of the teacher role? Place an asterisk by responses that indicate a deeper understanding and new learning about the teacher role.

Discussion Questions

1. How are today's responses to the questions similar to those you wrote earlier? In what ways are they different?
2. Now that you are teaching, what surprises you about being the teacher? What motivates you to be a "good" teacher? What delights you most about teaching?
3. Think about your earlier images of the teacher you hope to become. Which teacher responsibilities and expectations are easiest to assume? What is your reaction when your own or others' efforts do not meet these expectations?
4. After careful consideration, what would you like to change about your image of the ideal teacher? Why? How might you do this?

Focus Two

In **Focus One** you shared your perceptions of the teacher role after several weeks of daily experience in the classroom. You may not have had a clue as to all that teaching involves! Teachers today have a greater responsibility than ever for making solid decisions that affect curriculum. By focusing on what students know and are able to do, teachers believe that all students can learn at reasonably high levels. Experienced teachers who are flexible and vary their instructional strategies are found to be more interesting to students than inexperienced teachers who have no knowledge of alternative teaching strategies (Emmer, Evertson,

& Worsham, 2000). This is a time for you to learn and practice varied instructional strategies. Soon students will number you among the more interesting teachers they have known!

APPLICATION: VARYING INSTRUCTIONAL STRATEGIES

To engage learners from diverse cultural and socioeconomic backgrounds and with varied learning styles, teachers use many different instructional strategies. Using a variety of teaching strategies to help learners assimilate knowledge, assess the degree of learning taking place, and determine whether learners have transferred the strategies into personal learning tools is part of the teaching-learning process. Varied strategies can take students from basic recall of information to higher levels of thinking and learning. Inquiry, discovery, and exploratory learning are highly motivating strategies for both teacher and student. Selecting the instructional strategies that best suit your students requires that you examine, practice, and revise a variety of strategies before making the choice.

Arends (2001) suggests a model of four cognitive strategies—rehearsal, elaboration, organization, and metacognition—that help learners act on new information and connect it to prior information. Using this model as an introduction, Table 8.1 categorizes key instructional strategies from classroom practice into five groups:

1. **Cognitive** strategies move from basic memory techniques to self-assessment thinking techniques.
2. **Collaborative** strategies involve teacher and students in a cooperative approach to learning.
3. **Community-based** strategies take teacher and student outside of the classroom to a broader learning environment.
4. **Organizational** strategies give the teacher specific techniques to guide student learning in a structured or logical format.
5. **Problem-solving** strategies stimulate critical and creative thinking skills and involve both process and product.

Consider the purpose and examples summarized in Table 8.1. We suggest that you review strategies that are unfamiliar to you by examining teacher preparation texts and materials referenced in this chapter. Implementing these strategies and teaching students how to use these strategies will go a long way to ensure that the content and skills you teach are more accessible for all learners. Your students with different backgrounds can interact profitably if teachers use the students' diverse experiences to make classroom learning richer and are sensitive in treating students' individual and cultural differences (Good & Brophy, 2000).

Effective teachers use different strategies to achieve their learning outcomes as they prepare instruction. A strategy that is growing rapidly in its use within the classroom is cooperative learning. Your seminar may be organized in a cooperative learning format. Good and Brophy (2000) provide a broad summary of classroom research on cooperative learning and offer certain qualifications to teachers when using this strategy.

1. Cooperative learning is *not* a wholesale replacement of whole-class instruction by the teacher, but an adaptation in which follow-up activities are accomplished through group cooperation.
2. Cooperative learning approaches may be more effective in certain classes than in others.
3. There may be optimal levels of the use of cooperative learning groups within courses or across the school day or year.
4. Cooperative learning emphasizes cooperation and deemphasizes competition.

5. Modeling, demonstrating, and practicing the cooperative learning approaches (sharing, listening, integrating others' ideas, and handling disagreements) is essential. Collaboratively, teachers and students participate in evaluating behaviors within the groups.
6. Cooperative learning activities engage the learner in the content currently being taught.

Implementing cooperative learning into your classes calls for careful planning, modeling, direct instruction, and practice if the process is to be effective. If you plan to use cooperative learning groups meaningfully, select content and learning activities that are designed to generate meaningful learning among students, and that are worthy of the time and energy necessary to gain the most from this process. According to Dickmann (2002), the use of proven instructional strategies such as cooperative learning supports students' efforts to "construct knowledge and apply it to problem solving." The purposeful use of cooperative groups appears to have lasting effects; research reports that students learn to use the cognitive and social skills gained from this interpersonal interaction long after they leave the classroom.

Perhaps the strategy that is most familiar to you, one that you experienced most often in your own education, is the lecture method. Use of the lecture, if well planned, can stimulate student interest and engagement in the subject matter. Rather than use an entire class period for lectures, many teachers are using mini-lectures and mini-lessons (10 to 20 minutes of direct instruction) to emphasize material and engage students in the learning process.

A number of strategies can be used to get students involved in the material emphasized: advance organizers, outlining, note taking, mapping or webbing, KWL (what you know, what you want to know, and what you have learned), graphic models, questioning, and discussion. Your enthusiasm will only further ignite the students' interest!

Discussion, when well planned and directed, leads students to think beyond the textbook. Facilitating a discussion requires that you know the subject matter and can emphasize the connections of ideas or opinions expressed, elicit responses from the students, clarify or expand on the topic, and, finally, summarize and bring to closure the response to the topic. Providing students a discussion web or other means to record and clarify their thoughts, facts, or rationales elevates the quality of the discussion and allows all students to participate at varying degrees. The brain stores knowledge in two forms: linguistic and visual (Marzano, Pickering, & Pollock, (2001). Having students represent their learning linguistically and visually is necessary to constructing meaning and ownership of knowledge. Using symbols, words, and images and allowing students to create models and other visual representations of their learning (visual and performing arts) stimulates critical thinking and allows learners to process knowledge and extend it to other arenas of their lives.

Other instructional strategies you might try are:

- verbally walking the students step-by-step through a conceptual map or web
- identifying and defining a problem with the students, verbalizing the approach to take, subdividing the problem being investigated, deciding on an approach and listing alternate approaches, checking on the progress of the investigation, and assessing strategies used in the process
- demonstrating and modeling note taking, outlining, and storyboarding
- using a Venn diagram to picture the use of compare and contrast or fact and opinion, and summarize student responses
- providing multimedia approaches that connect content with the outside world

Instructional strategies can be used in many other ways:

- implementing resource or thematic units
- cultivating critical reading
- developing writing across the curriculum
- reinforcing skill-based learning

As you vary your teaching strategies, your students begin to think about complex issues from various points of view. Providing multiple approaches leads students to apply and increase their thinking in a holistic manner and extend learning beyond the classroom.

TABLE 8.1 *Key Instructional Strategies*

Strategy	Purpose	Example
Cognitive		
rehearsal	to commit materials to memory	repeating phrases, underlining key words
elaboration	to create associations and connections between new information and prior knowledge	note taking, using analogies
organization	to cluster ideas and identify key ideas or facts from large amounts of information	outlining, webbing, mapping
metacognition	to think about thinking, to select, use, and monitor learning strategies	asking students to reflect verbally or in writing an explanation of their solution
Collaborative		
cooperative learning	to encourage academic achievement, acceptance of diversity, and social skill development	assigning specific roles and tasks to group members
peer or cross-age tutoring	to encourage peer acceptance, academic achievement, and social skill development	student helping another with a difficult concept
reciprocal teaching	to teach students strategies to improve subject matter and reading comprehension	teacher models, then students learn to perform on their own
Community-Based		
field studies	to give students an opportunity to solve problems in the real world	assigning a science project that requires soil samples
mentoring/ apprenticeship/co-op	to provide opportunities for students to acquire skill from experts in a particular area	pairing students with business individual
service learning	to encourage volunteerism among youth	students assisting elderly people in a nursing facility
Organizational		
advance	to help students bridge new learning materials to prior knowledge	teacher or students reviewing or summarizing previous lesson
compare/contrast Venn diagrams, flowcharts, sequence chains, time lines, task analysis	to help students identify similarities and differences, to show specific information in logical form and relate it to the big picture	(drawing Venn diagram) giving students an overview of the lesson or task to complete
graphic representations	to highlight critical attributes of a concept	using a visual or media aid

TABLE 8.1 *Continued*

Strategy	Purpose	Example
KWL	to help students retrieve relevant background knowledge and learn with awareness of purpose and accomplishment	learners writing what they know, what they want to learn, and what they have learned about a topic
PQ4R	to preview, question, read, reflect, recite, review	assigning a reading
mapping, webbing	to outline or analyze a concept	attributes ← lake → definition / ↓ examples nonexamples
note taking	to listen or read and take notes on what was said or read	having students take notes during an oral presentation
storyboard	to relate a story or procedure by means of pictures attached to a canvas or board	depicting the three branches of government
story map	to elicit meaning from a text or story	central events ← title → central ideas
mnemonics	to assist the memory by developing association between new materials and familiar patterns	devising a pattern of letters to recall important information or processes
scaffolding	to reduce complex tasks to manageable steps	helping students concentrate on one step of the task at a time
learning centers	to provide opportunities to practice decision making and new skills, use resources, and review or reinforce learned material	creating a measurement center for practice or enrichment

Problem Solving

A. Process

Strategy	Purpose	Example
brainstorming	to elicit numerous imaginative ideas, solutions, or responses to open-ended question or problem	asking students to generate descriptive language for an item
discussion	to share opinions to clarify issues, relate new knowledge to prior experience	teacher facilitating interactive exchange with students
heuristics	to assist learners in conceptualizing problems and organizing their solutions	given verbal problems, students coming up with alternate solutions
inquiry, discovery	to lead students toward a previously determined solution or conclusion	leading students through questioning to arrive at the concept mountain
questioning	to stimulate critical and creative thinking	asking students to classify, compare, or contrast using, how, why, and what if

B. Product

Strategy	Purpose	Example
debate	to add competition to and create excitement in instruction	debating use of the World Wide Web as an educational tool
interviews	to relate writing tasks to real life	developing questions for interviewing a person who experienced the Great Depression
research	to direct students in locating and using primary and secondary resources	assigning students to locate print and nonprint resources on space exploration
role-play	to enable students to think, feel, and act as other persons	choosing character from history or story to portray
simulations	to represent reality as closely as possible	using computer simulations (Oregon Trail) or developing one suitable for grade level

Note. From *Learning to Teach* (p. 428), by Richard I. Arends, 2001, Boston: McGraw-Hill. Adapted with permission.

ASSIGNED ACTIVITIES

1. Observe your supervising teacher as he or she uses cooperative learning. If you plan and use this instructional strategy, reflect on its effectiveness. How were the students prepared for the tasks to be accomplished? In what ways were the students held accountable for the completion of the task? Journal the questions or reservations you have about using cooperative learning at this time.

2. Select an instructional strategy you have not yet practiced. Outline how you plan to use it in your teaching and tell what learner outcomes you expect to achieve.

3. Develop a web or concept map that contains key concepts of at least one lesson you are teaching this week.

SUMMARY

At the beginning of the school year your supervising teacher initiated and now continues to practice techniques contributing to the classroom environment. In addition to observing these practices your involvement with students requires that you make these strategies your own. The assignment activities asked you to take an in-depth look at what you observed and did, and to examine the reasons behind your actions. You reflected on teacher attitudes and characteristics that motivate students, communicating clear expectations, using different means for relating to students from a diverse population, promoting positive working relationships among students, and arranging a learner-friendly physical environment.

Identifying instructional activities to take students beyond rote learning into discovery and exploration is challenging! You note that instructional strategies help your students meet the outcomes selected in the planning phase of instruction. Trying several new strategies may have been a struggle at first, but realizing that "Rome was not built in a day," you begin to reflect on your daily progress. Students seem to be engaged and you are beginning to see results in their assignments and assessments. You are gaining confidence in your teaching and even find that working with your supervising teacher has allowed specific strategies to come alive for you. Because of your success and determination, you are willing to try new instructional strategies that motivate and challenge your students to think more critically.

FOLLOW-UP QUESTIONS AND SHARED INSIGHTS

You have identified a variety of teaching strategies in your experience working with learners. From your journal and school experiences as a beginning teacher, share your responses to the following:

1. Identify four different instructional strategies you use most often with your classes.

2. Discuss how using these instructional strategies encourages students to be actively engaged in the learning process.

3. Discuss the difficulties and successes you recognize when using these strategies within your classroom.
4. Describe how each strategy you selected affects student learning.
5. Which of the strategies you observe or practice enables you to connect the subject matter with the students' prior knowledge?
6. Describe a strategy you have implemented that required a team effort between you and your supervising teacher.

High School

"After watching the movie, *Bernice Bobs Her Hair,* an F. Scott Fitzgerald story, the students used their movie study guides (which they completed during the movie) for discussion within the small groups. Students presented their group response to the guided questions. After the first group presented, I clapped and told them they did a good job and asked a couple of questions to begin a discussion. The class responded positively to this verbal and nonverbal behavior and others began to point out the strong points that were reported by the groups."

"The students are writing oral histories. They picked a person to interview last Friday. I assigned the actual interview over the weekend. Following the book's suggestion, I asked the students to write notes from their interview on index cards. This will help to keep them organized."

"I am still struggling a little with the group discussions. It is hard to find a balance of discussion in the large group. They either make too many irrelevant comments or don't participate much. I'm trying to find a balance by monitoring the room, using proximity control, asking students to cite where the group is finding the answers, etc. I think using the think-pair-share strategy modeled by my professor will work here."

Middle School

"For this week, we prepared the students quite a bit because of the number of field trips. A couple of strategies that I use often are graphic organizers and brainstorming. Most of the time I use them in conjunction with one another. I am a big fan of webbing and use it in nearly every subject. I think it's not only a great way to organize thoughts but also helps students learn how to take notes. It also serves to help students with their writing."

"In second period, the algebra class used a balance and manipulatives to work 'Hands-on Equations.' The teacher prepared an actual model, but the students had a laminated paper drawing for their use. Everyone had the same set of materials to work the equation. They really enjoyed this and it helps them to see how to find the answer."

"Ms. I. and I taped an enlarged number line to the floor. Students walked it as a model for adding and subtracting in one-step equations. It was really effective, especially for visual and kinesthetic learners in the class."

"Some classes haven't finished reading *Anne Frank* yet; however, Ms. A. wanted to get a feel for what they thought about the story thus far. She led them in a discussion about the feelings they have. She asked them if they could empathize with Anne's feelings of loneliness and isolation from the outside world. Students seem to respond to discussion more openly than they do when they are assigned a learning log entry which is written. I see the value in both discussion and writing as one can provide fuel for the other!"

Elementary

"Today I read the poem 'Johnny Appleseed' to the class. I had the students do an activity sheet on sequencing the order of the growth of the apple tree. I also had the students do a writing assignment with cut-out apples and an apple stencil. They were to write a sentence describing their cut-out apple and on the back of the same paper they were to write a sentence using one directional word. For example, 'I see a worm inside my apple.' These writings were super!"

"One thing which Mrs. L. does (which I found excellent) is allow the children to bring closure to the lesson. She has one child come to the front of the room and explain what they did in that lesson for the day. Not only does this bring closure to the lesson, but it also presents the information and ideas in a way that may be different from the way the teacher actually presented the idea. After all, oftentimes children understand each other better than they understand an adult. This is an excellent way to include closure in a lesson and assess what the class knows or has learned."

"I have become rather brave, and I plan to allow the children to make sand paintings both today and tomorrow. I hope this will go over okay. Mrs. D. seemed rather surprised to see me undertake such a messy project, but she said she would be there to help me throughout the project. The children were extremely excited about painting. I had this dream that sand was going to be everywhere and that the children would run haywire through the school. Gladly, I was wrong. The children worked wonderfully on this project and created some of the neatest sand paintings I have ever seen."

Special Education

"G. and C. are now mainstreamed for math every morning. During this time we do calendar, DOL, journals, daily questions, states and capitals, and magic sentences. C. and L. are able to draw pictures for their journal, while J. must write his. J. has a difficult time staying on task during this time. I decided that I would set a timer for him to finish DOL and the journal. I explained to him that I was giving him fifteen minutes to finish each assignment. It should only take J. fifteen minutes if he stays on task. The strategy worked—wonderful!"

"Today we had computer. After the normal computer class Mr. D. demonstrated 'Wiggle Works' to the students. Soon they will start using it. Most of the students did well even though the demonstration made the class last longer than usual. Modeling is an important strategy to use with all students, not just learners with special needs."

"I had assigned a page for math with problems of greater than and less than. The students were to choose which item was of greater value. I made an alligator from construction paper and explained to the students that the alligator ate only the greater numbers. I then used the wipeoff board to show the numbers presented in pictures. The students then placed the alligator on the page so it could 'eat' the larger number. This activity went well. Using hands-on learning helped the students discover and visualize the concepts greater than and less than."

REFERENCES AND SUGGESTED READINGS

Anderson, L. (1989). Learners and learning. In M. Reynolds (Ed.), *Knowledge bases for beginning teachers.* Englewood Cliffs, NJ: Prentice Hall.
Arends, R. I. (2001). *Learning to teach* (5th ed.). Boston: McGraw-Hill.

Barell, J. (1995). *Teaching for thoughtfulness: Classroom strategies to enhance intellectual development* (2nd ed.). White Plains, NY: Longman.

Bliss, T., & Mazur, J. (2002). *K–12 teachers in the midst of reform: Common thread cases.* Upper Saddle River, NJ: Merrill/Prentice Hall.

Brooks, J. G., & Brooks, M. G. (1993). *In search of understanding: The case for constructivist classrooms.* Alexandria, VA: Association for Supervision and Curriculum Development.

Brophy, J. (1998). *Motivating students to learn.* Boston: McGraw-Hill.

Calderhead, J. (1992). The role of reflection in learning to teach. In L. Valli (Ed.), *Reflective teacher education cases and critiques* (pp. 139–146). Albany: State University of New York Press.

Callahan, J. F., Clark, L. H., & Kellough, R. D. (2002). *Teaching in the middle and secondary schools* (7th ed.). Upper Saddle River, NJ: Merrill/Prentice Hall.

Clark, L. H., & Starr, I. S. (1996). *Secondary and middle school teaching methods* (7th ed.). Upper Saddle River, NJ: Merrill/Prentice Hall.

Cruickshank, D., & Metcalf, K. (1994). Explaining. In T. Husen and T. N. Postlewaite (Eds.), *International encyclopedia of education* (2nd ed.). Oxford: Pergamon Press.

Dewey, J. (1916). *Democracy and education: An introduction to the philosophy of education.* New York: Macmillan.

Dickmann, M. (2002 Winter). Having the tools of instruction. *Curriculum Update.* Alexandria, VA: Association for Supervision and Curriculum Development.

Eby, J. W., & Martin, D. B. (2001). *Reflective planning, teaching, and evaluation in the elementary school* (3rd ed.). Upper Saddle River, NJ: Merrill/Prentice Hall.

Eggen, P. D., & Kauchak, D. P. (2001). *Strategies for teachers: Teaching content and thinking skills* (3rd ed.). Boston: Allyn & Bacon.

Emmer, E. T., Evertson, C. M., & Worsham, M. E. (2000). *Classroom management for secondary teachers* (5th ed.). Boston: Allyn & Bacon.

Evertson, C. M., Emmer, B. S., & Worsham, M. E. (2000). *Classroom management for elementary teachers* (5th ed.). Boston: Allyn & Bacon.

Freiberg, H. J. (2000). *Universal teaching strategies* (3rd ed.). Boston: Allyn & Bacon.

Gagne, E. D., Yekovick, C. W., & Yekovick, F. R. (1999). *The cognitive psychology of school learning* (2nd ed.). White Plains, NY: Longman.

Giordano, G. (1992). Heuristic strategies: An aid for solving verbal mathematical problems. *Intervention in School and Clinic, 28*(2), 88–96.

Good, T. L., & Brophy, J. E. (2000). *Looking in classrooms* (8th ed.). New York: Longman.

Green, M. (1995). Choosing a past and inventing a future: The becoming of a teacher. In W. Ayers (Ed.), *To become a teacher.* New York: Teachers College Press.

Harmin, M. (1994). *Inspiring active learning: A handbook for teachers.* Alexandria, VA: Association for Supervision and Curriculum Development.

Henderson, J. G. (2001). *Reflective teaching: Professional artistry through inquiry* (3rd ed.). Upper Saddle River, NJ: Merrill/Prentice Hall.

Hunter, M. (1982). *Mastery teaching.* El Segundo, CA: TIP.

Jacobs, H. H. (1989). *Interdisciplinary curriculum: Design and implementation.* Alexandria, VA: Association for Supervision and Curriculum Development.

Jacobsen, D., Eggen, P., & Kauchak, D. (1999). *Methods for teaching: A skills approach* (4th ed.). Upper Saddle River, NJ: Merrill/Prentice Hall.

Johnson, D. W., & Johnson, R. T. (1991). *Learning together and alone: Cooperation, competition, and individualization* (3rd ed.). Englewood Cliffs, NJ: Prentice Hall.

Kameenui, E. J., & Carnine, D. W. (1998). *Effective teaching strategies that accommodate diverse learners.* Upper Saddle River, NJ: Merrill/Prentice Hall.

Kottler, E., Kottler, J. A., & Kottler, C. J. (1998). *Secrets for secondary school teachers: How to succeed in your first year.* Thousand Oaks, CA: Corwin Press.

Lovitt, T. C. (2000). *Preventing school failure: Tactics for teaching.* Austin, TX: Pro-Ed.

Marzano, R. J., Pickering, D. J., & Pollock, J. E. (2001). *Classroom instruction that works: Research-based strategies for increasing student achievement.* Alexandria, VA: Association for Supervision and Curriculum Development.

Mendler, A. N. (2001). *Connection with students.* Alexandria, VA: Association for Supervision and Curriculum Development.

Moore, K. C. (2001). *Classroom teaching skills* (5th ed.). New York: McGraw-Hill.

Nelson, G. D. (2001). Choosing content that's worth knowing. *Educational Leadership, 59*(2), 12–16.

Newman, F., & Wehlage, G. (1993). Five standards of authentic instruction. *Educational Leadership, 50*(7), 8–12.

Orlich, D. C., Harder, R. J., Callahan, R. C., & Gibson, H. W. (2001). *Teaching strategies: A guide to better instruction* (6th ed.). Boston: Houghton Mifflin.

Ornstein, A. C., & Lasely, T. J. (2000). *Strategies for effective teaching* (3rd ed.). Boston: McGraw-Hill.

Post, T. R., Ellis, A. K., Humphreys, A. H., & Buggey, L. J. (1997). *Interdisciplinary approaches to curriculum.* Upper Saddle River, NJ: Merrill/Prentice Hall.

Richert, A. E. (1992). Voice and power in teaching and learning to teach. In L. Valli (Ed.), *Reflective teacher education cases and critiques* (pp. 187–197). Albany: State University of New York Press.

Rosenberg, M. S., O'Shea, L., & O'Shea, D. J. (1998). *Student teacher to master teacher: A practical guide for educating students with special needs* (2nd ed.). Upper Saddle River, NJ: Merrill/Prentice Hall.

Ross, D. D., Bondy, E., & Kyle, D. W. (1993). *Reflective teaching for teacher empowerment: Elementary curriculum and methods.* New York: Macmillan.

Schön, D. A. (1987). *Educating the reflective practitioner* (pp. 12–17). San Francisco: Jossey-Bass.

Stone, R. (2002). *Best practices for high school classrooms: What award winning secondary teachers do.* Thousand Oaks, CA: Corwin Press.

Wolfinger, D. M., & Stockard, J. W., Jr. (1997). *Elementary methods: An integrated curriculum.* White Plains, NY: Longman.

Zeichner, K. M. (1992). Conceptions of reflective teaching in contemporary U.S. teacher education program reforms. In L. Valli (Ed.), *Reflective teacher education cases and critiques* (pp. 161–186). Albany: State University of New York Press.

Creating a Learning Climate

> " *People who serve as models of behavior usually are admirable . . . or more competent than the learner or observer.* "

R. H. Zabel and M. K. Zabel

Expected Performance

- Identify examples of modeling used to teach appropriate attitudes and behaviors.
- Analyze modeling and other strategies for teaching character education.
- Discuss the complexities teachers and schools encounter with moral education.

TEACHER AS ROLE MODEL

Learning to teach is an ongoing process and one that suggests you are always continuing the journey to become a teacher. This process of becoming entails examining specific goals of teaching while keeping in mind the total, complex act of teaching. Reflective teaching asks that you as teacher also engage in moral deliberation as you face head-on the difficult questions about and good reasons for educational actions in your classroom and the demands society makes of public education (Zeichner, 1990).

Among the current and frequently cited societal needs from American schools is character education. Lickona (1999) describes character education as "the deliberate effort to cultivate virtue," and says "character education has three goals: good people, good schools, and good society" (p. 78). Popular press and professional journals advocate the role of the school as that of fostering good character in youth. That the school needs to play a unique moral role in a democratic society has wide public support, and character education is being emphasized in teacher preparation (Berkowitz, 1999; DeVries, 1999; Lickona, 1999). "For many students, character and virtues will be acquired in school—or not at all" (Kagan, 2001). Teachers must be able to model those character qualities that students need to develop (Jones, Ryan, & Bohlin, 1999).

Modeling: Fostering Positive Attitudes and Behaviors

Modeling is a powerful means for nonverbally communicating the positive attitudes and actions you want your students to learn and practice. Consider how you can use modeling in the classroom.

Just as your university professors and supervisors are urged to be models for you, so you are urged to act and deliberate on what it means to exemplify moral character for your students (Zeichner, 1990). The respect and cooperation shown you may have been powerful motivators for reexamining your current performance and may have challenged you to search for ways to develop and model attitudes and behaviors that children or adolescents need to learn. Fostering the construction of good character demands a certain kind of interpersonal context, the creation of an interpersonal atmosphere composed of the entire network of interpersonal relations that make up the learner's school experience (DeVries, 1999).

Modeling: Interpersonal Relationships

Interpersonal relationships are the foundation for the learner's construction and understanding of the self, of others, and of subject matter knowledge. Interpersonal relationships promote both character and intellectual development, and these relationships are important components of creating a learning climate that is conducive to student learning. As teacher, you act as a mentor and eventually increase students' decision making by promoting character education. The behaviors you model are critical for teaching the values that promote mutual respect for equitable human rights and responsible citizenship in everyday situations (Coyne & Coyne, 2001; Pastor, 2002). Children and adolescents experiencing this interpersonal atmosphere also receive a powerful foundation for learning.

Being a reflective teacher calls for an active, persistent, and careful consideration of your beliefs in light of your background and educational experiences (Zeichner & Liston, 1987). Because teaching offers opportunities to influence students' thinking about value-related issues and activities, it is laden with ethical and moral responsibilities and consequences.

Your personal experiences are influenced and molded by your values and principles. Perhaps you have chosen to do service learning and upon reflection you are amazed at your personal growth and the change in your worldview. In addition, employing a "multicultural mindset" enables you to help all students in your class function well and to feel individually valued in the learning environment you create. These broadened attitudes are now a part of you, and as teacher you model behaviors and use language to promote an atmosphere of mutual respect. Your students are likely to intuit or learn consistently modeled behaviors that are valued and reinforced in a "good" school and useful in a "good" society. Your growing experience and competency encourages and invites your students' admiration, and interactions between you and your students reinforce the values you want them to learn (Fennimore, 1995; Zabel & Zabel, 1996). Examining the quality of your interactions with students is an important step in determining the interpersonal atmosphere your words and actions promote within the classroom setting.

Modeling: Positive Values

Young people observe adult behavior and search for images that contribute to the development of their values and attitudes. Think about what you want students to observe about you as their teacher. Since you value learning and working in an environment characterized by respect and concern for others, you intentionally model for your students those attitudes. You want students to be interested and enthusiastic about learning. It's important that your students respect and care about themselves, each other, and you.

From their daily interactions with you, students learn what you know and value about others and how important learning is. A student reaches to pick up an object falling from a peer's desk, and you pause to say "Thank you, Devon." You interrupt someone who is speaking with, "Excuse me, Nicole. . . ." The tone and expression of your voice communicate a gentle, caring spirit of helpfulness and you follow with "Why am I interrupting my explanation?" asking the student to acknowledge her and own her behavior. You encourage students to

"Empowerment, compassion, justice, equity, and community must be directly experienced by preservice teachers if they are to compact the next generation of learner . . . for it is in their own classrooms that these values and practices must be enacted to assure the democratic future of this nation."
V. O. Pang

think critically for themselves rather than querying you for answers by saying to them, "That's a wonderful question. Now how are you going to find that answer?" You put the responsibility and initiative back into their hands. You are very conscious of what you do and say in the classroom; you realize that your students watch and listen to you, absorb every nuance. You are modeling for students the behaviors you want to see in their actions and speech in the classroom. Do your interactions and conversations with students invite them to adopt the behaviors you model?

This activity asks you to recall a time during the past week when you consciously used modeling to teach students, where you used verbal or nonverbal communication to relay a single message. Pause to recall a specific classroom event (one in which students were involved). Use the space below for writing what you did or said to students.

_____

_____

_____

Discussion Questions

1. Share examples of how you greet students each day: making eye contact with some of them, shaking hands or smiling at others, and so on. Observe their facial expressions or body language. Tell what you learned from initiating such behavior.
2. Appraise and describe a situation in which you intentionally used modeling to teach students. How has modeling been effective in establishing mutual respect among the students in your class?
3. Summarize what modeling requires of you as a teacher. To what extent are you comfortable in seeing yourself as a model for your students?
4. In response to the public's call for schools to teach children and adolescents moral character, how prepared do you feel to teach values? What teaching strategies would you use? Discuss with the group the issues you would want to avoid and why.

Focus Two

In **Focus One** you identified ways to use modeling to teach students appropriate behavior and to help them become responsible members of a learning community. A primary emphasis was on your modeling sensitive and caring interpersonal interactions and respect for equitable human rights as a basis for creating a desirable classroom environment. These components of character education seem periodically in demand when national disasters occur and the public looks to schools, and consequently to teachers, to teach democratic values and attitudes, ethics and caring. In your interactions with peers, you share and listen for ways they use modeling to teach appropriate behaviors to students. Modeling is one approach for teaching students appropriate behavior, and deliberate use of this strategy greatly enhances the classroom environment for maximum degree of teaching and learning.

Expected Performance

- Use an understanding of individual and group motivation and behavior to create a learning climate that encourages positive social interaction, active engagement in learning, and self-motivation.
- Communicate with and challenge students in a positive and supportive manner.
- Establish and maintain standards of mutually respectful classroom interaction by establishing the importance of shared expectations during individual and group responsibilities.
- Demonstrate flexibility and modify classroom processes and instructional procedure as the situation demands.

APPLICATION: CREATING A LEARNING CLIMATE

Creating the learning climate begins with you. Every day you practice multiple strategies and reflect on the effectiveness of your practice. As a student or intern teacher you are keenly aware of managing student behavior and your concerns about managing your class are typical. Classroom management is a priority for experienced teachers, and tops their list of concerns about teaching. According to Haberman (2000), classroom management is an accepted centerpiece of teacher training and if beginning teachers are asked why they don't apply to teach in urban districts or practicing teachers are asked why they quit or failed in urban schools, "they typically respond that they are afraid that they will be unable to manage the classroom or deal with the continuous stress" (p. 205). Classroom management has many dimensions and needs to undergird instruction. Teachers who have well-planned curriculum have fewer classroom behavior problems. By identifying, discussing, and reflecting on the different aspects of managing behavior, you are building confidence and improving ways for creating a learning environment (Good & Brophy, 2000).

The topics reviewed and practiced in this chapter are considered preventive classroom management techniques. In using preventive techniques you work to create a positive learning climate and reduce or eliminate a number of misbehaviors from occurring. Preventive discipline techniques, furthermore, promote and build student self-control and motivation. How does this happen? How do effective teachers prevent misbehavior from occurring? Five effective techniques for creating a learning climate are listed below (Goethals & Howard, 2000). Which are used by teachers you observe? Which do you intend to practice?

- Exhibits positive attitudes and characteristics
- Communicates clear verbal and nonverbal expectations
- Relates to diverse student populations
- Promotes working relationships among students
- Arranges a positive physical environment

Exhibits Positive Attitudes and Characteristics

Beliefs and attitudes teachers hold about themselves, about learners, and about their role powerfully impact their interactions with students. As a professional teacher, you are the primary determiner of the learning climate and tone of your classroom. What teacher attitudes and characteristics do you possess that contribute positively to the learning environment? Do you observe and model attitudes such as these: "I feel lucky to be here!" "I like what I'm doing!" "I believe in you!"? Students receiving these kinds of messages from you are likely to think learning is worthwhile and school can be exciting.

An inclusive atmosphere begins with positive initial interactions between the teacher and students in the class and needs to continuously build. Learners of all ages need assurance from you that being in your class is important to you and that you are able to help them perform academically. Communicating positive attitudes toward adolescents can be tricky if you are not aware of their need for peer recognition and the pecking order among students in the class (Kagan, 2001).

How do you communicate to students the importance of a task? Planning appropriate, challenging activities and enabling students to succeed boosts their confidence. Expect to assist students repeatedly and insist they complete tasks. Students who experience success feel more positive about themselves and you as the teacher. Your belief that students can learn, your positive words and actions, and confidence in your teaching ability nurture a prevailing can-do spirit that permeates your class. Reflecting on how you perceive and respond to your role as leader and manager of the teaching-learning setting contributes to a productive learning climate.

Communicates Clear Verbal and Nonverbal Expectations

Activities connected with rules and procedures require the teacher's most salient verbal and nonverbal communication skills. Stating and posting rules and consequences, procedures, and clear directions communicate to students your expectations concerning classroom behavior. In monitoring students you "catch" them behaving appropriately and reinforce them for doing so in specific terms. For example, thanking a student for holding the door because it allowed another student to hang on to his books or be on time for class clearly lets the student know why you value what he or she chose to do and how the community benefits from one person's actions. Odds are that behavior will be repeated.

You are observing and learning the impact nonverbal communication has on an uninterrupted flow of instruction. Your gestures, eye contact, facial expressions, and pointing to lists of rules communicate to students approval and reminders about your expectations. Continuously sending verbal and nonverbal messages keeps students mindful of the purpose for their involvement. These messages help create a rich learning environment.

Involves Students in Creating a Positive Learning Climate

Rules and procedures relate to both managing instruction and behavior. The list of classroom rules is generally short, not exceeding four or six rules, and addresses broad areas of behavior. Teachers often involve students in making and explaining rules while emphasizing the importance of clearly understanding what behavior is expected in the classroom. Involving students in the process of rule making promotes a sense of ownership and builds a community of learners. Current practice recommends that class rules be clearly and prominently posted.

Daily procedures address more specific routines and tell students what is expected of them at the beginning and ending of class and the school day. Outlining and practicing procedures help students to meet expected behaviors when joining the reading group, in obtaining and returning class supplies, and in responding to interruptions. New procedures may be introduced and others replaced as the year progresses. The process varies according to learners' age, instructional period, and student needs.

The supervising teacher may plan and conduct the rule-making process and invite you to give input. If you were not present for the rule-making process, the supervising teacher may review the classroom rules as a review for students or as a part of introducing you to the class. This introduction and discussion of rules with the supervising teacher allows you to gain a deeper understanding of the rules and procedures of your particular setting. Furthermore, it initiates you into the authority role, as you monitor the rules and remind students what you expect of them. Student teaching allows you the opportunity to apply prior knowledge about rules and procedures and to construct a deeper understanding and conviction about their importance in creating an environment that is respectful, tolerant, and fair to all.

How comfortable are you with having power and authority? If student teaching is the first time you are responsible for others' behavior, you may feel apprehensive and hesitant about speaking and acting in ways you recently identified as being "the establishment." If you teach high school, you may be just a few years older than your students, and you both know you are new to teaching! At the same time, you realize the responsibility and authority accompanying the teacher role; you believe that students need to respond to you as teacher. Clearly communicating your expectations (verbally and nonverbally) is an important part of the preventive stage of classroom management.

The seminar session offers an opportunity to share your questions and concerns openly about communicating your expectations and about the learning climate in your classes. Take advantage of your peers' suggestions, and during later sessions share management strategies you used that positively impacted on student behavior in your classes.

Relates to Diverse Student Populations

Earlier you examined and identified examples of differences that exist among the learners in your classes. Being sensitive to and informed about the varied cultural, social, economic, and ethnic backgrounds of students and their abilities or disabilities, you can plan instructional activities that connect with their life experiences. Have you included resources and activities highlighting different cultures into the content? Did you observe student response to information about a specific culture, race, special learner needs, or ethnic group? By integrating student experiences and prior knowledge into instruction you take advantage of the diversity existing among your students. In doing so you help your students feel they belong to the group and you create an opportunity for deeper understanding and tolerance among your learners (Gay, 2000; Ladson-Billings, 2000; Pang, 2001).

You may be engaged in cooperative learning groups or other types of groupings during part of a seminar session. You can talk more often and decide how you will perform a task within a given time frame. This experience allows you to think about how it feels to work within a group and what you want the group to accomplish. During student/intern teaching your reflection on the effective use of instructional groups is one means for meeting student needs. Students claim they work harder and enjoy participating in cooperative groups because they are socializing as they work (Gay, 2000, 2002; Glasser, 1990; Johnson & Johnson, 1996).

Group work is a favorite learning strategy for some (but not all) students. You can help students understand the process and reward those individuals and groups following the process outlined for them. We encourage you to consider how group instruction allows you to give greater attention to specific student needs as compared with using only a direct teaching approach. In assigning students to groups, you provide an opportunity for peer teaching and allow students to develop and strengthen social skills in performing different roles within a group. Well-planned and well-managed group activities positively contribute to the learning climate.

Promotes Working Relationships Among Students

Connected with the ability to work in groups are skills for resolving conflict nonviolently. Conflicts are natural and normal occurrences among persons working together (Bodine & Crawford, 1998). You may have already witnessed conflicts erupting into violent outbreaks among students in your school. Society looks to schools "to replace disparagement with respect, exclusion with inclusion, and lonely isolation with collaborative community" (Kagan, 2001). Because of the increasing number of violent incidents occurring, many schools now offer students peer mediation training and other conflict resolution programs. Although incorporating the total conflict resolution process into instruction may not be practical, you can model and directly teach the skills included in conflict resolution. For example, you may teach students to listen sensitively, work together, trust, help each other, express feelings of anger and frustration in nonaggressive ways, and respond creatively to conflict (Girard & Koch, 1996). You realize that attaining these goals requires you to teach, model, and practice the skills. Look for opportunities to reward students using these skills in their daily interactions with peers. Teaching students to view conflicts as situations they have the ability and choice to resolve allows you more academic class time. An accepting, inclusive learning environment increases the chances that the instructional activities you plan will interest and engage students in the content areas.

Arranges a Positive Physical Environment

Organizing and arranging the physical features of the classroom occurs as school begins and continues throughout the year. **Assigned Activities** in Chapter 1 asked you to observe physical characteristics and to get involved with arranging the classroom in preparation for students. Planning instruction includes thinking ahead and anticipating learner movement and use of space and is therefore included among the preventive actions you want to consider in creating a learning environment.

The physical arrangement of the classroom suggests the type of interaction between you and your students (Weinstein & Mignano, 1997). When two teachers work within the same classroom, consideration can occur so that their desks convey a collaborative working relationship between them (Vallecorsa, deBettencourt, & Zigmond, 2000). Deciding how to arrange desks, tables, and other classroom furniture accompanies your decisions about whether you use teacher-directed or student groups during your instructional activities. You may have student desks or tables in rows and later rearrange them into groups, thus providing flexibility during a single period of extended instruction.

Classroom displays convey messages about the students and your interests and values. Teachers often choose an array of action posters, motivational quotes, and assorted hangings to express their values and vision about school and learning (Weinstein, 1996). Messages selected and displayed on the walls and bulletin boards can energize and motivate you and your students. Displays of varied student work communicates to observers that you promote and value the varied talents of many students. Although displays of student work are more plentiful in elementary and middle school classrooms, you also see student work and informational materials displayed in most student-centered high school classrooms. Other messages about students appear, for example, in student writing samples, artwork, and other creative projects. What you exhibit in your classroom helps to show students the quality of work you expect, and most are thrilled to have their work publicly acclaimed. Creating a learning environment that encourages positive social interaction, active learning, and self-motivation challenges any teacher and is especially challenging for beginning teachers.

ASSIGNED ACTIVITIES

This week's assignment asks you to reflect on what you are observing and doing to create a learning environment in your classes.

1. Observe your supervising teacher during two teacher-directed classes or parts of classes. Using Figure 9.1, modify the rows and columns to show the seating arrangement of students in your class. Tally each time the supervising teacher interacts with a student. After a day or so, repeat the

activity using a different colored pen to show the separate markings. Place an *X* marking the supervising teacher's location during the class. In your journal respond to the following questions:
- In what part of the room does the chart show the most frequent interactions?
- For which section of the room are there fewer tallies?
- After examining the chart, what new insights do you have about teacher-student interactions?

2. In your journal describe how the teacher uses verbal and nonverbal communication to encourage, motivate, and involve students. Give specific examples, one from each day, and explain what the supervising teacher said or did. Describe how student behavior changed as a result of the supervising teacher's communication.

3. If you were not present when class rules were established, talk with your supervising teacher about *when, how,* and *by whom* rules and procedures are established. Describe how you monitored and reviewed rules and procedures with students this week.

4. Describe in your journal some cultural, social, or ethnic information or experience you have had during student teaching. What did you learn that helps you to teach all students from diverse backgrounds?
- Ask the supervising teacher to observe you during two different classes and use Figures 9.2 and 9.3 for tallying your interactive behaviors. We suggest that you not know when the observations are made.
- Use this data to name the actions you plan to take to enhance this component of your teaching.
- After conferencing with your supervising teacher and examining Figures 9.2 and 9.3, write your reflections in your journal as a beginning effort in developing a professional growth plan for yourself. Include comments on the strengths you demonstrated and areas you want to improve. Note the actions you chose to address to enhance your patterns of interaction with students.

You want to consider the following:
- In what ways would you change the nonverbal communication indicated by the tallies?
- How would the changes improve the interactions you have with students?
- What do the tallies indicate about your attitude toward students and what you are teaching?

FIGURE 9.1 *Seating Chart*

1	2	3	4	5
6	7	8	9	10
11	12	13	14	15
16	17	18	19	20
21	22	23	24	25
26	27	28	29	30
31	32	33	34	35

FIGURE 9.2   *Verbal and Nonverbal Teacher Behaviors*

Eye Contact ex. Looks at students while teaching them Eye range includes all learners		
Facial Expression ex. Matches verbal expression Pleasant, smiling, listening		
Posture ex. Alert and attentive to learner participants Confident		
Gestures ex. Nodding in agreement, shaking head in disagreement Placing hand on shoulder Pointing to charts, diagrams, etc.		
Voice ex. Clear, articulate Changes inflection, volume, and rate		
Position to Learner ex. Moves about the classroom to view all learners		

FIGURE 9.3   *Classroom Layout and Patterns of Interaction*

Illustrate the layout of the classroom and sketch your patterns of movement and interactions with students.

SUMMARY

Misbehavior affects you and your students and can destroy the learning environment of your classroom. When students behave inappropriately, the teaching-learning time is shortchanged and teachers become frustrated and discouraged.

Learning to anticipate, plan, and manage the complexities of teaching, including maintaining a learning environment, is a critical area that you and other student or intern teachers are eager to master.

FOLLOW-UP QUESTIONS AND SHARED INSIGHTS

From observations described in your journals, share with others your experiences based on the following questions.

1. After reflecting on verbal and nonverbal communication used by the teachers you observed, what communication techniques are important for competent teachers?
2. In this chapter you read that teacher attitudes toward students are communicated in a variety of ways. Describe examples of teacher expressions, signs displaying values and beliefs, or activities that evoked a positive response from students.
3. Name some successful approaches you used to engage students who have different backgrounds and learning styles.
4. Share with the group examples of learner behavior that you have promoted:

   - Listening to each other—Describe how you encouraged learners to listen to each other.
   - Working as a group on a joint project—What are some examples of directions that were specifically given?
   - Learner response to mistakes made—What did you say or do to teach the class an appropriate response to others' mistakes?

5. If you were in the class when rules were established, share what you now think are important components of the rule-making process. Share at least one significant insight you now have about the importance of establishing rules and consequences and outlining classroom procedures. Tell how this contributes to creating a learning environment.
6. After examining Figures 9.2 and 9.3, tell how you plan to sharpen your interaction with learners. What strengths did you demonstrate in teaching? What areas need improvement?

Portfolio Tasks

Effective teaching and learning depend on the teacher's ability to create and maintain the learning climate. As a beginning teacher, you recognize the challenge of managing instruction and student behavior. The portfolio tasks in this chapter emphasize your understanding of learners and instructional decisions you make as a teacher. In addressing these tasks you demonstrate how you meet the INTASC Performance Standards 3 and 5. Another New Teacher Standard II (State) located in Appendix C may also assist you.

Creating and Maintaining the Learning Climate

ITASC Performance Standards

Standard 3: The teacher understands how students differ in their approaches to learning and creates instructional opportunities that are adapted to diverse learners.

Standard 5: The teacher uses an understanding of individual and group motivation and behavior to create a learning environment that encourages positive social interaction, active engagement in learning, and self-motivation.

Performance Guidelines

1. You are to provide evidence of your ability to establish a climate that:
   a. promotes and maintains learning in your classroom
   b. shows how you teach, monitor, and follow up rules and procedures
   c. demonstrates sensitivity to individual differences
   d. shows flexibility and modifies instructional techniques
   e. uses media to enrich the teaching-learning process

2. Samples may include but are not limited to the following:
   a. list of your classroom rules, consequences, and procedures
   b. discipline strategies most often practiced
   c. brief narrative outlining a description of your class and how instructional tasks were adapted for this class
   d. pictures and/or videotape of your learning environment that include students engaged in multimedia projects, oral presentations, art, music, research, or lab activities

Performance Criteria

The quality of your entry will be assessed to the extent that evidence provided:

- demonstrates that communication with students is challenging, positive, and supportive
- establishes and maintains a standard of mutually respectful classroom interactions
- uses classroom management techniques that foster self-control and self-discipline
- encourages responsibility to self and to others
- demonstrates ability to use and manage individual and group inquiry

Journal Excerpts

High School

"Expectations of student behavior were made clear on the first couple days of class. The students were allowed to ask questions so I think expectations were clear. Students know that they are to enter the classroom prepared for learning tasks. The teachers begin class with a review of previous material and/or summary of learning tasks for the day . . . gets students focused on the class."

"J., my supervising teacher, is very outgoing and enthusiastic. She likes for her students to be 'pumped up' about everything and she often uses a 'cheerleader' type of approach! With freshmen, this seems to work particularly well, because they are already excited just to be in high school and they really want it to be fun. She tells them why she does everything and this really seems to help them comprehend why they are being encouraged to do certain activities! She uses a strong, loud voice that is full of enthusiasm. Still, it can be very firm when needed. Her eye contact is also very dominant. She really looks at her students when she is teaching or they are talking. She is obviously reading their comprehension levels and showing them her full attention. . . . She praises a lot and smiles a lot, but she also uses her 'looks' to get her point across."

"Mrs. P. put a poster on the board with the name of a song and a sort of practical connection alongside it! She explained that she had made a musical tape with a mixture of songs that describe things about herself and the feelings of the year. She began with a classical piece to explain that everyone finds time to 'nourish the spirit' by reflecting. Next she played Aretha Franklin's 'R-E-S-P-E-C-T' and she wrote on the poster 'What everyone needs'—this allowed her to subtly intro-duce classroom expectations. Next, she played 'Ain't too Proud to Beg' and wrote on the poster, 'What I want you to be . . .' —this was explained that she wanted the students to never be afraid to ask for her help. Finally she played 'Why Walk When You Can Fly,' a country song stressing the importance of always having a positive attitude. In this way Mrs. P. introduced herself, addressed different learn-ing styles, and suggested some of her expectations from the students."

"Today I had to talk to a student after school about his attitude. He has con-sistently turned in poor work and does not take any of the assignments seriously. I am nervous about talking to this student, so Mr. G. and I talked about it. He gave me great advice (as usual), and I think that I handled the situation well. I sat down and pulled a desk up next to me. I did not want to make it confrontational. I was honest with him about how I was feeling and I let him speak too. I hope that this little talk will help the student improve in the class. Only time will tell!"

Middle School

"I have to say that all of the students in this eighth grade class do perform what's expected of them. Mrs. D. is very effective this way. If they have trouble, then they get help, but all do experience success in the end. The students show con-sideration to one another by keeping silent while their classmates are talking. They try to help each other within cooperative group settings. One thing that I thought was kind of funny was that while they had time in class to work on their homework, they were extremely conscientious about the noise level."

"Some nonverbal interactions that I have witnessed would be the use of peer editing and editing marks. I know K. uses these marks quite a bit when grading their writing. She also uses them during their Daily Oral Language ac-tivity. They have picked up on these and use them frequently themselves. An-other is that when the students are asked to read another student's work, they read the entire story, essay, etc., entirely through once before commenting on it. Now, I know that this is also a behavior that K. exhibits. I don't blame them—I want to be like her too!"

"The skills I learned in peer mediation will be very beneficial to me in the future. Conflict (peaceful) resolution is an ability we all need to have. I think it is encouraging that these middle schoolers care enough to be a part of the solu-tion to the problem of violence in schools."

"When students come in, my supervising teacher handles business briefly and jumps into action. The students know then, it's time to get serious. With each lesson, she briefly states her plan and goals and usually reminds students of the lessons' purpose during and after it as well. She told them she never as-signs busy work and believes all work should be beneficial, so she makes her ob-jectives clear. Her attitude is also encouraging."

Elementary

"I have become very aware of how effective various forms of discipline can be in maintaining a creative learning environment. Mrs. W. and I have been im-plementing a new behavior management technique with the students this week. The students are very aware of their responsibilities using this method of record keeping. The students lose a letter from the word *celebrate* if their be-havior is inappropriate. I like this method very much. As a teacher I can quickly walk over to a student and mark out a letter when that student is not on task. I do not have to say a word to the student in order to gain his/her at-tention. The other students are very aware of my actions, but I do not have to say a word. This method is making students responsible for their own behav-ior and/or actions."

"We began the day with a class meeting. I think such meetings are necessary and are a wonderful way to get students involved in *their* classroom. It also equips the students with a sense of responsibility. Each class meeting begins with compliments. Each student compliments another. Next, they talk about 'happenings' within the classroom, whether good or bad. It is a time to review rules, especially those being broken most often. It is also a time to discuss positives."

"Ms. P's ability to communicate well can be attributed to her clear voice. She speaks so that all the students can understand her. She never raises her voice 'as a rule,' and she doesn't need to. She also maintains eye contact with the entire class during instruction. This keeps the students on task because they realize that she is aware of their behavior at all times. She almost always has a smile on her face and her enthusiasm is 'catching' for the students. Her expressions are very motivating for these first graders!"

Special Education

"I have a child who is mute. I have been using reinforcement when he responds to a question with verbal cues from an adult or peer. I also conned M. into eating his lunch. I sat by him and teased with him that I love all the things on his tray and if he wasn't going to eat them he could give them to me. He would eat them and it became a game. All the children at the table began to join in my game and by the end of lunch M. was laughing with the other students. I really think he will talk with time and intervention. Something is wrong, but what it is, is a mystery!"

"The rules were established at the beginning of the year through discussion and role play. She made sure the students understood that they were everyone's rules. There is a list of rules posted. I monitor, review and reinforce adopted rules by modeling (giving cues), adding visuals (pointing to list) and verbal reminders to instruction, and reinforcing good behavior through stickers."

"I have been thinking about the effectiveness of the class helpers. While I think the helper positions are an excellent way to teach students responsibility, sometimes I become frustrated because I know I could do their jobs much more efficiently by myself. Yet, this is a preoccupation that I must overcome not only in teaching but in every aspect of my life."

REFERENCES AND SUGGESTED READINGS

Berkowitz, M. (1999). Obstacles to teacher training in character education. *Action in Teacher Education, 20*(4), 1–10.

Bodine, R. J., & Crawford, D. K. (1998). *The handbook of conflict resolution education.* San Francisco: Jossey-Bass.

Coyne, K., & Coyne, R. (2001). Dispelling the myths of character education. *Principal Leadership, 2*(3), 58–60.

Deutsch, M. (1992). Typical responses to conflict. *Educational Leadership, 50*(1), 16.

DeVries, R. (1999). Implications of Piaget's constructivist theory for character education. *Action in Teacher Education, 20*(4), 39–47.

Duttweiler, P. C. (1995). *Effective strategies for education students in at-risk situations.* Clemson, SC: Clemson University, National Dropout Prevention Center.

Edwards, C. H. (1993). *Classroom discipline and management.* New York: Macmillan.

Emmer, E. T., Evertson, C. M., & Worsham, M. E. (2000). *Classroom management for secondary teachers* (5th ed.). Boston: Allyn & Bacon.

Emmer, E. T., & Hickman, J. (1991). Teacher efficacy in classroom management and discipline. *Educational & Psychological Measurement, 51*(3), 755–766.

Evertson, C. M., Emmer, E. T., Clements, B. S., & Worsham, M. E. (2000). *Classroom management for elementary teachers* (5th ed.). Boston: Allyn & Bacon.

Fennimore, B. S. (1995). *Student-centered classroom management*. Albany, NY: Delmar.

Gay, G. (2000). *Culturally responsive teaching: Theory, research, & practice*. New York: Teachers College Press.

Gay, G. (2002). Preparing for culturally responsive teaching. *Journal of Teacher Education, 53*(2), 106–116.

Girard, K., & Koch, S. J. (1996). *Conflict resolution in the schools*. San Francisco: Jossey-Bass.

Glasser, W. (1990). *The quality school*. New York: Harper and Row.

Goethals, M. S., & Howard, R. A. (2000). *Student teaching: A process approach to reflective practice*. Upper Saddle River, NJ: Merrill/Prentice Hall.

Good, T. L., & Brophy, J. E. (2000). *Looking in classrooms* (8th ed.). White Plains, NY: Longman.

Gordon, T. (1974). *Teacher effectiveness training*. New York: David McKay.

Haberman, M. (2000). Urban schools: Day camps or custodial centers? *Phi Delta Kappan, 82*(3), 203–208.

Hogelucht, K. S. B., & Geist, P. (1997). Discipline in the classroom: Communicative strategies for negotiating order. *Western Journal of Communication, 61*(1), 1–34.

Johnson, D. W., & Johnson, R. T. (1999). Learning together and alone: Cooperative, competitive, and individualistic learning. Boston: Allyn & Bacon.

Johnson, D. W., & Johnson, R. T. (1996). Conflict resolution and peer mediation programs in elementary and secondary schools: A review of the research. *Review of Educational Research, 66*(4), 459–509.

Johnson, D. W., Johnson, R. T., Dudley, B., & Burnett, R. (1992). Teaching students to be peer mediators. *Educational Leadership, 50*(1), 10–15.

Jones, E. N., Ryan, K., & Bohlin, K. (1999). Character education and teacher education. *Action in Teacher Education, 20*(4), 11–28.

Jones, V. F., & Jones, L. S. (1998). *Comprehensive classroom management: Creating communities of support and solving problems* (5th ed.). Boston: Allyn & Bacon.

Kagan, S. (2001). Teaching for character and community. *Educational Leadership, 59*(2), 50–55.

Kohn, A. (1996). *Beyond discipline: From compliance to community*. Alexandria, VA: Association for Supervision and Curriculum Development.

Kreidler, W. J. (1984). *Creative conflict resolution*. Glenview, IL: Scott Foresman.

Ladson-Billings, G. (2000). Fighting for our lives; Preparing teachers to teach African-American students. *Journal of Teacher Education, 51*(3), 206–214.

Lickona, T. (1999). Character education: Seven crucial issues. *Action in Teacher Education, 20*(4), 77–84.

Marshall, M. L. (2001). *Discipline without stress: How teachers and parents promote responsibility and learning*. Los Alamitos, CA: Piper Press.

McCarthy, C. (1992). Why must we teach peace. *Educational Leadership, 50*(1), 6–9.

Nimmo, D. (1997). Judicious discipline in the music classroom. *Music Educators Journal, 83*(4), 27–33.

Pang, V. O. (2001). *Multicultural education: A caring-centered reflective approach*. Boston: McGraw-Hill.

Pastor, P. (2002). School discipline and the character of our schools. *Phi Delta Kappan, 83*(9), 658–661.

Richert, A. E. (1992). Voice and power in teaching and learning to teach. In L. Valli (Ed.), *Reflective teacher education: Cases and critiques*. Albany: State University of New York Press.

Thayer-Bacon, B. J., & Bacon, C. S. (1998). *Philosophy applied to education: Nurturing a democratic community in the classroom.* Upper Saddle River, NJ: Merrill/Prentice Hall.

Vallecorsa, A. L., deBettencourt, L. U., & Zigmond, N. (2000). *Students with mild disabilities in general education settings.* Upper Saddle River, NJ: Merrill/Prentice Hall.

Weinstein, C. S. (1996). *Secondary classroom management: Lessons from research and practice.* Boston: McGraw-Hill.

Weinstein, C. S., & Mignano, A. J. (1997). *Elementary classroom management: Lessons from research and practice* (2nd ed.). Boston: McGraw-Hill.

Wolfgang, C. H. (2001). *Solving discipline and classroom management problems: Methods and models for today's teachers.* New York: Wiley.

Zabel, R. H., & Zabel, M. K. (1996). *Classroom management in context: Orchestrating positive learning environments.* Boston: Houghton Mifflin.

Zeichner, K. M. (1990). Educational and social commitments in reflective teacher education programs. *Proceedings of the Fourth National Forum, Association of Independent Liberal Arts Colleges for Teacher Education* (pp. 55–60).

Zeichner, K. M., & Liston, D. P. (1987). Teaching student teachers to reflect. *Harvard Educational Review, 57*(1), 23–48.

chapter 10

Maintaining the Learning Climate

> " We need nothing less than clear thinking, careful planning,
> excellent communication skills, and an overriding concern for
> the well being of students. Combining these skills with our
> current knowledge on effective practice will surely result in
> more efficient and more effective . . . practices. "
>
> T. R. Guskey

Focus One

Expected Performance

- Identify beliefs and expectations of yourself as teacher that you prize.
- Design a model that communicates the professional teacher.
- Discuss questions you have about teaching and how they relate to your future goals.

REEXAMINING YOUR REASONS FOR BECOMING A TEACHER

Why are you becoming a teacher? Do you want to work with youth? Do you like sharing knowledge with children? Do you enjoy working for youth's best interest? Are you hoping to help students learn how to care for themselves, each other, and the global community? How do you feel about working with teachers as colleagues? From watching and working with others who embody professional teacher characteristics, why do you feel drawn to teaching?

Teaching is a service-oriented profession. This means that people who choose teaching as a profession expect to derive job satisfaction from working with and for the well-being of others. Job satisfaction is evident in your enthusiasm for teaching and your positive mind-set toward the events and people within the school.

As you approach being inducted into the teaching profession, you see more clearly critical aspects of the teacher role. Your desire to work with youth now causes you to look at classroom policy and practices that are good for your students. You are concerned about their intellectual growth and are aware of your ability to help them learn ways to interact with and contribute to the global community. You understand what being of service to others means in the daily routine of classroom life. You reinforce your students' gestures of helpfulness and validate their contributions to the lives of others. You encourage them to build a better world, beginning with their own—the classroom. You realize the rewards of teaching lie mainly in seeing your students grow. As a result of your student teacher or intern experience, your understanding of teaching has reached a new level: you realize the impact you can effect on your students' lives, and this realization sharply focuses the teacher characteristics you value.

You find the social organization of schools to be an inviting atmosphere. Observing and interacting with other teachers help you gauge your own level of dedication to teaching. You enjoy working with peers, especially those who are caring and open and seem happy in their profession. You find yourself drawn to those willing to assume new perspectives and accept challenges. In working with a team of dedicated professionals you now identify numerous teacher behaviors worth emulating. Teachers engaged in study and professional development or actively involved in creating rich learning experiences for their students have all influenced your understanding of *teacher.* You want to be like those teachers. You think you have made progress in developing a solid relationship with your supervising teacher and with other members of the team or department. You feel like a professional, and a career as a professional teacher has multidimensional meaning for you.

Decisions! Decisions! Decisions!

Do you find yourself asking your supervising teacher or college coordinator "What do you do when . . . ?" You raised the question because you are searching for help in finding a specific, practical, and real answer for a situation or problems you encounter. You are eager to know the "answer," to know what you *should* be doing to alleviate a particular crisis, perhaps one that affects the climate of your classroom. Although knowledgeable outsiders can be resources, answers to problems and situations in the classroom and school must come from individuals in touch with the multiple inside variables (Wasserman, 1993). You are an "inside variable" and grasp the importance of resolving the problem yourself in conjunction with your students. Like other beginning teachers, you are concerned about maintaining a learning climate, and you recognize that your thinking and decision-making practices about daily classroom life are keys to meeting this goal.

As the teacher, you recognize that goals you have for your students are the major factors that influence your academic decisions and classroom policies designed to maintain the learning climate. Most likely you find yourself deciding between two approaches—a teacher-directed, information-dissemination model of teaching or a more constructive, student-centered approach (Jones & Jones, 1998). Considering what you want your students to know and do, you may choose to integrate both approaches during an extended class period. Your decisions and the goals pushing these decisions are guided by such considerations as the engagement and maturity levels of the students and the overall behavior patterns of the group. Rather than stopping and punishing misbehavior, you would rather reinforce positive behavior and capitalize on student strengths and interests.

You work hard to plan and systematically establish classroom groups that reflect your values and ideals, and challenge your students to maintain the quality work standards you put in place. Your reflective approach to planning enables you to better match activities to student interests, while allowing your expectations for individual students to remain high. Being an informed decision maker enables you to maintain a learning climate necessary to impact student learning.

What You Expect Is What You Get!

The goals and expectations you hold for yourself as teacher are guided by your beliefs about your students' needs and their responses when challenged to meet academic standards and goals. Your student teaching experience encourages you to recognize the connection between your curricular and instructional decisions and your beliefs about the academic ability of the class and of individual students.

High expectations and commitment to bring about student achievement are part of a pattern of attitudes, beliefs, and behavior that characterize schools that are successful in maximizing their students' learning gains, especially for children of color (Gay, 2000). Good and Brophy (2000) maintain that expectations you have about students can cause you to treat them in ways that make students respond just as you expect them. For example, you expect students to recognize the necessity of rules for a smoothly running classroom. In a class meeting students decide what rules they need to govern themselves. Considering classroom instructional experiences and the school climate where you now work, do you recognize the powerful impact of teachers' beliefs and expectations for students? Your search for answers to the question "What do I do when . . . ?" is an important one. You may find help from others who are closely connected with the internal variables of the classroom setting you so diligently strive to manage. Be aware that your own beliefs, expectations, and goals impact the routine responses you make.

You are engaged with the school on a personal level. These are your students and their activities occupy your thoughts and interests. You are aware of practices that promote ethical standards for you and your students. Daily, you make choices keeping in mind what is in your students' best interest. Your awareness of teachers' ethical practices grows day by day as you learn about school and state policies, and such routine tasks as grading, confidentiality of records, responsibilities toward student journals, and writing portfolios. Professional ethics carries new meaning for you as you struggle with these issues.

As a result of your experiences, do you have different expectations for yourself as teacher? Your satisfaction with the job you are doing as a teacher depends on the success you realize from meeting these expectations, while allowing yourself to learn by making mistakes. Ask yourself this critical question: Do you feel enriched by working with and for youth? If the answer is a resounding "Yes!" you understand more clearly than ever before the importance of the expectations you hold for yourself as teacher. Your student or intern teaching experiences allow you to describe specifically and work toward the professional teacher you aspire to become. Upon careful reflection, what teacher characteristics do you truly value? How do these contribute to the sense of satisfaction you experience as a result of your work as a teacher? What would your list of prized teacher characteristics contain? How might you symbolize these?

Facilitator Tasks

- Provide 4-by-6-inch pieces of high-quality paper for designing a monument.
- Make available or remind participants to bring pens or other drawing instruments.

Monumental Design: A Testimonial to your Growing Professionalism

We invite you to design a monument that captures you, the teacher. The monument may include words, phrases, symbols, and any other design elements you choose to communicate visually who you are and whom you want to become as teacher. You want persons viewing your monument to recognize the professional characteristics you value and the personality traits you cherish in a teacher. Viewers will immediately grasp and recognize the essence of your creation. You are the designer with an eye on the future!

Discussion Questions

1. In designing your monument, did you concentrate more on the present or on the future? How is the future represented?
2. Looking at your monument, are there certain characteristics or repeated themes? If so, what are they? Do you see terms such as *dedicated, decision maker, student advocate, risk taker, searcher,* and *student centered?* How do

these correspond to the beliefs and expectations you hold for yourself as teacher?

3. Share examples of how your expectations of students caused you or other teachers to treat students in ways that caused them to respond as you expected.

4. When your students remember you as one of their teachers from the past, what would you most like them to recall about you?

Focus Two

Expected Performance

- Show consistent sensitivity to individual academic, physical, social, and cultural differences and respond to all students in a caring manner.
- Use classroom management techniques that foster self-control and self-discipline. Encourage responsibility to self and others.
- Promote student willingness and desire to receive and accept feedback.
- Use instructional strategies that interest and challenge students in a positive and supportive manner.
- Motivate, encourage, and support individual and group inquiry.

Focus One encouraged you to consider yourself as a teacher having high and positive expectations about students' behavior and academic performance. You recognize that your talents and abilities positively affect students' interest, and engagement in activity boosts your self-confidence as a teacher. Hopefully, you got in touch with your own enthusiastic desires to make a difference in the lives of the children and adolescents, and that you are motivated to take risks in further exploring your response to being the teacher. You might also be motivated to take other risks in using a variety of teaching techniques. Varying teaching techniques and thus increasing the amount of time your students are engaged with instructional activities is at the very heart of creating and maintaining a learning climate.

APPLICATION: MAINTAINING THE LEARNING CLIMATE

In the last chapter you focused on the teacher attitudes and actions that contribute to a learning environment. Teachers deliberately choose preventive discipline approaches that are intended to promote student self-control and responsibility. Also fitting into the preventive stage of classroom management are rules and procedures that your supervising teacher, and perhaps you, introduced at the beginning of the school year. Monitoring rules and procedures and implementing consequences span the entire year and play an integral part in maintaining the classroom learning climate.

What does it mean to maintain a learning climate? You may hear teachers say, "I really like this school. I am able to teach every day." Teachers may be referring to their desire to spend most of each day engaged in instructional activities. Their greatest challenges are planning creative lessons, obtaining resources, teaching students, and assessing student work. Carefully planned instructional activities and meeting student needs take priority and help prevent misbehaviors from occurring. Does the above description fit your current teaching placement? People living and working together over a period of time can expect to encounter problems. Even in ideal school settings discipline problems occur.

Maintaining a learning climate depends on decisions you make when discipline problems interrupt classroom instruction. What is your initial reaction to the student who falls out of the desk? When students are poking, wrestling, or teasing one another? When they break into gales of laughter over a double entendre you unconsciously make in class? How does your supervising teacher respond to these types of problems? Have students disrupted instruction while you are teaching? How do you respond?

As the person in charge of classroom instruction, you are expected to resolve any disruption quickly and effectively and refocus students' attention on instruction. Your classroom observations provide examples of how experienced teachers respond to discipline problems. When a student acts out, you may act spontaneously and then observe the effects of your response on the individual. Later, you reflect on the incident and the results of your actions. After assessing your response, how satisfied are you with the action you took? Did you rely on a specific management theory or model you learned from an earlier course or classroom management class? What might you do differently the next time a student chooses to disrupt the class?

MODELS OF DISCIPLINE STRATEGIES

Summaries of selected models and theories are included below to help you connect theories with observations and practice in your classes. These models can assist you in clarifying your beliefs and applying your knowledge about classroom management strategies to the less-than-perfect situations you encounter in your classroom.

Instructional Management Strategies

The instructional management approach consists of appropriate instruction so carefully planned and implemented that it prevents most discipline problems and solves those not prevented (Weber, 1999). In addition to planning appropriate activities that address student needs, the instructional management approach also incorporates Kounin's research (1970). His studies found that teachers maintain quality instruction within the classroom through (1) preventing misbehavior, (2) managing movement, and (3) maintaining group focus.

- Preventing misbehavior refers to the teacher's ability to demonstrate:
  withitness—communicating general awareness of the classroom to students
  overlapping—attending to two or more simultaneous events
- Managing movement includes the two instructional skills:
  momentum—keeping lessons moving and avoiding slowdowns
  smoothness—staying on track
- Maintaining group focus is accomplished through:
  group alert—sustaining whole-class attention to ongoing activity
  accountability—communicating that participation will be observed and evaluated
  high-participation formats—engaging all students, those directly and not directly responding to tasks

Kounin's concepts for managing group instruction enable teachers to analyze and identify areas needing improvement (Evertson, Emmer, & Worsham, 2000). Practicing and using these methods in your classroom will allow you to move closer to the vision you hold for yourself as teacher.

Behavior Modification Strategies

Teaching students with special behavioral needs requires skillful use of behavior management skills. A number of strategies based on behavior modification are available to teachers in the regular classroom and those teaching in self-contained classrooms for special learners. We use the term *behavior modification* here in referring to any stimulus that maintains or increases the behavior exhibited immediately prior to the presentation of the stimulus. For example, in praising a student for raising a hand before responding, you increase the chances that every student in your class will raise their hands and wait to be called on before speaking.

Other strategies grounded in behavior modification theory include chaining, modeling, contingency contracting, and extinction.

- **Chaining** is a series of tasks you want students to perform independently and in a sequence. Its advantage is that you can teach and assess each task independently. Performing routine tasks is one example.
- **Modeling** means you demonstrate or publicly acknowledge actions and attitudes you want individuals or the entire class to display. You will want to be sensitive in using modeling with older students and not embarrass them before their peers.
- **Contingency contracting** is a written behavioral agreement between you and a student and can be applied to a variety of settings. Involving students in planning their own behavior improvement can lead to other positive results. Using positive reinforcement creates an inviting atmosphere, and you are likely to prefer these strategies.
- **Extinction** is withholding from the student a reinforcing event or object. This is used to decrease an inappropriate behavior. For example, if a student is acting inappropriately, withholding attention or assigning timeout from a reinforcing activity or situation may effectively reduce or eliminate an undesirable behavior.
- **Punishment** refers to using a strategy that decreases an undesirable behavior such as incompletion of assigned tasks. Most student and intern teachers find using punishment a difficult choice to make. You may even squirm when reading the word. What may appear to students as "punishment" (having the student complete an assignment before participating in a class activity) is simply providing them an opportunity to meet your expectations.

Socioemotional Climate Strategies

Appearing throughout the text are examples emphasizing the importance of strategies that contribute to the social and psychological (socioemotional) climate of the classroom. These strategies are appropriate for maintaining a learning climate and preventing discipline problems. Socioemotional strategies include skills such as listening attentively to others and teaching students to listen to each other (Weber, 1999). Think about the times when students come to your class with problems and you have the opportunity to help them. Most days you can relate to students in a positive and interpersonal manner and show empathy and understanding to students' expressing sadness, pain, and negative feelings about themselves. Modeling attentive listening and being present to students are powerful means toward establishing a positive learning climate.

Other strategies associated with creating a socioemotional climate call for honing interpersonal skills through one-to-one interactions, the use of conflict resolution, and other group processes. Teachers can model and teach students about Gordon's (1974) "I Messages" (clearly and without blame stating one's needs) and adopt suggestions from Glasser's **reality** and **control theories** (Glasser, 1969, 1986, 1990). You may want to research Glasser's suggestions for becoming personally involved, accepting the student but not the student's misbehavior, and confronting students with unacceptable behavior. Glasser also proposes a classroom meeting process that you can use to teach a whole class how to deal with the groups' behavior problems.

Assertive Discipline Strategies

Strategies from the assertive discipline model are authoritarian and directly address misbehavior. In using these strategies you convey to individuals and to the total group that you are in charge. When you observe that a rule is not being kept and you implement the consequence for breaking rules, you are using assertive discipline. Other strategies prevalent in the assertive model include

proximity control (standing close to a misbehaving student or one not engaged in the assigned activity) and **mild desist** (a brief statement of disapproval quietly, gently spoken). These actions convey the message that you see your role as being responsible for students behaving according to classroom rules and administering consequences (Canter & Canter, 2002; Weber, 1999).

Teacher implementation of classroom rules and procedures plays a pivotal role in maintaining a learning climate. Student and intern teaching offers you an opportunity to experience the effect class rules have in meeting students' personal and nonacademic needs. Have you been "tested" by students to see if you and your supervising teacher are in agreement with the class rules and procedures? When you see a student breaking class rules, what do you say and do? You are aware that teachers need to know and follow up students' responses to school and district rules. The student teaching or intern experience provides you opportunities to formulate, implement, and monitor rules both in the classroom and the entire school setting.

We encourage you to consult with other teachers and to read and review theories and suggestions by other educators as you continue to learn about classroom management. The section at the end of this chapter offers sources on models and theories and other discipline-related topics.

SAFE SCHOOLS

Even though crime has decreased in schools, the amount of crime committed continues to be a concern (National Center for Education Statistics, 2001). Schools reflect society, and the escalating seriousness of violence in schools corresponds with concern for what is happening in society. For example, the 33rd Annual Phi Delta Kappa/Gallup poll reported an approximate 50–50 split in the public's attitude toward firearms, firearm safety, and how to reduce the number of shooting deaths following numerous incidents of gun violence involving youth (Rose & Gallup, 2001). This emphasis matches the nation's concern for school safety and involves students, parents, educators, and the community at large and results in enacting such laws as zero tolerance designed to make schools safe.

Rather than focus on the word *violence,* many educators prefer a more positive term, *safe schools.* School safety includes and extends beyond the routine care you take in storing and using materials and in physically arranging furnishings as precautionary safeguards against classroom accidents. The emphasis is on dissipating situations and problems before they result in violence, a preventive approach to creating a safe school. Do you see yourself as being in the unique situation to teach tolerance in a diverse school setting? You have the opportunity to guide students in making choices, working collaboratively, and respecting themselves and their peers as responsible members of the school community (Kagan, 2001; Pastor, 2002; Raywid & Oshiyama, 2000).

Maintaining a safe learning environment for your students can be accomplished with foresight and planning. Part of learning and planning is to gather information about the school and the district's policies about safe schools and determine how the information involves you. What is expected of teachers when fights break out between students in the classroom or hallways? What are you expected to do if you suspect a student is carrying a weapon, using drugs, threatening another student or teacher? Providing a safe environment for all students regardless of physical or academic ability, social or economic background, sexual orientation, or religious beliefs is an imperative charge given schools.

Most boards of education are addressing issues pertaining to safe schools. Policies are adopted for possession of drugs, bringing guns, knives, and other weapons to school, and eliminating gang activity. Schools collaborate with community resources, especially law enforcement officers, on safety issues affecting children and adolescents. You might inquire about programs that exist for teachers in your school district and how you can become better informed about existing threats to safety in the community where you teach.

Learning about and obtaining available community resources, working with parents, and taking advantage of programs for preventing outbreaks of violence are some suggestions for promoting safe schools (Cohen, 2001; Woods, 2001/2002). What do you do when name-calling and verbal put-downs occur among your students in your presence? Perhaps you participate with your supervising teacher, team or department members, or school counselor in programs that teach skills such as problem solving, conflict resolution, verbal and nonverbal communication, anger management, and other long-range violence prevention programs. Your school may offer programs in collaboration with other community groups. Knowing about these valuable resources allows you to connect with strategies you use to include and acknowledge students who need extra attention from you (Adelman, 2002). By helping to build a sense of community and respect among the students you teach, you are contributing to a safe environment for teaching and learning.

Research findings and information about school violence and safe schools suggest that although circumstances vary for students and schools, there are recognized approaches for all schools. Components relevant to all students in every school are listed below. How are these components reflected in your school?

- Is the school a supportive learning community?
- Does the school provide systematic approaches to support positive behavior?
- To what degree are families, students, school staff, and surrounding community involved in the school?
- What data provide evidence that standards and measures are in place to support continuous improvement? (Learning First Alliance, 2001)

As a student or intern teacher you are adjusting to being in charge. We encourage you to take advantage of opportunities that prepare and protect you and your students. In accepting your role as leader, you are responsible for choosing strategies for managing student behavior and sustaining student involvement in learning. As teacher you join with others in creating a supportive learning school community while pursuing academic excellence. You will want to reflect on what you observe, examine the preventive and direct disciplinary strategies you use with students, and determine how you plan to proceed in subsequent times. Adjusting to the authority role and possibilities and responsibilities that accompany that role takes time and supportive assistance. We intend that these **Assigned Activities** offer you the opportunity to reflect on decisions you make for maintaining a safe and positive learning climate in your classes.

ASSIGNED ACTIVITIES

The following activities are intended to help you consider strategies for maintaining a learning climate. You are asked to respond to them as part of your reflections on what you are observing and implementing in the classroom and on the effects of your actions.

1. For which rules and procedures do you most frequently need to apply consequences? Which rules do you periodically review? How has your student or intern teaching experience changed your understanding about class rules and procedures?

2. From what sources can you learn the school and district policies for promoting a safe school? Examine student and teacher handbooks. Are policies of student behavior such as bullying, taunts, threats, and harassment discussed in these handbooks? Under what heading(s)?

3. Ask your supervising teacher for time to discuss safe schools. What evaluation has or does the school conduct to assess school climate and what changes have been made to improve school climate? How does the school involve families, students, school staff, and the surrounding community in promoting a safe learning environment?

4. Table 10.1 lists discipline techniques described in this chapter. While reflecting on your teaching each day, refer to the table and check those you used.

5. Describe three incidents that challenged you to resolve a discipline problem this week. What techniques did you use in resolving the problem? Under which model are the techniques listed? How effective are the techniques you use in maintaining a learning climate in your classroom?

Problem:

Technique used:

Under which model is the technique listed?

How effective was the technique you used in maintaining the learning climate in your classroom?

---

6. In assessing your growth as a teacher, discuss an important insight you now have about maintaining a learning climate? Name an area of classroom management that you want to strengthen.

SUMMARY

Over the past weeks you have reflected on the different components contributing to a learning climate. Your journal entries address the management of instruction and explain your reasons for decisions you made to meet student needs. Every day you monitor and apply rules and procedures established for the class. When looking back to your first days in the classroom and comparing that time with now, you perhaps sense an increase in student self-control and personal responsibility. Are you feeling a sense of ownership toward this shift? Are you sharing the responsibility for helping create and maintain a positive atmosphere? Do you feel "in charge"? You want your students to experience success in your class. You want students to be happy and behave! In your seminar you are encouraged to recognize what you know about discipline strategies and to consider *when* and *why* you apply them in the school setting. After sharing your concerns and questions with peers, you may discover that yours are quite typical. You realize that managing instruction and student behavior are skills that advance along a continuum and you have made progress in these areas. You may feel more confident about managing student behavior and find yourself better able to deescalate situations before they flare out of control.

TABLE 10.1 *Discipline Techniques*

Discipline Techniques	Times Used	Individual	Group	Effect on Individual Learner/Class Discipline
1 Ignores inappropriate behavior				
2 Rewards appropriate behavior				
3 Refers to another learner model ("I like the way…")				
4 Assigns timeout				
5 Assigns cleanup area				
6 Student compensates for damages				
7 Withholds privileges				
8 Assigns extra work				
9 Sends students to the office				
10 Calls parents, solicits support				
11 Demonstrates withitness/ overlapping				
12 Maintains group focus: alert-accountable-participative				
13 Manages movement				
14 Moves close to student				
15 Places hand on shoulder— behavior noticed while class continues				
16 Listens and encourages learner to express problems				
17 Encourages cooperation				
18 Student describes own behavior; states improved course of action				
19 Describes situation, expresses feelings, clarifies expectations				

FOLLOW-UP QUESTIONS AND SHARED INSIGHTS

Refer to your journal as you converse with your peers about the discipline techniques you observed and used. Discuss your knowledge of the school district's methods for promoting a safe learning environment. The following questions offer you an opportunity to share your experiences with preventing or eliminating unacceptable behavior in the classroom.

1. Which class rules do you most often remind students to observe? What seems to renew students' motivation to follow procedures? How

successful are the stated consequences in preventing repeated rule breaking?

2. What connections do you see between planning and managing instruction, and managing student behavior? You might consider specific topics: teacher enthusiasm, questioning techniques, group work, use of technology, and so on.

3. Using the discipline techniques in Table 10.1, share with others what you consider to be effective techniques in maintaining a learning climate. Explain why you think they are effective.

4. Name a technique that you were not successful in applying and explain why you think the technique failed to work. How might others help you to successfully apply this technique?

5. What discipline techniques do you want to acquire? You might describe specific events in your classroom and ask others' suggestions for dealing with them.

6. How do you see the emphasis on *safe schools* providing students the knowledge and awareness for living in a democratic society?

7. With which aspects of discipline are you now feeling more comfortable?

Journal Excerpts

High School

"Sixth period was the only class that gave me trouble today. The problem was not students talking too much but it was talking too little! That class does not like to participate! We were discussing a short story they had read in their books. I was using the discussion questions as my starting point. Then I moved away from prepared questions and lost the focus. Unfortunately, they would not respond to me! They would give me an answer from the book, but if I asked for any type of opinion-based answer they clammed up. I think one of the factors is that they are a quiet group, and I have not taught them very long. We just need to 'get used' to each other."

"I have been working hard at using myself to model behavior. I'm aware of my body position, location, eye contact, hand on shoulder, etc. This has been working well. Today in the 4th period I had a group of students who were easily distracted. I decided to pull up a desk and sit between them for part of the period. This really worked. They spent the remainder of the period working and utilizing every moment and were surprised at how much they had accomplished. I did this again in 5th period. Although I'm still not where I want to be with this class, I feel like I am well on my way. I think that I have come a long way in a week, and that mainly is because of my desire and determination to teach this class, and for my students to be successful."

"There are times that I need to ignore the students who are only 'acting up' to get attention from me. By always acknowledging them, they are receiving a message that reinforces their behavior. On the other hand, I also must pay attention to students who may need me but are too quiet or self-conscious to call their needs to my attention in any way. I have to make sure to always include them in my interactions. . . ."

"As I watched the students in small groups, I noticed one girl was talking with another about her boyfriend, while the others were trying to complete the group assignment. I slowly walked up to the group and pretended to intently study the group's guiding question. After a couple of seconds, the two not working looked at me. I said, 'Oh! I was just trying to figure out where (boyfriend's name) was in the question I gave you!' They both turned red and smiled nervously at me—they knew what I meant!"

Middle School

"As I watched the students come into the classroom, I mentioned to my supervising teacher that one student in our 6th period class had gotten in trouble every period today. Holding true to form, the boy shoved another boy and threatened him, and a serious shoving match ensued in the hall as they approached the classroom. Luckily, Mrs. A. was right behind them and she broke it up quickly (which she normally doesn't do—she's pretty small compared to these boys). She conferenced with the boys, calmed them down, and set up a peer mediation meeting between them for tomorrow."

"I was taken aback today when our notoriously loud and unfocused 4th period class performed so well. Normally they get one or two lectures about behavior and respect everyday. However, today for some reason, they focused beautifully, read well and acted out the words in an interesting manner. It was a pleasant way to end the day because it reaffirmed my belief that all students are capable of focusing on learning and succeeding! Because they were actively engaged in reading and acting out new vocabulary words, they were on task and focused."

"I did a lot of one-on-one work with students today. We have a student who seems to be a hyperactive student. He never does his work, sits still, or stops talking. Today, I sat down with him for a while and encouraged his ideas. I kept telling him he wasn't stupid (as he said), he could do it, and I praised him when he did. After a while, I left him on his own. When the class went on to the next activity, he came to show me that he had finished. I was stunned . . . so proud . . . of him and myself, too."

"What a day! I had the class by myself and looking back, I can tell I was tense about teaching. I gave one warning and then I threatened detentions if they weren't quiet. One student said I wasn't a teacher and couldn't give a detention. I said I could and then felt badly for being so harsh. Sometimes I worry they will take advantage of me, looking so young and being so small."

Elementary School

"I found that Mrs. J. uses a great number of management techniques. I have been watching and learning a great deal. I am very impressed by the way she handled a student that lied. Mrs. J. made it very clear to that student and the entire class that she would not tolerate lying in her class. She asked the other students what they thought about lying. She turned this situation into a true learning experience for everyone without causing the student who lied embarrassment."

"I do not feel good about how I managed behavior today. . . . I think I need to prepare myself better. I should look at the pages before I introduce them to the learners even though the book is on tape. I had serious problems with one student. For some reason I have the hardest time getting him to mind me. When I try to talk to him, he covers his ears or runs from me. I wonder if it's because he doesn't think there will be any solid consequences for disobeying me. I must decide how I want to discipline him and then follow through with my plan. It just gets to me because he intentionally misbehaves. I have a hard time dealing with this. Perhaps if I knew more about his background and experience I could get more insight about why this student behaves the way he does."

"After today, I feel much more confident. During my learning center time, I set rules and established consequences. I stuck to them and also used a lot of sticker reinforcement. The students responded well—met my expectations! I'm beginning to see the connection between solid planning objectives, high expectations and positive student behavior!"

"I'm still struggling to gain the respect of the children. While many of the children see me as their teacher, there are still those few who test me every single day. I give warnings, and I talk with each child, but they act as if they could care less about what I am saying. When I am with these students, I feel as though I am losing control quickly. I need to find ways to keep the ball in my court. I know I need to be in charge and maintain control. I just feel as though these few students are throwing me for a loop and holding me back. This is something I will work on during this placement."

Special Education

"C. had a rough day for the first time this year. I am not really sure what targeted his outburst today but he had to be placed in time-out twice. He ran around the room pulling books off the shelves and turning over chairs. I was in the room with the assistant when this first occurred. I began taking points from him and could see his behavior was escalating. It was very uncomfortable for me to feel I could place a child in time-out. I know Mrs. B. would support my action but it still was very scary. Mrs. B. returned to the room just as C. would have to be put in the time-out room. She came in and placed him in the time-out room without hesitation or question. She validated my action and I felt I had made a professional decision."

"I was talking to L. about appropriate behavior, since he had run to the chalkboard and charged me with his head. When I told him he could answer again if he were sitting in his seat, he asked, 'like the way I am sitting?' He squats down like he is sitting, however, there is no chair. This is when it becomes difficult to correct his behavior because his actions are so sporadic and funny. I continued to go on with the lesson and bragged about R. for sitting properly. L. jumped in his seat and said, 'I want to be good.' He is so funny, yet needs so much help. I know I must teach him appropriate behaviors if he is to be successfully mainstreamed."

"The fifth grade student who comes from the Behavior Disorders room wore me down today in reading class. Finally, after many cues and direct corrections, I deemed it necessary to explicitly conference with T. about appropriate and inappropriate behaviors. I think it is very difficult to instruct when you continuously have to stop and correct behavior. I have to learn to ignore a lot more of T.'s behaviors than I have been, but this is difficult when I am responsible for teaching him content (how to read) too!"

REFERENCES AND SUGGESTED READINGS

Adelman, H. S. (2002). School counselors and school reform: New directions. *Professional School Counseling, 5*(4), 235–248.

Allen, R. (2001). Classroom life after terrorism. *Education Update, 43*(8), 1–8. Alexandria, VA: Association for Supervision and Curriculum Development.

Aronson, E. (2000). *Nobody left to hate: Teaching compassion after Columbine.* New York: W. H. Freeman.

Bauer, A. M., & Sapona, R. H. (1991). *Managing classrooms to facilitate learning.* Englewood Cliffs, NJ: Prentice Hall.

Bey, T. M., & Turner, G. Y. (1996). *Making school a place of peace.* Thousand Oaks, CA: Corwin Press.

Burden, P. R. (1995). *Classroom management and discipline: Methods to facilitate cooperation and instruction.* White Plains, NY: Longman.

Canter, L., & Canter, M. (2002). *Assertive discipline: Positive behavior management for today's classroom* (3rd ed.). Los Angeles: Canter.

Center for Effective Collaboration and Practice. Early warning, timely response: A guide to safe schools. http://cecp.air.org/guide/

Charles, C. M. (2001). *Building classroom discipline* (7th ed.). Boston: Allyn & Bacon.

Cipani, E. (1998). *Classroom management for all teachers: 11 effective plans.* Upper Saddle River, NJ: Merrill/Prentice Hall.

Cohen, P. (2001). A focus on effective strategies for violence prevention. *Professional School Counseling, 4*(5), 379–380.

Cookson, P. W., Jr. (2001). Fostering moral democracy. *Educational Leadership, 59*(2), 42–45.

Dear, J. D. (1995). *Creating caring relationships to foster academic excellence: Recommendations for reducing violence in California schools.* Sacramento: California Commission on Teacher Credentialing.

Doyle, W. (1986). Classroom organization and management. In M. C. Wittrock (Ed.), *Handbook of research on teaching* (pp. 392–425). New York: Macmillan.

Edwards, C. H. (1997). *Classroom discipline and management* (2nd ed.). Upper Saddle River, NJ: Merrill/Prentice Hall.

Emmer, E. T., Evertson, C. M., & Worsham, M. E. (2000). *Classroom management for secondary teachers* (5th ed.). Boston: Allyn & Bacon.

Evertson, C. M., Emmer, E. T., & Worsham, M. E. (2000). *Classroom management for elementary teachers* (5th ed.). Boston: Allyn & Bacon.

Gay, G. (2000). *Culturally responsive teaching: Theory, research, & practice.* New York: Teachers College Press.

Glasser, W. (1969). *Schools without failure.* New York: Harper and Row.

Glasser, W. (1986). *Control theory in the classroom.* New York: Harper and Row.

Glasser, W. (1990). *Quality school: Managing students without coercion.* New York: Harper and Row.

Good, T. L., & Brophy, J. E. (2000). *Looking in classrooms* (8th ed.). White Plains, NY: Longman.

Gordon, T. (1974). *T.E.T. Teacher effectiveness training.* New York: David McKay.

Guskey, T. R. (Ed.). (1996). *Communicating student learning 1996 ASCD yearbook.* Alexandria, VA: Association for Supervision and Curriculum Development.

Hyman, I. A., & Snook, P. A. (2000). Dangerous schools and what you can do about them. *Phi Delta Kappan, 81*(7), 489–498.

Jones, V. F., & Jones, L. S. (1998). *Comprehensive classroom management: Creating communities of support and solving problems* (5th ed.). Boston: Allyn & Bacon.

Kagan, S. (2001). Teaching for character and community. *Educational Leadership, 59*(2), 50–55.

Koenig, L. (1995). *Smart discipline for the classroom: Respect and cooperation restored* (Rev. ed.). Thousand Oaks, CA: Corwin Press.

Kounin, J. S. (1970). *Discipline and group management in classrooms.* New York: Holt, Rinehart and Winston.

Learning First Alliance. (2001). Every child learning: Safe and supportive schools. Alexandria, VA: Association for Supervision and Curriculum Development.

Lee, C. (2002). The impact of belonging to a high school gay/straight alliance. *High School Journal, 85*(3), 13–26.

McAndrews, T. (2001). Zero tolerance policies. *ERIC Digest* (No. 146). Eugene, OR: ERIC Clearinghouse on Educational Management. Retrieved from http://www.ed.gov/databases/ERIC_Digests/ed451579.html

National Center for Education Statistics. (2001). Task force on school crime, violence, and discipline. Retrieved from http://nces.ed.gov/pubs2002/crime2001/9.asp?nav=3

Pastor, P. (2002). School discipline and the character of our schools. *Phi Delta Kappan, 83*(9), 658–661.

Raywid, M. A., & Oshiyama, L. (2000). Musings in the wake of Columbine. *Phi Delta Kappan, 81*(6), 444–449.

Rose, L. C., & Gallup, A. M. (2001). The 33rd annual Phi Delta Kappan/Gallup poll. *Phi Delta Kappan, 83*(1), 41–58.

Wasserman, S. (1993). *Getting down to cases: Learning to teach with case studies.* New York: Teachers College Press.

Weber, W. A. (1999). Classroom management. In J. M. Cooper (Gen. Ed.), *Classroom teaching skills* (6th ed.). Boston: Houghton Mifflin.

Weinstein, C. S. (1996). *Secondary classroom management: Lessons from research and practice.* New York: McGraw-Hill.

Weinstein, C. S., & Mignano, A. J., Jr. (1997). *Elementary classroom management: Lessons from research and practice* (2nd ed.). New York: McGraw-Hill.

Wolfgang, C. H. (2001). *Solving discipline and classroom management problems: Methods and models for today's teachers.* New York: Wiley.

Woods, J. (2001/2002). Hostile hallways. *Educational Leadership, 59*(4), 20–23.

Zabel, R. H., & Zabel, M. K. (1996). *Classroom management in context: Orchestrating positive learning environments.* Boston: Houghton Mifflin.

Zirpoli, T. J., & Melloy, K. J. (1997). *Behavior management: Applications for teachers and parents* (2nd ed.). Upper Saddle River, NJ: Merrill/Prentice Hall.

chapter

11

Assessing Student Learning and Communicating Learning Results

> " To gain in knowledge of self, one must have the courage to seek it and the humility to accept what one may find. "

A. T. Jersild

Focus One

Expected Performance

- Trace your journey through the student teaching experience.
- Describe your affective and cognitive responses to the different phases of learning to teach.
- Examine and discuss the different types of communication about your progress in becoming a teacher.

LOOK WHERE I AM!

Standing near the top of a hill and looking back at the path leading up, you clearly see where you've been. As you approach the end of your student or intern teaching journey, this may be an ideal time to look back at the past months and examine your personal experiences during your transition to teacher. These experiences include your reflections and discussions about the teaching-learning process and your concerns while moving through these experiences. Having the courage to engage in self-analysis and accept what you find has the power to motivate you to become a more effective teacher. Likewise, others' offers of professional expertise and interactions give you deeper insights into the effectiveness of your teaching. You are better prepared to communicate the value of what you learn about yourself as teacher to others. Giving voice to your increasing levels of understanding of a practicing professional and your involvement in the process validates and affirms your learning experience.

Questions! Questions! And More Questions!

What concerns about teaching have you had during this period of transition? Looking forward to student or intern teaching, you may have felt anxious. You had butterflies in your stomach. There were so many concerns and questions racing through your mind! You eagerly awaited the announcement of your assigned school and your supervising teacher, along with your university supervisor. Upon arriving at the school, you found yourself involved in various activities, and your concern about your evaluation escalated. "How do I find out when I succeed and when I fail? How will I ever be able to put it all together and really be a teacher?" Do you recall having these questions? Later, other questions about your teaching arose and you asked, "How effective am I?" You wondered if your voice was loud enough and if students would follow your directives and behave during class. Do you remember worrying about knowing the content well enough to respond to students' questions?

In the early weeks of student or intern teaching you may have been concerned about how your students felt about you and if you were becoming too personally involved with them. You may have been concerned about your lack of experience. There may have been times when your own status was unclear to you or you felt conflicting expectations were thrust upon you. By now you have discovered that individuals taking on new roles usually have these or similar initial reactions.

After several more weeks you began designing, planning, and teaching for extended periods. Along with additional instructional responsibilities came new questions: "Are students learning what I'm teaching?" "Are students learning what they need?" At this time you may have asked yourself, "How can I improve myself as a teacher?" You examined your instructional strategies, experimented with different methods, and assessed your teaching effectiveness against student success and productivity. This is exactly what you should have been doing! Questioning yourself as teacher is part of the process of your transition to teacher. According to Fuller (1970), these are the kinds of persistent questions of student teachers. These questions develop sequentially and accompany the growth of student teachers as they assume more of the teacher role. Seeing your questions in this light, do you feel more like a professional teacher?

Exploring Questions and Expanding Insights

Take a look at where you are. Are the above questions the same ones that have nagged you from time to time during this experience? We pose these questions for two reasons. First, we want you to realize that to ask questions like these is typical for student or intern teachers. Second, we want you to recognize the importance of such questions as you adapt to your new role. As you develop professionally, expect to encounter and respond repeatedly to changes in education that challenge you. Be prepared to have similar concerns and questions as you make transitions to other new roles within your school. Your response to these concerns is critical to your growth as teacher. When moving through change, you are encouraged to pay attention to your feelings and seek support (Rust & Freidus, 2001). Your journals, reflections, and conversations with peers and supervisors are intended to help you address your questions and personal concerns to understand yourself as a learner. Engaging in this process helps you adopt more complex behaviors as a result of your questions and expanding insights.

You have been invited to explore and analyze your affective and cognitive responses to student/intern teaching. Throughout the student teaching seminars, conversations with peers, and conferences with supervisors, you have assessed your professional progress on many levels. Further explorations lie ahead as you enter the teaching profession and your understanding of teacher continues to expand. New and creative approaches to professional growth are developing. Rust (2000) reports that teachers (beginning, experienced, and teacher educators) come together to research and learn actively and promote change in their professional lives. Within these supportive learning opportunities teachers from diverse groups reflect on their own experience and knowledge, explore their attitudes and beliefs about teaching and learning, and share a host of skills and strategies—those that form the underpinnings of their work.

Through professional conversations about classroom life new insights about the teaching and learning processes are deepened. As you look forward to your own professional growth, you will want to keep in mind that cognitive development is not automatic. Rather than growth happening as a result of accumulating years and experience, your growth as a professional depends largely on your interactions with other professionals and your ability to give voice to all you have learned. Self-reflection and interpersonal communication are catalysts for professional growth.

The **Focus One** activity presents the different phases of transition to the teacher role and invites you to examine your own experiences using these questions. Which ones match your experiences as a student or intern teacher moving toward becoming teacher? How is your experience similar to that of your peers? So much is happening each day, and one fast-paced day follows another! You may not even be aware of the progress you have made in your transition to teacher. You may not have taken time to compare your initial steps into student or intern teaching with your present performance. Noting events and identifying feelings associated with each turning point in your experience is valuable in sorting out all that you've learned so far. Perhaps you are now able to be more objective, to have different insights, and to take a broader perspective of prior events. Perhaps you've come to understand and value the processes necessary to learning. Perhaps you recognize the need to pause, to take stock of your professional journey thus far.

To help you connect your experiences with the sequence of development phases associated with professional growth, read the list outlined below along with brief descriptions of each. Make notes beside each description to recall specific situations from your experience to help you make connections and give voice to your growth as you interact with your group members.

Phase I *Concern About Self*

- I'm anxious. What do I need to be concerned about?

_____

_____

Phase II *Concern About Self as Teacher*

- What am I supposed to do?
- Will I know enough to teach? What if students ask questions I can't answer?
- What happens if I lose control?
- Where do I stand in this new situation as a teacher?
- How do my students see what I'm doing? Do they like me?

_____

_____

Phase III *Concern About Students*

- How can I explain this idea to students?
- Is what I'm teaching what students really need to know?
- How can I be a better teacher?

_____

_____

Discussion Questions

1. Which of the questions listed under the different phases match those you ask during your student or intern teaching experience? Which questions caused you the most anxiety? What other feelings about your new role resurfaced?
2. When you had questions similar to those listed under the various phases, what sources of support have you sought? What might have caused you to be hesitant about seeking support?
3. Looking back over this experience, what new insights have you gained about your progress toward the role of teacher?

4. When your students are happy with their accomplishments, you very likely feel proud of them and of yourself. Give examples of students' proudest moments, times when they met an instructional goal or performance standard you designed. Think about your response to your students' success. How might seeing your students succeed help you become a better teacher?

Focus Two

Expected Performance

- Promote student self-assessment using established criteria and focus student attention on what needs to be done to move to the next performance level.
- Systematically collect and analyze assessment data and maintain up-to-date records of student progress.
- Use formal and informal assessment strategies to evaluate and ensure the continuous intellectual, social, and physical development of the learner.
- Accurately assess student performance using established criteria and scoring guides consistent with the school system assessment program.

"[S]chools are vital when they have integrity: that is, when they are true to their mission. Schools with integrity practice what they preach; policies make real what is valued; adults model the learning sought in students; teachers assess what they value and value what they assess."

G. Wiggins

During this time of tremendous personal and professional learning about the different teacher roles, reflection has played a critical role in your ability to voice your strengths and areas of need. Self-assessment and feedback from students, your cooperating and supervising teachers help you clarify and prioritize your professional goals. Engaging in self-assessment contributes to your understanding of the vital role assessment plays in informing your instruction to facilitate your growth, as well as that of your students. One of the most demanding roles you experience as teacher is that of assessor. Understanding the assessment process is critical to your development as a professional educator. **Focus Two** addresses the importance of assessing what students know and have learned because of your instructional goals. Communicating these results to students and parents or guardians involves a thorough understanding of the assessment process.

The key to effective assessment connects the assessment with intended learner outcomes. All students learn differently and their needs vary. As educators, we want to take students beyond rote learning into discovery and higher levels of thinking. Teachers use a variety of teaching strategies to help students learn, assess the degree of learning, and determine how successfully learners have translated the strategy into personal learning.

Throughout your preservice education you have heard repeatedly that communication is essential to becoming an effective teacher. You are learning during this student teaching or intern experience that communication involves interacting not only with students and your supervising teacher, but also with other teachers, administrators, and parents or guardians. Communicating learning results means encouraging, challenging, listening, and providing the learners with information about their achievement and continuing progress. (Think for a moment of the valuable insights you had regarding your professional growth as a result of reflective communication!) Written or verbal comments on papers, projects, journals, portfolios, progress reports, and report cards communicate to the students what they have achieved. Much like conferences scheduled with your supervising teacher, individual conferences with the students give you opportunities to discuss questions, academic progress, and class behavior and to listen to their perspectives. This communicates to the students that you care. You are interested in their learning, you want them to succeed, and you are encouraging them to take charge of their learning. What a professional approach to establishing a trusting relationship and rapport with students!

APPLICATION: ASSESSING STUDENT LEARNING AND COMMUNICATING LEARNING RESULTS

As a professional teacher you will use multiple means for assessing student thinking, problem solving, and verbal and written responses to learning tasks. No process is more central to teaching than evaluation, a process that involves collecting information, forming judgments, and making decisions. Properly designed assessment instruments and procedures can improve decision making regarding learner performance. Assessment, therefore, is essential for improvement of the curriculum, of instruction, and of student learning.

You want to reflect with your students on the learning process, and their progress in achieving the stated expectations. The assessment methods (such as scoring guides or rubrics) you select will inform and challenge the learners to reach higher levels of thinking, self-learning, and self-assessment.

A number of methods of assessment can measure student performance and progress. Testing is the most conventional source of data, and probably the most familiar to you. Alternative assessments are becoming more common in classrooms today, and many educators design their own criteria and standards for student work.

One of the primary uses of assessment is to determine what students know or have learned with regard to specific instructional objectives. Multiple examples of assessment communicate clearly to students, to other teachers, and often to parents the range of the student's performance. Students receive feedback from teachers in a variety of ways. In considering how students are performing and assigning summary scores, Marzano (2000) makes the following suggestions:

- Use as much information as possible, even information not recorded in the grade book.
- Weigh the various scores using sound criteria.
- Assign summary scores if adequate information is available.
- Consider the nature of the standards issued by the state or learned societies (diversity of knowledge or skill and the consistency of knowledge or skill).

> *"When students and teachers make use of reflection as a tool for learning and assessment, they are creating an opening that allows them to enter into students' work, making sense of their endeavors and accomplishments, and learning how they judge their success."*
> R. Zessoules
> and H. Gardner

Alternative, Authentic, and Performance Assessment

The terms *alternative assessment, authentic assessment,* and *performance assessment* are often used synonymously, yet have different meanings. Reviewing the terms at this point gives you a broader picture of assessment.

- **Alternative assessment** usually applies to all assessments different from the multiple-choice, timed approaches that characterize most standardized and many teacher-made tests. Alternative assessment affects teachers and students in a number of ways. Teachers continually reflect on student needs and assessment results and begin to view every activity in light of assessment. Students become more reflective and self-assessing; they begin to take responsibility for their own learning.
- **Authentic assessment** conveys the idea that students are engaged in applying knowledge and skills to real-life situations and problems. The purpose of authentic assessment is intended to help students understand their own work in relation to that of others, to see new possibilities and challenges in their verbal and written assignments, and to refine and redesign their responses. Reflection and self-assessment are vital to this process. Planning for authentic assessment has a significant influence on the instruction provided the student.
- **Performance assessment** indicates students' progress through demonstrating their understanding and application of knowledge, skills, and attitudes. As instructional strategies become more diverse so must the form of assessment change. These assessments over time result in a tangible product or observable performance assisting the students to improve their learning.

Information gained from student performance assists the teacher with instructional decisions. Learner performance is evaluated to determine the extent to which your students meet your expectations; it also provides you with information to make sound instructional decisions. Once your assessment is designed to be educative, you no longer separate it from instruction. It is a major, essential, and integrated part of teaching and learning (Wiggins, 1998).

Standards for Authentic Pedagogy and Student Academic Performance

Newmann, Marks, and Gamoran (1995) have developed standards for authentic pedagogy and student academic performance. Their model is designed to determine the extent to which teachers use authentic assessment tasks and teach authentic lessons. These authors are clear that not every instructional or assessment activity need fulfill all three standards. But they encourage you to keep **authentic achievement** as your ultimate goal. Reflect on their criteria that serve as guides for student achievement:

- **Construction of knowledge**—students interpret, synthesize, and evaluate complex information producing new meaning for them.
- **Disciplined inquiry**—students demonstrate an in-depth understanding of a particular problem or issue.
- **Value beyond school**—students make connections between school activities and their own experiences and the world beyond the classroom.

At this point, your development of assessment activities may be at the novice or apprentice stage. Nevertheless, having a grasp of the relationship between the instructional objectives and the assessment activities is an important step toward authentic achievement, your ultimate goal!

Keep in mind several attributes related to assessments as you develop your assessment system. Effective assessment is:

- **Continuous or ongoing.**   Daily and weekly assessment of identified teaching goals and assessing the progress of each learner are the first steps toward authentic assessment. Redesigning the way the curriculum is taught to suit the learner's individual needs leads to success for the teacher and the learner.
- **Flexible.**   Assessment needs to concentrate on the identified areas of weakness or goals for each learner. Effective teachers are always adjusting their instructional activity to meet the needs of the individual learner.
- **Cumulative.**   A longitudinal approach to assessment puts the results of any one assessment into perspective. A sampling of student work (portfolio) over time is one example of implementing a cumulative approach to assessment.
- **Diverse.**   Multiple instruments should be used to assess learner progress. Combining a variety of views of performance paints a clearer picture of learner achievement. There simply is no *one* right way to assess students.

Your selection and use of the various assessment instruments involve much reflection and research. The choice of an assessment instrument depends on the evaluative decisions you want to make about student learning. When you assess what you value and value what you assess, you remain true to your mission of educating those in your care, challenging them to meet or exceed your expectations for them as learners. Educational integrity can only be met through instruments of authentic assessment, and begins with you—the classroom teacher.

TABLE 11.1 *Assessment Instruments: Type and Use*

Prior to (Diagnostic)	Ongoing (Formative)	Final (Summative)
Pretests	Quizzes	Teacher-made tests
Observations	Discussions	Portfolios
Journals/logs	Assignments	Projects
Discussions	Projects	Standardized tests
Placement tests	Teacher-made tests	Discussions
Standardized tests	Checklists	
Questionnaires	Observations	
Interviews	Portfolios Journals/logs Standardized tests	

The learner's response to any one of the assessment tasks can be influenced by a variety of environmental factors. Preparing learners by discussing the assessment strategies with them may give you new insights about the individuals and allay some learner anxiety. Your sensitivity and encouragement may increase their ability to stay on task, think for themselves, and complete the assessment with a positive attitude.

Table 11.1 provides a variety of assessment instruments and their use in making evaluative decisions to guide your instruction.

Forms of Assessment

Watts (1996) encourages the use of alternative forms of assessment for communicating student learning. To get a clearer and more comprehensive picture of student achievement, she outlines a formula for successfully and fairly assessing student learning:

1. Presenting visible evidence of student growth and achievement
2. Ranking or rating of student achievement against clearly stated, predetermined standards
3. Involving students in grading through self-assessment and/or peer evaluation
4. Conferencing with students and parents or guardians to open the lines of communication

Incorporating these assessment strategies may at first seem daunting to you. As you practice and use them with your students you may experience a new sense of purpose and direction in your lessons. You are empowering your students by having them experience assessment as a process rather than "giving" them a grade at the end of the quarter! These strategies enable you to work with individual students to help them set goals and engage them in learning. The learner is validated through this model, and learning is seen as real, tangible, and valuable.

Visible evidence of student growth and achievement is accomplished through a variety of exciting classroom performance tasks. Employing portfolios in the classroom and creating opportunities for exhibitions of student knowledge are sound assessment practices. Other highly visible alternative methods include displays of student work, student presentations, and anecdotal records. Videotaping your students' work, while they are working, is a remarkable record of their progress, achievement, and potential.

Portfolios are purposeful collections of student work and may include:
- student-selected works in progress illustrating their learning, application of knowledge, and risk-taking
- student rationale statement supporting selection of work
- student samples of their best work
- student reflection about their work
- criteria developed by teacher and student used for assessment
- teacher evaluative comments and student self-assessment

Presentations may include students conducting experiments, teaching a skill or concept to others, performing a play, or working as a cooperative group in solving a problem.

Exhibitions may include a visual display, chart, graph, concept map, written report, or science fair project.

Anecdotal records include teacher-recorded observations of individual student behaviors. Clipboard notes, index cards, and individual pages filed for each student's recordings are often used by experienced teachers to provide assessment information.

Keep in mind in recording effective anecdotal records that you record positive and negative indicators. Other points to remember:

- Be brief and record only the unusual behaviors.
- Be consistent.
- Be factual.
- Be careful not to draw inferences from a single incident.

Ranking or rating student achievement is difficult unless you prepare ahead of time clearly stated standards for student performance. Using report card checklists, rubrics or scoring guides, and standards found in work samplings helps to provide a road map for your students as they move toward achievement.

Scoring Guides or Rubrics

Different ways to label criteria for evaluating student performance include rubrics, scoring rubrics, scoring criteria, and scoring guides. Each describes the guidelines for evaluating learner performance and usually includes a scale of values for rating the quality of the task or performance and the learner expectation for a specified performance. The criteria that you develop or select for the task or performance depends on the purpose for the assessment. When criteria is clearly communicated to the learner and the parents or guardian, it helps them understand what you, as teacher, intend the learner to accomplish. In designing your own rubrics or scoring guides, some guidelines that may help you include:

- Behaviors described in the rubric are behaviors that reflect the learning outcomes.
- Include four to six points on a scale depending on the activity.
- Descriptors are clearly written. Avoid negative statements such as "cannot perform the mathematical operation."
- Students may contribute to the construction of rubrics. They may specify the expected behaviors for each point on the scale.

Peer and Self-Assessment

Involving students through self-assessment or peer evaluation gives them opportunities to become active learners. They become more articulate about their progress and what they need to work on to improve their performance. Early in the school year you will want to communicate to students your grading system and encourage them to take responsibility for tracking their personal progress and setting academic goals. Giving your students the opportunity to journal, reflect on their learning, and record their grades enables them to see progress in various areas over time.

Students can assess themselves and their peers in a variety of settings using rubrics, checklists, and performance criteria. Best practices in teaching writing include a step in the writing process where students are actively involved in learning. Each group member drafts a composition that will be read and responded to by peers. After responding to the piece and making suggestions for revisions, each composition is revisited for editing purposes. Students proofread each others' work, helping with necessary corrections, by using the criteria set by the teacher for this particular writing piece. Before the individual student writes the final copy, each student signs a statement that the criteria have been met. This process allows each student in the group to read, review, and rate another student's work against an established performance criteria. By using a peer's work as a model, students not only gain a better understanding of the performance criteria, but they also engage more deeply in the multifaceted processes of learning, oftentimes resulting in improvement in productivity, creativity, and accountability.

Peer assessment activities used for writing purposes are highlighted here as one example. Teachers use other self- or peer assessment activities in reading, math, learning logs, journals, and goal setting for behavior management. The bottom line is getting your students involved in self-assessment and peer evaluation across the curriculum. This involvement motivates students to take a more active role in their own learning.

Grading

Nothing seems to be more controversial in education than grading and communicating student learning results. Grades provide limited information about how the student is performing and are oftentimes misunderstood by the student and parent. In addition, teachers find the grading process very difficult and time consuming.

The meaning of the grade must be clearly defined and easily understood by the learner so that it clearly communicates the level of student achievement. Feedback regarding your students' performance should be continuous and allow your students to know where they stand. Although the teacher's subjective perceptions and insights inevitably influence the grading process to some extent, they should not be allowed to greatly distort the subject matter grade (Airasian, 2000).

Multiple measures provide a more complete picture of student performance. Skills and attitudes that a student is developing become part of your reporting system. Most subject matter assessment is done with teacher-made tests, papers, quizzes, projects, activity sheets, and homework. Some aspects of student achievement can be better assessed by performance rather than or in addition to a multiple-choice or essay test. Using scoring guides or rubrics for performance assessment tasks will assist you in making decisions and reporting the results of your learners' achievement. In addition, it will encourage student self-assessment and cooperative group reporting for accountability purposes. Finally, when conferencing with students and parents or guardians about results of performance assessment, scoring guides will provide a more sophisticated analysis of student achievement.

Reporting Guidelines

Guskey and Bailey (2001) recommend the following guidelines to help ensure that grading and reporting practices are equitable and useful to students, parents, and teachers:

- Begin with a clear statement of purpose. A statement of purpose would address why grading or reporting is done—for whom the information is intended, and how the information will be used.
- Provide accurate and understandable descriptions of student learning.
- Use grading and reporting methods to enhance, not hinder, teaching and learning.

Reporting to Parents

The report card is the most common form of communicating to parents or guardians a student's progress. Each school system usually has a set format. You may discuss with your supervising teacher the reporting form your school uses and the procedures used for grading and commenting to parents or guardians.

The written progress report is another method of communicating learner progress. Written in clear, easy-to-read, everyday language, the report communicates to parents or guardians specific areas indicating learner progress. Many teachers write student progress notes to parents or guardians periodically throughout the school year. In the near future, with electronic capabilities, you may be communicating with parents even more frequently.

Conferences

Conferencing is the most effective way of communicating with parents or guardians and the student. Conferencing will open the lines of communication and frequently save you time and trouble later. Although it is time consuming, careful planning is necessary to ensure productivity. Parent, guardian, and student response is usually positive. Conferencing is proactive! Your students see the connection between their performance and the need to talk about it and communicate the results of their hard work (or lack of it!) to their parents or guardians. Two-way communication ensures that the message received is the message sent. All parties feel secure and informed about academic expectations, goals, problems, and academic standing. When you invite parents or guardians for a conference, you are actually saying, "We would like to communicate what your son or daughter is learning in school. What would you like to know? There are many different ways to give you a picture of your son's or daughter's work. We invite you to see examples of classwork, research projects, and writing portfolios. We want you to examine your son's or daughter's academic performance thus far by reading a reader response journal, a learning log, or math portfolio."

Begin saving samples of students' work in a working portfolio (in upper levels, students take responsibility for them), and any other pieces of information that will enhance the discussion. Using an individual self-assessment form (designed by you) allows students to participate in the conference and take an active role in their development as learners.

Planning jointly for the student's benefit is the overall goal of the conference. At the conclusion of the conference you will want to review what was discussed and summarize the actions planned and agreed upon by all. Student-led conferences place the learner in the spotlight and require reflection about progress to this point. Teaching students to set academic goals pays off in the student-led conferences as students articulate their strengths and areas in need of improvement. Time is always a factor; therefore, it is highly recommended that you prepare an agenda of the items you wish to discuss.

During the conference you will want to listen to the parents' or guardian's concerns. This helps you learn about the student from their perspective and provides opportunities for sharing valuable information about the learner.

Linn and Gronlund (2000) suggest the following steps when planning for conferences:

1. Make a list of the points you want to cover and the questions you want to ask.
2. Begin the conference in a positive manner.
3. State the student's strong points before describing areas needing improvement. Present samples of student work.
4. Encourage parents or guardians to participate and share information. Actively listen to their questions and concerns and take notes.
5. Establish a cooperative partnership so that all can work toward assisting the student with a plan to achieve specific academic and/or social goals.
6. End the conference on a positive note, thanking the parents or guardians for coming.

It is important to conduct a follow-up report, keeping contact with the parents or guardians. Sending notes, making phone calls, and communicating via the Internet may help keep the lines of communication open and the student benefits from the shared experience.

Responsibility for completing report cards or preparing conference reports for parents or guardians may not be entirely your responsibility at this time. Assisting your supervising teachers with developing a reporting process greatly increases your competence and contributes to your confidence in this important area of teaching.

ASSIGNED ACTIVITIES

1. Select one assessment instrument from Table 11.2 that you are currently using or have recently used. The questions below are intended to help you examine the assessment process. Referring to the instrument you selected, respond to the questions about the assessment process you are conducting. Bring the instrument to the next session for peer analysis and evaluation.
   a. What outcomes are to be measured?
   b. Is it group or individual work? If group work, what roles are expected to be fulfilled?
   c. What options or choices are allowed? Describe the choices (e.g., written, verbal, action, and so on). Who makes the choice? The teacher, student, or both?
   d. What materials or equipment will be available to students? Are there any specifications?
   e. Are the activities given a time limit? How does the time affect student performance? Is peer assistance permitted?
2. Describe your involvement in the following assessment reporting methods.
   • Open house
   • Parent-teacher-student conferences
   • Report cards or progress reports

TABLE 11.2 *Assessment Instruments*

Assessment Instruments	Examined	Used
Observations		
Student interviews		
Written tests		
Performance events/exhibitions		
Journals		
Autobiographies		
Criterion-referenced tests		
Group work		
Checklists		
Standardized achievement tests		
Homework		
Videotapes		
Case studies		
Anecdotal records		
Portfolio entries		
Rubrics		
Conferences		
Rating scales		

- Individualized Education Plan (IEP)
- Performance events
- Parent-teacher organization meetings

3. Comment on the formative and summative evaluative reports given students this week. How were the results recorded, used, and analyzed? What was the follow-up for students who were not reaching their potential?

Reports

- Tests (written, oral, performance)
- Daily assignments (class presentations)
- Projects (problem solving, thematic)
- Group work
- Journals, notebooks, lab books, learning logs
- Home assignments
- Portfolio entries
- Student interviews
- Conferencing with student

Summary

Focusing on assessment, you are more conscious of the connection between learning strategies and student performance. Perhaps your reflections include questions about the academic levels of the learning strategies you use. Did you ask yourself: Were my students engaged in activities of value that produced new meaning? Do my students' activities reflect an understanding of a specific concept, problem, or skill? Did I meet the ability levels of all my students? Can my students relate or apply this task, this activity, to the world beyond the classroom?

If authentic assessment is to influence the learning process, then the various assessment instruments need to reflect the academic expectations of the teachers. You as the teacher, or with other team members, select the assessment instrument that matches the stated expectations. Through your choice of the appropriate assessment, you communicate to the learners what is important, what they are expected to know and be able to do, and what deserves their attention and focus.

To communicate learning results effectively it is imperative that you fully appreciate the processes involved in and the opportunities for individual growth that stem from reflective communication. Effective communication of learning results calls for the use of a number of assessment strategies and tools. As a professional, you engage in reflection, self-analysis, and other assorted ways to mark your progress. You recognize the need to communicate your growth and receive feedback from others. From this you better understand students' need to engage in communication about their progress as learners.

Current research suggests that a partnership between parents or guardians and teacher results in better planning and decision making and positively impacts student learning (Buttery & Anderson, 1999; Marzano, 2000). Conferencing with parents or guardians can be an effective means for creating and continuing cooperative relationships between home and school. You may have been present for the open house or parent night when your supervising teacher communicated with the parents for the first time this school year. Perhaps you have been present or even participated in scheduled conferences with parents or guardians. You observed as your experienced supervising teacher enabled parents to share mutual concerns, ideas, and opinions in a comfortable, secure setting. In a special education meeting you witnessed all committee members contributing to the Individualized Education Plan planning and reaching a consensus on reasonable expectations for the student.

Actively listening to students, parents, and others encourages communication rather than confrontation. Your understanding of effective communication skills can result in a more productive dialogue between you and parents or guardians. You have also discovered how essential it is to be well prepared and organized if parent conferences and meetings are to be successful. Positive, well-conducted conferences can serve as encouragement and direction for the learner if appropriate information is shared.

FOLLOW–UP QUESTIONS AND SHARED INSIGHTS

Using the following questions, share the results you found from examining, planning, and using assessment instruments.

1. Review Table 11.2 and determine which assessment instruments you have used this week. How does this information help you make decisions concerning learner progress, and how are those decisions reflected in your follow-up instructional planning?
2. What information is helpful for teachers to request from parents or guardians regarding the learner?
3. In what ways does the teacher communicate learner progress or achievement to the student?
4. Which reporting plans used by the school and teachers were valuable in building and strengthening the partnership among the parents, teachers, and students?

5. What suggestions do you have for getting parents more actively involved in the student's educational achievement?
6. How is student progress determined? What provisions are made for students with different learning styles?

Portfolio Tasks

Providing students, parents, and guardians with systematic information about your assessment strategies and how you plan to help students achieve at their highest potential is addressed in your response to the Portfolio Tasks for this chapter. These tasks are based on INTASC Performance Standard 8. New Teacher Standard IV (State) located in Appendix C may also be of assistance.

Assessing and Communicating Learning Results

INTASC Performance Standards

Standard 8: The teacher understands and uses formal and informal assessment strategies to evaluate and ensure the continuous intellectual, social, and physical development of the learner.

Performance Guidelines

1. Briefly address the social, cultural, and physical diversity of your class and school community. Specify the content areas you are teaching.
2. Describe how you help students understand the performance level you expect of them and what is needed to progress to the next level.
3. Draft a letter to the parents helping them understand the assessment process used with your classes.
   a. Name and briefly describe the different assessment instruments you plan to use with your students.
   b. Explain how grades for assessment activities will be decided.

Performance Criteria

The quality of your entry will be assessed to the extent that evidence provided:

- Proposes both formal and informal assessment experiences that are developmentally appropriate for learners, allowing different accommodations for student response, and reflecting the specific content being taught.
- Makes appropriate provision for assessment processes that address social, cultural, and physical diversity.
- Provides students with information about a systematic way of assessing student work that is consistent with the school system's performance assessment program.
- Focuses student attention on what needs to be accomplished to progress to the next performance level.

Journal Excerpts

High School

"The assessment tool I designed for my freshman English class was a scoring guide to help me grade their independent novel projects. I made up this rubric before I ever introduced the independent novel project to the students and tied it to the objectives I had written for the unit. I wanted to make sure that they knew exactly what was expected of them. When I introduced the project, I gave each student a handout which stated the specific criteria on which I would be grading the project. The next time I create a rubric, I will have students use it as a self-evaluation tool and together we'll assess the process, progress, and product."

"Today we had Parent-Teacher Conferences. It was quite fascinating to experience this aspect of teaching. I got to see how Mr. R. prepared and dealt with specific situations. It was wonderful to meet the parents. No one was mad or frustrated with me so I felt really good. After these conferences, I feel much more comfortable and confident about my interactions and relationships with parents. In general, they are very supportive of their sons and daughters and also our efforts. Wonderful learning experience!"

"Portfolio entries are the major form of evaluation we used this week. Students handed in their portfolio pieces to be given a revision grade. They will eventually be graded on their final portfolio—complete with four writing pieces. For now, though, students are only able to see their progress in the revision stage of their writing. After the revision of the portfolio piece is evaluated, students have the option of coming to a peer or teacher conference about their writing to gain a more complete understanding of the revision process, and their grade at this point for a work in progress. This ongoing evaluation and feedback continually allows the students to improve their work, yet makes them accountable to meet deadlines and writing process expectations."

Middle School

"We had Open House tonight. I was nervous, but I did not have to speak to the entire group of parents. In a way, I wish I would have had the practice. I'll be so nervous when I do have to face parents on my own. I need to work on being assertive. Parents are scary! I felt so proud when Ms. P.J. would turn to me for specifics about an individual student. Since I grade so much of their work, I know them well and know how they're doing. Luckily, I only had to speak of good things and Ms. P.J. handled the tough cases. I learned a lot about approaching problems because my supervising teacher is great with parents. Tonight was very beneficial for me."

"I was pleased to read the limericks from those students who handed in their homework. I found that most of the limericks the students turned in did fit the qualifications for being a limerick. However, the most common mistakes were: (1) there were too many or too few syllables in a particular line, (2) the words at the end of the lines didn't rhyme. To address this, I commented on each student's paper accordingly and deducted points for limericks with errors in rhyme, form, syllabication, and humor qualifications. They have an opportunity to revise them for their final drafts. I'm curious to see if my comments will impact their choice to revise or not."

"Today's test offered a new challenge. I caught one of my favorite students cheating on the exam. He had made a cheat sheet with all of the formulas in small, block print. I took his exam from him and told him to see me after class. I knew if I tried to handle it right then I would have lost my temper and would not have thought rationally. As I walked to the back of the room, I began thinking to myself, 'I wonder how many of my other students have cheated on my exams? Have I paid close enough attention?' After class, I called him over to talk about the situation. I talked to him for at least fifteen minutes. I asked him, 'What do you think I should do?' He would only respond with 'Give me a zero.' I wasn't going to give him a zero because I did not want to destroy him, but I wanted to teach a lesson. So I told him to be at study skills the next day to take a new test that would be much harder than the previous. He then had to take the grade he received on the test. I hope it works."

Elementary Education

"One method of formative evaluation that I use often is journaling. I give them a topic to journal at the end of every class period. The topic usually flows directly from the lesson/discussion and is in addition to homework (as they are given the last few minutes of class time to complete it). I take these up every day and make comments on every one before I return them. This allows me to gauge their progress in grasping crucial elements and also to direct their thinking in the direction of deeper meanings."

"I taught Reading formally today for the first time. It went okay, but I'm trying to think of ways to spice up the discussion. I think I might allow them to act out scenes tomorrow. I think that would also be a neat assessment activity instead of the formal test that would normally follow the completion of a unit."

"Ms. W. uses a weekly recording journal that is sent home with the students. I am very interested in this procedure and I think it works very well. I was involved in charting these reports today and recording their results in the grade book. I also gave and graded their spelling tests. The students work hard and I enjoy grading the tests so I can see the results."

Special Education

"I was asked to give another Brigance test. So first thing this morning, I gave the test. I almost cried. This little boy should already be in a self-contained unit. He is in the second grade and he does not have accurate letter recognition. On the test, he could only recognize four to five letters. I cannot believe a child has gotten this far in his education without services. I was told that last year he was not tested because his attendance was so poor. He is a sweet child that tries hard, but I can see that if we do not get him some help soon he is going to acquire behavior problems due to the frustration level."

"I was working independently with one student in particular because they were making pictionaries. This required writing, and he needed a lot of help. After this, they took a spelling test. The test was on homophones; a word was used in a sentence and the students had to decide whether or not it was correct. I read the test to him. I realize it is hard to read a test, without hinting at the answer. After he would answer, he would look at me to see if it was correct. Of course, I would not tell him, but he would watch my face and try and figure it out. I just looked away. He knew most of the answers, but I do not think he trusted himself."

"I was able to sit in on G.'s IEP meeting. While in the meeting with his mom and stepdad, Mrs. B. asked me to explain the intervention I started with G. today. I started a stamp book. I explained to G. that each time he responded to a question with verbal cues from an adult or peer he would receive a stamp in his book. After five stamps he would receive a treat from the treat box. This was a great hit! Before the IEP meeting he had already earned two treats. So, I shared with Mom and Dad that the general idea was to start with G. receiving a treat after only five stamps, but that number of stamps needed to receive a treat would be increased over time."

REFERENCES AND SUGGESTED READINGS

Airasian, P. (2000). *Assessment in the classroom: A concise approach* (3rd ed.). New York: McGraw-Hill.

Allman, J., & Brophy, J. (1998). Assessment in a social constructivist classroom. *Social Education, 62*(1), 32–34.

Arter, J., & McTighe, J. (2001). *Scoring rubrics in the classroom.* Thousand Oaks, CA: Corwin Press.

Buttery, T. J., & Anderson, P. J. (1999). Community, school, and parent dynamics: A synthesis of literature and activities. *Teacher Education Quarterly, 26*(4), 111–122.

Caine, R. N., & Caine, G. (1997). *Education on the edge of possibility.* Alexandria, VA: Association for Supervision and Curriculum Development.

Carpenter, S. L., & King-Sears, M. E. (1998). Classroom assessment practices for instruction. In M. S. Rosenberg, L. O'Shea & D. J. O'Shea (Eds.), *Student teacher to master teacher: A practical guide for educating students with special needs* (2nd ed.). Upper Saddle River, NJ: Merrill/Prentice Hall.

Countryman, L. L., & Schroeder, M. (1996). When students lead parent-teacher conferences. *Educational Leadership, 53*(7), 64–68.

Danielson, C., & McGreal, T. L. (2000). *Teacher evaluation to enhance professional practice.* Princeton, NJ: Educational Testing Service.

Davies, M. A., & Wavering, M. (1999). Alternative assessment: New directions in teaching and learning. *Contemporary Education, 71*(1), 39–48.

Diez, M. E. (Ed.). (1998). *Changing the practice of teacher education: Standards and assessment as a lever for change.* Washington, DC: American Association of Colleges for Teacher Education.

Fuller, F. F. (1970). *Personalized teacher education for teachers: An introduction for teacher educators.* Austin: University of Texas, R & D Center for Teacher Education. (ERIC Document Reproduction Service No. ED048105)

Gallagher, J. D. (1998). *Classroom assessment for teachers.* Upper Saddle River, NJ: Merrill/Prentice Hall.

Guskey, T. R. (1996). *Communicating student learning 1996 ASCD yearbook.* Alexandria, VA: Association for Supervision and Curriculum Development.

Guskey, T. R. (2002). Computerized gradebooks and the myth of objectivity. *Phi Delta Kappan, 83*(10), 775–780.

Guskey, T. R., & Bailey, J. M. (2001). *Developing grading and reporting systems for student learning.* Thousand Oaks, CA: Corwin Press.

Hart, D. (1994). *Authentic assessment: A handbook for educators.* Menlo Park, CA: Addison-Wesley.

Herman, J. L., Aschbacher, P. R., & Winters, L. (1992). *A practical guide to alternative assessment.* Alexandria, VA: Association for Supervision and Curriculum Development.

Jamentz, K. (1994). Making sure that assessment improves performance. *Educational Leadership, 51*(6), 55–57.

Jersild, A. T. (1955). *When teachers face themselves.* New York: Teachers College Press.

Johnson, D. W., Johnson, R. T., & Holubec, E. (1993). *Cooperation in the classroom* (6th ed.). Edina, MN: Interaction Book.

Linn, R. L., & Gronlund, N. E. (2000). *Measurement and evaluation in teaching* (8th ed.). Upper Saddle River, NJ: Merrill/Prentice Hall.

Martinello, M. L., & Cook, G. E. (1994). *Interdisciplinary inquiry in teaching and learning.* Upper Saddle River, NJ: Merrill/Prentice Hall.

Marzano, R. J. (2000). *Transforming classroom grading.* Alexandria, VA: Association for Supervision and Curriculum Development.

Marzano, R. J., Pickering, D., & McTighe, J. (1993). *Assessing student outcomes: Performance assessment using the dimensions of a learning model.* Alexandria, VA: Association for Supervision and Curriculum Development.

Newmann, F. M., Marks, H. M., & Gamoran, A. (1995). Authentic pedagogy: Standards that boost student performance. *Issue Report* (No. 8). Madison: Wisconsin Center for Education Research.

Orlich, D. C., Harder, R. J., Callahan, R. C., & Gibson, H. W. (2001). *Teaching strategies: A guide to better instruction* (6th ed.). Boston: Houghton Mifflin.

Pellegrino, J. W., Chudowsky, N., & Glaser, R. (Eds.). (2001). *Knowing what students know: The science and design of educational assessment.* Washington, DC: National Academy Press.

Perrone, V. (2000). *Lessons for new teachers.* Boston: McGraw-Hill.

Popham, W. J. (1997). What's wrong and what's right—with rubrics. *Educational Leadership, 55*(2) 72–75.

Popham, W. J. (2001). *The truth about testing: An educator's call to action.* Alexandria, VA: Association for Supervision and Curriculum Development.

Reineke, R. A. (1998). *Challenging the mind, touching the heart: Best assessment practices.* Thousand Oaks, CA: Corwin Press.

Rich, D. (1998). What parents want from teachers. *Educational Leadership, 55*(8), 37–39.

Rust, F. O. (2000). Professional conversations: New teachers explore teaching through conversations, story, and narrative. *Teaching and Teacher Education, 15*(4), 367–380.

Rust, F. O., & Freidus, H. (2001). *Guiding school change: The role and work of change agents.* New York: Teachers College Press.

Salvia, J., & Ysseldyk, J. E. (1998). *Assessment* (7th ed.). Boston: Houghton Mifflin.

Stiggins, R. J. (1998). *Student-centered classroom assessment* (2nd ed.). Upper Saddle River, NJ: Merrill/Prentice Hall.

Stiggins, R. J. (2002). Assessment crisis: The absence of assessment for learning. *Phi Delta Kappan, 83*(10), 758–765.

Taggart, G. L., Phifer, S. J., Nexon, J. A., & Woods, M. (1998). *Rubrics: A handbook for construction and use.* Lancaster, PA: Technomic.

Urban, V. D. (1999). Eugene's story: A case for caring. *Educational Leadership, 56*(6), 69–70.

Wasserman, S. (2001). Quantum theory, the uncertainty principle, and the alchemy of standardized testing. *Phi Delta Kappan, 83*(1), 28–40.

Watts, K. H. (1996). Bridges freeze before roads. In T. R. Guskey (Ed.), *Communicating student learning 1996 ASCD yearbook.* Alexandria, VA: Association for Supervision and Curriculum Development.

Wiggins, G. (1998). *Educative assessment: Designing assessments to inform and improve student performance.* San Francisco: Jossey-Bass.

Zessoules, R., & Gardner, H. (1991). Authentic assessment beyond the buzzword. In V. Perrone (Ed.), *Expanding student assessment.* Alexandria, VA: Association for Supervision and Curriculum Development.

Zmuda, A., & Tomaino, M. (1999). A contract for the high school classroom. *Educational Leadership, 56*(6), 59–61.

chapter

12

Collaborating With Colleagues, Parents, and Community

> 66 *[U]nderstanding and teaching the complexities associated with collaboration will avert putting the proverbial bandwagon before the horse and ultimately keep us on the bandwagon known as collaboration.* 99

M. Welch

Focus One

Expected Performance

- Identify the ways you see yourself as a team player.
- Engage in a problem-solving activity with peers.
- Apply your understanding of cooperation and collaboration to your current teaching situation.
- Discuss the necessity for cooperation and collaboration within the changing role of teachers.

AM I A COLLABORATOR, A TEAM PLAYER?

New expectations are emerging for schools in the 21st century and for individuals working in schools. Many schools are changing from a hierarchical pattern of organization and structure to one more decentralized, thus changing the traditional roles of administrators and teachers. Beginning teachers are learning about ways that families and the community can benefit them and their students, and of the need to work positively with parents and with community agencies and institutions (Davies, 2002). These changes in structure are made for promoting a sense of community in schools and are focused on meeting human needs. The roles and responsibilities of the administrators, teachers, and others in these schools are more general and flexible than in the past.

Today, quality teachers are seen as professionals who demonstrate their expertise within the school and are given opportunities to provide input for the larger school community. You may have heard teachers' roles referred to as guides, leaders, decision makers, learners, student advocates, and colleagues. In your student teaching placement you may be working with administrators, the curriculum coordinator, a number of special educators, and a social worker; in addition, you may be a member of an instructional team. Each of these teacher roles supports the idea of teacher as collaborator—part of a collective group contributing to the school's overall climate.

Creating the school community and establishing a healthy climate (one in which teachers, students, and staff come together to learn and to teach) requires cooperation and collaboration. In the text there are extensive descriptions and suggestions for structuring and maintaining cooperative group activities. You may be using these techniques and observing group members working and showing mutual respect toward each other. Likewise, new teacher roles such as leader and colleague require that teachers collaborate. Henderson (1996) explains that "when teachers collaborate, they support one another's professional

161

autonomy and celebrate their diversity in the context of shared pragmatic reconsiderations and critical examination. Collaborating professionals treat one another as fellow inquirers" (p. 187). You may already be engaged in collaborative activities to provide services for learners with special needs and English as a second language (ESL) students in your school. You join the efforts of others in addressing students' needs and school-related problems (Zabel & Zabel, 1996). Does this resemble the school where you are now teaching? How do you interact with professionals and paraprofessionals at your school site?

EXAMINING COLLABORATIVE STRATEGIES AT THE SCHOOL LEVEL

The working relationship between the school-based professional and paraprofessional is often labeled as collaboration and teamwork. Are you a team player? Do you collaborate with others? Individuals engaged in this collaborative relationship share and promote a common goal. In the school the common goal is generating and maintaining a teaching-learning climate for all members of the school community where all learners can learn in deep and meaningful ways. Consider your own student or intern teaching situation and the collaboration and teamwork that exist within your classroom, the team, and the school and reflect on the following questions:

- What elements are present that create the interdependent relationships you experience?
- Are you and others willing to participate actively in the formation of a dynamic community?
- Is there recognition and respect for each other's competence?
- Is diversity celebrated among the community members, individually and collectively?
- Do members interact with each other to communicate pragmatic concerns and identify common problems?
- Are conflicts resolved through a critical examination process that promotes a wise and decisive course of action?

Whether you are a regular classroom teacher, a special educator, a bilingual or ESL teacher, these components necessarily supply the impetus and motivation inherent in working collaboratively toward a common goal.

Being fully cognizant of expectations you hold for yourself (and others working with you) is an important starting point for reflecting on collaboration and teamwork. **Focus One** offers a hands-on activity that demonstrates the elements critical to effective collaboration and teamwork. It invites you to participate with your group in working toward a common goal and analyze the process involved, the underlying framework that encourages success. During the activity you work with your group members to solve a problem, and then determine a course of action for solving the problem. Specific directions serve as parameters in which the task is performed. By adhering to the confines of this activity, you will experience your personal feelings and actions during the interaction with others and, from this, better understand the challenges associated with real-life problem-solving events in the school or in your classroom.

Directions for the Rectangular Puzzle Activity

Each member assembles a rectangular puzzle that has the same dimensions when completed. No two puzzles have pieces with the same shape. Using the pieces given by the Facilitator and those received from others, group members

Facilitator Tasks

- Prepare puzzles using the diagram found in Appendix A. Puzzle pieces can be made of tagboard.
- Provide each student with an envelope. Each envelope contains one or more geometric pieces. The pieces may or may not fit the same rectangle.
- Form groups of five students each.
- Monitor and check the accuracy of puzzles assembled by each group.

work independently solving the problem and are aware of what other members need for completing their puzzles. When the Facilitator confirms that yours and other members' puzzles are accurately assembled, your group has completed the activity (Goethals & Howard, 1985).

Puzzle Pieces

- All correctly completed puzzles have the same size.
- Pieces to each puzzle have different shapes.
- Edges of all correctly placed puzzle pieces fit together smoothly.

Directions

- Remove puzzle pieces from the envelope.
- Examine puzzle pieces to see if the pieces fit together to form a rectangle.
- Pass puzzle pieces you do not want to the person on your right.
- Receive puzzle pieces *only* from the person to your left.
- Mentally picture the completed rectangle, yours and others'.
- Engage in the activity without gesturing or verbally communicating with other group members.
- Be aware of how you feel toward yourself and toward others while performing the task.

Helping Other Group Members

- Pass puzzle pieces you are not using.
- Allow others to work assembling their own puzzle.
- Be mindful that other group members are capable of completing their task.
- Be willing to restructure your rectangle to help other members try out other solutions.
- When your group completes its task, reflect on the process and your participation.

Discussion Questions

1. Describe the myriad feelings you experienced while you and your group assembled the puzzles. How did you feel toward yourself? Toward others in the group?
2. When you observed that others in the group needed help, what did you do? How did your interactions with others during the activity mirror your attitude toward them as capable and competent professionals?
3. To what extent did you remember the group's common goal? What caused you to lose focus of the goal?
4. Consider your experience of this activity and analyze which collaboration and teamwork elements are most important to individual and group success.
5. Apply what you have learned to a current situation in your school and analyze the effectiveness of collaborative effort.

Focus Two

In your **Focus One** activity, you worked together as a team to build a puzzle, which demonstrated a way to collaborate. You needed to complete your task and simultaneously observe others' needs. There were tense moments, humorous times, frustrating moves; you may have wanted to just take charge! In your discussions that followed, you began to relate this experience to real-life

Expected Performance

- Foster relationships with school colleagues, parents, and agencies in the larger community to support students' learning and well-being.
- Demonstrate leadership or team membership skills that facilitate the development of mutually beneficial goals.
- Demonstrate tolerance for alternative perspectives and options, and encourage contributions from school and community resources.
- Demonstrate sensitivity to differences in abilities, modes of contribution, and social and cultural backgrounds.

situations for you as a teacher. Working with your supervising teacher has its ups and downs. Teaming with other teachers can be frustrating and time consuming. When conferencing with the learners' parents or guardians, you may want to take charge and dismiss their concerns, setting a course with yourself in charge. You may think it is quicker and easier to do it yourself rather than involve everyone else in decisions about a student's academic concerns. You may recall that it takes a large number of people to educate a single individual.

APPLICATION: COLLABORATING WITH COLLEAGUES, PARENTS, AND COMMUNITY

Collaboration is the shared responsibility of teachers, parents, administrators, and community members. As a participant in conferences and meetings with colleagues, parents or guardians, community, and other agencies, your desire to become an effective collaborator is confirmed. You realize the ability to work collaboratively within diverse groups takes great sensitivity and patience. Likewise, making joint decisions, resolving conflicts, setting goals, and following through on assigned tasks is a real commitment of time and energy. True collaboration with colleagues, parents, and others is a great feeling of accomplishment, especially when objectives are met and actions are taken. Working together for the benefit of the learner generates a genuine sense of community and purpose.

Collaboration Skills

Sometimes the collaboration process seems overwhelming. Your supervising and team teachers may have collaborated for years and may continue to work on overcoming specific roadblocks to effective communication. Good collaborators, according to Pugach and Johnson (1995), are willing to invest the time and energy necessary to improve their own professional practice. Improving collaborative skills leads to a sense of collegiality, creating a climate for successful student achievement.

Throughout your beginning teacher experience you realize the importance of interpersonal skills, communication skills, organizational abilities, flexibility, joint problem solving, decision-making strategies, and conflict resolution strategies in working with others. These skills are necessary for purposeful collaboration with others to more effectively provide the most productive learning climate for all your students.

Howard, Williams, Port, and Lepper (1997) describe factors discussed in the literature necessary for successful collaboration:

- trust
- face-to-face interaction
- interpersonal skills on the part of all team members
- voluntary collaboration
- equity among participants

You may find yourself more skilled in some areas than in others. This student or intern teaching experience provides a safe environment in which you can continue to practice and engage in collaboration.

Collaboration With Your Supervising Teachers

Your university supervisor and cooperating teacher are charged with guiding and supporting your student or intern teacher experience. They *want* you to succeed and become an effective teacher. Working together collaboratively provides you the opportunity for positive growth as an effective teacher. Your supervising team will encourage you to reflect on your lessons and ask questions, will offer suggestions, and will provide information that will give you a broader picture of your development as teacher. It is important that you remain open and share your self-assessment. If you are not receiving feedback from your cooperating or supervising teacher, ask for assessment of your lessons either verbally or in writing. Regular meetings with your cooperating teacher and university supervisor give you continuous feedback on your teaching and learning. This allows you to set and meet goals to improve any number of areas associated with quality teaching from planning and implementing lessons to classroom management and assessment.

We recommend that you communicate your lesson plan to your supervising team prior to teaching it. This will help your supervising team recognize your objectives, rationale for the instructional techniques used, type of assessment, and accommodations you make to meet the needs of all learners. Submitting your lesson plans electronically may be another means of receiving feedback regularly. As you receive feedback and suggestions from either your cooperating teacher or supervisor, ask questions to clarify what is being said and expected of you. Taking notes may be helpful. At the close of a conference (electronic or face to face), set one or two goals that relate to your teaching behaviors and put these in writing to review as you plan your lessons and practice your lesson presentation. Your level of confidence will grow as you set and reach these professional and academic goals.

Collaboration With Colleagues

Friend and Cook (1996) define collaboration as interaction between parties sharing resources to reach a common goal. Collaboration may take many forms within the school. Gable and Manning (1997) list the more popular teacher collaboration arrangements to include:

- grade-level collaboration, where first-grade teachers are paired with a reading specialist or resource teacher.
- subject-area collaboration, where teachers teach specific subjects.
- "cluster" collaboration, where teachers are located in the same wing.

General and special education teachers are participating in more collaborative teaching arrangements whereby two teachers share responsibility for planning, teaching, and assessing students. This provides the teachers involved with numerous problem-solving and cooperative teaching opportunities. Research shows that both students with and without disabilities benefit (Gable & Manning, 1997). Teachers begin to develop flexibility and are more creative in developing and using strategies to meet the needs of all students. Wood (1998) found that in initial stages of an inclusive or collaborative environment, teachers maintained discrete role boundaries, but as the year progressed, role perceptions became less rigid and the teaming became more cooperative. Contradicting previous results suggesting that educators prefer pull-out programs, a comprehensive assessment of general and special education teachers and administrators indicated the respondents from 32 school sites favored full inclusion of all students (Villa, Thousand, Meyers, & Nevin, 1996). True collaboration forces teachers to let go of preconceived notions about who teaches what and to whom, so only the highest quality of instruction is delivered to all learners.

Whether you are in a collaborative situation or general classroom, there are numbers of students and learners with special needs from diverse backgrounds and experiences. It is essential that you learn to consult with other colleagues and seek their assistance when you need it. Tap into others' area of expertise and ask how you might accommodate the needs of your students, what techniques or grouping patterns work best with particular groups of learners, and how you might design assessment for such a diverse group. Familiarize yourself with the various special resources and learn how to obtain the available services that will benefit you and ultimately all of your students.

Collaboration With Parents

Collaboration extends beyond the environs of the school. Parents are a valuable asset to the school, and their involvement and support needs to be fostered. Encouraging parents to express their concerns and soliciting their ideas and support in making academic or behavior decisions regarding their child or adolescent benefits the learner, the parent, and the teacher. When we fail to include parents as full partners in school affairs we limit successful achievement among students. The Metropolitan Life Survey of the American Teacher (Harris & Associates, 2001) found that students who perform better academically are more likely than students who experience academic difficulties to feel that their parents take an active interest in their school lives, provide them with the home support they need to succeed academically, and encourage them to pursue their dreams.

Parent involvement is a critical component of student success. You may find yourself smiling as you read this statement and asking obvious questions: How do we get more parents involved as active partners in the education process? How do I encourage a collaborative partnership among myself, my students, and their parents? How do I make the home-school connection become a reality in my teaching? Listed below are 10 approaches adapted from Giannetti and Sagarese (1998) to use right now (and in the future) to turn parents into partners in education.

1. Welcome and invite the parents to the classroom.
2. Advertise your expertise through newsletters and other media.
3. Implement an early warning system with frequent progress reports.
4. Show parents a positive picture of their child. Call to report a positive observation or behavior of their child or adolescent.
5. Convey to parents your shared values—effort, discipline, responsibility, standards, and integrity.
6. Cast yourself as a child advocate.
7. Share your inside information about the learner's world.
8. Empathize with parents that parenting is a tough job.
9. Be an effective and fair disciplinarian.
10. Be a consistent role model.

It is not surprising that parents' wishes and your professional judgment sometimes conflict. This can be frustrating and difficult to resolve, especially among new teachers who may lack the experience or assertiveness veteran teachers enjoy. It is important that you invite parents to state their concerns and the nature of their inquiry. When speaking with a parent or guardian, the student's welfare is the common denominator—that is, the focus should be on the student and his or her particular accomplishments and needs. After listening to the parent, explain your rationale for using the technique or program in question. If the parent is still dissatisfied you should arrange a meeting with the principal or counselor, the parent, yourself, and the student to resolve the conflict in a professional way.

Events and Opportunities for Collaboration With Parents

Open House and Parent's Night

Teachers are asked to collaborate with parents or guardians in a number of ways throughout the school year. Early in the year, an **open house** or **parent's night** is scheduled in elementary, middle, and high schools to invite parents and community to visit the school and classroom teachers. You may find yourself introduced to parents and visitors, and called on to describe the curriculum and upcoming events your classes will experience. This is an opportunity to meet parents and share your vision and academic goals for the coming school year. It is a time to state your expectations and garner parent support by keeping them informed about classroom matters. It is also a time to validate their commitment as an educational partner and set the tone for the academic school year.

Parent Teacher Associations and Organizations

Parent teacher associations and organizations involve parents and teachers in meetings scheduled to bring a better understanding of the unique responsibility both school and home share in the learning experience of each student. Parents and community representatives are important resources for meeting the mission and goals of schools. Many times members of these organizations are involved in the governance of the school either as an elected position on the decision-making council or board. Site-based decision making engages parents and teachers working together in planning school improvement. In addition, parents volunteer to assist teachers with academic and social events as tutors, chaperones, library assistants, and other positions.

Weekly Newsletters and Messages

Inform parents or guardians about school policies and curriculum experiences by making a connection between home and school through weekly newsletters and messages. When time is taken to send messages home, communication between home and school is enhanced. As a student or intern teacher you may be asked to write a parent newsletter to inform them of student learning experiences and announce future plans or themes that center around teaching and learning. The newsletter may include special dates, invitations, homework assignments, reminders, and small samples of student work or responses to class work and projects.

Homework Hotline and E-mail Messages

In addition to newsletters and messages sent home, parents or guardians and students access homework hotlines for reminders of assignments and due dates. Many of your students may have access to e-mail outside school, and you may want to set up a listser to send messages to your students outside school hours regarding academic progress, reminders of projects, or field trips. Likewise, picking up the phone to call a parent or guardian or student is a quick and effective way to communicate and reinforce the connection between school and home. Think how thrilled a parent, guardian, or student would be to receive a call or message from you to praise the student for a job well done!

Collaboration With School and Community

Schools are an integral part of a larger community. Schools need to value the knowledge and skills of community members. Involving the community as partners in education increases the learning opportunities for students. Inviting different members of the business and service community to speak to the class or school or demonstrate skills in a specific area provides students with a broader view of their world. Visiting the immediate area on foot or making field trips to a particular site allows students to interact with adults in a real-world setting as they learn about how and why things work within their own community. Accessing the arts (visual and performing) is another way for your students to expand their knowledge and experience of the world.

Increased emphasis is being placed on an expanding relationship between the school and community. Some parents serve on school councils and work cooperatively to include different parental and community interests, values, and expectations on establishing school policy. In efforts to close the huge gap between White and minority students, and between middle-class students and those with lower social status, the home, community, and schools sometimes share responsibilities of care and education (Davies, 2002). These and other changes vary in degree and emphasis and their influence affects all involved.

Collaboration With Other Agencies

There are many resources at the school and community level that may contribute to your students' learning or positively impact their experience in social and behavioral ways. These resources are available to you and require you to involve yourself as a student advocate if they are to maximize their potential to reach children and adolescents in times of need, stress, or desperation.

Many schools have family resource centers and personnel available to parents and guardians to help with intervention in family crises or times of need. These centers often provide counseling, training, and resources to families with documented needs and focus on strengthening the family unit (regardless of composition) so children and adolescents can experience more academic success while in school. Visit the family resource center to discover how it operates at your school and the benefits it provides to families, the school, and in turn, the larger community.

The family resource center cannot meet all the needs of families in distress. You may find that other outside agencies work within the families of some of your students to create a degree of stability and structure in their lives. Some of your students may be in residential group homes, foster care, or family shelters. Some may be bussed to your school to participate in academics only. It is important that you understand the significant role these atypical homes play in each student's development cognitively, socially, and emotionally. You may be asked for input regarding their status as students in the areas described above. Knowing beforehand your students' family backgrounds can give you insights into their school performance and prepare you to meet with personnel assigned to cases.

Likewise, you may find a number of students are in counseling or participate in treatment centers. Some students may take prescribed medication to help them stay focused in school or behave appropriately for their ages and ability levels. Parents and physicians may consult with you or have you document behavior (cognitive, emotional, physical) to help them determine the effectiveness of a medication dosage or therapy. It is your responsibility as a student or intern teacher to be aware of students' medical needs, especially if these needs interfere with their academic performance.

Developing appropriate relationships with colleagues, parents, and others within the community is a significant segment of teaching. The quality of interactions between you and colleagues, parents, and others within community agencies involved with learning programs affects your success as teacher. Your experience as beginning teacher provides extensive opportunities for interacting with a variety of professionals. Sharing insights, efforts, and resources enhances the quality of instruction provided to learners. As an effective collaborator, you contribute to—and benefit from—exchanging views, opinions, and experiences with those who play important roles in the success of your students.

School, Family, and Community Collaborative Resources

Many times you are asked to give resource information that will assist your colleagues, a parent, or others in the community. There are innumerable research centers and resources offering invaluable information to teachers, parents, and community on student learning. The following list gives you some ideas:

- Information Resource Center (IRC) links families, schools, and communities to information on student learning and provides updates on the U.S. Department of Education programs, funding opportunities, teleconferences, and other events. Call toll free 1-800-872-5327, or visit the Web sites.
  http://www.ed.gov/offices/OIIA/IRC
  http://usa_learn@ed.gov
- Harvard Family Research Project (HFRP) provides strategies for family involvement and community collaboration to support student achievement through ongoing research.
  http://gseweb.harvard.edu/hfrp
- National Center for Family Literacy (NCFL) provides literacy services for families to gain the resources they need to support their childrens' education. The NCFL literacy model integrates adult education instruction, children's education, Parent and Child Together Time, and Parent Time into a comprehensive program for families with preschoolers.
  http://www.famlit.org
- Community Family Club, designed by Camp Fire USA, offers a unique opportunity for parents to find a community support group. Outcome based, the program tracks the progressive learning experiences and developmental assets acquired by both youths and adults.
  http://www.campfire-sc.org

ASSIGNED ACTIVITIES

Recall the number of professionals and others with whom you relate as a teacher. The activities below are intended to guide your reflection on the quality of your interactions, how you have benefited and contributed to a collaborative effort.

1. Review the list of professionals in Figure 12.1. With whom have you collaborated? Indicate the date(s) you met and the topics or issues you discussed with each professional.
2. Using Figure 12.1, select at least one individual with whom you have collaborated.
. Use the blank spaces for your reflective response to the following:
   a. What I learned by collaborating with the selected individual(s) about instruction, assessment, and accommodations to greater impact student learning.

   _____

   _____

   _____

   _____

   b. Strengths I Acknowledge (teaching, communication, initiative, etc.)

   _____

   _____

   _____

FIGURE 12.1 *Record of Collaboration Activities*

	Date(s)	Topic(s)
Supervising Teacher		
University Supervisor		
Team and Department Members		
Students' Parents or Guardians		
School and District Staff		
Principal(s)		
Counselor(s)		
Other School Personnel		
Community or Agency Member		
Information Sought or Presented		

c. Areas for My Growth as Teacher

_____

_____

_____

d. My New Goals

_____

_____

_____

_____

SUMMARY

Focus One invited you to continue to interact with your students, your colleagues, your supervising teacher, parents or guardians, and others with a new awareness of the numerous personal benefits derived from refining your collaborative skills. As you gain confidence and a sense of belonging, you are more likely to contribute to the valuable insights you have received from observations and daily interaction with the students. Developing collaboration skills takes practice and is an ongoing process. **Focus One** provided ways to pool your resources, clarify your ideas, share and receive suggestions, and make decisions in the form of an action plan. This cooperative, collaborative interpersonal activity allowed you to practice collaborative skills and analyze the underlying framework necessary for effective collaboration among members of a community.

Effective communication skills and positive interaction in collaborative settings lead to shared decision making, benefiting students, parents, and families. No one course or workshop can prepare you adequately to work effectively with families and agencies. Activities that may help you increase your confidence and competence may include the following:

- Attending guest lectures and discussions led by teachers, parents, or community experts provides opportunities to interact and learn different approaches to collaboration.
- Peer-sharing of case studies and school and community experiences presents a type of action research where your responses can be analyzed and discussed against learning theories presented in your preservice courses.
- Serving on a school or community committee with a variety of teachers, parents, and community consultants is a great experience and allows you insights into collaboration and its workings outside the classroom.
- Working cooperatively with other group members by actively listening, determining when to question for clarification, or initiating an action leads to joint decision making and productive problem solving.

FOLLOW-UP QUESTIONS AND SHARED INSIGHTS

As a beginning teacher you have been observing and participating in curriculum integration efforts in a variety of collaborative approaches to accommodate learner needs. Reflect on your own family background, your basic assumptions about social and cultural differences of your students' backgrounds, and your attitude toward working with all your students and their families as you share insights and discuss the following:

1. Describe collaborative efforts in which you are presently engaged (e.g., student portfolio development, thematic units, Individualized Education Plan (IEP), school-based decision making, conferencing).
2. When conflicting ideas and opinions are expressed, how do partners, team members, administrators, parents, and other group members respond?
3. Examine Figure 12.1 showing the number of your interactions with other professionals during the past 5 days. With whom do you most frequently interact? Share an experience about when collaboration was necessary to your decision making.
4. Which skills do you most frequently use or would like to use in all collaborative activities? Describe the degree of success you experienced in applying these skills.
5. Role-play one of the following situations. Alternately play the roles of parent and teacher. Discuss the collaborative behaviors demonstrated by each in the role.

   - Discuss a son's or daughter's performance or behavior with a parent or guardian.
   - Talk with parents or guardians who are upset about their son's or daughter's grades.

Portfolio Tasks

Reflecting on and documenting your collaboration experiences with colleagues, parents or guardians, and other agency personnel are portfolio tasks for this chapter addressed in INTASC Performance Standard 10. You may also consult New Teacher Standard VI located in Appendix C.

Collaborating With Colleagues, Parents, and Community

INTASC Performance Standards

Standard 10: The teacher fosters relationships with school colleagues, parents, and agencies in the larger community to support students' learning and well-being.

Performance Guidelines

During your education program you have had various experiences that provided opportunities for collaboration. You have interacted with instructors and colleagues in university classes, and as a student or intern teacher you are working extensively with supervising teachers and other support personnel in the schools. In addition, you are increasingly involved with the school community and social service agencies. When addressing the collaboration section of your portfolio, you will want to describe these and similar experiences. The three tasks below are intended to guide your reflective experience with collaboration.

1. Identify three different types of collaborative experiences you have had in university classes, school settings, and with community or social service agencies.
2. Describe when and where the collaboration occurred, the purpose and scope of the collaboration, and your specific contributions to the effort.
3. Critique the effectiveness of each collaboration in terms of:

   - How the collaborative effort met its stated goals. Notes taken from the Record of Collaboration Activities (Figure 12.1) will help you.
   - What was learned from your experience about negotiation, conflict, and compromise.
   - How you use what you learned in working collaboratively with parents, colleagues, and others.

Performance Criteria

The quality of your entry will be assessed to the extent that evidence provided:

- Identifies the purpose and scope of the collaborative effort.
- Demonstrates tolerance for alternative perspectives and options, and encourages contributions from parents and community resources.
- Demonstrates sensitivity to differences in abilities, modes of contribution, and social and cultural backgrounds.

Journal Excerpts

High School

"I will be conferencing with all my students' parents this evening. Mr. T. and F. will assist me in preparation, provide input, and answer any questions I can't handle. T. and F. said we'll get about 30% of our parents, with more coming in the Spring to concentrate on scheduling. Most all the parents I have met are very supportive and enthusiastic. They said I'll get a few apologetic parents concerning their child and perhaps a few hostile ones. I'm excited to meet with the parents, but also very nervous."

"Today was a busy and long day. I met at 7:15 with my supervising teachers to discuss my upcoming schedule at school and my soccer schedule. They never seem to be impatient or uninterested in helping me. I am thankful for this. Mr. G. has helped me get acquainted with Resource Period which means I supervise students' study time. I now understand the sign out/in process and I think I'll be fine. We also began planning with Mr. S. for the new classes I am assuming responsibility for teaching. During first and second periods the guidance counselor came in to speak to the sophomores about the PSAT they will be taking later this month. I think several in Mr. G.'s class are beginning to trust me. This makes me feel more confident."

"Teacher education can prepare you for many things except for the tragic event that happened today at our high school. One of the school's outstanding students and a football player was killed while waiting for his bus. First, the players were called down and told; then, the vice principal came around and told each teacher before making an announcement over the P.A. After the announcement bursts of screams, yelps, and loud crying were heard throughout the building. Upset students were asked to go to the library where there were counselors to talk with and comfort students. Crises members from the school district office came, police officers, and some gang specialists were all available. Teachers and staff were there to counsel, comfort and love the hurting friends, team members, and classmates. Not only were the student's family and friends affected by his death, but the entire school and community. I can't begin to describe the hurt I felt these students were going through and the many unanswered questions of 'Why?' Although none of us has the answer, many teachers stopped class and dealt with the issue in different ways. Some students were asked to write journal entries, some just sat quietly, and some teachers just hugged and comforted those students who needed a shoulder to cry on. I was very impressed at the way the staff, faculty, and school district representatives handled this tragic event and the way they were there for each student. College classes can't prepare you for such tragedies and all week I've been asking God, 'Why?' and I have learned a lot. It seems that what helps most is that teachers, schools, businesses and community members all pull together for the kids and changes happen. I can't imagine how incredibly well students would do if they always had this kind of love and support from all!"

Middle School

"I had a great day! Dr. S. observed me and had positive things to say about my teaching. Ms. N., the Principal, sent my recommendation letter to the school district office, another middle school called to set up an interview, and the newspaper called and said it was publishing the article I sent. I'm elated!"

"Another student teacher and I collaborate quite a bit. He gave me a really creative lesson plan on irony that I tried with this class today. Of course, they loved it. It involved listening to music. S. is so creative in so many ways. I thought I would miss talking with him when I move, but then I remembered we both have e-mail. Another thing we talked about was my eighth grade class. He sensed that I was frustrated with them. I can't help it; I try not to get irritated with them, but I always seem to anyway. Their behavior definitely needs work. It's getting to the point where I worry about doing hands-on lessons and cooperative learning with them. They're fine in small groups but when the entire class is there, for example language arts, I have to keep a very tight reign or they get out of control. S. gave some suggestions that I plan to try."

"Yesterday we met as a team to discuss upcoming field trips. We are going to the zoo and later we will take a three-day camping trip. I expect it to be a lot of work. Field trips require so many forms, especially the over-night camping trip. There are packing lists, permission slips, money to be paid, and plans for students staying at school during this time. The list seems endless and each one has a deadline. Fee waivers cover the zoo trip but not the camping trip. Most students sold candy to go to the camp for free. Parents are also involved. Our school holds 'Chit-Chat' sessions with parents and most of their questions this week were about the upcoming camping trip."

Elementary

"One problem with the lesson occurred when students who received special help returned after I began teaching the class. Everything is orderly and all students are working until these two students come into the room. I lose all control and everyone loses focus on what they are doing. As I see it, the rules and consequences are not followed for these students and this bothers me. If they get two or three marks, it doesn't matter because nothing happens to them. I know I need to stick to my guns and apply consequences."

"Today was my first day with Mrs. W. and the third grade class. It was very new and interesting. I came in and was greeted with a warm welcome. The day was spent getting familiar with routine procedures in the room. I charted students' names and drew seating charts to help me learn the names of the children. The class was reading their *Storybook* magazine. This is an extra that she uses for reading. The magazine is full of short stories and clever activities. I noticed that after reading the magazine, Mrs. W. asked them to identify the genre of the story. Later she filled me in and told me she is emphasizing the genre this year and including it in the assessment process. I learned the markings that she uses in her grading system; A+ means very good and a check mark means adequate. This is a bit different from what I have been using to grade homework."

"I arrived early today to share my plans with Mrs. R. I have completed the plans for my lessons for next week and I wanted to show her my ideas to make sure that she approved of the plan and the activities I had selected. She seemed pleased with the plan and the activities."

Special Education

"My day began with an ECE Meeting. This session was very informative. We talked about a number of issues, specifically the new IEP forms and how to complete them. Actually I shared some of the things I knew from the classes I've taken on campus."

"I was very happy to be with Ms. M. on Friday. We didn't have time to really discuss my role but I know it is a conversation we will soon have. With her I think I will really experience what team teaching is like."

"We had another parent volunteer again today. I've met this mother before and really like her. Apparently she paid a compliment about me to Ms. L. It felt good to hear something positive because very often I only think the worst. Although I don't feel as though I change my style when parents come in, I am very aware of their presence."

REFERENCES AND SUGGESTED READINGS

Balli, S. J. (1998). When mom and dad help: Student reflections on parent involvement with homework. *Journal of Research and Development in Education, 31*(3), 142–148.

Behrman, R. E. (1996). Special education for students with disabilities. *Center for the Future of Children, 6(1).*

Berger, E. H. (2000). *Parents as partners in education: The school and home working together* (5th ed.). Upper Saddle River, NJ: Merrill/Prentice Hall.

Berres, M. S., Ferguson, D. L., Knoblock, P., & Woods, C. (Eds.). (1996). *Creating tomorrow's schools today: Stories of inclusion, change, & renewal.* New York: Teachers College Press.

Chamberlin, C. R. (2000). Nonverbal behaviors and initial impressions of trustworthiness in teacher-supervisor relationships. *Communication Education, 49*(4), 352–364.

Davies, D. (2002). The 10th school revisited: Are school/family/community partnerships on the reform agenda now? *Phi Delta Kappan, 83*(5), 388–392.

Dryfoos, J. (2002). Full-service community schools: Creating new institutions. *Phi Delta Kappan, 83*(5), 393–399.

Finn, J. D. (1998). Parental engagement that makes a difference. *Educational Leadership, 55*(8), 20–24.

Friend, M., & Cook, L. (1996). *Interactions: Collaboration skills for school professionals* (2nd ed.). White Plains, NY: Longman.

Gable, R. A., & Manning, M. L. (1997, Summer). The role of teacher collaboration in school reform. *Childhood Education,* 219–223.

Giannetti, C. C., & Sagarese, M. M. (1998). Turning parents from critics to allies. *Educational Leadership, 55*(8), 40–42.

Goethals, M. S., & Howard, R. A. (1985). *Handbook of skills essential to beginning teachers.* Lanham, MD: University Press of America.

Harris, L., & Associates, Inc. (2001). Building family-school partnerships: Views of teachers and students. *The Metropolitan Life Survey of the American Teacher (1998).* New York: Metropolitan Life Insurance.

Henderson, J. G. (1996). *Reflective teaching: The study of your constructivist practices.* Upper Saddle River, NJ: Merrill/Prentice Hall.

Hollingsworth, H. L. (2001). We need to talk: Communication strategies for effective collaboration. *Teaching Exceptional Children, 33*(5), 6–9.

Howard, V. F., Williams, B. F., Port, P. D., & Lepper, C. (1997). *Very young children with special needs: A formative approach for the 21st century.* Upper Saddle River, NJ: Merrill/Prentice Hall.

Kosmoski, G. J., & Pollack, D. R. (2001). *Managing conversations with hostile adults: Strategies for teachers.* Thousand Oaks, CA: Corwin Press.

Lytle, R. K., & Bordin, J. (2001). Enhancing the IEP team. *Teaching Exceptional Children, 33*(5), 40–45.

Menlove, R. R., Hudson, P. J., & Suter, D. (2001). A field of IEP dreams: Increasing general education teacher participation in the IEP development process. *Teaching Exceptional Children, 33*(5), 28–33.

Neuman, M., Fisher, S., & Simmons, W. (2000). Leadership for student learning. *Phi Delta Kappan, 82*(1), 8–12.

Pugach, M. C., & Johnson, L. J. (1995). *Collaborative practitioners: Collaborative schools.* Denver, CO: Love.

Rosenberg, M. S., O'Shea, L., & O'Shea, D. J. (1998). *Student teacher to master teacher: A practical guide for educating students with special needs* (2nd ed.). Upper Saddle River, NJ: Merrill/Prentice Hall.

Rubin, H. (2002). *Collaborative leadership.* Thousand Oaks, CA: Corwin Press.

Villa, R. A., Thousand, J. S., Meyers, H., & Nevin, A. (1996). Teacher and administrator perceptions of heterogeneous education. *Exceptional Children 63*(1), 29–45.

Welch, M. (1998). Collaboration: Staying on the bandwagon. *Journal of Teacher Education, 49*(1), 26–37.

Wood, M. (1998). Whose job is it anyway? Educational roles in inclusion. *Exceptional Children, 64*(2), 181–195.

Zabel, R. H., & Zabel, M. K. (1996). *Classroom management in context: Orchestrating positive learning environments.* Boston: Houghton Mifflin.

chapter

13

Reflecting On and Evaluating Teaching

" To cultivate good teaching we must begin with ourselves. "

C. M. Clark

Focus One

Expected Performance

- List gifts, talents, abilities, and sources of these gifts in your life.
- Examine ways these gifts allow you to fulfill some aspect of the teacher role.
- Share with others your insights about gifts and their effect on who you are and what you do as a teacher.

FOR WHO I AM AND WHAT I HAVE, THANKS!

Welcome to the changing profession of teaching! You join the profession at a time when the teacher role is expanding its terrain, encompassing new expectations for you as collaborator, colleague, leader, decision maker, and learner. Throughout the student or intern teacher experience you reflect on teaching practices, collect data, and share your understandings and insights with colleagues. Performing the teacher role requires you to have a broad knowledge base, effective methodologies and teaching strategies, and critical thinking skills. To be an effective teacher it is also necessary to have a focused understanding of yourself as an individual.

Focus One activities invite you to share with peers your perceptions and feelings about your development as a teacher. We intend that these activities allow you to highlight the positive feelings you have about your growth as a professional and your ever-widening perceptions of the teacher role. Your group and seminar discussions may even extend into the school and generate conversations with other teachers willing to share their insights about teaching! As you look to yourself and others, your understanding of the teacher role continually expands and changes. You clarify your beliefs about teaching and highlight those aspects you value and intend to acquire. You are changing, developing, advancing, and experiencing the joys and disappointments of life as a teacher.

Understanding yourself and valuing your beliefs influences your teaching, and this ongoing process is critical to your development. We teachers need help from others, urges Clark (1995), and we learn to respect our students by learning to respect and love the novice learner within ourselves. To connect with students it is important to remember what learning and life was like for you when you were their age. Awareness of yourself as a learner allows you to better understand and define the reciprocal nature of the teaching and learning processes (Collier, 1999). To cultivate good teaching we must begin with ourselves and learn to identify and reflect on what we believe, where these beliefs come from, and how they impact who we are as teachers. As members of the profession, we are also charged to consider these beliefs in light of principles associated with the teaching profession: honesty, fairness, protection of the weak, and respect for all people. The ongoing exploration of yourself as a teacher calls you to recognize and appreciate others, assist and encourage those in need, and appraise and direct others with integrity and courage.

SELF EXPLORATION

One dimension of exploring self is to consider the gifts you bring to the teaching career. These gifts are the characteristics and abilities that make you unique and special. Do you think of yourself as a gift? Webster's definition of *gift* is "something given; talent." Implied in the definition is the existence of a receiver. In how many ways do you as a teacher give of yourself? Is your ability to give to others the result of someone giving to you? Coles (1993) describes people who provided models of service for him: Dorothy Day, Simon Weil, Anna Freud, Erik Erikson, his mother and father. He describes his parents as gifts in their modeling of service:

> "I have been given so much, and shown so much, by so many individuals. My parents still hover over, even haunt, this subject matter. . . . I have heard my mother's and my father's voices . . . I have a tape of a radio interview done with my father, discussing his extraordinary work with ailing and poor elderly people, and I have a tape of a talk my mother gave to a charitable group devoted to the needs of children." (p. xxvi)

Who are the people in your life you consider gifts? How did the values they embody and their principled living influence your development?

Your reflections, conversations, and journal writing act as a wetstone in sharpening your awareness of gifts you bring to others each day. As a student or intern teacher, do you discover being and doing things you never expected of yourself? Are you moved to act, to help, to instruct and assist students and colleagues? These experiences are invitations to learn about the abilities and characteristics—gifts—that you may not have been aware of possessing! Have you thought or said, "I didn't know I could do it!" Can you name a gift you recently discovered? Teaching uses all of your gifts, and your awareness of these gifts better enables you to direct and expand their use.

From whence did these gifts come? Your talents and abilities are justifiably treasured and remembering them you feel enriched. Perhaps earlier generations passed these gifts to you and they became your heritage. Preservice teachers involved in service learning are reported to have gained in their social and personal responsibility, moral reasoning, and self-esteem. Opportunities to reflect on what they learned from service-centered activities and the total impact of these experiences contributed even more to their personal development (Root, 1997). Do your experiences within the school community bear out this type of learning for you? Acknowledging and using your talents and gifts enables you to develop an attitude of gratitude.

RECOGNIZING YOUR GIFTS AND SYSTEMS OF SUPPORT

The media repeatedly reminds us that we are a nation of power and luxury compared with many other countries throughout the world. Once a year, particularly at Thanksgiving, we are reminded to count our blessings. Among these blessings are the founding fathers' and mothers' ideals of freedom, human rights, and justice for all. You can name heroes, heroines, and saints whose lives and words embody these ideals and continue to inspire. Taking time to reflect briefly and affirm ourselves reminds us that our gifts are indeed bountiful.

On a more personal basis, consider the support systems you have come to count on: your family, your education, your moral convictions. Contrast these with what you may see in the classroom. As a student or intern teacher you may be surprised at the level of isolation some children and adolescents live with daily. Some may know little of the "good life," and you marvel at their resilience. You may be surprised at the amount of neglect experienced by children and adolescents in your school. In this land of plenty you recognize that a sense of family is not necessarily present in the lives of some youth. Perhaps you note that a sense of pride and approval is not part of every student's experience. Their eyes and their interactions tell you volumes about their needs to communicate and longing to be accepted.

TREASURING YOUR GIFTS

This activity asks you to take a few minutes to consider your gifts, and name two or three that you prize. These could be people who have always been there for you—your parents, extended family members, friends, a teacher, a neighbor, or a member of your church, synagogue, or mosque. There may be events and memories you treasure, times when others recognized and praised your special abilities. From conversations and interactions with others you realize that you have a positive attitude toward yourself, toward others, and toward life's challenges. You take risks, possess a vision of what you want to become, and are determined to move ahead. What gifts have brought you to this time in your life? Who are the people who inspired, motivated, supported, and believed in you? Using the space below, list the persons, abilities, and events you consider the treasured gifts to which you credit much of who you are and what you have to give as a teacher.

Seminar Facilitator Task

You may want to provide student or intern teachers with special materials for listing their gifts. Appendix B contains a wrapped-gift design that may be copied and distributed to students.

_____

_____

_____

Discussion Questions

1. Describe some gifts you deeply value and are most grateful to have. Which of your gifts do you want to share with students? With teachers and other members of the school community?
2. What student or intern teaching experiences have helped you recognize your gifts? Without your current experiences, which gifts might you ignore and take for granted?
3. Consider these principles of the teaching profession: honesty, fairness, protection of the weak, and respect for all people. Select the principles you see as especially important for you to practice and explain the reasons for your choice.
4. When considering the role of teachers in preparing citizens for a democratic society, what would you add to the list of professional teaching principles?

Focus Two

You are assuming a more active role as teacher and becoming responsible for the class instruction. How exciting! What an awesome feeling! You have worked so hard to develop the necessary characteristics and skills to become an effective teacher. In **Focus One** you may have found it easy to identify the strengths, gifts, and talents you have as a classroom teacher. **Focus Two** challenges you to identify areas of need in terms of the professional knowledge, skills, and dispositions that enable you to positively impact student learning. After identifying these areas, you may feel at a loss about how you can get the advice, assistance, and support necessary to transform yourself into the teacher you dream of becoming. One route to this transformation is through critical reflection.

Throughout your beginning teaching experience, you are reviewing and monitoring your goals and expectations, assessing what progress is made, and deciding what reinforcement is needed. All strengthen your critical reflective practice because they increase your confidence and competence in the teaching role. As a perceptive observer and a full participant in the learning process, you gradually assume more responsibility for all aspects of instruction and assessment. You are planning, preparing all the materials and activities, and teaching learners with varied talents and needs. You are also realistic and realize the commitment and energy it takes to fulfill this demanding role of teacher.

We have defined critical reflection as a reasoned response through either preplanned or spontaneous but conscious actions. In recalling learning from liberal arts and educational courses and previous work with students, you are developing your teacher behaviors within the classroom and integrating your knowledge and experience. Critical reflection on your classroom practices encourages growth. Learning to teach well is a result of critical reflective practice.

APPLICATION: REFLECTING ON AND EVALUATING TEACHING

Critical reflection requires looking back, reviewing goals and priorities, and continually asking questions: What have I learned? How has this learning helped me? What are the implications embedded in this teaching experience for my students? What external or environmental forces are at work helping shape what I/we do in the classroom? How do I bring about change in the classroom that may benefit student learning when it is not *my* classroom? Bridging theory and practice is a gradual process requiring continuous and systematic focus, trial and error, and critical reflection.

Reflection and Self-Assessment

Reflection and self-assessment are highly regarded among researchers as useful tools to record your professional journey, progress, and levels of mastery of the teaching tasks you are expected to perform: planning, implementing instruction, assessing learning, creating and managing the learning environment, and reflecting on and evaluating instruction. Reflecting on specific learning activities you make available to students offers you the opportunity to review what you planned and carried out in the classroom and assess its effectiveness with regard to its impact on student learning. Self-analysis through reflective journaling can lead you to ask yourself critical questions about your teaching methods, the content, the students you teach, and the environment in which teaching and learning take place historically, politically, economically, and socially. Deep reflection leads to critical reflection about pedagogy and best practice, and ultimately affects your intellectual decisions and the moral and ethical actions you take in the classroom.

According to Farrell (2001) and Yost, Sentner, and Forlenza-Bailey (2000), critical reflection challenges you to move beyond what they call stage one in your reflective journal writing toward more critical reflection.

- **Stage one** refers to reflections that are primarily descriptions of classroom activities and learners, or reports about the applications of skills and technical knowledge you have gained.
- **Stage two** of reflection is deeper, and a higher level of consciousness and interaction with teaching and learning is revealed by your responses to assumptions and beliefs you have about teaching, the reality of classroom life, and your understanding about your impact on student learning, motivation, and classroom climate.
- **Stage three** is termed critical reflection. The writer is able to engage in self-dialogue more purposefully and analytically to reveal the holistic nature of teaching and learning by examining, questioning, and investigating through action research what is taught, how it is taught, why it is taught, and the possibility of teaching differently. At this level of inquiry you begin to interact more deeply to fully experience and learn from teaching, and seek answers to classroom problems, issues, and challenges.

New information, knowledge, and insights gained through experience and analysis of the teacher's roles and responsibilities enable novice teachers to take the steps necessary to place learners and their needs at the forefront of instructional practice. Content, pedagogy, and practice are more synergetic and student or intern teachers are better prepared to teach and learn if they use critical reflection as a tool to enhance their performance as professionals. The purpose of critical reflection is to provide yourself a mirror or lens through which you can critically examine the interlocking variables at play in your day-to-day experience as teacher, and use your insights and knowledge to make informed ethical and moral decisions relative to classroom life (Yost et al., 2000). Levels one and two speak to "reflection on actions" in the classroom; level three involves "reflection for action." The ultimate goal of critical reflection is individual cognitive change that leads to action—action taken to empower your own students by providing an equitable and quality education for each of them.

Moving Toward Critical Reflection

Quality performance and continuous growth require critical self-reflection, assessment, and analysis. Conferences with your classroom and university supervising teacher—in which you share reflections, successes, concerns, suggestions, and future plans—are intended to help you progress and become comfortable, competent, and confident. Supervisors' encouragement and constructive comments reinforce your efforts in the classroom, but there is a need for you to look beyond these exchanges to analyze the underlying structure of what, how, and why you teach the way you do.

- Are you able to connect what you do with researched-based best practices and articulate the rationale for your actions in the classroom?
- Are you innovative in your teaching because you have a solid philosophical foundation and understanding of theories that drive your practice?
- Do you imitate what your supervising teachers do in the classroom, or an old favorite you had as a third grader or sophomore in high school?

These are important questions to ask yourself as you move ever forward toward the professional teacher you dream of becoming. Responding to these questions will help you understand the "why" of what you do in the classroom and challenge you to cross-examine yourself, your thinking, your philosophy of teaching and learning, and your practice. It is our hope that you experience some sort of cognitive dissonance or disequilibrium, for that is the place in which new opportunities for learning are born!

Making the Implicit, Explicit

One of the best ways to begin a critical examination and reflection about classroom teaching and learning is to share with peers and other professionals your questions and concerns, and even the action research you are undertaking. Feedback from others is critical to developing new questions and gaining new insights and information. You may have meaningful conversations with your supervising and cooperative teachers; documenting that which you find helpful will allow you to keep constructive feedback in your conscious mind and work toward desired outcomes in your teaching. Articulating and writing about your concerns, successes, and questions during your student/intern teaching experience, and making connections about what you know and do in the classroom to current educational research, brings you to the threshold of critical reflection. You are explicitly stating what may have been hidden from you earlier in your experience. Making what is implicit in your teaching explicit allows you to critically examine all of the corners of your praxis to find patterns and gaps in your teaching so you can respond to them appropriately (Ethell & McMeniman, 2000). This can allow you to challenge your old assumptions about teaching and learning so you can get about the business of improving your teaching in ways that impact student learning.

Making what is implicit explicit is a tall order. We recommend that you watch your cooperating teacher or other educators in your building teach a lesson and then engage them in dialogue not only about the content taught, but also about the decision-making process that led to *how* it was taught and *why* it was taught. Getting inside your cooperating teacher's mind-set by asking her to model her thinking processes or walk you through a decision-making process is instrumental in your growth as a professional. Tom (1997) calls this "transparency of practice" and you can immediately see the implications for you as student or intern teacher. Your ability to articulate *why* you choose an instructional method or strategy to use in a particular class with a particular set of learners places you on the high road toward professionalism. You understand the critical difference between explaining to a peer or superior your rationale or justification for implementing a new strategy or method of teaching, instead of saying, "The students love it! And it's *so* much fun!" The measure is in the degree or level of professional language used to express your theoretical knowledge and its connection to best practice. That sets you apart from those who teach for "fun" and puts you in the league of those who teach purposefully and mindfully and still manage to make learning fun for students.

Helping Learners Become Reflective

Influencing the development of your students' learning each day is a tremendous opportunity for you as teacher. When students see you excited and eager to learn new things, they become motivated to become active learners. Reflecting with students, probing to find out what they learn from assigned activities, who their favorite character is and why, how the experiment could have different results, and what approach the students used to solve the problem encourages the reflective process. Reflection is actually modeled for the students. Such thinking, open-mindedness, discernment, rational judgment, and creativity transfers to other aspects of students' lives. Teaching students to become critical reflective thinkers enables them to take more responsibility for their learning and become active participants in the process.

What are some strategies to increase reflective practice among your students? Adapting Van de Walle's (2001) suggestions to structure mathematical lessons promoting reflective thought, are generalized to address all areas of the curriculum. You may find them useful in assessing whether you are encouraging reflective thinking among your students. To what degree do you:

- create a rich and safe learning climate?
- pose worthwhile, engaging instructional tasks?
- use well-planned cooperative learning groups?
- use models, multimedia, and physical materials as "thinker tools"?
- encourage thoughtful discussion and writing?
- require students to defend and explain their responses?
- listen actively?

Careful analysis and reflection are necessary to guarantee learning. Journal writing, group work, higher level questions, projects, presentations, problem-based learning, discussions, and creative homework assignments are ways students may demonstrate reflective critical thinking. Students who are critical thinkers (students who think about their own processes for thinking and decision making) and independent learners are the hallmarks of quality education. Incorporating reflection into your objectives leads students toward deeper insights, whatever the topic of study. Helping young people become reflective and discerning learners gives them a sense of confidence and ownership about personal learning. It also makes them accountable and more responsible for learning, individually and collectively.

Internalizing Reflective Practice

You want to try so many new strategies and classroom activities! Looking at the assessment results of your lesson or unit, you might ask yourself a number of questions to direct your instruction in meaningful ways:

- Was this the best strategy to use for the content I taught?
- Did I know the backgrounds of my students, recognize the experiences they bring to class with them, and discern how those experiences impact or impede their individual learning?
- Did I build or extend the background knowledge of my students by creating learning experiences to help them better grasp the new concepts I presented?
- Perhaps if I used cooperative learning groups students would be more engaged in the discussion . . . but am I prepared to implement this type of learning in my classes?
- Why was student writing not up to standard?
- Have I modeled my own writing and thought processes to help my students make the connections between writing in school and outside school?
- Have I given them purposes for reading and writing by connecting these skills to the real world in which they live?
- What cultural or socioeconomic barriers or roadblocks are keeping some students from learning to the degree they should to function in mainstream society?

Questions such as these demonstrate how you are internalizing reflective practices and becoming a more critical reflector with each new teaching and learning experience.

Reflective Teaching Techniques

You are in a setting with extensive opportunities to practice reflection. During this beginning teacher experience, trying out new ideas, instructional strategies, and assessment instruments and sharing your planning and self-assessment with your supervising teacher and university supervisor reveal your commitment to reflective practice. You have a desire to hone your critical reflective skills, and wonder how to assess your own strategies.

Yost and Sentner (2000) and Ross, Bondy, and Kyle (1993) describe characteristics and abilities essential to developing critical reflective techniques:

- Demonstrate introspection, responsibility, and open-mindedness.
- See things from multiple perspectives.
- Use adequate evidence to support or assess decisions.
- Use educational, ethical, and practical criteria.
- Implement critical self-evaluation and metacognitive practices, and make a connection between theory and practice.

You are asking reflective questions:

- What do my students need?
- How will I plan for these needs?
- Why am I selecting these activities?
- What approach will I use to communicate this concept?
- Which assessment instruments will I use to determine how well my students are learning?
- Why are some students still not engaged?
- What can I do differently to keep my students focused?

All of these questions assist you in looking at ways to expand and deepen your knowledge of the learners, content, and instructional and management skills. Reflective questions result in answers or movement toward more student-centered teaching.

Journaling and conferencing with your classroom and university supervising teachers, administrators and other school personnel, colleagues, and parents provide extensive opportunities for reflective practice. You have been asked to share specific responses to questions relating to best practice throughout your student or intern teaching experience. By writing journal entries regarding specific assigned activities, you are analyzing classroom events, testing your beliefs, and building your educational philosophy. Participating in cooperative groups, and testing and discussing educational issues with your colleagues, brings you into contact with new ideas and different perspectives, and assists you as you engage in critical reflection. Continually collecting evidence about student learning leads you to make wise choices and ethical decisions in the classroom, identify strengths and weaknesses in your instructional decisions, and analyze ways to improve your teaching. As a promising effective teacher, you will never be satisfied with the status quo.

As a reflective beginning teacher, you are aligning instructional practices with major outcomes designed to facilitate effective instruction outlined by state and national standards. Learning to teach using those outcomes and standards allows you to review and reflect (self-assess) your teaching. To what extent are you impacting student learning by:

- designing and planning instruction and learning climates that develop student abilities?
- introducing, implementing, and managing instruction that develops student abilities?
- assessing and communicating learning results to students and parents or guardians?
- reflecting and assessing teaching-learning situations or programs?
- collaborating with colleagues, parents, and others?
- engaging in professional development?
- demonstrating knowledge of subject matter?

Beliefs about teaching and learning are built over a lifetime. Teachers who approach teaching and reinvent themselves through critical reflection often view themselves as problem solvers and even change agents. Meeting the challenges of today's classrooms in terms of diversity among learners, national and state standards, and accountability will require you to have a solid knowledge base, strong philosophical beliefs, and interactions with learners from diverse backgrounds and experiences. Your talents and resourcefulness, resiliency and knowledge, experience and vision are all necessary to the future of education.

There is a sense of movement in the field—movement toward change and innovation in teaching due to the influx of current educational research that cries out for educational change. According to Rust (1993) there is often a sense of excitement and apprehension in the way individuals greet change. We expect you to meet the challenges of your student or intern teaching experience by analyzing it through critical reflective practice. We expect you to take on leadership roles today and in the near future as education struggles to redefine itself amid the political and economic forces bent on shaping policy.

ASSIGNED ACTIVITIES

In your journal, critically reflect (for self-assessment purposes) on your instructional behaviors and examine class instruction during one setting each day from lesson preparation through assessment and reflection. Include the following components:

- grouping for instruction
- content area and concept, skill, or process
- instructional resources and materials
- students' special needs
- objectives, outcomes, expectations
- introduction, anticipatory set, advance organizer
- strategies and procedures (direct instruction, group investigation, cooperative group discussion, learning centers, creative problem solving, multimedia presentation)
- management of learning environment and student behavior
- closure, transition
- learning assessment
- assignment

SUMMARY

Focus One provided you an opportunity to examine your individual talents and gifts as teacher. In addition to seeing your role as collaborator, colleague, leader, decision maker, and learner, you can also identify the skills you have that guarantee your success in these roles. Naming and owning your gifts and talents is not an easy task for some, especially if you are gradually becoming aware of what you have to offer others. You may have surprised yourself by more freely sharing your ideas, asking for suggestions, and voicing your beliefs. You realize that to become the teacher to which you aspire, you cannot flourish in isolation. Reaching out to others validates your gifts and talents as you begin to establish a close network of colleagues. This network paves the way toward collaborative endeavors such as solving school problems and making long-term decisions that affect learners.

When you become self-reflective, self-evaluative, you think deeply about every aspect of your teaching. Your everyday teaching provides ample experiences to analyze and determine strengths and areas needing improvement. Keeping a journal of your thoughts and feelings about your teaching is an additional means of self-evaluation. Studying and analyzing your teaching moves you toward becoming, as Cruickshank (1987) says, "a thoughtful and wise teacher."

FOLLOW-UP QUESTIONS AND SHARED INSIGHTS

Throughout your beginning teacher experience the activities emphasized reflection and evaluation of your teaching behaviors. You journaled comments on specific components of your instructional performance and initiated change where necessary. The following questions will aid in sharing your reflective evaluation of the lesson using the components from your **Assigned Activities.**

1. To what extent did you consider the diversity among learners in preparation for this lesson? How are you providing for the individual learner?
2. Do the materials and procedures match your objectives or learning outcomes for the lesson taught? What is the learning value of the activities planned for this lesson?
3. To what extent do you assess student performance using the established criteria and scoring guides consistent with the school system performance assessment program?
4. In what ways do you promote student reflective self-assessment?
5. What are the strengths you exhibit in your teaching performance? What teaching strategies reinforce your creativity?
6. What areas of the curriculum present your greatest challenge?
7. Discuss your growth as a reflective self-evaluator in making decisions about curriculum content, classroom management, collaborative teaching, and performance assessment.

Portfolio Tasks

Throughout this text you are encouraged to practice reflection on the complex task of learning to teach. The portfolio tasks in this chapter ask you to demonstrate your ability to self-assess as addressed in INTASC Performance Standard 9. New Teacher Standards V and VII (State) may also be of assistance in your documentation.

Reflecting On and Evaluating Teaching and Learning

INTASC Performance Standards

Standard 9: The teacher is a reflective practitioner who continually evaluates the effects of his or her choices and actions on others (students, parents, and other professionals in the learning community) and who actively seeks out opportunities to grow professionally.

Performance Guidelines

Teachers as reflective learners accurately assess, analyze, and make appropriate changes to instruction. Read the following guidelines and submit the evidence described in step 7.

1. Provide three lesson plans you have taught with learner academic expectations or objectives, course content, and core concepts identified.
2. Refer to your lesson plans as evidence of meeting performance criteria for your first portfolio task as you make your selection.
3. Reflect on different classes or content areas in your choice of plans.

4. Evaluate the effectiveness of the learning experiences for your students.
5. Reflect on your instructional strategies and your interaction with students throughout the lesson.
6. Describe how you would improve student learning.
7. Submit **evidence** to include the following:
   - a copy of three lesson plans (refer to lesson plans from Portfolio Tasks in Chapter 3)
   - evaluation of student learning experiences in the lesson
   - self-evaluation as you reflect on the teaching experience
   - description of changes you would make

Performance Criteria

The quality of your entry will be assessed to the extent that evidence provided:

- Accurately assesses, analyzes, and communicates the effectiveness of instruction and makes appropriate changes to improve student learning.
- Analyzes and evaluates the effects of learning experiences on individuals and on the class as a whole, and makes appropriate changes to improve student learning.

Journal Excerpts

High School

"I am now responding to freshmen and sophomores concerning their writing portfolios. I really enjoy learning to do this and I feel it's one of my strengths. I do have a tendency to put too much information on student evaluations and this can overwhelm them. So, I'm really working on choosing the most important things the students need to work on. I try to stay positive and always find something good about each piece I see. It is hard, draining work to respond to everything; however, students have put a lot of time into their writing and it deserves my time as well. This is making me feel much more prepared to teach and evaluate."

"I think I showed productive leadership in an English Department meeting today. I shared with others a creative group activity for teaching my freshmen how to write a letter to the newspaper editor. All freshmen have to write this letter. I suggested topics such as sports, teen smoking, and others they were interested in. I made copies of some examples of student work and handed them out at the meeting. Sharing ideas is what being a good department member is all about."

"I went over the answers to the Diagnostic Tests for grammar using basic presentation skills. I discussed *why* we review grammar since I wanted them to know the *purpose* of this lesson and see its relevance. I had to review basic grammar rules before feeling comfortable answering the students' questions. I had written out reasons, page numbers for all answers so I could effectively explain it to the students. As a form of reinforcement I asked students to explain *why* they answered as they did. Teaching grammar at first glance seems a very simple task. I thought, 'I'm an English major. This should be easy.' Once again I was wrong. I had to go back and relearn basic grammar rules in order to be confident in teaching them to the sophomores. I had to write grammar rules and page numbers just to teach the basic rules I take for granted!"

"Wow! I think my emotions, fatigue, confidence, cluelessness, happiness, compassion, anxiety, detachment, etc. . . . are all swirling around endlessly! My student teaching is rapidly drawing to a close and I think I have grown tremendously. It is going to be extremely sad to leave. I'll miss it."

Middle School

"The peer mediation activities were excellent. It was such a valuable educational experience for the students and for me! I was totally engaged in the discussions and I enjoyed participating every chance I got. Mrs. H. and I even participated as disputants in a mock mediation. The students got a big kick out it. I think it helped them grasp the idea. These skills will benefit me in the future. Conflict resolution is a skill we all need. I think it is encouraging that these middle schoolers care enough to be part of the solution to the problem of violence in schools."

"After I taught sixth period Ms. P.J. gave me a note about my teaching and I asked for more critiquing. She helped me out by saying that I had left out some minor details, and when I used the overhead I looked at students to my left, but needed to keep eye contact with others as well. She praised my getting a girl on task who was talking and couldn't answer the question I asked. I had stayed with the student until she responded to the question."

"I used to think closure came at the end of the lesson—boy was I wrong! I sometimes use closure as part of a transition at the end of each activity such as a review and before giving new material. I have also used closure after explaining projects and writing assignments and at the end of class or group discussions. This is something that I have gotten good at over the last few months. I often use the agenda that is written on the board to help students make the transition from one activity to another. Closure is important because it gives students a sense of accomplishment and if done well is a form of reflection."

Elementary School

"I taught the math lesson and it went well. I am continuing to focus on my strengths—planning well, providing an overview, and I even included closure. I have found that keeping students involved in the lesson by varying the responses keeps them on-task. I'm also working on some of my 'weaknesses,' such as circulating more."

"I taught a chapter review preparing students for tomorrow's test. I felt rushed and forgot to go over the directions for each problem. The students had many questions so we spent extra time. Mrs. D. was called out by the vice principal and couldn't help me deal with the problem at the time. This lesson went poorly but I think it was good for me to experience this. I think that I recovered and the important thing for me to remember is to take my time and not get rushed."

"I accomplished another goal that was that I pretended that I was the only teacher in the room, and many times I was! I directed the instruction and moved students to and from places such as the bathroom and P.E. I took initiative in beginning and ending tasks, and in following through with rules and consequences. I had a much better day because of this. The students listened to me because I asserted myself and believed that I was in charge. I feel much better about myself when I assume my role in this way."

Special Education

"Student behavior was not awful today but it was not as good as usual. We had three students go to the center, but they all walked themselves. Although I had been responding to student behavior pretty well before, I got more forceful today. For some reason they were wound up. I never had to be very forceful before, but they responded well to me when I was. I took more points than usual and gave two students tickets (a few problems on a worksheet). This calmed down the students and things went well."

"I am getting very attached to some of these kids. Every day it gets harder and harder to leave their problems at school. The environment some of these kids live in—it's a wonder they behave as well as they do. In order to reach these students I realize I have to relate to them personally while remaining professional. When I do this, it is very difficult to separate myself from their problems."

"Today was a good day although I have come to realize that I really need to set goals and a schedule for myself. I feel that by setting a schedule I can keep the students and myself in line. I really have a hard time moving the learners along, but I think setting time limits on activities contributes to their ability to attend to tasks."

REFERENCES AND SUGGESTED READINGS

Barth, R. S. (1990). *Improving schools from within.* San Francisco: Jossey-Bass.

Brubacher, J. W., Case, C. W., & Reagan, T. G. (1994). *Becoming a reflective educator: How to build a culture of inquiry in the schools.* Thousand Oaks, CA: Corwin Press.

Burn, K., Hagger, H., Mutton, T., & Everton, T. (2000). Beyond the concerns with self: The sophisticated thinking of beginning student teachers. *Journal of Education for Teaching, 26*(3), 259–278.

Clark, C. M. (1990). The teacher and the taught: Moral transactions in the classroom. In J. I. Goodlad, R. Soder, & K. A. Sirotnik (Eds.), *The moral dimensions of teaching.* San Francisco: Jossey-Bass.

Clark, C. M. (1995). *Thoughtful teaching.* New York: Teachers College Press.

Clift, R. T., Houston, W. R., & Pugack, M. C. (1990). *Encouraging reflective practice in education: An analysis of issues and programs.* New York: Teachers College Press.

Coles, R. (1993). *The call of service.* Boston: Houghton Mifflin.

Collier, S. T. (1999). Characteristics of reflective thought during the student teaching experience. *Journal of Teacher Education, 50*(3), 173–181.

Cruikshank, D. R. (1987). *Reflective teaching: The preparation of students of teaching.* Reston, VA: Association of Teacher Education.

Eby, J. W., & Martin, D. B. (2001). *Reflective planning, teaching, and evaluation for the elementary school* (3rd ed.). Upper Saddle River, NJ: Merrill/Prentice Hall.

Ethell, R. G., & McMeniman, M. M. (2000). Unlocking the knowledge in action of an expert practitioner. *Journal of Teacher Education, 51*(2), 87–101.

Farrell, T. S. C. (2001). Tailoring **reflection** to individual need: A **TESOL** case study. *Journal of Education for Teaching, 27*(1), 23–39.

Harmin, M. (1994). *Inspiring active learning: A handbook for teachers.* Alexandria, VA: Association for Supervision and Curriculum Development.

Henderson, J. G. (2001). *Reflective teaching: The study of your constructivist practices* (3rd ed.). Upper Saddle River, NJ: Merrill/Prentice Hall.

Jersild, A. T. (1955). *When teachers face themselves.* New York: Teachers College Press.

Osterman, K. F., & Kottkamp, R. B. (1993). *Reflective practice for educators.* Newbury Park, CA: Corwin Press.

Posner, G. J. (2001). *Field experience: A guide to reflective teaching* (5th ed.). White Plains, NY: Longman.

Root, S. C. (1997). School-based service: A review of research for teacher education. In J. A. Erickson & J. B. Anderson (Eds.), *Learning with the community.* Washington, DC: American Association of Colleges for Teacher Education.

Ross, D. D., Bondy, E., & Kyle, D. W. (1993). *Reflective teaching for student empowerment: Elementary curriculum and methods.* New York: Macmillan.

Rust, F. O. (1993). *Changing teaching, changing schools.* New York: Teachers College Press.

Rust, F. O. (2001). Professional conversations: New teachers explore teaching through conversation, story, and narrative. *Teaching and Teacher Education, 15*(4), 367–380.

Schön, D. A. (1987). *Educating the reflective practitioner: Toward a new design for teaching and learning in the professions.* San Francisco: Jossey-Bass.

Shartrand, A. M., Weiss, H. B., Kreider, H. M., & Lopez, M. E. (1997). *New skills for new schools: Preparing teachers in family involvement.* Cambridge, MA: Harvard Family Research Project.

Stern, B. S. (1997, March). *Relations among college supervisors, cooperating teachers, and student teachers in a reflective teacher education program.* Paper presented at the annual meeting of the American Educational Research Association, Chicago.

Tom, A. (1997). The deliberate relationship: A frame for talking about faculty-student relationships. *Alberta Journal of Educational Research, 43*(1), 3–21.

Van de Walle, J. A. (2001). *Elementary and middle school mathematics: Teaching developmentally.* New York: Longman.

Wilson, J., & Jan, L. W. (1993). *Thinking for themselves: Developing strategies for reflective learning.* Portsmouth, NH: Heinemann.

Yost, D. S., Sentner, S. M., & Forlenza-Bailey, A. (2000). An examination of the construct of critical reflection: Implications for teacher education programming in the 21st century. *Journal of Teacher Education, 51*(1), 39–49.

chapter
14

Continuing the Professional Journey

> " *Being a good teacher is not an end point; it is a continuous process—a process of action, a process of reflection and planning, and a process of collaboration.* "

L. A. Baloche

Expected Performance

- Examine short- and long-term goals of a professional teacher.
- Identify professional goals attempted or met.
- Share insights gained from engaging in the process of reflective practice.
- Provide evidence of performance levels achieved as student or intern teacher.
- Create a professional development plan to improve performance.

You are becoming a professional teacher! What does the descriptor *professional* mean? Your journey thus far has provided you many new and challenging experiences. Throughout this student/intern teaching experience you have participated in a variety of activities reinforcing your professional and personal growth. You are expected to develop new instructional techniques, refine your practice, and continually grow as a teacher and individual. These expectations may be imposed internally and externally. You may be quite familiar with state or local school system standards. Professional organizations offer curriculum frameworks and formats for designing and implementing instructional practices. Decisions and actions by these external groups influence your short- and long-term goals. As a partner with your supervising teacher and others, you have set professional goals for yourself prior to each lesson, and following each lesson you used these goals to assess your teaching. Critically reflective teaching and learning encourages and scaffolds lifelong learning (Rodriguez & Sjostrom, 1998). Reflective teaching promotes your dream of becoming truly professional.

PROFESSIONAL GROWTH: LOOKING INWARD

In previous chapters you examined your stages of growth beginning with the concerns you have about yourself as teacher and moving on to the concerns you hold about students' learning. This chapter engages you in the total reflective process. Asking reflective questions like "How can I change the approach to engage more of my students?" and "In what way did I improve my questioning strategies?" gets to the very heart of reflective teaching. "A teacher's understanding of others can be only as deep as the wisdom possessed when looking inward" (Jersild, 1955). Becoming increasingly critical and reflective of your teaching enhances professional growth and an understanding and acceptance of yourself and others. Likewise, your reflective modeling enables your students to become more critical and reflective in their learning tasks.

PROFESSIONAL GROWTH: PARTNERS IN THE PROCESS

Your supervising teacher and university supervisor are instrumental in guiding you on your professional journey. The feedback addressed in your conferencing with them provides specific insights into the progress you are making. These professionals, observing your instruction and interaction with students, help you consider the impact of your teaching on student learning. You have no doubt relied on their advice and suggestions in designing, planning, and implementing instructional improvements. These kinds of opportunities enhance your ability to reflect and analyze your teaching. Making curriculum and instruction adjustments necessary to ensure maximum student learning is essential for professional growth.

Administrators also help you clarify and establish your professional growth goals and assess progress toward reaching them. Communicating with these individuals as often as opportunities arise demonstrates your strengths in interpersonal skills. Requesting and preparing for classroom observations by the principal, team leader, and/or department chair provide you a variety of evaluation experiences. Observation reports and recommendations from these individuals can become part of your university credential file and give a prospective administrator a broader picture of your instructional performance. In selecting effective teachers, administrators consider teaching performance during an applicant's student or intern teaching the most important indicator of their future success as teacher (Ralph, Kesten, Lang, & Smith, 1998).

PROFESSIONAL GROWTH: A CRITICAL REFLECTION

Throughout this student or intern teaching experience you have been actively engaged in sequentially examining the process of transitioning from student or intern to teacher. Each week you considered one or more parts of this whole process. The group activities and the application sections encouraged your growth through active involvement. You continue to build a repertoire of best practice and learn to cope with many challenging situations. As you come closer to completing this student or intern teaching experience, we provide you a reflection for connecting the teaching-learning process with your next big step—becoming a professional teacher. This reflective activity is designed to help you holistically view your process and progress toward becoming a professional teacher.

You may feel pride in your past accomplishments and be energized with new perspectives for what lies ahead. The journey toward professionalism has begun! Your student or intern position has provided you numerous opportunities to document your growth toward the title *professional*. Your reflective processes have enabled you to recall with ease your experiences with planning, students, collaboration, and more. We have provided competencies to help you document your activities as an educator and showcase your work by creating a professional portfolio. The professional teacher competencies representing your student or intern teacher experience are presented in the following sections. You might want to jot down your thoughts as you move through each criteria. Onward with the journey!

Designs, Plans, and Implements Instruction (Chapters 1–13)

Compiling your portfolio during the past months is one means to connect professional development with teaching practice. Through conversations, seminar discussions, and journals you have reflected on the teaching strategies that you design, plan, and implement. You communicate evidence of your performance in all of these areas through the portfolio.

- What do you want others to know about your teaching?
- Do you see yourself as a professional teacher able to identify, plan, and implement teaching practices that are recognized as "best"?
- Which lesson plans demonstrate your best instruction?
- In what ways were you able to introduce and use technology across the curriculum?
- How does your portfolio present this aspect of you, the professional?

_____

_____

_____

_____

Accommodates Diversity (Chapters 3–11)

Believing that all students can learn is the first step in developing instructional strategies adapted to diverse learners. Treating all students with sensitivity and promoting racial unity and gender equity requires establishing a positive learning environment. Creating plans to include literature, art, music, multimedia, cooperative learning groups, community speakers, and other resources and activities contributes to cultural knowledge. Designing multiple learning experiences prepares students for working and living within a multicultural, pluralistic society.

- In what ways have you provided for classroom diversity in adapting your instruction to the cultural background, learning styles, and multiple intelligences of your students?
- How has your own ethnic, racial, gender, and cultural experiential background prepared you for teaching in a multicultural classroom?
- Would persons viewing your portfolio gain insight into your understanding and sensitivity toward other cultures and ethnic groups?

_____

_____

_____

_____

Assesses Performance (Chapters 3, 11, 13)

Reflection implies that as a professional teacher you continually assess your performance. Your student or intern teaching experience provides numerous opportunities to assess your performance class by class and to examine your teaching over a learning sequence and instructional units. Perhaps your supervising teacher and college supervisor provided suggestions and models for assessing best practice. As professionals, they observed your teaching and later in conferences guided you in looking at individual strategies and the overall instructional objectives as criteria for making assessment.

- How does your portfolio present you as a reflective professional?
- Which criteria included in your portfolio document the breadth and depth of your self-assessments?
- Have you solicited comments from administrators and others who observed your teaching?
- What written comments did you receive?
- How did these comments affect your subsequent planning and teaching?

_____

_____

_____

Identifies Personal and Psychological Needs (Chapters 1–13 Focus One)

The Focus One group activities and action plans encouraged you to identify your personal feelings, perceptions, and insights you experienced as you adjusted to different aspects of the teacher role. Role taking implies learning a set of new skills and adjusting to accompanying emotions.

- How might you communicate coping skills learned and growth in self-knowledge acquired through activities, conversations, and sharing with a variety of other professionals?
- How does your portfolio represent the growth and stretching that has occurred as the result of this student or intern teaching experience?
- How have you changed personally and professionally as a result of this experience?

_____

_____

_____

Seeks and Receives Support (Chapters 1–3, 12–13)

Professional growth occurs when persons seek and receive support. On a daily basis you engage with peers, colleagues, and other professionals within and outside the school. Perhaps you share your perceptions and learn from others through their experiences from earlier teaching years. You observe their ongoing efforts to grow as directors, guides, and advocates of students, learners, and leaders.

- How have your interactions with these individuals encouraged you to pursue self-growth and consistent improvement professionally?
- In what way have you grown more interdependent as a result of this experience?
- Toward what growth areas do you aspire?

_____

_____

_____

Collaborates With Parents, Colleagues, and Community (Chapters 2, 4, 9–12)

Collaborating with parents, assisting a colleague in presenting a school program, sponsoring a student group, and participating on a school committee would be additional evidence that you are growing professionally. Parents and guardians look to you as expert in knowing how to direct and help their son or daughter. You experienced opportunities to communicate with them about their child and to work with them toward meeting a goal you shared. Perhaps you collaborated with other teachers on your team or in your department. Your portfolio allows you to demonstrate these and other collaborating activities you engage in now and throughout this experience.

- How do you see yourself as a collaborator?
- What portfolio entries present you as a partner and team or department member?

_____

_____

_____

_____

Engages in Professional Growth Opportunities (Chapters 5, 14–15)

Perhaps you attended workshops and inservice activities during student/intern teaching. You may belong to professional groups and have even shared ideas and strategies you used successfully with your students.

- How proficient are you with integrating technology into your classes?
- What evidence is there that you continue learning a variety of teaching techniques?
- How can your portfolio communicate to those viewing it that you are a learner?

_____

_____

_____

_____

PROFESSIONAL GROWTH: THE PORTFOLIO (CHAPTERS 3, 7, 9, 11–13, 15)

Your reflection using these seven performance outcomes as guides helps you to see just where this whole process has brought you. Your portfolio is the visual demonstration of your reflections and accomplishments. We have suggested a structured format to assist you with organizing your experiences. You are free to make choices that portray your "best" practice, your rationale for the choices you make in managing your classroom, your selection of assessment instruments, your reflective response to your collaborative experiences, your problem-solving and creative approaches in working with diverse learners, and your own philosophy—what you believe about your role as teacher at this time.

Continuing the Journey: A Professional Growth Plan and Continuing Education

The reflective process used in building your portfolio is actually professional development, an ongoing process. What an outlay of effort and energy is spent in this accomplishment! You have a well-prepared document demonstrating your growth in professional knowledge and expertise.

Setting goals for your students is an experience you practice daily. Setting goals for yourself, following up your instruction with self-assessment, and determining your strengths and areas needing further improvement are part of the ongoing process for professional development. As an example, the following may be a framework for your plan:

- List one professional development goal for increasing the level of learner expectations that you set for yourself.
  Example: Provide more activities that involve problem solving.
- Name the evidence you will use to determine the level of growth made toward reaching the goal.
  Example: Introduce problem-solving activities each day as a regular part of my lessons. I will make an effort to assess one group of students each week.
- Determine a time line you will use for performing these activities.
  Example: I will research math and science ideas for a variety of examples. I plan to begin on Monday with total group and assess Group #5 on Thursday. After one month I will assess the class with a written test. The results will determine the intervals for the next month.
- Name the external monitors that will provide feedback on progress made toward the professional goals.
  Example: In this case, my plan depends on continued practice and research by retrieving information from more experienced teachers. I will ask my supervising teacher to assess my progress in this area. I am comfortable in developing a lesson for my university supervisor and conferencing about my problem-solving strategies.

Onward and Upward! Journey On!

Developing a plan of action now demonstrates commitment to professional growth. Some of the documentation will change as you meet future challenges in your first teaching position. Many states have a well-designed induction or internship program, which includes a professional development plan created by the beginning teacher. Having completed a professional development plan at this stage of your journey places you at an advantage. You are well on your way!

Continuing education is a critical component of living a professional life. As a proponent of lifelong education you value education and realize the impact learning has on cognitive development and one's ability to transform thinking that leads to thoughtful actions personally and professionally. The state in which you desire to teach may require you to obtain a master's degree in education within a given amount of time to continue teaching in the system. If so, the exit portfolio you create while student or intern teaching may be part of the application process to the college or university you apply to continue your education.

Your teaching life will be transformed by the new experiences you take on in higher education, but more important, you have classroom experience on which to anchor new learning theories and engage in action research. As a teacher, your master's work adds a deeper dimension to what you do in the classroom and provides you additional research to support the practices you choose to implement. The master's degree serves to validate your growth as a professional while it moves you forward in your praxis. Odds are, your students will cheer you on as you embark on this continuing journey, and you may never know the impact your modeling of lifelong education has on the learners in your class, their parents or guardians, and other professionals in your building.

PROFESSIONAL ORGANIZATIONS AND YOU

Teachers are members of numerous professional organizations and engage in a wide range of development initiatives with peers. Organization members formulate standards for teaching and learning for specific content areas, generate and share teaching techniques, and address issues affecting the different age levels of learners. You may already hold membership in one or more of the local, state, or national groups. Your involvement with any of these groups is a rich and ongoing source for learning and developing teaching strategies and exploring evolving issues in education.

Are you considering joining a professional organization? Will the next phase of your journey as a professional teacher involve you as a participant? Professional organizations provide multiple resources. As a member you receive journals and other publications produced by the organization and attend workshops and conferences sponsored by the organization. Members are invited to present research, ideas, and strategies at local and national sites throughout the year. Exchanges with other teachers are available through the World Wide Web. Using the Internet, you can access the Web site for each group and then join chat lines to dialogue current issues and teaching techniques with other members across the nation. The list below suggests several groups, journals, mailing lists, and Web site addresses.

American Alliance for Health, Physical Education, Recreation and Dance (AAHPERD)

> 1900 Association Dr.
> Reston, VA 20191-1598
> http://www.aahperd.org

AAHPERD consists of six national and district associations with the research consortium:

> American Association for Active Lifestyles and Fitness (AAALF)
> American Association for Health Education (AAHE)
> American Association for Leisure and Recreation (AALR)
> National Association for Girls and Women in Sport (NAGWS)
> National Association for Sport and Physical Education (NASPE)
> National Dance Association (NDA)

American Association for the Advancement of Science (AAAS)

> 1200 New York Ave. NW
> Washington, DC 20005
> http://www.aaas.org

American Chemical Society (ACS)

> Publications Support Services
> 1155 16th St. NW
> Washington, DC 20036
> http://jchemed.chem.wisc.ed

American Council on the Teaching of Foreign Languages (ACTFL)

6 Executive Plaza
Yonkers, NY 10701
http://www.actfl.org

Association for Childhood Education International (ACEI)

17904 Georgia Ave., Ste. 215
Olney, MD 20832
Journal: *Childhood Education*
http://www.udel.edu/bateman/acei

Association for Supervision and Curriculum Development (ASCD)

1703 N. Beauregard St.
Alexandria, VA 22311-1714
Journal: *Educational Leadership*
http://www.ascd.org

Council for Exceptional Children (CEC)

1110 N. Glebe Rd., Ste. 300
Arlington, VA 22201-5704
Journals: *Exceptional Children, Teaching Exceptional Children*
http://www.cec.sped.org

International Reading Association (IRA)

IRA headquarter office address:
800 Barksdale Rd.
PO Box 8139
Newark, DE 19714-8139
Journals: *The Reading Teacher;* others are available at
http://www.reading.org

International Technology Education Association (ITEA)

ITEA headquarters:
1914 Association Dr., Ste. 201
Reston, VA 20191-1539
http://www.iteawww.org

Music Teachers National Association

441 Vine St., Ste. 505
Cincinnati, OH 45202-2814
http://www.mtna.org

National Art Education Association (NAEA)

1916 Association Dr.
Reston, VA 20191-1590
Journal: *Journal of Art Education*
http://www.naea-reston.org

National Association for Gifted Children (NAGC)

1707 L St. NW, Ste. 550
Washington, DC 20036
http://www.nagc.org

National Association for the Education of Young Children (NAEYC)

1509 16th St. NW
Washington, DC 20019
Journal: *Young Children*
http://www.naeyc.org

National Association of Biology Teachers (NABT)

> 12030 Sunrise Dr., Ste. 110
> Reston, VA 20191
> http://www.nabt.org

National Council for the Social Studies (NCSS)

> 8555 16th St., Ste. 500
> Silver Springs, MD 20910
> Journal: *Social Education*
> http://www.ncss.org

National Council of Teachers of English (NCTE)
(Educators in English studies, literacy, and language arts)

> 1111 W. Kenyon Rd.
> Urbana, IL 61801-1096
> Journals: *English Journal, Primary Voices K-6, Voices from the Middle*
> http://www.ncte.org

National Council of Teachers of Mathematics (NCTM)

NCTM headquarters:

> 1906 Association Dr.
> Reston, VA 20191-1502
> Journals: *Arithmetic Teacher, Mathematics Teacher*
> http://www.nctm.org

National Council on Economic Education (NCEE)

> 1140 Avenue of the Americas
> New York, NY 10036
> http://www.nationalcouncil.org

National Middle School Association (NMSA)

> 4151 Executive Pkwy., Ste. 300
> Westerville, OH 43081
> Journal: *National Middle School Journal*
> http://www.nmsa.org

National Science Teachers Association (NSTA)

> 1840 Wilson Blvd.
> Arlington, VA 22201-3000
> Journals: *The Science Teacher, Science and Children*
> http://www.nsta.org

School Science and Mathematics Association (SSMA)

> 16734 Hamilton Ct.
> Strongsville, OH 44149-5701
> Journal: *School Science and Mathematics*
> http://www.ssma.org

Teacher Organizations: American Federation of Teachers (AFT)

> 555 New Jersey Ave. NW
> Washington, DC 20001
> Journals: *American Educator, American Teacher*
> http://www.aft.org

National Education Association (NEA)

> 1201 16th St. NW
> Washington, DC 20036
> Journals: *Today's Education, NEA Reporter*
> http://www.nea.org

Journal Excerpts

High School

"My student teaching experience has really proven how much I do know and also how much more I have to learn and develop. I realize I have certain strengths and weaknesses. As far as professional development, I think this is an ongoing (never-ending) process in becoming an effective educator. Some areas I should focus on include: classroom management and discipline, planning, less reliance on the textbook, more original and unique approaches, integration of content, the balance of quantity with quality in the English classroom. I must make future decisions such as where I want to teach and live. I guess my priorities will center around preparing my files for future employment. I've never even designed a resume. I need to decide where I want to be, and when, and how, and. . . . "

"I must admit that I was nervous about being observed this week by so many different people but everything went really well. The principal could only come to observe me during the time I was teaching freshmen. Two university supervisors from English and Education Departments came, and I had already scheduled a class for the department chair to observe me. I am very used to people coming in and observing me, so when the principal came, I was not really that nervous. I did worry about his visit because I would really love to teach here and I wanted to impress him by teaching a fine lesson. My class was very well organized and I kept students engaged the entire class period. The principal later told me he was really impressed and made other positive comments on the report that he gave me. I was on 'cloud nine' the entire day! I'm even thinking of asking the president of the school to observe me since his teaching area is English. The more people who see me teach and give me feedback the better!"

"Today was a fun and unusual day! It's the end of the quarter and we had a faculty retreat. The first talk was on mission effectiveness as it applies to our school, and then in small group discussions we tried to generate practical ways for applying the ideas. We took time to reflect and journal for ourselves. For me the day was relaxing and a great experience!"

Middle School

"Overall, I was happy with the results of the lesson. They seemed to really retain what I want them to know. A few students even offered examples of ironic things that have happened to them. Speaking of ironic, the inservice we attended was on reading in the content areas. The speaker mentioned that a good way to help students develop a schemata was to relate the reading to a story or song, which I have been doing all semester. Even if I didn't learn anything I didn't already know, the in-service was informational and validating. I was able to talk with professionals and experience a different side of school and teaching through professional development."

"I think I feel better now about how things went when I was observed today. It's hard for me to separate my personal and professional feelings. I had prepared well, I was having a *blast,* and the kids were so excited. These same students who constantly say they don't like to write or can't write were writing beautiful poetry. It makes me want to cry. I know I'm too much a perfectionist and I wanted everything to be perfect. I should know better. There's always something that can be improved. I agree with all of the comments that were made on my observation form—positive things I did in the lesson and areas needing improvement. This is the purpose of 'reflective teaching'! The lesson wasn't perfect, but I will continue to learn and refine my skills."

Elementary School

"Our inservice today was given by a teacher from another college who gave a workshop on Claris Works. We created spreadsheets, made graphs, and inserted spreadsheets into a word processing document. Some teachers became frustrated and gave up. Since this was somewhat a review for me from our education classes, I did not get much new information from the meeting. In fact, I was helping others around me who were not as familiar with this program as I am. I felt good being able to do so. Computers are a difficult tool to master and quite frustrating when one doesn't catch on quickly and the instructor moves ahead. It is interesting to note that adults are like students when first learning a new skill."

"This past week I had the opportunity to attend the Regional Conference. We spent the evening talking in our hotel rooms. It was so interesting for me to see how different these teachers were outside of the classroom. My supervising teacher and I walked to the conference center and I visited the exhibits before the general session began. Seeing so much free stuff was exciting! I wanted to attend a session on Portfolios but there wasn't room. I went to a session on integrating Science and Literature and another on Mathematics and Literature. I received copies of several lesson plans which may be useful in the future. A session on phonics was terrific and the presenter provided a packet of wonderful ideas for creatively teaching it. I never knew there were so many interesting ways to teach phonics. Throughout the conference people commented on how young I looked and some took a personal interest in talking with me. Teachers from the school told me they were impressed that I was willing to attend the conference. I responded that I was impressed that they provided me the opportunity to attend."

"An area in which I am a bit cautious is Science, and more specifically knowing how to help students' understand scientific methods to solve real-life problems. There is no doubt that becoming more comfortable and confident with the subject of science is vital to my becoming a successful teacher. I find throughout my student teaching experience that when there is an area where I am uncomfortable, the best thing to do is get help and assistance from those who are comfortable and successful in that area. In this case my plan involves requesting information from more experienced teachers. It would also be helpful when planning a lesson to consult more than one source for ideas such as NCTS, and journal articles. In this way I will have 'more than one trick in my bag' . . . "

Special Education

"After school we had departmental meetings. It was neat to meet the other ECE teachers. I felt overwhelmed hearing them talk about the paper work they had to do for some students. The new IEP forms will take some getting used to, but will be worth our effort for our students. They did find out that they fill out a different form for the three-year review than they complete for the original form. There are so many forms for different things and it's easy to be confused. I plan to watch Ms. K. as she completes a few forms and ask questions so I will better understand how to do it."

"I was privileged to attend the Council for Exceptional Children national conference these past two years with a group of Education students. This year I went to a presentation by a specialist in behavior disorders. He had researched strategies to help retain student attention. His research was current and reality based giving us the best intervention techniques to use with students. I always learn so much at these sessions."

"I can see that I have grown professionally by implementing a variety of teaching strategies. This enhances the learning process because every child has his or her own unique learning style. I believe that good teachers use different methods and also integrate technology to make learning more interesting. Special education students need more visuals and hands-on experiences and I try to have them in cooperative groups each day. As a result, I have noticed the students are gaining confidence as well as feelings of success. I want to set high expectations for my students and challenge them to go beyond the requirements of each lesson."

References and Suggested Readings

Baloche, L. A. (1998). *The cooperative classroom: Empowering learning.* Upper Saddle River, NJ: Prentice Hall.

Beattie, M. (1997). Fostering reflective practice in teacher education: Inquiry as a framework for the construction of a professional knowledge in teaching. *Asia-Pacific Journal of Teacher Education, 25*(2), 111–128.

Borko, H., Michalec, P., Timmons, M., & Siddle, J. (1997). Student teaching portfolios: A tool for promoting reflective practice. *Journal of Teacher Education, 48*(5), 345–357.

Brennan, S., Roberts, R., Thames, W., & Miller, K. H. (1998). *Guiding and assessing teacher effectiveness: A handbook for Kentucky teacher internship program participants* (5th ed.). Frankfort, KY: Office of Teacher Education and Certification Education Professional Standards Board.

Bullough, R. V., & Gitlin, A. (1995). *Becoming a student of teaching: Methodologies for exploring self and school context.* New York: Garland.

Danielson, C., & McGreal, T. L. (2000). *Teacher evaluation: Enhancing professional practice.* Alexandria, VA: Association for Supervision and Curriculum Development, and Princeton, NJ: Educational Testing Service.

Darling-Hammond, L. (1997). *Doing what matters most: Investing in quality teaching.* New York: National Commission on Teaching & America's Future.

Davies, R., & Ferguson, J. (1997). Teachers' views of the role of initial teacher education in developing their profession. *Journal of Education for Teaching, 23*(1), 39–56.

Fuller, F. F. (1970). *Personalized education for teachers: An introduction for teacher educators.* Austin: University of Texas, R&D Center for Teacher Education. (ERIC Document Reproduction Service No. ED048105)

Huling-Austin, L. (1992). Research on learning to teach: Implications for teacher induction and mentoring programs. *Journal of Teacher Education, 43*(3), 173–180.

Jersild, A. T. (1955). *When teachers face themselves.* New York: Teachers College Press.

Louis, D. S., Marks, H. M., & Kruse, S. (1996). Teachers' professional community in restructuring schools. *American Educational Research Journal, 33,* 757–798.

Ralph, E. G., Kesten, C., Lang, H., & Smith, D. (1998). Hiring new teachers: What do school districts look for? *Journal of Teacher Education 49*(1), 47–56.

Rodriguez, Y. E. G., & Sjostrom, B. R. (1998). Critical reflection for professional development: A comparative study of nontraditional adult and traditional student teachers. *Journal of Teacher Education, 49*(3), 177–186.

Wolf, K., Whinery, B., & Hagerty, P. (1995). Teaching portfolios and portfolio conversations for teacher educators and teachers. *Action in Teacher Education, 17*(1), 30–39.

Zeichner, K. (1987). Preparing reflective teachers: An overview of instructional strategies which have been employed in preservice teacher education. *International Journal of Educational Research, 11*(5), 565–575.

Zeichner, K., & Tabachnick, B. R. (Eds.). (1991). *Issues and practices in inquiry-oriented teacher education.* London: Falmer Press.

Zubizarreta, J. (1994). Teaching portfolios and the beginning teacher. *Phi Delta Kappan, 76*(5), 323–326.

chapter
15

Searching for a Professional Teaching Position Begins With You!

" . . . unlike the paper-based portfolio, the electronic portfolio is a multimedia approach that allows the teacher to present teaching, learning, and reflective artifacts in a variety of formats . . . "

P.M. Costantino and M.N. De Lorenzo

Expected Performance

- Create a professional portfolio— hardcopy, electronic, or digital.
- Contact your career services center.
- Develop a resume and cover letters.
- Inquire about teaching positions.
- Prepare for interviews.
- Complete the certification process.

Your journey now takes you beyond your student or intern teaching experience. Equipped with materials for compiling your professional portfolio, you are eager to continue moving into your first teaching position. The search for a professional teaching position begins with you! We intend that this chapter guide you in efficiently and effectively designing and creating materials you will use in pursuing a teaching position. The chapter format changes to accommodate the different activities that engage you as you step into a different whirlwind, that of entering the profession of teaching. You will want to consider tasks such as creating a portfolio, contacting the career services center at your college or university, developing a resume and cover letters, inquiring about teaching positions, preparing for interviews, and completing the certification process. Some questions to ask yourself include:

- How do I create a professional portfolio?
- Will the career services center assist me with inquiries about teaching positions in selected schools or school districts?
- How do I go about developing a resume?
- What is the best way to prepare for an interview?
- Who can answer my questions about completing the state certification process?

This chapter provides information and suggestions on these important questions. In addition, the chapter provides both print and electronic sources to assist you in researching, planning, and developing materials. These will enable you to seek that position you have dreamed about for years!

PROFESSIONAL PORTFOLIO

Portfolios are given different names and descriptions depending on the purpose they serve. During your teacher education program you may have developed portfolios for different purposes, for example, to communicate your goals and attitudes about teaching and to document your growth in the process of becoming a teacher. Some teacher preparation institutions require portfolios of their graduates, and some states require portfolios as partial assessment of program-completers having met state or national standards. Beginning with **Portfolio Tips** in Chapter 3 of this text and throughout your student or intern teaching experience, you have had the opportunity to document your teaching performance and the way you met the criteria stated by state or national standards that are recognized "good practice" by professional educators. A **professional portfolio** can help communicate to prospective employers your disposition, knowledge, skills, and overall competence as teacher. What impression do you want to leave with prospective employers as they read your portfolio to determine if you are a teacher who would be a good fit at their school? Where do you begin?

Throughout your student or intern teaching experience you consistently collected samples of your planning and teaching. In addition, you collected examples of student work and accompanying assessments, examples of your collaborations with parents and experienced teachers, and your written reflections about your performance. **Portfolio tips** and assignments from prior chapters are intended to help you create and collect illustrations, photos of classroom events, students' musical performances, and your own self-assessments to lend more credibility to your portfolio. Some refer to this collection as a "working" portfolio, created as evidence of performance, goal setting, and personal growth. As a beginning professional these are materials you may have stored as hard copies in files, in notebook binders, and on computer discs (Campbell, Cignetti, Melenyzer, Nettles, & Wyman, 2001).

On the other hand, you may have created and organized evidence of your performance to meet certain criteria labeled an "exit portfolio," a partial requirement documenting that you have met a certain level of mastery related to performance standards and the goals of your teacher education program (Costantino & De Lorenzo, 2002). If you have completed either an exit or working portfolio, you now have splendid resources for creating what others would call a presentation portfolio (Campbell et al., 2001) or an interview portfolio (Costantino & De Lorenzo). Because you may need to present your portfolio as part of an employment process and use it during an interview, we are calling it a professional portfolio.

We describe the professional portfolio as a compilation of your best work—completed during your student or intern teaching experience. The carefully selected entries document your performance during student or intern teaching and the professional portfolio will enhance your job-search effort. We encourage you to create, describe, and arrange these items using the Interstate New Teacher Assessment and Support Consortium (INTASC) standards or standards required by your particular state's professional standards board. While creating and organizing this easy-to-read display of your professional competence, you will want to keep in mind some of the following questions as you select and assemble the contents of your professional portfolio.

"Making portfolios an integral part of a teacher education program ... encourages ongoing professional development through reflective practice ... portfolios offer programs a tool for assessing effectiveness in promoting professional growth ..."
E.M. Willis and M.A. Davies

- **The audience:** Who will examine your professional portfolio?
- **The medium:** Is a 3-inch notebook binder, a CD-ROM, or a Web page the best medium to present materials that showcase your work with learners and other professionals?
- **Employers:** How do you determine which prospective employers prefer receiving electronic portfolios (Flanagan, 1999)?
- **Standards:** In addition to addressing the INTASC or state standards, what else would enhance the portfolio?

You are entering the teaching profession at a time known for its teacher shortage. Is there a particular school, district, or assignment with a specific group of children or youth you especially desire? Preparing a thorough portfolio requires that in addition to gathering materials, you know what prospective employers want and deeply understand how these characteristics and skills meet the needs of children and youth of the school or district. What educational issues are being addressed by the school or district where you are applying to teach? How have your teacher preparation program and your work in schools, especially student or intern teaching, enabled you to acquire the dispositions, knowledge, and skills needed to address student learning and any other issues and concerns for the school or district at this time? If the school or district where you want to teach has as its major goal the integration of technology into instruction, you might consider converting your portfolio from hard copy to an electronic or digital portfolio. Whatever you choose, you want to prepare a display that captures the interest of persons charged with the hiring process. How can you make your professional portfolio communicate and quickly inform readers about what you offer children and adolescents, and the teaching profession?

Electronic or Digital Portfolio Considerations

You might use a high-tech medium, known as the *electronic* or *digital portfolio,* for displaying your professional portfolio. The literature reports that preservice teachers displaying their abilities through electronic portfolios have an advantage in securing a teaching position and are more likely to integrate technology into instruction (Costantino & De Lorenzo, 2002; Goldsby & Fazal, 2000; Wiedmer, 1998). The electronic portfolio, like the traditional hard-copy portfolio, is a purposeful collection of work you electronically assemble and present as an exhibit of your efforts, growth, and achievements in various stages of your learning to teach. You may choose the CD-ROM format for including digital versions of assessments, photographs of working groups, illustrations, students' art and musical performances, bulletin boards, and multiple other classroom projects with accompanying narratives. A second option is the Web-based digital portfolio that incorporates Internet materials into lesson plans you taught students during your student/intern teaching experience. The CD-ROM and Web-based portfolios enable you to go beyond collecting and displaying evidence of teaching-learning tasks to provide as complete as possible a representation of your teaching competencies and a holistic view of yourself as a teacher (Goldsby & Fazal, 2000; Hurst, Wilson, & Cramer, 1998).

Benefits of the Electronically Produced Professional Portfolio

Many components of electronic portfolios are similar to those you follow in producing a hard-copy professional portfolio; however, a multimedia capacity offers additional ways to display your unique talents and abilities. For example, you may produce a Web-based digital portfolio including all the elements of a traditional portfolio and in addition, a unit with an actual set of lessons you taught in the classroom with links to photography of activities from this lesson and student work. You can link a lesson plan with other lessons, the unit overview, and to the teaching standards' criteria demonstrated throughout this lesson. Lesson plans that include embedded Web sites provide the viewer samples of your knowledge and creativity along with rationale for choosing the instruction, your assessment, and ways you might change things the next time you teach.

The electronic portfolio allows you to communicate your *reflective,* critical thinking about your reflective capabilities. During student or intern teaching you practiced through journal writing, seminar discussions and focused conversations, and dialogue with your supervising teacher or university supervisor. These can communicate your practices extremely well using the electronic portfolio (Goldsby & Fazal, 2000). Selecting resource materials from the Internet demonstrates your knowledge of content and creativity in connecting the class-

room with the outside world. The vast assortment of sources from the Internet requires you to analyze and critically choose those that truly enhance and deepen your students' understanding and learning. Using the electronic portfolio can capture the expanse of your growth, your passion for teaching, and challenges that teaching holds for you.

You benefit from developing an electronic portfolio. You have been challenged to integrate technology into instruction, reviewed and selected resources, and continuously assessed your students' success in meeting objectives you outlined. Just as you encourage self-assessment in your students, the electronic portfolio offers you an ongoing process of self-assessment. As creator of the electronic portfolio, you can acquire a deeper sense of the important role assessment plays in your development by using criteria developed by professional educators. It allows you to see your progress over a period of time.

For Whom Is the Electronic Portfolio Intended?

Teacher portfolios serve a variety of purposes and can satisfy a number of goals. Viewing electronic portfolios, employers gain insight into your knowledge and use of technology along with your personal and professional abilities, knowledge, and disposition as a teacher. Through the experience of creating an electronic portfolio you learned new ways to organize and present ideas and means for ongoing self-assessment, and have expanded your understanding of educational technology (Bartlett, 2002; Fazal, Goldsby, Cozza, Goethals, & Howard, 2001; Goldsby & Fazal, 2000).

As a student or intern teacher you are looking for a professional position. Many educators eager to bring cutting-edge ideas into the school are looking for technology-literate teachers. Viewing your electronic portfolio and interacting with you about its contents, the interviewer gets an understanding about your level of expertise and attitude toward integrating the use of technology into your teaching. An electronic portfolio can serve your needs as you enter teaching and be modified as evidence of professional growth during your first year of teaching and beyond.

Organizing Your Portfolio

Deciding whether to create a traditional-type portfolio using a large notebook binder or an electronic portfolio is an important decision. You most likely made this decision early during your student or intern teaching experience. The following considerations can help you decide on the type of portfolio to select, and ways to organize the contents of your professional portfolio.

Traditional or Electronic Medium

Determine the medium you will use depending upon the resources available. A traditional professional portfolio requires you to have a notebook binder large enough to accommodate all of the contents. Deciding to develop an electronic professional portfolio demands that you consider needs in these areas:

1. Knowledge of technology; perhaps a prior course or a technology workshop taken concurrently
2. Extensive access to different equipment and software programs
3. Sufficient time for entering and arranging the materials you have decided to include
4. Direction from individuals knowledgeable of the technology used and of the contents portfolios need to display
5. Sufficient lead time to complete your portfolio prior to sending it to prospective employers

Organizational Categories   Select and organize materials around standards or core propositions (National Board for Professional Teaching Standards [NBPTS]) that demonstrate your knowledge, skills, dispositions, and commitments that enhance student learning. Study the criteria stated under each of the standards and determine what evidence you want to provide that addresses each criterion.

Collection of Materials   Set aside all materials that may be included in your professional portfolio and make a diagram listing them; for example, you might include lesson plans and your assessment of student work and your self-assessment, photographs of projects, and examples of inclusion activities and accommodations made to impact the learning of all students.

Quality, Not Quantity   Carefully select the materials, and organize the contents in such a way that readers quickly grasp the instructional and assessment practices you use and your knowledge of content. We suggest that you select those materials and accompany them with succinct, effective narratives that address INTASC or state standards. Organize all entries making an obvious connection between them and the standards or core propositions that serve as an organizing framework.

Time Line   Sketch out an estimated time when certain tasks will be attempted. For example, decide on a number of lesson plans and if you will include a unit of study or an instructional sequence. Consider the criteria listed under the different standards and note how these will be addressed.

Portfolio Checklist   Below is a list of different items that you may want to include in your portfolio. Adapt the list to best suit your individual situation and purpose and be mindful of time limits on individuals reading a large number of portfolios.

- Letter to the reviewer explaining the purpose and the process used in compiling the contents the reader will find in the portfolio. As briefly as possible you want to inform readers about what they can expect to learn from reading and inspecting the display.
- Your philosophy or educational beliefs about teaching and learning in particular.
- Introduction to the school, classroom, and teacher where you were assigned as an intern or student teacher.
  - Concise description of teaching behaviors that explains the connections between a particular entry and evidence of criteria.
  - Examples of planning lessons appropriate to students you teach and suitably connected with knowledge of content taught.
  - Complete lesson plans including activities and materials demonstrating accommodation and inclusion of all learners.
  - Evidence of assessment and communication of learning results.
  - Evidence of collaborative activities with others: teachers, administrators, parents, and supervisors and the impact on teaching and learning.
  - Evidence of self-assessment and reflections that result in changes, and the actions and impact these changes contributed to meaningful teaching and learning.
  - Evidence of technology use by students and teacher and integration into teaching-learning environment.

Additional Resources

With the increased use of electronic portfolios by preservice teachers, education and technology publications are focusing more on the topic. You may find the sources listed below helpful in planning and creating an electronic portfolio.

Electronic Portfolios

- American Association for Higher Education. This site features electronic portfolios and provides links to additional sources http://www.aahe.org/
- Barrett, H. (2001). Features Electronic Portfolio Handbook retrieved from http://www.electronicportfolios.com/
- Bartlett, A. (2002). Preparing preservice teachers to implement performance assessment and technology through electronic portfolios. *Action in Teacher Education, 25*(1), 90–97.
- Costantino, P. M., & De Lorenzo, M. N. (2002). *Developing a professional teaching portfolio.* Boston: Allyn & Bacon.
- Fazal, M., Goldsby, D., Cozza, B., Goethals, S., & Howard, R. (2001). Implementing web-based digital portfolios in three teacher preparation programs. *Academic Exchange, 5*(1), 25–30. Washington, DC: American Association of Higher Education.
- Kovalchick, A., Milman, N. B., & Elizabeth, M. (1998). Instructional strategies for integrating technology: Electronic journals and technology portfolios as facilitators for self-efficacy and reflection in preservice teachers. (ERIC Document Reproduction Service No. ED421115)
- Wiedmer, T. L. (1998). Digital portfolios: Capturing and demonstrating skills and levels of performance. *Phi Delta Kappan, 79*(8), 586–589.

CAREER SERVICES CENTER

If this is your first experience seeking a professional position, you will want to explore all areas having available assistance. Perhaps you have visited your campus career services center, introduced yourself to the personnel there, and sought their assistance. Among the first tasks you undertake prior to seeking a position is to begin assembling your credential file. Establishing a credential file allows you to organize the observations and evaluations by supervising teachers, the college or university supervisor, team leaders, department chair, and letters of recommendation. A single packet of these materials can be sent to the personnel specialists in the school district where you desire to teach. You are the owner of your credential file and you will need to request that it be sent to whomever you wish.

Career services centers provide a number of other services. You will want to make a personal or virtual visit to the career center located at your college or university and explore these available services. Most colleges and universities have special career counselors to assist you in assembling your file and in completing other tasks in the job-seeking process (e.g., creating a resume and writing a cover letter). You may also take advantage of practice-interview sessions as a means of strengthening your communication skills. Have an expert career counselor review your resume, practice interview techniques with you, and make other suggestions that allow your resume to take on a more professional appearance. This increases your confidence in future interviews.

You may find that the career center provides listings of teaching positions in local school districts, the state, the nation, and international schools. On a virtual visit to the career center at your college or university, you will likely find career center links to major job search databases. Many of the databases provide resume, cover letter, and interviewing advice, and free samples. For a fee, you can purchase assistance from different online career sites for compiling a resume. Through using the Internet you can also benefit from career services departments in other colleges and universities. Some career services centers will post your resume on the Internet. You will want to plan ahead, allowing enough time for writing your resume and obtaining all materials needed for your credential file, and you must be ready to promptly follow up on all teaching position openings from prospective employers.

Web Sites: Resume, Cover Letter, Interview, and Selected Print Sources

Web-based career tools are plentiful and many offer useful advice to you when seeking employment. Some Web sites offer you access to sample resumes and cover letters, and may link to other sites posting teaching positions nationally and internationally. You may want to browse the Web sites or obtain a copy of the books listed below for helpful information.

Electronic Sources

http://www.CollegeRecruiter.com—Free samples of resumes for the classroom teacher, cover letter strategies, and thank-you letters are available.

http://www.Ednow.com—Links to K–12 Job Search which displays position listings by subject or position, state, then city. Site allows you, for a fee, to post or view your resume.

http://www.collegegrad.com—Dedicated to college students and recent-graduate job searches. Provides information on many unique career areas for college students (for free). Information is also available on topics such as resumes, cover letters, and interview preparation.

http://www.bls.gov/oco/—*Occupational Outlook Handbook* (2002–2003) (Bureau of Labor Statistics, U.S. Department of Labor). Descriptions of work done by K–12 teachers, working conditions, training and education needed, and current and future projections of job descriptions across the United States. Web site links to teachers of preschool, kindergarten, elementary, middle, and secondary school, and special education.

http://www.jobhuntersbible.com—Author Richard Bolles created an online supplement to the *What Color Is Your Parachute?* series. In addition to providing quick advice, the site links to related sites.

Print Sources

Sparks, K. (2002). Web watch. *Library Journal, 126*(8), 28–30.

Enelow, W. S., & Kursmark, L. M. (2001). *Expert resumes for teachers and educators.* Indianapolis, IN: Jist Works.

INQUIRY ABOUT TEACHING POSITIONS

Let's start with your making inquiries about possible teaching positions within the school systems of your choice. Most school districts require an application form, which may be requested by mail, phone, accessed through the Internet, or directly retrieved from the personnel office of the school system. Otherwise, an application and/or letter of introduction is necessary to get your enclosed resume read and generate an interview.

A cover letter may accompany your application and resume to expedite the hiring process. Communication skills are most important in your letter; it is the first introduction to your writing competency. Banis (1997) provides timely tips for writing and producing job-search correspondence and samples of several types of letters. Editing your own responses and giving careful attention to style, punctuation, and spelling may give the reader a strong first impression of you, the applicant.

INTERVIEWING FOR A POSITION

Personal contact with the prospective personnel specialist or director is likely to culminate in an interview session. Make sure you provide the personnel office with a phone number where you can be reached when you are out of town. When you are contacted and given an interview, make sure you are prompt for your appointment. You may be interviewed by an administrator, a group of administrators, a group of teachers and principal from the school, or a group of teachers from the district. Their goal is to find the best possible candidate to fill a position for their school or district.

How do you prepare for a successful interview? Prior to the interview session you will want to research and consider materials you find at suggested Web sites and in print materials. The following questions may be helpful to use either as a role-playing activity or an opportunity to mentally prepare for an interview. Writing an outline and making brief comments can help you recall specific strategies to support beliefs you have about teaching and learning, and research that supports the beliefs and practices you describe.

Suggested Interview Questions

- What specific talents do you bring to the teaching profession that will benefit students?
- How do you think students learn? How do you stimulate their thinking?
- How would you go about maintaining discipline and creating an environment conducive to learning?
- Give an example of a time when you had to deal with a difficult student.
- If I were to encounter you 3, 6, and 9 years from now, what would you be doing?
- To what extent are you willing to explore and share new ideas with others?
- In what ways have you integrated technology in your teaching?
- Describe any opportunities you have experienced to develop unit or interdisciplinary teaching.
- What can be learned from observations by supervisors and principals?
- Tell me about your student teaching experience.
- How prepared are you to work with diversity among learners?
- What resources have you used effectively in the classroom?
- What types of student assessment have you used? What were the results?
- How would you get parents involved in their child's learning?
- What is your philosophy of education?
- What do you consider your greatest strengths? Any areas in need of improvement?
- Describe your collaborative relationships with your supervising teacher and university supervisor.

Questions for the Interviewee

In addition to preparing for the response to interviewing questions, you may want to generate a list to ask the interviewer or use the following:

- What types of professional development and supervisory programs does the school or district provide?
- What is the beginning teacher's salary? Are salary increments based on merit pay or automatic yearly increases?
- What is the school district policy for teacher evaluation?
- What opportunities will I have to demonstrate my leadership ability?

Keep in mind that an interview is significant in the hiring of new personnel. It is important that you arrive promptly for your appointment, dress professionally, and speak distinctly when responding to the questions.

Some schools and school districts use the Teacher Perceiver Interview Instrument in hiring teachers. The instrument, administered during an interview, is taped and later scored by the interviewer. The SRI Teacher Perceiver Instrument includes questions asked of the interviewee over 12 categories: mission, empathy, rapport drive, individualized perception, listening, investment, input drive, activation, innovation, gestalt, objectivity, and focus. In preparing for an interview of this type you would want to reflect on your convictions, beliefs, and experiences of teaching. You may find it helpful to review your professional portfolio described below.

Obtaining Certification

Teaching licensure or certification is required in all 50 states and the District of Columbia and is confirmation that you have met the necessary requirements of that particular state department of education. Recent reforms have brought about many changes in teacher certification and it is advisable that you contact the state department of education in the state you are seeking employment. By clicking on a particular state's department of education Web site, you can access information about certification and teacher licensure requirements for that state. (See Appendix H for the mailing addresses, phone numbers, and Web sites for U.S. state offices of certification.) In addition, the teacher certification official on your campus can provide a listing of certification requirements in your state and for information about other states. Many states accept the requirements of another state, granting what is called *reciprocity*. You can find the states with reciprocal agreements and a listing of individual state requirements for certified personnel in the following publication.

Tryneski, J. (1999). *Requirements of certification of teachers, counselors, librarians, administrators for elementary and secondary schools: Sixty-second edition, 1999–2000.* Chicago: University of Chicago Press.

Tests

Many states require preservice teachers to earn a minimum score on specified tests. A majority of states require one or more levels of the Praxis series. Praxis I measures your reading, writing, and mathematics skills and is required by some states and institutions prior to admission to a teacher education program. Praxis II is considered an entrance-into-the-profession type exam measuring your knowledge of content and the principles of teaching and learning. Praxis III is designed to assess a beginning teacher's classroom performance and usually takes place during the first year of teaching. Information about the Praxis series, state requirements for certification and licensure, test dates, and registration forms are available from the Educational Testing Service at http://www.ets.org/praxis. If you have a question about registration, scoring, or other Praxis series services you may call 609-771-7395, or e-mail praxis@ets.org.

Other tests may be required by schools or districts or be mandated by different states. For example, many require that all prospective employees who work directly with children or adolescents have a criminal records check and finger prints made. You will want to contact the personnel specialist in the particular school or district to inquire about the tests required and any costs you can be expected to pay prior to being employed.

CAREER ADVANCEMENT

Your journey onward takes you beyond your initial teaching experience, advancing to higher levels of instructional, interpersonal, and collaborative skills and knowledge of content. Advanced degrees or developing specialization areas for certification are in your future. As you gain at least 3 years of experience you may want to consider being certified by the National Board for Professional Teaching Standards (NBPTS). NBPTS has established standards for teaching practice and developed board certification assessments based on these standards. Many educators believe that NBPTS certification will mean higher salaries and contribute to creating a profession of superior teachers. Although NBPTS is for experienced teachers, it is wise to continue on your journey forward reaching for high standards as a professional.

Your immediate need is to plan ahead for your most immediate stop on your journey—procuring a professional teaching position. This chapter presents several steps to take and some are intricate and require a series of actions. Making a chart that lists these different steps and planned dates can help you organize and realize progress toward this goal (Table 15.1).

TABLE 15.1   *Organizer for Pursuing Your Teaching Position*

Activities	Beginning Date	Completion Date
Professional Portfolio Tasks to complete (lesson plans, etc.)		
Credential File		
Resume		
School District Inquiry Letters		
School District Application Forms		
Certification Application Forms		
Praxis/State Teacher Examination		
Interview 1		
Interview 2		
Thank-You Letter		
Acceptance Letter		
Letter Informing Other Interviewing Schools of Your Decision		

REFERENCES AND SUGGESTED READINGS

Backer, P. R. (1997). The use of portfolios in professional education: A multimedia model of instructional methodology. (ERIC Document Reproduction Service No. ED408356)

Banis, W. J. (1997). The art of writing job-search letters. *Planning job choices: 1998* (41st ed.). Bethlehem, PA: National Association of Colleges and Employers.

Campbell, D. M., Cignetti, P. B., Melenyzer, B. J., Nettles, D. H., & Wyman, R. M. (2001). *How to develop a professional portfolio.* Boston: Allyn & Bacon.

Costantino, P. M., De Lorenzo, M. N. (2002). *Developing a professional teaching portfolio: A guide for success.* Boston: Allyn & Bacon.

Fazal, M., Goldsby, D., Cozza, B., Goethals, S., & Howard, R. (2001). Implementing web-based digital portfolios in three teacher preparation programs. *Academic Exchange, 5*(1), 25–30.

Flanagan, L. L. (1999). Portfolio management. *Education, 120*(1), 128–129.

Gatlin, L., & Jacob, S. (2002). Standards-based digital portfolios: A component of authentic assessment for preservice teachers. *Action in Teacher Education, 23*(4), 35–41.

Goldsby, D. S., & Fazal, M. B. (2000). Technology's answer to portfolios for teachers. *Kappa Delta Pi Record, 36*(3), 121–123.

Holt, D., Claxton, C., Dresch, L., Ley, M., McAllister, P., & Myrick M. (1997). Integrating preparation and practice through a technology-based approach to portfolios for professional development using IBM technology. (ERIC Document Reproduction Service No. ED405325)

Hurst, B., Wilson, C., & Cramer, G. (1998). Professional teaching portfolios: Tools for reflection, growth, and advancement. *Phi Delta Kappan, 79*(8), 578–582.

Niguidula, D. (1997). Picturing performance with digital portfolios. *Educational Leadership, 55*(3), 26–29.

Riggsby, D., Jewell, V., & Justice, A. (1995). Electronic portfolio: Assessment, resume, or marketing tool. (ERIC Document Reproduction Service No. ED387115)

Ryan, C. W., Cole, D. J., & Mathies, B. K. (1997). Teacher education field experiences: Impact on self-esteem of professional year program interns via electronic portfolios. (ERIC Document Reproduction Service No. ED405329)

Ryder, R. J., & Hughes, T. (1997). *Internet for educators.* Upper Saddle River, NJ: Merrill/Prentice Hall.

Sparks, K. (2002). Web watch. *Library Journal, 126*(8), 28–30.

Wilcox, B. L., Tomei, L. A., & Manner, B. M. (1997). Intelligent portfolios for professional development. (ERIC Document Reproduction Service No. ED408250)

Willis, E. M. (2002). Promise and practice of professional portfolios. *Action in Teacher Education, 23*(4), 18–26.

appendix

A

Guidelines and Forms for Cooperative Learning Groups

" Cooperative learning taps into students' natural capacities to be engaged socially and emotionally and supports their efforts to construct knowledge and apply it in problem solving. "

M. Dickmann

WHY COOPERATIVE GROUPS?

Teaching in the 21st century encourages teachers to use active learning strategies with students of all ages and across all disciplines. Cooperative learning is recognized as an effective approach to involve learners actively. As a future educator, you will most likely incorporate cooperative learning within your repertoire of instructional strategies. Instructional group strategies designed for teaching academic and social learning continuously evolve as you implement and assess their impact on student learning. By designing and managing the group structure, you can determine the learning outcome for your students. "Cooperative learning strategies properly structured have proven to be efficient and effective in promoting mastery of knowledge and skills among students of all abilities and ages" (Leighton, 1999).

Certain cooperative group structures strengthen social interaction skills and have shown that learning can be individual and quite worthwhile. One of the primary reasons for promoting cooperative learning groups is to teach those skills that contribute to productive working groups. Five basic elements generally associated with effective cooperative learning groups include:

- positive interdependence
- face-to-face promotive interaction
- individual accountability
- interpersonal and small-group skills
- group processing (Rhem, 1992)

The best way to implement cooperative learning group structures is to engage personally in the process. We invite you to interact weekly with peers in sharing the similar and diverse experiences you encounter. Participating in cooperative learning groups at this time enables you to learn about the attitudes and skills you want to teach students and analyze the concepts and theories about cooperative learning groups. Cooperative learning encourages interdependence and interpersonal interaction and strengthens social skills (Goodwin, 1999). As you engage in the process, you will analyze and draw conclusions about the concepts and theories associated with implementing cooperative learning groups.

In achieving group goals, Johnson and Johnson (1989–1990) recommend group members practice the following skills:

- getting to know and trust each other
- communicating accurately and unambiguously
- accepting and supporting one another
- resolving conflicts constructively

Teaching social and interpersonal skills to all age learners is fundamental to the cooperative learning process. These skills positively produce student learning. Studies show that when cooperative groups are used, the achievement of these students exceeds that of students taught with other methods (Newman, 1992, Stevens & Slavin, 1995). Practicing these affective skills leads you to a deeper understanding of the foundations of effective group learning. Therefore, we provide a structure that emphasizes interdependence and interpersonal interaction and builds social skills.

From the many cooperative learning structures that are available, we selected Johnson and Johnson's Learning Together model (1999), which promotes working together to produce a single group product. In face-to-face interactions you are invited to promote positive relationships with your group members and create opportunities for interdependence within your group. The most effective means for individual growth with your group is to acknowledge and genuinely praise one another's accomplishments, including your own! This creates a sense of community and allows meaningful dialogue to occur. You are experiencing the powerful impact that individual feedback has on you. Later you can teach your students how to give individual feedback that increases their use of targeted social skills and higher achievement levels within the group (Archer-Kath & Johnson, 1994). In this type of environment you are free to become a risk taker, sharing not only your successes but also your questions, mistakes, and fears about teaching. As beginning teachers, identifying and integrating the theories and beliefs that you have about teaching calls for an open forum where discussion encourages you to step freely into the role of teacher. Discussion along with deep reflection allows you to take on that role more freely. You have a built-in support system—your cooperative group!

The Group Process

Cooperative group activities expose you to different perspectives and attitudes. Furthermore, these new perspectives can be very helpful in the development of teaching strategies in the classroom. For this reason, interaction is very important. Your active participation and contributions offer support and encouragement to your peers in ways you might not imagine. We believe that your experiences help to make explicit your implicit theories and beliefs about teaching. Group members should try to share as many insights and experiences as possible. Speaking will be easier for some, and more difficult for others within the group. If your group creates an open, respectful, and accepting environment, then everyone will interact more freely. This in turn will enable all members of the group to benefit from the experiences of others and apply these insights to their classroom practices.

Within your cooperative group, you are also learning about two important components of the Learning Together model. First, as an individual member of the group, you are accountable for your share of the work and contributions to the group's success. Individual accountability is the hallmark of successful group process. Second, your input enables your group to put into action a plan that allows each member to grow. Your group's focus for each session is a written action plan that becomes the building block for your personal development as a professional.

Who Participates?

To simulate the collaboration concept observed in schools, each group consists of three to four individuals who work with different ages and content areas. The seminar director, or facilitator, suggests group membership. Each group remains in place for three or four sessions, rotating roles each session. Assuming different roles enables everyone to participate in the group process from a different perspective. Your active involvement in the group allows you not only to experience how cooperative learning groups work, but also to determine how the group process can best be incorporated into your classroom.

What Are the Roles?

Each member of the group will assume a specific role: initiator-reader, encourager, summarizer, or observer.

Initiator-Reader

The initiator-reader is responsible for the group beginning its work promptly and using time productively. Other responsibilities include:

- clarifying the task
- making sure everyone in the group understands the activity and the supplied information
- moving the group toward task completion

Encourager

The encourager promotes positive interpersonal relations through acknowledging the team-building contributions of group members. Other responsibilities are:

- restating group member comments
- connecting the comments of two or more group members
- reminding other members of appropriate social skills when necessary
- assembling and returning all materials that the group uses during the activity (if the group does not have an observer)

Summarizer

The summarizer makes sure the group completes all assigned tasks. Other responsibilities are:

- monitoring time and alerting group members to the time remaining in each session
- restating group member comments
- writing the action plan and the follow-up report to the action plan during the succeeding session
- obtaining group consensus on content of the action plan

Observer

The observer serves as a guide for the group and focuses on the success of the group and its members. Other responsibilities are:

- observing and reminding other members of their roles within the group
- giving reactions to specific behaviors of the group and its members when asked
- assembling and returning all materials that the group uses during the activity

"Teachers who receive frequent, systematic feedback based on observations of their performance do a better job of implementing cooperative learning methods."
D. B. Strother

Facilitator

The facilitator teaches the course or seminar and also collects and gives written feedback to each group's action plan and to the individuals' accountability reports. Other responsibilities include:

- providing outside measure of accountability to the group
- commending the group for the quality of its interactions
- providing reinforcement and directions for the cooperative learning group process
- articulating how group members might apply this model of cooperative learning within their classrooms

PRACTICING THE COOPERATIVE LEARNING GROUP PROCESS

Now that you have read the information about the cooperative learning groups, you are ready to get involved as a member of a group. This first interaction moves you slowly through a series of steps aimed at helping you learn the process. You are then asked to engage in reflections about your learning, recalling what you did and the outcomes you obtained and comparing these with outcomes expected from the "learning together" group activities. The first activity is an introduction to the cooperative group process.

Step 1. Forming Groups   Your facilitator suggests your group membership. After the groups are formed, the facilitator makes some introductory comments explaining what the activity is, how much time is allotted to complete it, and when the activity will officially begin. Unless otherwise directed, assume your role within the group as soon as the facilitator concludes the opening remarks and the activity begins. Throughout each session, the facilitator is available for any questions about this process. The facilitator also may modify any of the activities or process steps.

Step 2. Choosing Roles   After reading each role description, choose your role and obtain group consensus. Think about the responsibilities of this role.

Step 3. Getting Into Action   As the group gathers, the observer (or encourager if there is no observer) obtains a group number and a role marker for each member. (Markers with the group numbers can be made of folder paper and kept in a central location for routine use.) The observer also distributes any other materials needed by the group prior to the task at hand. In addition, the observer designates space for materials. This saves time and allows individuals to fulfill their roles in a timely manner.

Using Discussion Questions

Discussion questions appear in each of the cooperative learning group activities in Focus 1 for each session. Each set of questions focuses on different concerns many believe that new teachers experience in adjusting to the teacher role. The questions emphasize the affective aspects you are experiencing. The discussion format invites you to share your personal insights and feelings about becoming a professional teacher. To derive the greatest benefit from the discussion questions, consider the following:

- thoroughly read the introductory information provided
- clarify the meaning about what is stated
- respond openly to the initiator-reader's invitation to share
- attend to peers' sharing and feed back the messages received

Individual Accountability Report (Sample)

Name __Jack Doe__   Date __9/21__   Group No. __4__

Circle your role in the group. Review the tasks associated with your role.

Initiator-reader   Encourager   Summarizer   Observer

Communication rating
(0 indicates Not at All; 5 indicates Highest Quality)

Sent accurate, unambiguous message	0	1	2	3	4	⑤
Actively listened to others	0	1	2	3	④	5
Assisted another with his/her role	0	1	②	3	4	5
Degree of involvement	0	1	2	3	4	⑤

Comment on your performance in the group during this session:

At times I forgot I was the encourager. Next time I hope to notice the others' role a little better and say supportive type things to them.

Signatures of other group members:

Initiator-reader __Marti__   Observer __Corey__

Encourager __Jack__   Summarizer __Latosha__

Facilitator comments:

Your comments are candid. You will have many opportunities to assume the different roles. You might review the role of encourager; read the description above and take a few minutes to reflect on what you might say.

Initiator-reader
The initiator-reader is responsible for the group beginning its work promptly and using time productively. Other responsibilities:
- clarifies the task
- makes sure everyone in the group understands the activity and the supplied information
- moves the group toward task completion

Encourager
The encourager promotes positive interpersonal relations through acknowledging the team-building contributions of group members. Other responsibilities:
- restates group member comments
- connects the comments of two or more group members
- reminds other members of appropriate social skills when necessary
- assembles and returns all materials that the group uses during the activity (if the group does not have an observer)

Summarizer
The summarizer makes sure the group completes all assigned tasks. Other responsibilities:
- monitors time and alerts group members to the time remaining in each session
- restates group member comments
- obtains consensus from the group on each report
- writes the action plan and the follow-up report to the action plan

Observer
The observer serves as a guide for the group and focuses on the success of the group and its members. Other responsibilities:
- observes and reminds other members of their roles within the group
- gives reactions to specific behaviors of the group and its members when asked
- assembles and returns all materials that the group uses during the activity

Before stating the first discussion point, the initiator-reader checks to see that members of the group understand their roles and are ready to discuss the questions provided. If group members choose, more time can be spent on some questions than on others. The time allotted for each cooperative learning activity is stated at the end of each **Focus One** activity. The initiator-reader confirms this time with the group.

The encourager verbally acknowledges members using positive interdependence, face-to-face interaction, social skills, and group processing. If the interaction among group members strays from the assigned discussion, the encourager reintroduces the topic.

The summarizer keeps the group aware of the time remaining in the session and initiates summary comments that include key ideas shared by group members. These may be written for quick reference on the **focused conversation sheet.**

The observer of the group gives the group members some feedback. At least one comment about the performance and effectiveness of each group member's role is recommended.

"If I feel I belong, I know I have a place in that group that only I can fill; that I contribute something that is necessary to the group and is valued by other members."
L. Graves

Practice Discussion Questions

1. Have you previously participated in a cooperative learning group? If so, was it a learning together model? What kind of structure did you follow in the group process?
2. As a student or intern teacher, what do you expect to learn from participating in the cooperative learning group?
3. Do you anticipate any difficulties involved in being a group member?
4. Since you will be meeting as a group two to three more times, what would help you work together as a group?

What Is an Action Plan?

The **action plan—group accountability report** is a summary of the group's discussion designed to create a collective goal that guides your thoughts and actions during the coming days. Although stated in practical terms, the plan focuses your thoughts and actions toward the lofty ideals you have about becoming a professional teacher. You and each member of your group need to contribute to and endorse the plan written by the summarizer. In producing an effective action plan you want to include components such as:

- insights you hear from other members during the session that motivate and inspire you
- ideas and actions you can practice in the school setting
- means for remembering to implement the plan during the week (for example, using your journal as a place to write about ways you implement the action plan)

The action plan serves as a means of accountability for your cooperative group; hence, the action plan is written on the group accountability form. In naming a specific action you will practice until the next session, you are naming a short range goal for yourself. You make public your plan by having the facilitator read and comment on the plan. At the following session you review the plan and share with others your experience with carrying out the plan. At the same time you examine the facilitator's comments and in closing write a response that summarizes your group's discussion of personal experiences with implementing the plan. For example, you can state how you might have made the plan more helpful or the ways you found the plan useful in moving you toward a desired goal. At the end of the session each group completes an action plan—group accountability report and the observer or encourager returns it to the designated location. The facilitator reads, responds in writing, and returns the action plan to the group the following session.

ACTION PLAN
Group Accountability Report (Sample)

Date ___*9/21*___   Group no. ___*4*___

Action plan statement:

In this session our group decided to work on initiating and participating by making our presence known in the classroom. We plan to step up our role, do more in the room such as taking roll or teaching lessons. We will document this in our journals.

Signature of cooperative working group members:

Initiator-reader ___*Marti*___   Observer ___*Corey*___

Encourager ___*Jack*___   Summarizer ___*Latosha*___

Facilitator comments to the group's action plan:

Great plan! You will no doubt be noticed and observed as partner teacher by your students. Assisting the teacher in any capacity will be recognized and appreciated. Good that you make yourselves accountable to one another. Onward!

Group members' follow-up comments to the action plan: *9/28*

Yes, we followed up on our plan. Each explained the process and actions that he or she took with the students.

What Is the Individual Accountability Report?

Assessing the quality and quantity of your participation as a group member is the purpose for the **individual accountability report.** The report guides you in marking personal progress in performing the different cooperative group roles. Allow yourself the opportunity to grow; do not expect to rate yourself as performing at the highest level at all times and in every role. By stating a specific interpersonal skill you want to strengthen, you are likely to improve this skill in subsequent sessions. Each time you complete the individual accountability report, keep in mind:

- your role in the cooperative group as described in the preceding pages
- the level and degree of your verbal and nonverbal interactions
- the encouragement and support you offer other group members
- your strengths as a group member (or areas needing improvement)
- peer assessments regarding your performance within the group

The rating you give your performance in the group is written on the individual accountability report. You read and sign the report of other group members and they sign yours. Self-assessment is more likely to occur with peer encouragement and support.

The observer or encourager collects all materials from the group and deposits these in the designated location.

The total time allotted for this and most cooperative learning group activities is approximately 30 minutes.

Beginning Time _____   Ending Time _____

- Since the above exercise is a practice of the cooperative group structure, writing an action plan for the coming week is optional.

Focused Conversation

When conversation is purposeful and focused it can enhance learning among all group members. It is important to record group members' thoughts and insights to clarify or raise more questions about the teaching and learning processes. All group members must participate in the conversation and be accountable to the group to facilitate individual as well as collective learning. Each group's summarizer is asked to record group members' names on the form provided below, and to jot notes about the strains and directions the **focused conversation** takes. This will enable the group to analyze the key concerns voiced by members and point the way for the actions you may take in the coming week to address issues or areas of need. This first session is a learning time for all group members. You are learning not only about performing a specific role, but also about the people in your group. Being patient with yourself and allowing time for multifaceted learning to occur is critical to the process.

REFERENCES AND SUGGESTED READINGS

Archer-Kath, J., & Johnson, D. W. (1994). Individual versus group feedback in cooperative groups. *Journal of Social Psychology, 134*(5), 681–694.

Cooper, J. L. (1991). Cooperative/collaborative learning: Research and practice primarily at the collegiate level. *Journal-of-Staff, Program, & Organization Development, 7,* 143–148.

Dickmann, M. (2002, Winter). Having the tools of instruction. *Curriculum Update.* Alexandria VA: Association for Supervision and Curriculum Development.

Goodwin, M. W. (1999). Cooperative learning and social skills: What skills to teach and how to teach them. *Intervention in School and Clinic, 35*(1), 29–33.

Graves, L. (1992). Cooperative learning communities: Context for a new vision of education and society. *Journal of Education, 174*(2), 57–69.

Johnson, D. W., & Johnson, R. T. (1989–1990). Social skills for successful group work. *Educational Leadership, 47*(4), 29–33.

Johnson, D. W., & Johnson, R. T. (1999). *Learning together and alone: Cooperation, competition and individualization.* Boston: Allyn & Bacon.

Kagan, S. (2001). Teaching character and community. *Educational Leadership, 59*(2), 50–55.

Leighton, M. S. (1999). Cooperative learning. In J. M. Cooper (Ed.), *Classroom teaching skills.* (p. 270). Boston: Houghton Mifflin.

Newman, F. M. (1992). *Making small groups productive.* Madison, WI: Center on Organization and Restructuring of Schools (Issue Report No. 2).

Rhem, J. (1992). Elements of cooperative learning, *National Teaching & Learning Forum, 2*(1), 3.

Stevens, R. J., & Slavin, R. E. (1995). The cooperative elementary school: Effects on achievement, attitudes, and social relations. *American Educational Research Journal, 32,* 321–351.

Strother, D. B. (1990). Cooperative learning: Fad or foundation for learning? *Phi Delta Kappan, 72*(2), 162.

ACTION PLAN

Group Accountability Report (duplicate for groups)

Date _____   Group no._____

Action plan statement:

Signature of cooperative working group members:

Initiator-reader _____   Observer _____

Encourager _____   Summarizer _____

Facilitator comments to the group's action plan:

Group members' follow-up comments to the action plan:

Individual Accountability Report (duplicate for participants)

Name _____   Date _____   Group No._____

Communication rating
(0 indicates **not** at all; 5 indicates **highest** quality)

Sent accurate, unambiguous message	0............1............2 ....3............4............5
Actively listened to others	0............1............2 ....3............4............5
Assisted others with their role	0............1............2 ....3............4............5
Degree of involvement	0............1............2 ....3............4............5

Comment on your performance in the group during this session:

Signatures of other group members

Initiator-reader _____   Observer _____

Encourager _____   Summarizer _____

Facilitator comments:

Materials needed
- Role markers (5-by-8 inch role identification markers)
- Group accountability report (action plan statement)
- Individual accountability report

appendix

B

Facilitator Tips Using the Cooperative Group Approach and Other Processes for Focus One Activities

A Note to the Facilitator

The **Focus One** section of each chapter may be facilitated with a number of different approaches that best suits the needs of your group.

For example:

1. You may choose to act as facilitator or director for the student or intern teachers engaged in the cooperative group process as described step-by-step within the text. Your role is to monitor and assist student or intern teachers as they process Focus One content. You provide written feedback to individual and group self-assessment tasks, and challenge groups to think more critically through focused conversation that probes their affective responses to teaching.

2. A university instructor or supervisor of student or intern teachers might facilitate the seminar in a whole-group setting by using the Focus One portion of each chapter. As such, you may select probes and prompts to engage preservice teachers in reflection about teaching and the way it impacts their perception of teaching as a profession.

Whichever model you employ, Focus One readings, reflections, discussions, and student or intern teacher action plans are designed to engage student or intern teachers in connecting reflective practice and action. Each chapter is briefly reviewed for the cooperative group process, and step-by-step suggestions are made to move the process along and engage participants in discovery, personally and professionally.

Before you begin, you may find it helpful to review the group process and procedures described in Appendix A. The more comfortable you are with the process, the more comfortable your student or intern teachers will be when expected to engage in collaborative activities and discussions in the seminar. The main objective for the use of cooperative groups in Focus One activities is to have the student or intern teachers experience the process and thus help them grasp the significance of purposefully designed group tasks and interactions. They are further challenged to employ the practice in their own classrooms to better impact student learning.

REVIEW OF THE COOPERATIVE GROUP PROCESS

Since the cooperative learning group process in Focus One may still be new to members of the seminar, review the roles and expectations for the group members. Keep in mind the **Expected Performance goals** for the group and expectations for individual members of the group as listed prior to Focus One activities in each chapter.

The Facilitator's Role and Responsibilities

- Selects appropriate discussion questions and activities
- Provides materials for seminar activities
- Sets time frame for seminar (no more than 30 minutes is necessary to give reasonable attention to selected content in Focus One)
- Monitors student or intern teachers' interactions and grasp of Focus One content
- Nudges student or intern teachers to higher levels of thinking by bypassing the obvious to examine the deep structures of teaching
- Responds in writing to student or intern teachers' individual accountability and action plan—group accountability reports

Tasks for the Group Process

1. **Decide on roles for each group member.**
   - Initiator-reader
   - Encourager
   - Summarizer
   - Observer
2. **Obtain materials for group—encourager (observer in a four-member group).**
   - Action plan—group accountability reports from prior session
   - Role markers
   - Action plan—group accountability report forms (blank form found in Appendix A)
   - Individual accountability report forms (blank form found in Appendix A)
3. **Reflect** on facilitator's response to group action plan.
4. **Hold a group discussion:** The initiator-reader checks with other group members to see if all are ready to begin the discussion portion of the session.
   - Initiator-reader directs group members to the **Discussion Questions** (Focus One in each chapter).
   - All other group members assume and review their role for this session.
   - Summarizer attends to the content of the discussion and monitors the time and tasks the group is to complete.
5. **Write the action plan:** The action plan is a summary of the most significant discussion points made by the group members. Consider the meaningful insights shared during this session, and review the **focused conversation in Appendix A.**
   - Name one idea that motivates and inspires the group to action. Be realistic and choose a practical teaching goal—one that is attainable with consistent practice and reflection.

   The group's **action plan** must:
   - Be written in specific terms that are observable in the practices or behaviors of the student or intern teacher.

- Reflect the steps the group plans to implement to reach their collective goal.
- Promote a professional attitude or a teacher action.
- Allow the student or intern teacher to mark progress toward or attainment of a goal.
- Be recorded in the teacher or intern student teaching **journal** for reference and reflection on action during the coming week.
- Be written by the summarizer and signed by all group members to indicate their agreement to practice the plan.

To Conclude the Activities

6. **Complete the individual accountability report.** The quality of individual participation as a group member is the focus of the individual accountability report. It serves as a guide to mark progress in the different roles participants assume during each session. Individuals are expected to:
   - Review specific tasks assigned in accordance with individual's role.
   - State a specific and desired interpersonal skill to practice during subsequent sessions.
   - Read and sign the individual accountability report of other group members.
   - Encourage participants in their efforts toward mastery learning of group process.
   - The encourager or observer must return the action plan—group accountability report, the individual accountability report, and other materials completed during the seminar to a location designated by the facilitator.

7. The facilitator will read and return the Action plan-Group Accountability Report to the group to start the following session.

Follow-Up to Action Plan

- At the beginning of each session the facilitator returns the action plans to the groups.
- Groups discuss the effectiveness of their plan and the comments of the facilitator.
- Individuals or groups articulate their growing understanding and greater motivation for learning to teach in effective ways.

CHAPTER 1 FOCUS ONE: COOPERATIVE GROUP APPROACH

First Observations

Focus One cooperative learning group activities promote greater self-understanding. These activities ask student or intern teachers to share their classroom experiences with their peers. Through intensive dialogue they let others get to know who they are, what they are learning, and the feelings they attach to their experiences in the classroom. Sharing and attending to others promotes a sense of trust within a small-group setting, and promotes open-mindedness among participants and an opportunity for learning. Facilitators may wish to use the following guidelines for successive seminar sessions, especially as group membership changes after each member has experienced a new role and responsibilities within the originally as-signed group.

Seminar Procedures

- Allow time for the student or intern teachers to feel comfortable with members of their group.

- Set the tone for cooperative group process by stating expectations, time limits, and personal and professional boundaries that emphasize respect for all members.
- Post an agenda or format with clearly stated objectives for the seminar to inform student or intern teachers of the goals for the session.
- Model the attitudes and skills student or intern teachers are expected to use in their classroom settings: rituals, procedures, and other cues to promote a learning environment.
- Follow the guidelines for the seminar in "A Note to the Facilitator" section above. This list may also be copied, blown up to poster size, and laminated for quick procedural references during the seminar.
- Provide paper and envelopes for the number of student or intern teachers in the seminar.
- Collect student or intern teachers' written and sealed responses to questions regarding teacher characteristics they wish to attain as a result of the student or intern teaching experience.
- Designate particular procedures, and places or containers for seminar participants to place completed forms (individual accountability and action plan—group accountability reports, and journals) for easy identification and return of materials.

Seminar Follow-Up for Facilitator

- Review individual accountability reports and each group's action plan—group accountability report. Provide clear comments and purposeful feedback to groups regarding the plan as a means toward their professional development as effective teachers.

CHAPTER 2 FOCUS ONE: COOPERATIVE GROUP APPROACH

Am I Initiating or Am I Hiding Behind the Bookcase?

Seminar participants meet to share and reflect on meaningful learning experiences and insights about becoming a professional teacher that they encountered, since the last session. This session each participant is asked to assume a new role within the same group, paying close attention to the requirements of the role description.

Seminar Procedures

- The facilitator opens the session and distributes to each group the individual accountability and action plan—group accountability reports collected during the last session.
- Participants are given an opportunity to read the facilitator's comments individually and as a group.
- The initiator-reader assumes leadership in the group and all other group members are expected to take on new roles and responsibilities.
- Groups review and discuss the prior session's action plan and assess their individual and collective success in achieving their goal.
- Within the same cooperative groups, participants discuss personal experience (attempts, trials, and triumphs) with using the action plan to focus day-to-day teaching life in the school. Consider questions such as: Did group members remember the plan? If so, how useful was it in naming specific strengths? What aspect of the teacher role demanded the most attention and reflection?

- The summarizer records the group's experience with using the action plan and its contribution to individual and collective learning as professional teachers. Student or intern teachers are now ready to reflect on another aspect of becoming a teacher—taking initiative.

Group Discussion

The initiator-reader checks with the group members to see that they have had sufficient silent time to read the narrative in **Focus One** and are ready to begin the discussion.

- The initiator-reader directs group members to the **Discussion Questions** in **Focus One** to guide the analysis of student or intern teachers' performance at this time.
- All other group members assume and review their roles for the session.
- Members of the group share insights about taking charge in the classroom and to what degree they see themselves as initiators.
- The summarizer monitors the discussion and alerts other group members to recognize common topics and concerns that they may include in their action plan.

Writing the Action Plan

What actions does your group plan to take as a result of your discussion about taking charge?

- Group members decide on the professional action that needs to be taken or practiced in the coming week.
- Specific self-assessment measures are included so group members are held accountable to one another for the implementation of the action plan.
- The summarizer writes the group's action plan, and group members sign, indicating that all agree to practice the plan.
- The action plan—group accountability report (Appendix A) along with the individual accountability report (Appendix A) and other materials are returned to the facilitator.

Seminar Follow-Up for Facilitator

- Review individual accountability reports and each group's action plan—group accountability report. Provide clear comments and purposeful feedback to groups regarding the plan as a means toward their professional development as effective teachers.

CHAPTER 3 FOCUS ONE: COOPERATIVE GROUP APPROACH

Analyzing Your Emotional Response to Beginning Teaching

Focus One offers another group activity designed to help student or intern teachers examine and learn more about their growth as beginning professionals by acknowledging the feelings and attitudes they experience as they work with learners and teachers in the school setting.

Seminar Procedures

- The facilitator opens the session and distributes to each group the individual accountability and action plan—group accountability reports collected during the last session.

- Groups review and discuss the prior session's action plan. Below are guiding questions for review and discussion.
  1. Did individual members of each group remember the plan?
  2. Did group members find the means the group chose for remembering the plan workable?
  3. To what degree are the group members' experiences and the facilitator's comments about the plan connected?
- Assign New Groups. For the next part of this session student or intern teachers are assigned to a new group. Joining different groups offers an opportunity to learn more about oneself and other people by practicing the different roles and by interacting with others who respond in different ways to their roles in the group.
- Read group assignments and have participants move to the new group.
- Have participants introduce themselves by telling new group members about the school, students, faculty, and staff with whom they work.
- Direct each student or intern teacher to select the role he or she will perform and review the responsibilities of that role.

Group Discussion

The initiator-reader checks with the group members to see that they have had sufficient silent time to reflect and are ready to begin the discussion.

- The initiator-reader directs group members to the **Discussion Questions** in **Focus One** to guide the analysis of student or intern teachers' emotional response to beginning teaching.
- All other group members assume and review their roles for the session.
- Members of the group share insights about the deep feelings they experienced during student or intern teaching concerning the roles and responsibilities assigned to them. The summarizer monitors and assists members in recognizing the common threads of the discussion that may lead to creating an action plan.

Writing the Action Plan

How do student or intern teachers plan to practice the insights gained from the discussion about becoming professional teachers? If you need additional help with writing your action plan, refer to action plan examples in this Appendix.

- Group members decide on the professional action that needs to be taken or practiced in the coming week.
- Include specific ways individual members will be accountable to the group for implementing the action plan. Share these within the group and listen to others' ideas.
- The summarizer writes the group's action plan, and group members sign, indicating that all agree to practice the plan.
- The action plan—group accountability report along with the individual accountability reports and other materials are returned to the facilitator.

Seminar Follow-Up for Facilitator

- Review individual accountability reports and each group's action plans— group accountability report. Provide clear comments and purposeful feedback to groups regarding the plan as a means toward their professional development as effective teachers.

**EXAMPLES: ACTION PLAN, FACILITATOR'S RESPONSE,
FOLLOW-UP TO ACTION PLAN**

Action plan

This week we will try to be more positive with what we do and to write about this in our journals. We need to focus more on positive things to help boost our confidence in ourselves. We all seem to focus on the negative more than the positive.

Facilitator's response

Your group appeared to openly share your stories and your plan gives you a specific, practical goal. Best to you in following it!

Group response to action plan

We all focused on our strengths and progress as student teachers. This forced us to think about positives while still thinking about improvements to be made.

CHAPTER 4 FOCUS ONE: COOPERATIVE GROUP APPROACH

Analyzing the Affective Dimensions of Inclusion

Focus One offers a variety of group activities designed to help student or intern teachers examine and learn more about their growth as beginning professionals by examining their personal histories and looking deeply at the ways in which those histories impact who they are as teacher. Student or intern teachers are challenged to engage with students to discover the diversity that abounds in the classroom, and discuss ways in which teachers meet the needs of individual learners.

Seminar Procedures
- The facilitator opens the session and distributes to each group the individual accountability and action plan—group accountability reports collected during the last session.
- Groups review and discuss the prior week's action plan and assess their individual and collective success in achieving their goal.
- Each student or intern teacher selects the role he or she will perform and reviews the responsibilities of that role.

Group Discussion
The initiator-reader checks with the group members to see that they have had sufficient time to read the narrative in **Focus One** and are ready to begin the discussion.

- The initiator-reader directs group members to the **Discussion Questions** in **Focus One** to guide the discussion of student or intern teachers' responses and reactions to diversity. All other group members assume and review their roles for the session.

- Members of the group share insights about diversity and the feelings they experienced in the classroom as they interacted with people different from themselves. Topics may include gender, ability, disability, race, culture, religion, and socioeconomic and sexual preference.
- The summarizer monitors the time and tasks for the group and restates the common threads that are spoken throughout the discussion.

Writing the Action Plan

How do student or intern teachers plan to practice the insights gained from the discussion about becoming professional teachers?

- Group members decide on the personal or professional action that needs to be taken or practiced in the coming week.
- Along with the action to be taken, include the means the group will use for remembering the plan. (For example, in the **journal** student or intern teachers may comment on new insights gained by acknowledging diversity and working with learners to find out about their backgrounds.)
- Include specific ways individual members will be accountable to the group for implementing the action plan. Share these within the group and listen to others' ideas.
- The summarizer writes the group's action plan, and group members sign, indicating that all agree to practice the plan.
- The action plan—group accountability report along with the individual accountability reports and other materials are returned to the facilitator.

Seminar Follow-Up for Facilitator

- Review individual accountability reports and each group's action plan—group accountability report. Provide clear comments and purposeful feedback to groups regarding the plan as a means toward their professional development as effective teachers.

CHAPTER 5 FOCUS ONE: COOPERATIVE GROUP APPROACH

Handheld, or Holding On to the Tools of the Past?

Focus One allows student or intern teachers to reflect on their experiences using technology with a special emphasis on *how* they first learned to use different technologies. They are encouraged to share their excitement about using technology in the classroom as well as the fears and frustrations they may have about teaching students to employ technology as a means toward enhanced learning.

Seminar Procedures

- The facilitator opens the session and distributes to each group the individual accountability and action plan—group accountability reports collected during the last session.
- Groups review and discuss the prior session's action plan and assess their individual and collective success in achieving their goal.
- Each student or intern teacher selects the role he or she will perform and reviews the responsibilities of that role.

Group Discussion

The initiator-reader checks with the group members to see that they have had sufficient silent time to read the narrative in **Focus One** and are ready to begin the discussion.

- The initiator-reader directs group members to the **Discussion Questions** in **Focus One** to guide the discussion of student or intern teachers' emotional responses and reactions to technology and its use in the classroom. All other group members assume and review their roles for the session.
- Members of the group share their experiences of and feelings about using different types of technology in the classroom.
- The summarizer monitors the time and assists the group by restating members' comments and other consensus building remarks of the group.

Writing the Action Plan

How do student or intern teachers plan to practice the insights gained from the discussion about becoming a professional teacher who is required to use technology in everyday teaching, planning, and communicating?

- Group members decide on the professional action that needs to be taken or practiced in the time following the seminar.
- Along with the action to be taken, include the means the group will use for remembering the plan.
- Include specific ways individual members will be accountable to the group for implementing the action plan. Share these within the group and listen to others' ideas.
- The summarizer writes the group's action plan, and group members sign, indicating that all agree to practice the plan.
- The action plan—(group accountability report) along with the individual accountability report and other materials are returned to the facilitator.

Seminar Follow-Up for Facilitator

- Review individual accountability reports and each group's action plan— group accountability report. Provide clear comments and purposeful feedback to groups regarding the plan as a means toward their professional development as effective teachers.
- Prepare a copy for the one- and two-way communication activity. (See Figures B.1 and B.2.) For the person selected to be the sender. Provide each member 2 sheets of drawing paper.

  Small Group (optional)
- Prepare enough copies of the communication diagrams sheet (Figures B.1 and B.2) so each group has a copy. Provide two sheets of drawing paper for each group member.

CHAPTER 6 FOCUS ONE: COOPERATIVE GROUP APPROACH

What Am I Saying? What Am I Hearing?

Focus One invites student or intern teachers to reflect on their preferred communication styles and challenges them to explore ways to strengthen two-way communication as teachers.

FIGURE B.1 *Communication Diagram #1*   **FIGURE B.2** *Communication Diagram #2*

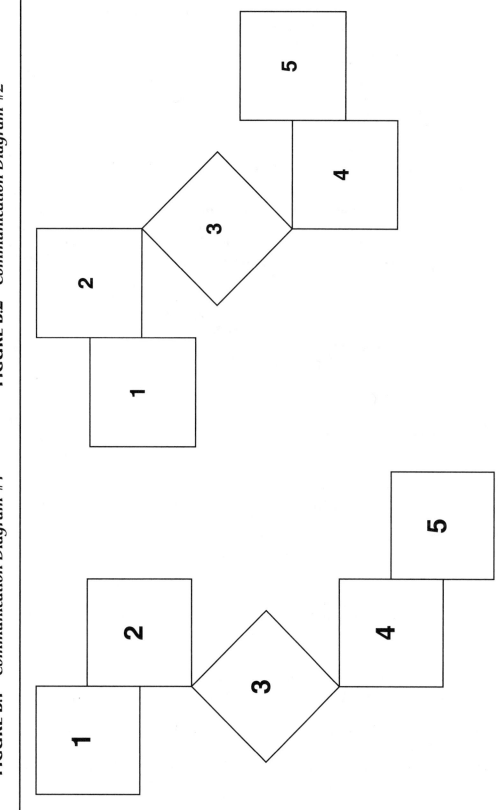

Source: Adapted from Exhibits 9.6 and 9.7, Directions for Communicator, pp. 205–206. Harris, B. M., Bessent, W., & McIntyre, K. E. (1969). *In-Service Education: A Guide to Better Practice.*

Seminar Procedures: A Communication Activity to Set the Stage for Discussion Groups

- The facilitator opens the session and distributes to each group the individual accountability and action plan—group accountability reports collected during the last session. (You may direct student or intern teachers to *not* read comments at this time, or allow a few minutes for reading facilitator comments without discussing them.)

Large Group
- Student or intern teachers are seated in stadium formation and have a flat surface for drawing.

Small Group
- Student or intern teachers are randomly assigned a partner with whom to work to test their preferred style of communication.

Large and Small Group Directions
- Student or intern teachers are asked to complete the drawing portion of the activity using one- and two-way communication skills in Figures B.1 and B.2. (See "Directions for the One-Way Communication Process" and "Directions for the Two-Way Communication Process" in **Focus One** of Chapter 6.)

- After completing the communication activities, student or intern teachers are invited to join members of their cooperative learning group to share experiences with each style of communication.
- Each student or intern teacher selects the role he or she will perform and reviews the responsibilities of that role.

Group Discussion

The initiator-reader checks with the group members to see that they are ready to begin the discussion.

- The initiator-reader directs group members to the **Discussion Questions** in **Focus One** to guide the discussion of student or intern teachers' preferred styles of communication and ways to enhance communication in the classroom. All other group members assume and review their roles for the session.
- Members of the group share their experiences with the effectiveness of different types of communication, and ways they might strengthen their means of communication.
- The summarizer attends to group members' comments, uses rephrasing and other approaches to assist the group.
- Groups may read the facilitator's comments regarding their action plan from the last seminar before developing a new plan of action for the coming week.

Writing the Action Plan

How do student or intern teachers plan to practice the insights gained from the discussion about one- and two-way communication in the classroom?

- Group members decide on the professional action that needs to be taken or practiced in the coming week.
- Along with the action to be taken, include the means the group will use for remembering the plan.
- Include specific ways individual members will be accountable to the group for implementing the action plan. Share these with the group and listen to others' ideas.

- The summarizer writes the group's action plan, and group members sign, indicating that all agree to practice the plan.
- The action plan—group accountability report along with the individual accountability reports and other materials are returned to the facilitator.

Seminar Follow-Up for Facilitator

- Review individual accountability reports and each group's action plan—group accountability report. Provide clear comments and purposeful feedback to groups regarding the plan as a means toward their professional development as effective teachers.

CHAPTER 7 FOCUS ONE: COOPERATIVE GROUP APPROACH

The Teacher's Journey: Balancing the Ideal With the Real

Focus One allows student or intern teachers to reflect on their evolving professionalism as they share classroom experiences that demonstrate how they currently view themselves as teacher. Student or intern teachers are challenged to compare their current status as teacher to their future vision of themselves as teachers extraordinaire.

Seminar Procedures

- The facilitator opens the session and distributes to each group the individual accountability and action plan—group accountability reports collected during the last session.
- Groups review and discuss the action plan and assess their individual and collective success in achieving their goal.
- Each student or intern teacher selects the role he or she will perform and reviews the responsibilities of that role.

Group Discussion

The initiator-reader checks with the group members to see that they have had sufficient silent time to read the narrative of **Focus One** and are ready to begin the discussion.

- The initiator-reader directs group members to the **Discussion Questions** in **Focus One** to guide student or intern teachers' discussion about insights and feelings about themselves as teachers. They are invited to share their new-found perceptions of the teacher's role including their surprises, disappointments, challenges, and emotional responses to the demands of teaching. All other group members assume and review their roles for the session.
- Members of the group share their experiences with teaching and compare the methods they use with those of their supervising teacher. They share questions they still have about effective teaching.
- The summarizer attends the conversation among the group and alerts the members to common threads.

Writing the Action Plan

How do student or intern teachers plan to practice the insights gained from the discussion about becoming a professional teacher who is required to use technology in everyday teaching, planning, and communicating?

- Group members decide on the professional action that needs to be taken or practiced in the coming week.
- Along with the action to be taken, include the means the group will use for remembering the plan.
- Include specific ways individual members will be accountable to the group for implementing the action plan. Share these within the group and listen to others' ideas.
- The summarizer writes the group's action plan, and group members sign, indicating that all agree to practice the plan.
- The action plan—group accountability report along with the individual accountability reports and other materials are returned to the facilitator.

Seminar Follow-Up for Facilitator

- Review individual accountability reports and each group's action plan— group accountability report. Provide clear comments and purposeful feedback to groups regarding the plan as a means toward their professional development as effective teachers.
- Bring to the seminar letters (in sealed envelopes) that student or intern teachers wrote about the ideal teacher when the seminars first began.

EXAMPLE: ACTION PLAN

During the coming week we will look at the characteristics we think the ideal teacher possesses and ask ourselves the following questions: How close am I to becoming this ideal teacher? What is one major weakness I still see in myself? What is one way in which I've improved? We will write our reflections on these questions in our journals.

Example: Response to action plan

Ideal teacher

In control, consistent, confident, "with-it," flexible, sensitive to diverse needs, organized, devoted, motivational to self and students, collaborative, and at times crazy!!!

How close am I?

Light years away, baby! I feel good about myself and where I stand—but the teachers I work with are seasoned veterans who know this game. They are on top of the game! I will strive to get to this point but for now, I will take it one step at a time.

One major weakness

I still have trouble adapting to sudden changes in the classroom. I can handle interruptions, but last-second schedule changes and such get me all out of whack. I must learn to be more flexible in these types of situations.

One area of progress

I see a marked improvement in my own abilities as a classroom manager. I toughened up and they responded.

CHAPTER 8 FOCUS ONE: COOPERATIVE GROUP APPROACH

The Power of Reflection: What Do I Now See?

Focus One allows student or intern teachers to reflect on their accomplishments as teacher and compare their earlier perceptions of the teacher's role to their more recent experiences in the classroom.

Seminar Procedures: A Reflective Activity to Mark Time and Personal Growth as a Teacher

- The facilitator opens the session by inviting student or intern teachers to engage in a reflective activity designed to have each participant reexamine his or her goal to become a teacher.
- The facilitator distributes to each group the individual accountability and action plan—group accountability report collected during the last session.
- Groups review and discuss the prior session's action plan and assess their individual and collective success in achieving their goal.
- Each student or intern teacher selects the role he or she will perform and reviews the responsibilities of that role.
- The facilitator returns the sealed envelopes to individual participants.

Group Discussion

The initiator-reader checks with the group members to see that they have had sufficient silent time to complete Questions 1–3, compare their current with previous responses to these questions, and are ready to begin the discussion.

- The initiator-reader directs group members to the **Discussion Questions** in **Focus One** to guide student or intern teachers' discussion about insights and feelings about themselves as teachers, and the changes they would like to make in themselves based on new knowledge and experience in the classroom. All other group members assume and review their roles for the session.
- Members of the group share their experiences with teaching and their motivations for being a "good" teacher. How have their expectations of themselves as teachers changed with the experiences of teaching?
- The summarizer monitors the group conversation, rephrasing the comments and restating questions being discussed.

Writing the Action Plan

Where do student or intern teachers go from here? What actions will increase their understanding of the teacher role? How do student or intern teachers plan to practice the insights gained from the discussion about becoming professional teachers who have high expectations of self and students?

- Group members decide on the professional action that needs to be taken or practiced in the classroom.
- Along with the action to be taken, include the means the group will use for remembering the plan.
- Include specific ways individual members will be accountable to the group for implementing the action plan. Share these within the group and listen to others' ideas.
- The summarizer writes the group's action plan, and group members sign, indicating that all agree to practice the plan.
- The action plan—group accountability report along with the individual accountability reports and other materials are returned to the facilitator.

Seminar Follow-Up for Facilitator

- Review individual accountability reports and each group's action plan—group accountability report. Provide clear comments and purposeful feedback to groups regarding the plan as a means toward their renewed motivation to engage in developing professionally.

CHAPTER 9 FOCUS ONE: COOPERATIVE GROUP APPROACH

Teacher as Role Model

Focus One calls student or intern teachers to reflect on the impact modeling has on learners and others. Intentional modeling of attitudes, skills, and behaviors by the student or intern teacher and other professionals at the school are examined in light of the recent demand that values and moral training be reinstituted in school curriculum.

Seminar Procedures

- The facilitator opens the session and distributes to each group the individual accountability and action plan—group accountability reports collected during the last session.
- Groups review and discuss the prior week's action plan and assess their individual and collective success in achieving their goal.
- Each student or intern teacher selects the role he or she will perform and reviews the responsibilities of that role.

Group Discussion

The initiator-reader checks with the group members to see that they have had sufficient silent time to read the narrative of **Focus One** and are ready to begin the discussion.

- The initiator-reader directs group members to the **Discussion Questions** in **Focus One** to guide student or intern teachers' discussion about the effectiveness of modeling in the classroom, and share insights about themselves as models for students. All other group members assume and review their roles for the session.
- Members of the group share their experiences with modeling (intentional or not) and the results or impact on students in the classroom. Are student or intern teachers beginning to see themselves as teacher-models?
- The summarizer monitors the time and tasks to perform and assists with identifying common threads in discussion.

Writing the Action Plan

Where do student or intern teachers go from here? What actions will increase their understanding of the teacher role? How do student or intern teachers plan to practice the insights gained from the discussion about teacher as model?

- Group members decide on the professional action that needs to be taken or practiced in the coming week.
- Along with the action to be taken, include the means the group will use for remembering the plan.

- Include specific ways individual members will be accountable to the group for implementing the action plan. Share these with your group and listen to others' ideas.
- The summarizer writes the group's action plan, and group members sign, indicating that all agree to practice the plan.
- The action plan—group accountability report along with the individual accountability report and other materials are returned to the facilitator.

Seminar Follow-Up for Facilitator

- Review individual accountability reports and each group's action plan—group accountability report. Provide clear comments and purposeful feedback to groups regarding the plan as a means toward their professional development as effective teachers.
- Gather materials necessary for student or intern teachers to design a monument that symbolizes and communicates their ideals of teacher as professional. (See Chapter 10 for more details.)

EXAMPLES: ACTION PLAN

Try to be open and willing to accept new challenges as they arise. Try to be positive as we move to the second half of the semester. We will journal our feelings about the new surroundings. We will compare how we feel today with how we feel we handle situations in the classroom next week.

Facilitator comments:

Excellent plan—you are anticipating this coming week's reflection! What a positive attitude and attempt to accept what is coming— "come what may."

You seemed to really enjoy sharing with one another even though your responses were similar. Since you stepped away—do the similarities say more to you today than they did a week ago?

Group member's follow-up comments:

Things have been different, but we have tried to be positive every day. Although it's sometimes difficult to be positive, to let ourselves be negative would only be self-defeating.

Sample: Implementing action plan

For my action plan, I believe I have been VERY flexible and will be all this week. Today also could have been quite discouraging, but I am even surprised at how well I am handling negative attitudes (toward me and the class, etc.) and poor behavior. I think at the beginning some of these challenges would have gotten me down. Now, however, I take it with a grain of salt and learn what I can from it!

CHAPTER 10 FOCUS ONE: COOPERATIVE GROUP APPROACH

Reexamining Your Reasons for Becoming a Teacher

Focus One calls student or intern teachers to reflect on their beliefs about the teaching and learning processes, and their expectations of themselves as teacher. They are asked to highlight the characteristics of an effective teacher, and look at themselves in light of those characteristics with an eye on the present as well as the future.

Seminar Procedures

- The facilitator opens the session and distributes to each group the individual accountability and action plan—group accountability reports collected during the last session.
- Groups review and discuss the prior week's action plan and assess their individual and collective success in achieving their goal.
- Each student or intern teacher selects the role he or she will perform and reviews the responsibilities of that role.
- The facilitator provides the materials individual group members will need to create a monument that symbolizes the characteristics they most prize in professional educators and teachers who inspire them. Remind participants that they may draw, use a word splash, or implement other ways to create the monument.

Group Discussion

The initiator-reader checks with the group members to see that they have had sufficient time to complete their illustration, and are ready to begin the discussion.

- The initiator-reader directs group members to the **Discussion Questions** in **Focus One** to guide student or intern teachers' discussion about the characteristics they have chosen to describe the teachers they aspire to become. All other group members assume and review their roles for the session.
- Members of the group share their monuments and discuss the themes they have in common and the implications for their professional journeys.

Writing the Action Plan

Where do student or intern teachers go from here? What actions will increase their understanding of the teacher role? How do student or intern teachers plan to practice the insights gained from the discussion about becoming a professional teacher who has high expectations of self and students?

- Group members decide on the professional action that needs to be taken or practiced in the coming week.
- Along with the action to be taken, include the means the group will use for remembering the plan.
- Include specific ways individual members will be accountable to the group for implementing the action plan. Share these within the group and listen to others' ideas.
- The summarizer writes the group's action plan, and group members sign, indicating that all agree to practice the plan.
- The action plan—group accountability report along with the individual accountability reports and other materials are returned to the facilitator.

Seminar Follow-Up for Facilitator

- Review individual accountability reports and each group's action plan—group accountability report. Provide clear comments and purposeful feedback to groups regarding the plan as a means toward their professional development as effective teachers.

CHAPTER 11 FOCUS ONE: COOPERATIVE GROUP APPROACH

Look Where I Am!

Focus One asks student or intern teachers to examine how far they have come as teachers since the beginning of the student or intern teaching experience.

They are asked to compare their feelings of success to those of their students when accomplishing learning. They are invited to acknowledge the different phases of their affective and cognitive learning, and share responses and insights within their cooperative learning groups.

Seminar Procedures

- The facilitator opens the session and distributes to each group the individual accountability and action plan—group accountability reports collected during the last session.
- Groups review and discuss the prior week's action plan and assess their individual and collective success in achieving their goal.
- Each student or intern teacher selects the role he or she will perform and reviews the responsibilities of that role.

Group Discussion

The initiator-reader checks with the group members to see that they have had sufficient time to read the narrative of **Focus One** and are ready to begin the discussion.

- The initiator-reader directs group members to the **Discussion Questions** in **Focus One** to guide student or intern teachers' discussion about their individual growth over time as educators and the supports they sought to guide them toward becoming more effective in the role of teacher. All other group members assume and review their roles for the session.
- Members of the group share their journeys through the student or intern teaching experience and assess their affective and cognitive responses as they proceeded through different phases of learning to teach. Are student or intern teachers able to acknowledge their growth and articulate areas of need?
- The summarizer attends to the time and the content being discussed, assisting the group in recognizing common understandings about their learning to teach

Writing the Action Plan

What actions will increase student or intern teachers' understanding of the teacher's role and responsibilities for designing curriculum, teaching to individual learning styles and needs, and assessing student learning to design new instruction? How will student or intern teachers implement their plans to practice the insights gained from the group discussion?

- Group members decide on the professional action that needs to be taken or practiced in the coming week.
- Along with the action to be taken, include the means the group will use for remembering the plan.
- Include specific ways individual members will be accountable to the group for implementing the action plan. Share these within the group and listen to others' ideas.
- The summarizer writes the group's action plan, and group members sign, indicating that all agree to practice the plan.
- The action plan—group accountability report along with the individual accountability reports and other materials are returned to the facilitator.

Seminar Follow-Up for Facilitator

- Review individual accountability reports and each group's action plan—group accountability report. Provide clear comments and purposeful feedback to groups regarding the plan as a means toward their professional development as effective teachers.

FIGURE B.3 *Puzzle Activity*

Source: From *Handbook of Skills Essential to Beginning Teachers*, by M. S. Goethals and R. A. Howard,1985, Lanham, MD: University Press of America.

- Gather materials and copy puzzle pieces (see Figure B.3) for collaborative learning activity for the next session.

CHAPTER 12 FOCUS ONE: COOPERATIVE GROUP APPROACH

Am I a Collaborator, a Team Player?

Focus One invites student or intern teachers to engage in a problem-solving activity designed to give them insights into the importance of collaboration in the classroom and at the school level. They are asked to analyze and reflect on the elements necessary to effective teamwork and collaboration, and challenged to implement those in their own classes.

Seminar Procedures

- The facilitator opens the session and distributes to each group the individual accountability and action plan—group accountability reports collected during the last session.
- Groups review and discuss the prior session action plan and assess their individual and collective success in achieving their goal.
- Each student or intern teacher selects the role he or she will perform and reviews the responsibilities of that role.

Cooperative Group Learning Activity

The facilitator provides each student or intern teacher with an envelope containing one or more geometric pieces. In groups of five, student or intern teachers correctly assemble the puzzle while the facilitator monitors group progress. Facilitators will want to assemble all rectangles (squares) and place an assortment from each into five different envelopes.

- Groups complete puzzles according to directions in Chapter 12. These directions may be given by the facilitator or the initiator-reader in each group.
- Group size can be reduced and the number of different rectangular designs reduced accordingly.
- One or two seminar participants may assist the facilitator in monitoring the groups following the rules for the puzzle activity.

Group Discussion

The initiator-reader checks with group members to see that they have had sufficient silent time to correctly complete the puzzle and are ready to begin the discussion.

- The initiator-reader directs group members to the **Discussion Questions** in **Focus One,** to guide student or intern teachers' discussion about the collaborative problem-solving activity just completed, and to identify the elements of teamwork as well as some of the pitfalls associated with loosely structured collaborative problem-solving and project work. All other group members assume and review their roles for the session.
- Members of the group share their insights about collaborative learning and teamwork and apply it to the school setting and their own classrooms.

Writing the Action Plan

What actions will increase student or intern teachers' understanding of teacher as collaborator and team player? In what ways does collaboration impact student or intern teachers' responsibilities for designing curriculum, teaching to individual learning styles and needs, and assessing student learning? How will student or intern teachers implement their plan to practice the insights gained from the group discussion?

- Group members decide on the professional action that needs to be taken or practiced in the coming week.
- Along with the action to be taken, include the means the group will use for remembering the plan.
- Include specific ways individual members will be accountable to the group for implementing the action plan. Share these within the group and listen to others' ideas.
- The summarizer writes the group's action plan, and group members sign, indicating that all agree to practice the plan.
- The action plan—group accountability report along with the individual accountability reports and other materials are returned to the facilitator.

Seminar Follow-up for Facilitator

- Review individual accountability reports and each group's action plan— group accountability report. Provide clear comments and purposeful feedback to groups regarding the plan as a means toward their professional development as effective teachers.
- Make copies of Figure B.4 for student or intern teachers and provide materials and markers, and so on for next session.

Chapter 13 Focus One: Cooperative Group Approach

For Who I Am and What I Have, Thanks!

Focus One invites student or intern teachers to reflect on the ways their individual gifts, talents, and abilities help fulfill aspects of their role as teacher. They are asked to share their insights about the impact their specific gifts have on their teaching and their students' learning. Student or intern teachers are challenged to consider their principles in conjunction with their role as teacher in preparing citizens for a democratic society.

Seminar Procedures

- The facilitator opens the session and distributes to each group the individual accountability and action plan—group accountability reports collected during the last session.
- Groups review and discuss the prior week's action plan and assess their individual and collective success in achieving their goal.
- Each student or intern teacher selects the role he or she will perform and reviews the responsibilities of that role.

Cooperative Group Learning Activity

- The facilitator provides each student or intern teacher with a photocopy of a gift (see Figure B.4). Students are asked to write words or illustrate the gifts, talents, and abilities they have to set the tone for the cooperative group discussion. The facilitator monitors groups' progress and sets the time limit for the discussion.

Group Discussion

The initiator-reader checks with group members to see that they have had sufficient time to illustrate their gifts, and so forth and are ready to begin the discussion.

- The initiator-reader directs group members to the **Discussion Questions** in **Focus One** to guide student or intern teachers' discussion about the individual gifts, talents, and abilities each member possesses and the responsible use of them. All other group members assume and review their roles for the session.
- Members of the group share their insights about their gifts, and so on and discuss the impact their gifts have on the students they teach as they educate them to act as citizens of a democracy.
- The summarizer monitors the time and assists the group in recognizing common threads from the discussion.

Writing the Action Plan

As their last opportunity for adopting an action with their cohorts, student or intern teachers may want to consider a plan that extends beyond the coming week. As professional teachers, how might they approach challenges they will encounter during the following weeks? What support systems are available to them that would benefit them in transitioning to Teacher?

- Group members decide on the professional action that needs to be taken or practiced in the coming week.
- Along with the action to be taken, include the means the group will use for remembering the plan.

FIGURE B.4   *Monument to Your Special Gifts*

- Include specific ways individual members will be accountable to the group for implementing the action plan. Share these within the group and listen to others' ideas.
- The summarizer writes the group's action plan, and group members sign, indicating that all agree to practice the plan.
- The action plan—group accountability report along with the individual accountability reports and other materials are returned to the facilitator.

Seminar Follow-Up for Facilitator
- Review individual accountability reports and each group's action plan—group accountability report. Provide clear comments and purposeful feedback to groups regarding the plan as a means toward their professional development as effective teachers.

appendix
C

New Teacher Standards: National (INTASC); New Teacher (State); and Technology (ISTE)

INTERSTATE NEW TEACHER ASSESSMENT AND SUPPORT CONSORTIUM (INTASC) STANDARDS FOR BEGINNING TEACHER LICENSING

1. The teacher understands the central concepts, tools of inquiry, and structures of the discipline(s) he or she teaches and can create learning experiences that make these aspects of subject matter meaningful for students.
2. The teacher understands how children learn and develop, and can provide learning opportunities that support their intellectual, social, and personal development.
3. The teacher understands how students differ in their approaches to learning and creates instructional opportunities that are adapted to diverse learners.
4. The teacher understands and uses a variety of instructional strategies to encourage students' development of critical thinking, problem solving, and performance skills.
5. The teacher uses an understanding of individual and group motivation and behavior to create a learning environment that encourages positive social interaction, active engagement in learning, and self-motivation.
6. The teacher uses knowledge of effective verbal, nonverbal, and media communication techniques to foster active inquiry, collaboration, and supportive interaction in the classroom.
7. The teacher plans instruction based upon knowledge of subject matter, students, the community, and curriculum goals.
8. The teacher understands and uses formal and informal assessment strategies to evaluate and ensure the continuous intellectual, social, and physical development of the learner.
9. The teacher is a reflective practitioner who continually evaluates the effects of his/her choices and actions on others (students, parents, and other professionals in the learning community) and who actively seeks out opportunities to grow professionally.
10. The teacher fosters relationships with school colleagues, parents, and agencies in the larger community to support students' learning and well-being.

NEW TEACHER STANDARDS FOR PREPARATION AND CERTIFICATION

Adopted June 1993, Revised November 1994. The Kentucky Education Professional Standards Board.

New Teacher Standard I: Designs and Plans Instruction

Standard Statement I: The teacher designs/plans instruction and learning climates that develop student abilities to use communication skills, apply core concepts, become self-sufficient individuals, become responsible team members, think and solve problems, and integrate knowledge.

New Teacher Standard II: Creates/Maintains Learning Climates

Standard Statement II: The teacher creates a learning climate that supports the development of student abilities to use communication skills, apply core concepts, become self-sufficient individuals, become responsible team members, think and solve problems, and integrate knowledge.

New Teacher Standard III: Implements/Manages Instruction

Standard Statement III: The teacher introduces/implements/manages instruction that develops student abilities to use communication skills, apply core concepts, become self-sufficient individuals, become responsible team members, think and solve problems, and integrate knowledge.

New Teacher Standard IV: Assesses and Communicates Learning Results

Standard Statement IV: The teacher assesses learning and communicates results to students and others with respect to student abilities to use communication skills, apply core concepts, become self-sufficient individuals, become responsible team members, think and solve problems, and integrate knowledge.

New Teacher Standard V: Reflects/Evaluates Teaching/Learning

Standard Statement V: The teacher reflects on and evaluates specific teaching/learning situations and/or programs.

New Teacher Standard VI: Collaborates With Colleagues, Parents, and Others

Standard Statement VI: The teacher collaborates with colleagues, parents, and other agencies to design, implement, and support learning programs that develop student abilities to use communication skills, apply core concepts, become self-sufficient individuals, become responsible team members, think and solve problems, and integrate knowledge.

New Teacher Standard VII: Engages in Professional Development

Standard Statement VII: The teacher evaluates his/her overall performance with respect to modeling and teaching Kentucky's learning goals, refines the skills and processes necessary, and implements a professional development plan.

New Teacher Standard VIII: Knowledge of Content

Standard Statement VIII: The teacher demonstrates a current and sufficient academic knowledge of certified content areas to develop student knowledge and performance in those areas.

New Teacher Standard IX: Demonstrates Implementation of Technology

Standard Statement IX: The teacher uses technology to support instruction; access and manipulate data; enhance professional growth and productivity; communicate and collaborate with colleagues, parents, and the community; and conduct research.

NATIONAL EDUCATIONAL TECHNOLOGY STANDARDS (NETS)

Technology Performance Profile for Student Teaching/Internship

Web site: http://cnets.iste.org

Upon completion of the culminating student teaching or internship experience, and at the point of initial licensure, teachers:

Numbers in parentheses following each performance indicator refer to the standards category to which the performance is linked. The categories are:

I. Technology Operations and Concepts

II. Planning and Designing Learning Environments and Experiences

III. Teaching, Learning, and the Curriculum

IV. Assessment and Evaluation

V. Productivity and Professional Practice

VI. Social, Ethical, Legal, and Human Issues

1. apply troubleshooting strategies for solving routine hardware and software problems that occur in the classroom. (I)
2. identify, evaluate, and select specific technology resources available at the school site and district level to support a coherent lesson sequence. (II, III)
3. design, manage, and facilitate learning experiences using technology that affirm diversity and provide equitable access to resources. (II, VI)
4. create and implement a well-organized plan to manage available technology resources, provide equitable access for all students, and enhance learning outcomes. (II, III)
5. design and facilitate learning experiences that use assistive technologies to meet the special physical needs of students. (II, III)
6. design and teach a coherent sequence of learning activities that integrates appropriate use of technology resources to enhance student academic achievement and technology proficiency by connecting district, state, and national curriculum standards with student technology standards (as defined in the ISTE National Educational Technology Standards for Students). (II, III)
7. design, implement, and assess learner-centered lessons that are based on the current best practices on teaching and learning with technology and that engage, motivate, and encourage self-directed student learning. (II, III, IV, V)
8. guide collaborative learning activities in which students use technology resources to solve authentic problems in the subject area(s). (III)
9. develop and use criteria for ongoing assessment of technology-based student products and the processes used to create those products. (IV)
10. design an evaluation plan that applies multiple measures and flexible assessment strategies to determine students' technology proficiency and content area learning. (IV)
11. use multiple measures to analyze instructional practices that employ technology to improve planning, instruction, and management. (II, III, IV)
12. apply technology productivity tools and resources to collect, analyze, and interpret data and to report results to parents and students. (III, IV)
13. select and apply suitable productivity tools to complete educational and professional tasks. (II, III, V)
14. model safe and responsible use of technology and develop classroom procedures to implement school and district technology acceptable use policies and data security plans. (V, VI)
15. participate in online professional collaboration with peers and experts as part of a personally designed plan, based on self-assessment, for professional growth in technology. (V)

INTERNATIONAL SOCIETY FOR TECHNOLOGY IN EDUCATION (ISTE) NATIONAL EDUCATIONAL TECHNOLOGY STANDARDS FOR STUDENTS

1. **Basic operations and concepts**
   - Students demonstrate a sound understanding of the nature and operation of technology systems.
   - Students are proficient in the use of technology.
2. **Social, ethical, and human issues**
   - Students understand the ethical, cultural, and societal issues related to technology.
   - Students practice responsible use of technology systems, information, and software.
   - Students develop positive attitudes toward technology uses that support lifelong learning, collaboration, personal pursuits, and productivity.
3. **Technology productivity tools**
   - Students use technology tools to enhance learning, increase productivity, and promote creativity.
   - Students use productivity tools to collaborate in constructing technology-enhanced models, prepare publications, and produce other creative works.
4. **Technology communications tools**
   - Students use telecommunications to collaborate, publish, and interact with peers, experts, and other audiences.
   - Students use a variety of media and formats to communicate information and ideas effectively to multiple audiences.
5. **Technology research tools**
   - Students use technology to locate, evaluate, and collect information from a variety of sources.
   - Students use technology tools to process data and report results.
   - Students evaluate and select new information resources and technological innovations based on the appropriateness for specific tasks.
6. **Technology problem-solving and decision-making tools**
   - Students use technology resources for solving problems and making informed decisions.
   - Students employ technology in the development of strategies for solving problems in the real world.

appendix
D

Getting Organized

BEGINNING TEACHER CHECKLIST

Are you concerned about how to get started? To facilitate organization and planning for this important venture, the following list is provided for you to consider.

1. Call the principal and cooperating teacher of your school prior to appearing at the school. Introduce yourself as a student or intern teacher. Let the principal know you would like to be present for any meetings held prior to the first day of class. Ask that you be informed of dates and times. These meetings can be essential to your becoming partner teacher and member of the faculty in the school setting.
2. Keep a schedule of all important dates to remember. Be on time and appear in professional dress for any meetings.
3. Work as partner with your supervising or team teacher in such activities as:
   arranging the classroom
   scheduling classes
   preparing and organizing materials
   designing bulletin boards
4. Examine the student or intern teacher handbook from your college or university. You may have questions regarding the required competencies, legal status of your role, or personnel involved in the student or intern teacher experience.
5. Record the time spent in observation, participation, and actual teaching experience. You will find a Log of Hours chart for recording time in this Appendix.
6. Enter the observations, reflections, activities, and suggestions made each day in a separate journal or log.

STUDENT TEACHER OBSERVATION GUIDE

This outline is intended to help you become a more perceptive observer. You are encouraged to use any part or all of the outline when observing teaching activities. The questions may be used following an observation as you reflect on what you recalled and examined.

I. Planning Procedures

- Can you tell by listening to and observing the teacher what the student learning outcomes are for this lesson?
- Is the purpose of this lesson to develop skills, convey information, or help the students develop attitudes and values?
- Can you write the objectives or outcomes of this lesson, using the criteria for complete instructional objectives?

- Is there evidence that the students were involved in planning the lesson? Were motivating activities planned and used? Culminating activities?
- Can the specific objectives or outcomes of this lesson be synchronized with the goals of the unit?

II. Content

- Is the subject matter adapted to meet the diverse needs of the students? Is the integrity of the content or concept preserved? Are adaptations and extensions appropriate to ensure achievement of the lesson's objectives for all learners?
- What is the source of subject matter: textbooks, other books, films, handouts, others?
- Is the subject content used as an end in itself or as a vehicle for achieving desired learning outcomes?

III. Teaching Strategies

- What teaching strategies are used? Does the teacher lecture, lead class discussion, ask questions, use technology or webbing, or use small-group procedures? Is one strategy used exclusively or is there a variety of techniques?
- How are students motivated? Does the teacher gain interest and maintain it? Are the procedures appropriate for the attention span and developmental levels of the students?
- Are reinforcement techniques used? In what ways? What is reinforced?
- Is the text used? What other materials would be effective?
- Was momentum established and maintained? Are transitions accomplished smoothly?

IV. Student Activities

- Are students interested, involved, active, and challenged?
- What percentage of the time is used in student-centered activities?
- Is appropriate student behavior rewarded? How? Are students praised?
- Do students initiate responses? Are students' ideas accepted? Must students be prodded for answers?
- Are students interacting with one another? Positively? Negatively?

V. Evaluation of Teaching-Learning

- Did the evaluation of today's lesson set the stage for the next lesson?
- Was evaluation done in terms of the skills, knowledge, and attitudes developed?
- Was evaluation done by the teacher? Students? Both?

SNAPSHOTS OF MY STUDENTS

(Parent or Guardian Information Sheet)

Dear Parents or Guardians:

Greetings to you from _____ School! It is especially exciting for me to begin this school year, and I am looking forward to meeting your son or daughter. I invite you to help me know more about your child/adolescent by filling out the short survey questions listed below. This will enable me to better meet the needs of your child/adolescent and assist him or her in reaching academic goals. Please return the questionnaire by September 1. I look forward to meeting you at our first parent orientation and open house. Thank you for your support and encouragement.

Sincerely,

Ms. Sanders

Name _____

1. Which subject does your son or daughter most enjoy?

2. Which subject does your son or daughter find the most difficult?

3. What are your son's or daughter's favorite books?

4. Does he or she have any special interests?

5. Are there any circumstances (family, academic, physical, social, or other) you would like to share with me that would allow me to better meet the needs of your son or daughter?

6. Tell me any other information you'd like to share to help me get to better know your son or daughter.

Log of Hours

Student/Intern teacher:

School:

Cooperative teacher:

Month: _____

Week One	Monday	Tuesday	Wednesday	Thursday	Friday
Observed:					
Participated:					
Taught:					
Other activities:					

Week	Monday	Tuesday	Wednesday	Thursday	Friday
Observed:					
Participated:					
Taught:					
Other activities:					

OBSERVED ____ HOURS

PARTICIPATED ____ HOURS

TAUGHT ____ HOURS

____ **Totals**

Student/Intern teacher signature   Date

Cooperating teacher signature   Date

(may be duplicated for additional weeks)

appendix
E

Lesson Plan Models

LESSON PLAN FORMAT

Name: _____ Date: _____

Age/Grade level: _____

Subject: _____ # of students _____ # of students: with

IEP (Individualized Education plan):

Major content: _____ Unit Title: _____

CRITERIA FOR PLANNING LESSONS

Essential Question(s)

Identify essential questions you want to address in terms of student learning. For example: Why is it important for me (the learner) to know how to write a business letter using the proper format? Essential questions guide the teaching and learning process, and as they are answered provide the rationale for learners to meet the objectives you have written. Essential questions usually begin with *how, why, what if,* and so on to relay the importance of what is learned in the classroom to the real world.

Goals and Objectives

Clearly state broad goals and specific objectives that identify the content and skills or processes you plan to teach and formally assess. What are the academic and social expectations you have for all students?

Student Assessment

Clearly state how you will assess student progress in meeting the lesson's listed objectives. Will you provide a performance criteria or rubric for students, use checklists or anecdotal records, or use a teacher-made or publisher's test to assess the effectiveness of the lesson? Will learners participate in the process through self-reflection and self or peer assessment? If so, attach sample(s) to the lesson.

Adaptations or Extensions to the Lesson

Scaffold learning in such a way that all learners can meet the objectives you have for the lesson, including students with IEP or Section 504 plans, without sacrificing the integrity of the content. Specifically state what you intend to do or make available for learners with special and other needs to guarantee their access to the curriculum.

Connections

List targeted learning objectives and explain how your objectives relate state goals and standards for learning content provided by professional organizations: NCTE, NCTM, NCSS, and so on. What will teaching look like in your class to the observer, and why are you doing what you are doing?

Context

Describe how the objectives in your lesson relate to the broad goals you outlined for teaching the topic. Explain the major focus of the unit to which the lesson belongs, and how the lesson relates to the unit. Are there personal, social, cultural, or global concerns that are relevant to student learning in your class? If so, address the circumstances or issues to clarify and contextualize learning for students.

Resources

List all materials, including technology and technology applications, necessary for the full implementation of your lesson. Are you using handouts and other printed material with learners, including adapted materials designed to meet the specific needs of individual learners? If so, attach them to the lesson.

Procedures

Describe the steps and strategies you plan to use to actively involve students in learning to accomplish your objectives for the lesson. How will you activate prior knowledge or build background knowledge with your students? What motivation (other than the essential questions for the lesson or unit) will set the stage for learning among your students? What steps are necessary for the successful implementation and closure of your lesson? Include strategies you plan to teach, model, or use to reach your objectives. What adaptations, organizers, concept diagrams, or other tools of intervention will you use with students to ensure meaningful learning occurs in your classroom? How will you (or students) close the lesson and return to the essential or guiding questions to bring learners full circle with what you have taught and what they have learned?

Reflection and Analysis of Teaching and Learning

Did the students learn what you intended them to learn? How are they progressing? What are the indicators of their achievement? Did you impact learning among low- and high-achieving students with what you taught in your lesson? Include students' samples of work (high, average, low) for analysis to direct your next phase of instruction. What worked well with your students? What do you plan to do differently the next time you teach? What are your expectations for the learners?

Refinement of a Lesson

Based on your reflection, what do you plan to do in subsequent lesson plans to reinforce, reteach, or extend learning for all students?

LESSON PLAN EXAMPLES

Elementary School Lesson Plan: Science

Name: Mindy Ashford   **Date:** October 14

Lesson length: 45 MINUTES

School: ELEMENTARY   **Age/Grade level:** 2   **# of students:** 22

Subject: Science   **Topic:** Life science—   **# of IEP students:** 3
organisms

Objectives

Broad Goals

The students will:

1. Work cooperatively in small groups of 4–5 students.
2. Participate in large-group activities by answering questions posed by the teacher and other students.
3. Identify in writing the difference between organisms and objects that are not organisms.

Specific Objectives

The students will:

1. Write a definition of an organism with 90% accuracy.
2. Write the four basic needs of an organism with 90% accuracy.
3. Identify organisms in writing when given examples with 85% accuracy.
4. Create a collage with examples of organisms and objects that are not organisms.

Student Assessment

1. Using anecdotal records, check the degree to which individual students work cooperatively in a group setting and perform individual roles.
2. Using teacher observation and a checklist, check the level of participation of individual students as they respond to teacher and student questions.
3. Using an activity sheet, students will be assessed on their ability to distinguish between living organisms and inanimate objects, with 95% accuracy the target.
4. Students' work (collages) will be assessed to determine the quality of the product created by a small group. Individual and collective marks will be assigned.

Connections: Kentucky Learning Goals

1.2   Students make sense of a variety of materials they read.
1.3   Students make sense of the various things they observe.
1.4   Students make sense of the various messages to which they listen.

1.10 Students organize information through development and use of classification rules and systems.

2.1 Students understand scientific ways of thinking and working and use those methods to solve real-life problems.

2.2 Students identify and analyze systems and the ways their components work together or affect each other.

2.3 Students use the concept of scale and scientific models to explain the organization and functioning of living and nonliving things and predict other characteristics that might be observed.

Context

This lesson is an introduction to organisms and their characteristics. The students will learn what an organism is and what organisms need to survive. This lesson leads into the life cycles of organisms and habitats.

Materials and Technology

1. magnetic cards with examples of organisms as well as items that are not organisms
2. chart paper
3. magazines and newspapers
4. glue and scissors
5. poster paper
6. scrap paper

Procedures

- Before the class assembles, write "What is an organism?" on the board. Make two columns, one labeled "Organisms" and the other labeled "Not Organisms."
- Review the procedures of the classroom routines and structures. The lesson will begin with large-group instruction and exploration of the concept, and end with small-group work where students will have time to work together to discuss what they are seeing and learning as they decide how to arrange their collage to demonstrate the concepts of living organisms and inanimate objects.
- Read the focus question on the board with the whole class.
- Ask if anyone has heard the word "organism" before by show of hands.
- Ask if anyone knows what an organism is by a show of hands.
- Place pictures of organisms in the appropriate columns on the board. With the class, decide which column each picture belongs in.
- Pass out scrap paper for each group.
- In small groups, have students talk about what they think organisms are and write their ideas on paper. Definitions and examples are acceptable.
- Have groups share what they have recorded and write their ideas on the board.
- Brainstorm to create a class definition and record it on chart paper. Make sure students know that an organism means a "living thing." Record or draw examples on the chart paper to illustrate their ideas.
- Explain to students that they will now work in small groups to create an organism collage. Model or show my example as a work in progress.
- State expectations for group behaviors and quality of work.
- Pass out poster paper for each group. Assign one person in the group to be the recorder and instruct that person to write the names of the members of the group on the back of the poster. The recorder will fold the poster in half and label each column as on the board.

- The materials collector gathers magazines and newspapers for the group, scissors, and glue.
- Monitor students as they make their collage and take anecdotal records on group participation checklists.
- Give students a 10–minute reminder before time is up for work on the collage. This will allow them time to glue the pictures they have found under the correct column on the poster paper.
- Present collages to the large group for feedback and discussion.
- Hand out an activity sheet to be completed by individual students and used to assess their understanding of organisms and nonliving things.

Impact and Refinement

After the lesson, write an impact analysis and refinement follow-up to be reviewed during the conference with my cooperating and university supervisor.

Impact—Reflection and Analysis of Teaching and Student Learning I was pleased with the lesson and the way it was implemented. This group worked at a slower pace than the previous two groups; however, all of the instructional goals were met. I was extremely impressed with the way these children worked together in their small groups. This was my first lesson, and even though the students have been taught about roles and working together, I was not sure about the dynamics because I had placed them randomly in groups and assigned new roles. Within minutes of adjusting to the new arrangement, they were actively engaged and participating in the lesson and group work. The students were very responsive during large-group instruction, and I had little problem with discipline.

Refinement—Lesson Extension and Follow-Up The follow-up lesson involves the students brainstorming what basic needs of organisms are. We will discuss the differences between wants and needs (I need one million dollars versus I need a house to live in). This lesson also engages the students by reinforcing basic needs through an activity I plan to use. Some of the students will be birds, some worms, waters, and so on. The students will need to connect with others to have their basic needs met. This supply and demand for resources will help students make connections about how systems work in the world, and what happens when needs are not met.

ELEMENTARY SCHOOL LESSON PLAN: LANGUAGE ARTS

Course level: Third or fourth grade

Name: JULIE HALL

Period of day: 10:00 a.m.

Type of lesson: Language arts integrated with science

Guiding and Essential questions

- How can I get students involved in the story *Peter's Place?*
- After observing an oil spill experiment, will the students be able to write their observations?

Objectives

After completing this lesson the students will be able to:

1. Identify unfamiliar vocabulary words.

2. Listen to the story, *Peter's Place,* and answer specific questions.
3. Observe and participate in an oil spill experiment.
4. Write about what they observed during the experiment and what was learned about oil spills during the lesson.
5. Reflect on their participation and complete a self-assessment form.

Assessment

Complete the attached performance rubric regarding student participation in reading and writing observations.

Multiple Intelligences Challenged

The intelligences that were challenged by this lesson include Verbal/Linguistic, Visual/Spatial, Intrapersonal, and Interpersonal.

Materials Needed

Bring the following materials: A copy of *Peter's Place* by Sally Grindley, pocket chart, sentence strips, oil, paprika, dish detergent, two bowls, water, spatula, feathers, cotton balls, copies of self-assessment form, pencils, and paper.

Modification for Special Needs

The students in cooperative groups will actually be involved in an oil spill experiment. All students with special needs will actively participate with a particular group responsibility (e.g., M. will be the timer for his group; S. will be materials handler for her group; J. needs guided notes). The oral discussion allows the students' individual responses to be heard. I will choose responders from cards I shuffle after every class period.

Procedure: Lesson Initiation

Overview: Brief synopsis of the story, including previewing the vocabulary in the story; reading of the story; discussion; culminating activity in which an experiment is conducted based on the story; completion of written observations; and self-assessments.

Lesson Development Before reading, discuss unfamiliar words with students. Words will be displayed on sentence strips for the students to identify and learn the meanings (e.g., *ravaged, turbulent, haven, crevice,* and names of birds). Story is read to the students.

Questions Generate a discussion of the story with the following:

How do you think Peter feels about his place at the beginning? After the spill?
Why did Peter help with the cleanup effort and rescue?
What would you have done?
What were your feelings at the end of the story?

Guided Practice Discuss oil spills with the students, including how oil is transported, spilled, the damage a spill causes, and how it is cleaned and removed. Allow for their questions to surface.

Students will observe and participate in the model experiment. I will create a miniature oil spill and try different methods of cleaning it up. Colored cooking oil will be placed in a bowl of water, and several objects will be placed in it so students may see the damage a spill can cause. Students will then create their own models in their cooperative groups. I will demonstrate three methods of cleaning up an oil spill—skimming the surface of the water, absorbing the oil around the edges, and adding detergents. After the students have completed their experiments, we will discuss the effectiveness of each method.

Independent Practice Explain the writing activity to students. They will write about what they observed during the experiment and what they learned about oil spills. For those who may finish before others, they may also write about any feelings they have about what they observed and learned.

Closure Pass out self-assessments for students to complete independently. Explain the directions, and remind students to be honest in their responses. If time permits, have students share something they learned today.

Reflection To what degree were the students actively involved in reading the story *Peter's Place?*

    After observing an oil spill experiment, to what degree were the students able to clearly write their observations?

Performance Criteria/Rubric

4—Student participated in the discussion of the story. The student participated in discussion of and experiment demonstrating oil spills. The student demonstrated an understanding of the experiment by writing 3–4 paragraphs discussing their observations. Student completed self-assessment.
3—Student participated in the discussion of the story and oil spills. Student demonstrated an understanding of the experiment by writing 2–3 paragraphs discussing their observations. Students completed self-assessment.
2—Student participated, although very little, to the discussion. Student demonstrated some difficulty in understanding the experiment, and the 1–2 paragraphs about the experiment were sketchy. Student completed assessment with assistance.
1—Student did not participate in discussion of story or oil spills. Student demonstrated much difficulty in understanding the experiment, and was only able to write a few sentences about his or her observations. Student did not complete self-assessment even though assistance was offered.

Elementary School Lesson Plan: Math

Name: Pam Naylor   **Date:** September 20   **Lesson length:** 60 minutes

School: ELEMENTARY   **Grade/Age level:** 5TH GRADE   **# of students:** 29

                                 # of IEP students: 5 (includes speech)

Subject: MATH   **Topic:** MULTIPLICATION AND DIVISION

TYPE OF LESSON: INTRODUCTORY: RAISINET RENDEZVOUS

Broad Goals

1. To provide students with real-world problem-solving opportunities.
2. To provide students an opportunity to work cooperatively to problem solve.
3. To engage students in discussing the multiplication and division processes.
4. To engage students in critical thinking as they reflect on and record their thought processes.

Specific Objectives

The students will:

1. Work the steps of a problem and record the strategies used for each step of the problem-solving activity on a "group think" chart paper.

2. Estimate the number of Raisinets in an unopened bag and record their estimates on chart paper and write reasons that support their estimation.
3. Open the bag of Raisinets to view the contents and revise their estimates if they wish, while recording why they changed the original estimate.
4. Collectively determine the number of Raisinets in the bag and record the amount using sentence format on chart paper.
5. Record on chart paper individual estimates each group member would have if they divided them equally among themselves.
6. Compare their estimates and reach a group consensus stating the amount each member of the group would receive after equally dividing the bag of candy.
7. Record their thought processes as they worked the problem together.
8. Produce a written map or flow chart to describe their thinking as they solved the problem.

Assessment

Use the scoring guide (attached) to assess the degree (0–4) to which each student records all steps of the problem-solving process used. Does the student include accurate details that support the process? Engage in reflective thinking about the process? Complete individual work samples and contributions in writing to the group's chart paper?

Connections

Kentucky Core Content for Assessment Student will describe properties of, give examples of, and apply to real world situations: whole numbers (0–100,000,000), fractions, mixed numbers, and decimals through thousandths.

1.1.1 Students will describe properties of, give examples of, and make applications to real world situations operations of addition, subtraction, multiplication, and division.
1.1.4 Student will describe properties of, give examples of, and apply to real world situations: place value, expanded form, number magnitude (order, compare) to decimals through thousandths.
1.1.5 Student will describe properties of, give examples of, and apply to real world situations: multiple representations of numbers (e.g., drawings, manipulatives, symbols).
1.2.1 Student will perform mathematical operations and procedures accurately and efficiently, explain how skills work in real world or mathematical situations and are able to: read, write, and rename whole numbers.
1.2.2 Student will perform mathematical operations and procedures accurately and efficiently, explain how skills work in real world or mathematical situations and are able to: add, subtract, multiply, and divide whole numbers using a variety of methods (e.g., mental, paper and pencil, calculator).
1.2.5 Student will perform mathematical operations and procedures accurately and efficiently, explain how skills work in real world or mathematical situations and are able to estimate quantities of objects.
1.2.6 Student will perform mathematical operations and procedures accurately and efficiently, explain how skills work in real world or mathematical situations and are able to estimate computational results using an appropriate strategy.

Kentucky Learning Goals and Academic Expectations

1.5–1.9 Students use mathematical ideas and procedures to communicate, reason, and solve problems.

2.7	Students understand number concepts and use numbers appropriately and accurately.
2.8	Students understand various mathematical procedures and use them appropriately and accurately.
2.37	Students demonstrate skills and work habits that lead to success in future schooling and work.
5.1	Students use critical thinking skills such as analyzing, prioritizing, categorizing, evaluating, and comparing to solve a variety of problems in real-life situations.
6.2	Student use what they already know to acquire new knowledge, develop new skills, or interpret new experience.

Context

We have been reviewing multiplication for the past week. Most of the students have done very well. Students have mastered the process, but still need multiplication practice. We use the acronym Dead Mice Smell Bad to represent the steps of the division process (**D**ivide, **M**ultiply, **S**ubtract, **B**ring down). This lesson connects prior knowledge to new learning about thinking processes necessary to dividing three- and four-digit numbers.

Materials

- poster board or chart paper for each group
- Raisinets for each group (medium-sized bag)
- individual papers for students to record their findings and reflect on strategies they used to come to an answer
- several colors of markers for recording information (whole group) on chart paper
- paper plates or napkins
- clean hands

Procedure

Instruct students to get out a clean piece of paper and clear their desks. Pass out napkins or plates, one for each student in each group.

Say: "Today we are going to really think about math, and we are going to show our thinking by writing down our thoughts. Each of you will work independently on some things, work together on others to solve a problem."

Pass out Raisinets and instruct students not to eat them, or even open the bag. Assure them that they will eat them, once the activity is completed by each individual in each group.

Model the behavior. Take one bag of Raisinets, walk around the room quickly, and allow all students to see the bag. Have them guess how many Raisinets are in my bag. Record the number on the board or chart paper. Have the students do the same in their small groups without touching the bag of candy.

After they record their estimates, open my bag of Raisinets, look inside, and decide whether to change the first estimation. Use think-aloud to model my decision-making process, and write what I am thinking on the board.

Have the students do the same, and give time for recording their new estimates and rationales.

Pour my Raisinets on the overhead where they can be counted by students. Record the actual number on the chart paper. Remind students that I'd like to eat my Raisinets, too, but I won't because it will mess up my data collection. Discuss how my estimate and the actual number might be different, the reasons why, and record some of our thinking as we talk about the problem.

Have students open their bags, pour the candy on the paper plate, and count each individual piece. Compare their estimates with the actual count and record their thinking on the group's chart paper. Have each student select a different color marker with which to record his or her response (accountability!) and write his or her name by the response.

Say: "Now we have a problem. I want each member of the group to have an equal number of Raisinets as a treat this afternoon!" Remind them that now that they have an accurate total, they must divide the candy equally among the group members. Instruct them to think about *how* they are going to go about solving the problem, and write on chart paper their ideas, methods, and so on. Ask them to remember to show their work, and describe their thinking to show others in the class how they solved the problem. Tell each step you took in the process.

Discussion

Ask students: Did you find a fair way to share the candy? Why or why not? How many pieces of candy did each member get? How do you know that you are right?

Once charts and individual papers are checked, allow students to eat the Raisinets. After finishing the snack, invite each group to share their group's work and thinking process with the large group to compare strategies used by each group.

Have students write a reflective piece about the activity and their thinking as closure to the lesson.

Impact and Refinement of Lesson

Not only did I teach this lesson, I also had it videotaped. Wow! It is too bizarre to watch yourself teach. I was aware of the camera and the fact that my university supervisor was observing this lesson. Overall the lesson went well, but there were some lulls in the timing. I think it will go much better when I do it again with another group of students. As I reflected on the video, I noticed places where I didn't follow up on some students' comments. As I watched, I thought, "Why didn't I say this or that?" I wish I had paid more attention to the individual papers the students were writing so I could have corrected some thinking at strategic points. There are 29 students in this class, and it is difficult to give the attention each of them needs. I felt pressured to finish on time, too, so I rushed through some parts, especially toward the end of the lesson. The children enjoyed the lesson, and reflecting about their own thinking was challenging for many of them. In this lesson, I was able to meet a number of learning styles and preferences. I used verbal instructions, models, and hands-on activities. The students worked individually and in small groups, and presented their thinking to the large group for discussion and comparison purposes.

Next time, I would tweak the lesson and make my objectives clearer to the students, and discuss the importance of knowing how we think and make decisions in school and in the real world.

High School Lesson Plan: English

Name: Kathy Knopf Schum

Type of Lesson:	INTRODUCTION TO SHORT STORY UNIT—CHARACTERIZATION AND PLOT
Level:	9TH GRADE
Materials:	OVERHEAD OR BOARD, COPIES OF ELEMENTS WORKSHEET
Time:	50 minutes

Objectives

Given teacher's explanation, students will:

1. Identify at least three characteristics of the short story genre and the seven methods of characterization.
2. Define the terms *setting, tone, antagonist,* and *protagonist.*
3. List three different forms of conflict.

Assessment

Assessment will include student responses to oral question, written notes, and writer response on in-class activity.

Motivation

Students will use dramas and TV sitcoms to introduce short stories.

Procedure

Teacher Activity	Student Response
Short stories are like dramas and sitcoms in that their primary *purpose is to entertain.* What TV programs fit this description?	Take notes and respond to questions relating to analogy. *Ally McBeal* *Dawson's Creek*
Second, they usually *focus on one theme or event* (everything contributes to one outcome).	
Third, there are a limited number of characters.	
Fourth, they have a tightly structured plot (introduction exposition, rising action, climax, falling action, denouement).	Write characteristics on the board for students to copy into notes.
Finally, they are short and complete in themselves.(Even *Cheers* has a story told each episode.)	
What is one of the first things you need when you write?	
Characters must be developed by authors (they don't just happen). They can be developed at different levels, from simple to complex, flat to round.	Listen and respond to questions.

List Seven Methods of Characterization

1. What does the character look like?
2. Where does the character live, work, and play?
3. What does the character think about?
4. How does the character speak?
5. How does the character react to people, places, and things?
6. How do other characters react to this character?
7. What does the author think about the character?

Take notes on methods of characterization.

Walk to empty chair and announce that Stanley Realbozo (or some other character) is seated there. Explain that we as a class will bring him to life.

Lead discussion in which all previous questions are answered in order to flesh out Stanley.

Assemble a composite picture of Stanley and "decide what to do with him." We will write a story with Stanley as our main character. He is now a member of our class. We have enrolled him in 9th-grade English.

Answer questions on the board to develop this character.

Explain: Stories have to be planned like a blueprint of a house. In a short story, the plot is the blueprint in the writer's plan for writing the story. Point of view: We will be third-person omniscient, that is, we will know everything about the character. (Other options: first-person or third-person objective.)

Write out the five stages of plot in question form:

1. What is the situation of the story? (Discuss the terms *setting* and *mood.*).
2. What is the main conflict of the story? What are the generating circumstances and what gets the actions going? (Discuss the different

Take notes in class.

forms of conflict—(person versus person, person versus self, and person versus God, nature, or humankind.) Also, discuss the terms *protagonist* (main character) and *antagonist* (one or ones who try to thwart the main character). What events in the story increase the conflict and push forward action? What is the theme or purpose?

3. What is the climax or highest point of the story?
4. How is the conflict resolved?
5. How does the story end?

Discuss these five questions in terms of the Stanley Realbozo story.

Completion of questions will result in a full-blown short story.

What is the theme or purpose?

Reflection

Students seemed to listen more to each other after I began writing their comments on the board. I still need to allow more wait time after asking higher level questions.

High School Lesson Plan: Computer Applications

Name: Stacy Johnson   **Grade level:** 9th grade

Subject: COMPUTER APPLICATIONS   **# of students:** 16

Major content: SPREADSHEETS AND CHARTS INTEGRATED WITH ECONOMICS

# of Students with IEP: 8   **Unit title:** Microsoft Excel

Objectives

1. Students will review the steps for creating Excel spreadsheets and charts.
2. Students will demonstrate knowledge of vocabulary orally and in writing.
3. Students will apply the steps for creating Excel spreadsheets and charts by working with a partner to complete a stock market project.

Connections

3.4 *Students demonstrate ability to be resourceful and creative.* Students will have the opportunity to be resourceful and creative by designing a cover page for their stock market project. They will be able to pull from what they learned in Microsoft Word and from their own unique style.

5.3 *Students organize information to develop or change their understanding of a concept.* Students will be working with partners to gather information from the newspaper and then organize it by developing an Excel spreadsheet. They will have the opportunity to see firsthand a real-life application.

5.4 *Students use a decision-making process to make informed decisions among options.* Students will be working cooperatively with partners to decide on the types of stock they wish to purchase as well and the number to reach their goal of "Closest to $10,000." They will have many options and will need to weigh each decision carefully.

6.1.1 *Students connect knowledge and experiences from different subject areas.* In completing the stock market project, students will be able to draw on experiences they had in grade school, their current math classes, and other knowledge they may have with respect to Excel or the stock market. By drawing on these experiences they are enhancing their ability to complete a successful project.

Context

Students have been studying vocabulary and learning how to create, format, and develop formulas through step-by-step instruction and one-on-one interaction and by practicing with Excel spreadsheets and charts on their own. They have been formally assessed on spreadsheets by taking a written and skills test. Before they will be formally assessed on charts they will complete a project that demonstrates their total understanding of Excel spreadsheets and charts.

Resources
- overhead projector
- example of stock market information (teacher demonstration)
- 17 computers
- computer and television
- stock market project rubric
- Excel charts quiz

Procedures

5 minutes	Take attendance, assign homework and review class agenda and goals and objectives.
3–5 minutes	Assigned student gives Tech Tip presentation. (Students select and prepare 3–minute reports on technology topics read from current newspaper, magazine, etc.)
5–7 minutes	Review with students how to create charts and graphs and printing procedures, and answer any questions they may have. Allow for several minutes to review notes and handouts before quiz. (Some students need time to quietly prepare; this usually increases their success with a written vocabulary quiz.)
15–20 minutes	Administer quiz to students. As they finish, have them turn over their paper and sit quietly until everyone has finished. Once everyone has finished, students will grade their own paper and correct errors using a marker or different color pen. I will collect them to record in grade book.
Transition	Explain to students that it is important not only to be able to complete activities and take tests on various topics and concepts, but also to be able to see how they can be beneficial in real-life situations.
5–6 minutes	Introduce the stock market project. Start out by asking students questions about previous experiences with the stock market. Clarify their understanding and solicit feedback in the form of both positive and negative experiences. Students need to be successful and have an idea of any obstacles they may have experienced in the past so it does not happen now.
3–5 minutes	Demonstrate how to read the stock market information in the newspaper using the overhead projector, and answer any questions students may have.
5–6 minutes	Hand out the rubric used to grade students and go through the requirements with them step by step. Stop and check for understanding and answer any questions. Also assign the due date and have students write that on their rubric.
Transition	Instruct students on what the procedure will be for this project: First, they will be assigned a partner; second, they will get a folder (from me); third, they will need to find some space at the tables with their partner to choose stocks and write down closing costs; fourth, they will return their folder to me and then go to a computer with their partner to complete the assignment. (Assigning partners allows me to match students so those who need peer assistance have it.)
2–3 minutes	Allow students time to meet with partner, get their folder, and find a place to work. Then remind students to return folders

	with newspapers neatly folded before going over to the computers.
20–25 minutes	Allow students time to work with partners at the tables and then the computers. Visit the partners at the tables to answer questions. Once students have chosen stocks and amounts, they will move to the computers where the technology leader will assist me in answering questions.
5 minutes (wrap-up)	Remind students of homework assignment: skills test on March 25 and written test on March 27, both covering spreadsheets and charts. We will have a workday on March 19 for the stock market project and a review day on March 21 for tests. Give a final reminder that the project is due on March 25.

Student Self-Assessment

Students will evaluate themselves as they correct their own quiz. This will help them to check understanding of vocabulary. The student who presented her Tech Tip will also evaluate herself on her presentation including being on time, having a neat copy of the article, creating a representation of the article, and delivering the presentation. As the teacher I reserve the right to adjust the grade based on my evaluation of the presentation.

Teacher Assessment

I will be able to informally assess students by observing them as they work with their partners at the tables gathering information to complete the stock market project. I will formally assess students by grading their completed projects. Additional formal assessments will take place the week before spring break as students take a written and skills test covering Excel spreadsheets and charts to complete this unit.

Impact

At the end of each unit students are assigned a project to demonstrate their understanding of concepts that were learned in previous lessons. The stock market project was designed to use real-life scenarios to produce a product using Excel spreadsheets and charts.

The major focus of this lesson was to explain, in detail, the expectations of the project, distribute and explain the rubric for grading the project, and provide time for students to get started working with their partners. In addition, this project was a life lesson, which gave students the opportunity to work with a partner and to gain valuable insight about how to make decisions and how to communicate with each other to complete an assignment on time.

Refinement

Overall I was pleased with the lesson, the pace of the class, and the students' response to the assigned project. After having time to reflect on this lesson and talk with my college supervisor, there are a couple of adjustments that I will make when I teach this lesson again: (1) check students' understanding of the project *prior to* assigning partners—I seemed to lose them once they found partners; and (2) when asking questions, use "Do you want to . . . " or "Make a mental note of what you need to work on." Some students seemed not to hear what I was asking them to do.

In addition, it was difficult for me to find the time to get around to all the groups. As some finished the first part of the assignment and moved to the computers to complete the rest of the assignment, I had to rely on the technology leader to assist the students at the computers while I worked with the groups still choosing their stocks. Sometimes I am frustrated that I am not able to assist all students.

Ninth-Grade Computer Applications
Stock Market Project Rubric

Name _____ Date due _____

Possible points _____   Your score_____

  I. Cover Sheet   10
     _____

    a. Appropriate clip art
    b. Names of partners
    c. Neat and creative

 II. Spreadsheet   15
     _____

    a. Eight to ten stocks
    b. Worksheet completely filled in
    c. Printout showing correct formatting
    d. Printout showing formulas

III. Charts   15
     _____

    a. Correct representation of data
    b. Appropriate title, legend, and labels
    c. Pie chart
    d. Bar chart

IV. Miscellaneous   10
     _____

    a. Rubric for each partner
    b. Worked together
    c. Good use of class time
    d. Completed on time

Total possible points   50
     _____

Comments:

_____
_____
_____
_____
_____
_____
_____
_____
_____

Stock Market Directions

Task One: Getting Started
- You and your partner have been given $10,000 to spend on purchasing stocks. You need to see me for a folder with a newspaper.
- Sitting at the tables or desks with your partner, go through the newspaper and choose 8–10 stocks and then complete the table below. You will do your calculations at the computer.
- Return to me the folder and newspaper neatly folded before going to a computer.

Stock Market Project by Partners Names			
Stock name (abbr.)	Number of shares	Cost per share	Value of stock
1.			(number of shares × cost per share)
2.			
3.			
4.			
5.			
6.			
7.			
8.			
9.			
10.			
Totals	(sum number of shares)	(sum total cost)	Sum value (not to exceed $10,000)

Task Two: Creating a Spreadsheet with Calculations
- At the computer, you and your partner need to create a spreadsheet with the above information.
- If necessary, in the *Cost per Share* column use decimals (to two places) versus using fractions. Example: 63 2/3 should appear as $63.75.
- Calculate the value of each share by multiplying the number of shares by the cost per share.
- Calculate the total number of shares, cost per share, and the value of stock. If necessary, add or delete the number of shares you are purchasing to get your total amount as close to $10,000 as possible. You cannot exceed that amount. The group getting closest will win a special prize.
- Save the file as STMARKET on the G drive.

Task Three: Creating Pie Charts
- Using the information from your spreadsheet in Task Two, create the following three pie charts. Be sure to label them properly.
  1. Create a pie chart that shows percentage of shares.
  2. Create a pie chart that shows percentage of cost.
  3. Create a pie chart that shows percentage of value of each share.
- Format all charts so that text, labels, and values are displayed.
- Save each chart to the G drive.

Task Four: Creating a Cover Page
- Create a cover page with an appropriate clip art—adjust to fill the page.
- Add names of partners and title the paper "Stock Market Project."

Task Five: Printing Spreadsheet and Charts
- Print the spreadsheet using proper formatting (it is not necessary to put a header with cover page):
  - Row and column headings
  - Gridlines
  - Spell Check
  - Fit to one page
  - Print Preview
- Print the spreadsheet showing formulas:
  - Fit to one page
  - Print Preview
- Print the three charts as "Chart1," not as embedded charts. Make sure to check "sheet."
- Print the cover page:
  - Spell Check
  - Check margins
  - Print Preview

Task Six: Putting It All Together
- Assemble the materials in the following order, staple, and turn it in:
  - Cover page
  - Formatted spreadsheet
  - Formula spreadsheet
  - Three pie charts
  - Rubric for each partner

Rubric for Designing Lessons and Instructional Materials

Distinguished	Proficient	Apprentice	Novice
Learner Goals			
1. Focuses instruction on one or more learning goals and outcomes.	1. Learning outcomes are well developed according to the concept being taught.	1. Learning outcomes are limited and lack sources.	1. Learning outcomes are unrelated to procedure.
Integration of Curriculum			
2. Integrate skills, thinking processes, and content across the disciplines.	2. Evidence of integration of skills, thinking processes, and content across disciplines.	2. An attempt to integrate skills.	2. Minimal attention to integrate across disciplines.
Instructional Materials			
3. Proposes learning experiences that challenge, motivate, and actively involve the learners.	3. Proposes learning experiences that involve the learner.	3. Random learning experiences that involve the learner.	3. Random and/or weak organization or plan involving the learner.
4. Proposes learning experiences that are developmentally appropriate for learners.	4. Proposes learning experiences that are appropriate for learners on the level being taught.	4. Unelaborated development of ideas and details of learning experiences for learners on the level being taught.	4. Minimal development of ideas and disciplines of learning experience for learners on the level being taught.
5. Incorporates strategies that address physical, social, and cultural diversity.	5. Demonstrates sensitivity to differences.	5. Little or no attention to cultural diversity.	5. Cultural diversity inclusion is missing.
6. Includes comprehensive and appropriate school and community resources that support learning.	6. Includes appropriate school and community resources that support learning.	6. Few school community resources are included to support learning.	6. No mention of school and community resources to support learning.
7. Includes learning experiences that encourage students to be adaptable, flexible, resourceful, and creative.	7. Includes learning experiences that encourage students to be flexible and resourceful.	7. Learning experiences are controlled and unelaborated.	7. Learning experiences lack focus.
Use of Computers/Technology			
8. Includes creative and appropriate use of technology as a tool to enhance student learning.	8. Illustrates use of technology with learners.	8. Little mention of technology use by learner.	8. No technology is mentioned.
Learner Assessment			
9. Includes appropriate assessment strategies and processes.	9. Includes acceptable assessment strategies and processes.	9. Assessment strategies and processes are simplistic and do not match outcomes.	9. Assessment is inappropriate.

Professional Portfolio Assessment Criteria

The student teaching/intern experience provides you with multiple opportunities to perform and reflect on your progress under the guidance of supervising teachers from the school and college setting. Professional portfolio development tasks and the rubric are designed to assist you in becoming an excellent teacher candidate who can compile an outstanding teaching portfolio. Performance of the criteria stated after each of the standards is rated using code numbers 1 through 4. An explanation of the code numbers is given below.

Code 4—Outstanding

The portfolio contains all important components and communicates ideas clearly.

The portfolio samples and narratives demonstrate in-depth understanding of the relevant concepts and processes needed in teaching and learning.

Where appropriate, the student offers insightful interpretations or extensions (generalizations, applications, analogies) of effective teaching and assessment.

Code 3—Competent

The portfolio contains most important components and communicates ideas clearly.

The portfolio samples and narratives demonstrate understanding of major concepts of teaching; omits or misrepresents some less important ideas or details.

Code 2—Developing

The portfolio contains some important components and communicates these clearly.

The portfolio samples and narratives demonstrate that there are gaps in his or her conceptual understanding of teaching and learning.

Code 1—Beginning

The portfolio shows minimal understanding of necessary components.
The portfolio samples lack evidence of concepts/processes necessary in effective teaching and learning.

EXAMPLE: PORTFOLIO RESPONSE

(Eighth-grade social studies and language arts)

Standard: Creating and Maintaining a Learning Climate

In creating and maintaining a learning climate, teachers are faced with a tough task. To be an effective classroom manager, a teacher must be well prepared and exhibit good planning techniques. As an educator, I must first be in touch with my own feelings about life, culture, children, and the educational process. I bring with me to the table a set of values and beliefs shaped by my own background, upbringing, and experiences. I must first see myself as a person, as someone with feelings, emotions, and beliefs. It is imperative that I am aware of these factors and how they influence my teaching. Students are going to have a whole different set of backgrounds and experiences of their own. This fact shouldn't be taken lightly.

I am able to effectively communicate with my students; therefore, I must understand from where they come. Communication is key. It is the essential component of teaching and learning, and without it neither can occur. I must communicate what is and isn't acceptable in my classroom, and I also have to set and enforce rules (via consequences). My goal as classroom manager is to maximize the amount of student learning time, and unacceptable behavior jeopardizes this goal. Therefore, my expectations of student behavior must be clear and firm. It is vital that I create an atmosphere conducive to learning and immediately discourage any behavior that threatens that atmosphere.

I use preventive disciplinary approaches and have found that the best way to deal with a problem is to identify it immediately, label it as unacceptable, and implement subsequent consequences. During the first days of classes, I post a set of classroom rules and make sure that students know and understand these and the consequences. This process helps them realize that they are accountable for their actions. I have also discovered that establishing daily routines is helpful in minimizing distractions. Clearly stating to students that they are expected to come into the class, sit down, take out a pen and some paper, and begin quietly writing a response to a question displayed on the overhead has worked beautifully for me. If the students aren't awarded opportunities to misbehave at the beginning of class, it will be much easier to hold their attention for an extended period of time. As I've been told and have learned through my own experience, "once you've lost them, it's very difficult to get them back!"

During my student teaching experience I have taught several special needs students. I have students who have impaired hearing disabilities, muscular dystrophy, and cerebral palsy. I wear a highly sensitive microphone attachment so the one student can listen as I speak and I make sure he can see the TV captions and writing on the board. The student in the wheelchair needs other physical arrangements and special books with enlarged print. I am grateful to have had the opportunity to teach these special needs kids. I am inspired by their determination and work ethic. They will not be denied anything! They believe in themselves and are determined to achieve whatever they set their minds to.

There are also cultural and social differences among the students I teach. I have students who live in fancy neighborhoods with elaborate homes and those who live in inner-city housing projects. It has been an eye-opening experience observing these students as they develop their cliques and discuss their common experiences. In walking by (in the lunchroom) a group of students from the projects, I heard them discuss their relatives being associated with and being killed by gangs. At the same table the suburban students were discussing what they were planning for the weekend or what happened last night on *The X-Files*. It is imperative that I recognize differences among students' experiences and invite students to share these.

In a lesson on limericks I encouraged them to write on any topic and use humor, and I found that the freedom to choose actually enhanced the quality of students' work.

I have planned and taught lessons that require students to perform in many different ways. In a mini-lesson about amiable characteristics, I had students create their own epitaphs and include all the amiable characteristics they thought they possessed. When they had finished writing, we began sharing their epitaphs. However, two students were talking and creating a disruption, so I exclaimed in a weeping voice, "Excuse me, Ebony, but it seem that someone is being so rude as to speak during this solemn occasion. Have you no respect? We are paying our respects to the late, great, wonderful Ebony! How rude—and you're not even wearing black!" I then briefly discussed the importance of listening to one another out of respect. It worked wonderfully and I think the students responded well.

Students work individually and within the large group. Each class period begins with a learning log activity in which the students respond to a question related to the day's lesson. I often organize students into small groups and they act as peer editors of each other's written work. When dealing with groups, I think I display an awareness of the on-goings within the classroom ("withitness"— Kounin). It was clear to the students that I would seek out and correct undesirable behaviors. Students were aware of my expectations concerning classroom behavior. They knew that I would circulate, monitor their behavior, and hold them accountable for their work in small groups. I always checked to be certain that each member was contributing to the completion of the task. I sometimes observed them closely and used proximity control to influence their participation. Other times I would observe from a distance and quietly approach individuals and ask that they join in. I would stand there until they cooperated. I also reminded students that working together often results in higher quality work and that each member's participation was essential to the completion of the task (positive interdependence).

Finally, I think I engaged in teacher/student interactions that contributed to establishing a learning environment. I really pushed some students as group members, and being persistent I was able to get each student to contribute. I give students options, ask them to choose, and then circulate to observe how they follow through with their decisions. I have learned that keeping students engaged contributes much to the classroom environment.

appendix

G

Evaluation Forms

Student Form

Student name _____ Language arts teacher _____

Date _____ Class _____

We have been reading the book _____ by _____

It is _____ fiction, written in _____ style.

While reading this book, I learned _____

We have kept a reader response journal while reading the novel. A good reader response entry includes _____

_____

Parent-Teacher-Student Conference Notes

My reader response journal is interesting to read. The entry dated _____ is my best entry

because _____

The entry dated _____ needs more reflection because _____

My writing portfolio includes _____

from _____ grade. To date, _____ grade pieces include: _____

At this point, I think my strength in written communication is _____

As a writer, I would like to be able to _____

In order to reach this goal, I will _____

I could rework this entry as a(n) _____

The entry dated _____ needs more reflection because _____

I could make this more interesting by _____

I have participated by _____

One way I could improve my participation is to _____

As an independent reader, I would rate myself as

   Outstanding _____   Satisfactory _____   Needs Improvement _____

I have read the following books and selected one for a book talk, book review, or presentation in class.

Title _____ Author _____ No. of pages _____ Rating _____

WRITING

Student and Teacher Evaluation

Student Evaluation

Date _____ Title of piece _____

Name_____ Grade _____ Section _____

1	2	3	4	The idea for my writing is creative. I have brainstormed and selected my best ideas to write an original piece.
1	2	3	4	This piece of writing "sounds" like me. It has style!
1	2	3	4	My writing makes sense. There is an introduction, a middle, and an ending.
1	2	3	4	Events happen in a logical and sequential order.
1	2	3	4	Each paragraph is indented.
1	2	3	4	Each paragraph has a topic sentence and supporting details.
1	2	3	4	Each sentence is interesting to read. The length is varied, and the thought is complete.
1	2	3	4	My choice of vocabulary is perfect for my piece of writing. The words are exciting and colorful. I have used a thesaurus.
1	2	3	4	I have reread my piece and added details, explanations, adjectives, and/or dialogue to make my writing electric.
1	2	3	4	I have checked: possessives, plurals, subject and verb, and person.
1	2	3	4	I have capitalized proper nouns and adjectives.
1	2	3	4	I have checked my writing for punctuation. [., ?, !," ", ( ) _____].
1	2	3	4	I have checked my writing thoroughly for misspelled words.
1	2	3	4	I have rewritten my final draft using my best handwriting.
1	2	3	4	I think this piece is my best work yet, and I am ready to publish.

I am (satisfied/not satisfied) with this piece of writing because _____

_____

Teacher Evaluation

1   2   3   4   Idea: _____

_____

1   2   3   4   Voice: _____

_____

1   2   3   4   Content: _____

_____

1   2   3   4   Organization: _____

_____

1   2   3   4   Sentences: _____

_____

1   2   3   4   Vocabulary: _____

_____

1   2   3   4   Grammar: _____

_____

1   2   3   4   Punctuation: _____

_____

1   2   3   4   Spelling: _____

_____

MIDDLE GRADES INDEPENDENT READER RESPONSE QUESTIONS

Independent Reading Log

Daily Minimum Requirement

20 Minutes Reading + A written response to the literature = a healthy lifelong habit that is fun!

Select an appropriate question and respond to what you have read by writing a reader response in your independent reading notebook. (If you would like to respond to the story on your own, that is acceptable.)

The questions are designed to help you get started writing and focus your thinking. Have fun! I am very interested in what you have to say. Remember to write the date at the top of each entry and the pages you have read. Example: April 16 (Pages 1–22).

1. . . . Based on the title, what do you think the book will be about?
2. . . . After scanning the chapter titles, what are some things you noticed?
3. . . . What comes to mind (image or idea, feeling, sensation, memory) now that you have read the title and opening paragraphs?
4. . . . What questions might you have after reading the first few pages or the first chapter?
5. . . . What are you expecting from this writer now that you have read the first couple of chapters?
6. . . . As you read, what caught your attention?
7. . . . As you read, what new images did you form?
8. . . . Were there words you did not understand or parts that did not make sense?
9. . . . What is in your mind (image, idea, feeling, sensation, memory) now that you have read further?
10. . . . As you read, what happened to your first impression of a character?
11. . . . Now that you have completed the entire novel (story), what realizations do you have?
12. . . . What interpretations and ideas have you gotten from the book?
13. . . . Now that you have completed the entire book, what do you think about a character's actions? About his/her decisions?
14. . . . If you were to write the author of this text (book, story, poem), what would you say to him/her?
15. . . . What tips would you give to readers who are just starting to read this story or novel?

Additional Response Suggestions

1. Design a character map—illustrate the relationship between the main character and minor characters.
2. Illustrate how a character changes over time or responds to events in the story or book.
3. Trace the plot of the book or story by creating a story ladder. (The above suggestions will need to be added to as the story unfolds.
4. Illustrate a favorite scene and write the book's description beneath your drawing.
5. Select favorite quotes from the book or story and tell why they were interesting to you.

6. Select phrases or passages from the book that you would like to imitate in your own writing.
7. Write a new ending to the book.
8. Write a dialogue between two characters that could have taken place. Be sure to use quotation marks.
9. Jot down anything you noticed about the author's style of writing: adjectives, a special theme, use of odd words, suspense, and so on.
10. Compare the book to another you have read by the same author or a different author.

Still Stuck?

1. I began to think of . . .
2. I wonder why . . .
3. I know the feeling . . .
4. I noticed . . .

EVALUATION OF STUDENT ORAL PRESENTATION

Name _____ Date _____

Type of Presentation

1. Voice is pleasant—natural tonal quality   1 _____ 2 _____ 3 _____ 4 _____

Comments _____

2. Voice is projected   1 _____ 2 _____ 3 _____ 4 _____

Comments _____

3. Speech is at conversational speed   1 _____ 2 _____ 3 _____ 4 _____

Comments _____

4. Words are clearly enunciated   1 _____ 2 _____ 3 _____ 4 _____

Comments _____

5. Fillers are avoided (*ah, like, you know . . .*)   1 _____ 2 _____ 3 _____ 4 _____

Comments _____

6. Vocal emphasis used for key words, sentences   1 _____ 2 _____ 3 _____ 4 _____

Comments _____

7. Enthusiastic, vibrant   1 _____ 2 _____ 3 _____ 4 _____

Comments _____

8. Volume and rate of speed varied to show emotion   1 _____ 2 _____ 3 _____ 4 _____

Comments _____

9. Able to hold audience's attention   1 _____ 2 _____ 3 _____ 4 _____

Comments _____

10. Appropriate gestures and facial expressions   1 _____ 2 _____ 3 _____ 4 _____

Comments _____

11. Posture is erect, comfortable, appropriate   1 _____ 2 _____ 3 _____ 4 _____

Comments _____

12. Eye contact with audience is maintained   1 _____ 2 _____ 3 _____ 4 _____

Comments _____

H

Addresses for State Offices of Certification

Alabama
Teacher Recruitment and Placement
State Dept. of Education
Montgomery, AL 36130-2101
334-242-9935
FAX: (334)-242-4998
http://www.alsde.edu/general/SDE_Directory.pdf

Alaska
Applications and Vacancies
Dept. of Education
801 W. 10th St., Ste. 200
Juneau, AK 99801-1894
907-465-2831
http://www.alaskateacher.org Fax: 907-465-2441

Arizona
Teacher Certification
Unit-70016
PO Box 6490
Phoenix, AZ 85005-6490
602-542-4367
http://www.ade.state.az.us/cert_emp.asp

Arkansas
Office of Professional Licensure
Arkansas Dept. of Education
4 State Capitol Mall
Little Rock, AR 72201-1071
501-682-4342
http://www.arkedu.state.ar.us/teachers

California
Commission on Teacher Credentialing
Box 944270
Sacramento, CA 95814
916-657-2451
http://www.ca.gov/ctc

Colorado
Educator Licensing
State Dept. of Education
201 E. Colfax Ave.
Denver, CO 80203-1799
303-866-6600

FAX: 303-830-0793
http://www.ctc.ca.gov
http://cde.state.co.us/index_license.htm

Connecticut
Connecticut State Dept. of Education
Bureau of Certification and Professional Development
PO Box 150471, Rm. 243
Hartford, CT 06115-0471
860-713-6969
FAX: 860-713-7017
http://www.state.ct.us/sde/dtl/cert/indes.htm

Delaware
Delaware Dept. of Education
Teacher Certification
PO Box 1402
Dover, DE 19903
302-739-4686
FAX 302-739-4654
http://www.doe.state.de.us

District of Columbia
State Education Office
441 Fourth St., NW, Ste. 920 S
Washington, DC 20001
(202)-727-6436
http://www.dc.gov/citizen/sec/index.htm

Florida
Florida Dept. of Education
Bureau of Educator Certification
Ste. 201, Turlington Building
325 W. Gaines St.
Tallahassee, FL 32399-0400
850-488-2317
800-445-6739
http://www.firn.edu/doe/edcert

Georgia
Georgia Professional Standards Commission
Two Peachtree St., Ste. 6000
Atlanta, GA 30303
404-657-9000
800-869-7775

FAX: 404-651-9185
E-mail: mail@gapsc.com
http://www.doe.k12.ga.us/index_teacher.asp

Hawaii
Office of Personnel Services
Teacher Recruitment Unit
PO Box 2360
Honolulu, HI 96804
808-586-3420
800-305-5104 (Cont. U.S. & Alaska)
http://www.K12.hi.us~personnl/license.html

Idaho
Teacher Certification
Idaho Dept. of Education
PO Box 83720
Boise, ID 83720-0027
208-332-6680
FAX: 208-332-6880
http://www.sde.state.id.us/certification

Illinois
Illinois State Board of Education
Division of Professional Certification
100 N. First St.
Springfield, IL 62777
800-845-8749
217-524-1289
http://www.isbe.state.il.us/teachers/Default.htm

Indiana
Indiana Professional Standards Board
101 W. Ohio St., Ste. 300
Indianapolis, IN 46204
317-232-9010
FAX: 317-232-9023
http://www.in.gov.psb/licensing

Iowa
Board of Educational Examiners
Dept. of Education
Grimes State Office Building
Des Moines, IA 50319-0146
515-281-5294
515-242-5988
http://www.state.ia.us/educate/boee/require.html

Kansas
Certification and Teacher Education
Kansas State Dept. of Education
120 S.E. 10th Ave.
Topeka, KS 66612-1182
785-291-3678
FAX: 785-296-7933
http://www.ksbe.state.ks.us

Kentucky
Kentucky Dept. of Education
Division of Certification
1024 Capital Center Dr.

Frankfort, KY 40601
502-573-4606
http://www.kde.state.ky.us

Louisiana
Louisiana Dept. of Education
Teacher Certification, Rm. 700
PO Box 94064
Baton Rouge, LA 70804-9064
504-342-3490
877-453-2721
http://www.doe.state.la.us
http://www.teachlouisiana.net

Maine
Certification Services
Dept. of Education
State House Station 23
Augusta, ME 04333
207-287-5944
http://www.state.me.us/education/cert

Maryland
Maryland State Dept. of Education
ATT: Certification Branch
200 W. Baltimore St.
Baltimore, MD 21201
410-767-0412
http://www.msde.md.us/certification

Massachusetts
Massachusetts Dept. of Education
Office of Teacher Licensure
350 Main St.
Malden, MA 02148
781-388-3000
http://www.doe.mass.edu/educators

Michigan
Michigan Dept. of Education
Office of Professional Preparation & Certification
PO Box 3008
Lansing, MI 48909
517-373-3310
http://www.michigan.gov/mde

Minnesota
Minnesota Dept. of Children, Families and Learning
Personnel Licensing
1500 Hwy. 36 W
Roseville, MN 55113-4266
651-582-8691
FAX: 651-582-8809
http://cfl.state.mn.us

Mississippi
Mississippi Dept. of Education
Educator Licensure/Certification
PO Box 771
359 N. West St.
Jackson, MS 39205-0771

601-359-3515
http://www.mde.k12.ms.us/license

Missouri
Missouri Dept. of Elementary and Secondary
    Education
Teacher Certification
PO Box 480
Jefferson City, MO 65102
573-751-3486
FAX: 573-751-8613
http://www.dese.state.mo.us

Montana
Certification Division
Montana Office of Public Instruction
PO Box 202501
Helena, MT 59620-2501
406-444-3150
888-231-9393
http://www.opi.state.mt.us

Nebraska
Teacher Certification
Nebraska Dept. of Education
301 Centennial Mall S
Box 94987
Lincoln, NE 68509-4987
800-371-4642
http://www.nde.state.ne.us

Nevada
Nevada Dept. of Education
Teacher Licensing Office
700 E. Fifth St.
Carson City, NV 89701
775-687-9115
FAX: 775-687-9101
http://www.nde.state.nv.us/licensure

New Hampshire
Bureau of Credentialing
State Dept. of Education
101 Pleasant St.
Concord, NH 03301
603-271-2407
http://www.ed.state.nh.us/certification/teacher.htm

New Jersey
New Jersey Dept. of Education
ATT: Office of Licensing and Academic
Credentials
100 River View Plaza
CN 503
Trenton, NJ 08625-0500
609-984-0905
http://www.state.nj.us/njed/educators/license

New Mexico
State of New Mexico Dept. of Education
Professional Licensure

300 Don Gaspar
Santa Fe, NM 87501-2786
505-827-6587
http://www.sde.state.nm.us

New York
New York State Education Dept.
Office of Teaching
Albany, NY 12224
518-4740-3901/2/3/4
E-mail:tcert@mailnysed.gov
http://www.nysed.gov/tcert

North Carolina
North Carolina Dept. of Public Instruction
Center for Recruitment & Retention
301 N. Wilmington St.
Raleigh, NC 27601-2825
919-733-4125
http://www.dpi.state.nc.us

North Dakota
North Dakota Dept. of Public Instruction
Teacher Licensure
State Capitol Bldg., 9th Floor
600 E. Boulevard Ave., Dept. 202
Bismarck, ND 58505-0080
701-328-2264
FAX: 701-328-2815
http://www.state.nd.us/esph

Ohio
Ohio Dept. of Education
Office for Certification/Licensure
25 S. Front St.
Columbus, OH 43215-4183
877-644-6388
http://www.ode.state.oh.us

Oklahoma
Oklahoma State Dept. of Education
2500 N. Lincoln Blvd.
Oklahoma City, OK 73105-4599
405-521-3301
FAX: 405-521-6205
http://www.sde.state.ok.us

Oregon
Oregon Dept. of Education
ODE Personnel Services
255 Capitol Street NE
Salem, OR 97310-0203
503-378-3569
FAX: 503-378-5156
http://www.ode.state.or.us

Pennsylvania
Pennsylvania Dept. of Education
Teacher Certification System
333 Market St.
Harrisburg, PA 17126-0333

717-783-6788
http://www.pde.state.pa.us

Rhode Island
Rhode Island Dept. of Education
Office of Teacher Certification
Shepard Building
255 Westminster St.
Providence, RI 02903-3400
401-222-4600
http://www.ridoe.net/teachers/ed_employment.htm

South Carolina
South Carolina Dept. of Education
Division of Teacher Quality
1015 Rutledge Building
1600 Gervais St.
Columbia, SC 29201
803-734-7896
http://www.sde.state.sc.us

South Dakota
South Dakota Dept. of Education and Cultural Affairs
Division of Education
Office of Policy & Accountability
700 Governors Dr.
Pierre, SD 57501-2291
605-773-5410
FAX: 605-773-6139
http://www.state.sd.us/deca

Tennessee
Tennessee Dept. of Education
Office of Teacher Licensing
710 James Robertson Pkwy.
5th Floor, Andrew Johnson Tower
Nashville, TN 37243-0377
615-532-4885
http://www.state.tn.us/edu.html

Texas
State Board for Educator Certification
Information and Support Center
1001 Trinity
Austin, TX 78701
888-863-5880
http://www.sbec.state.tx.us/index.htm

Utah
State Office of Education
Educator Licensing
250 E. 500 South
PO Box 144200
Salt Lake City, UT 84111-2400
801-538-7740
http://www.usoe.k12.ut.us

Vermont
Vermont Dept. of Education
Educator Licensing
120 State St.
Montpelier, VT 05620-2501
802-828-2445
E-mail: licensing@doe.state.vt.us
http://www.state.vt.us/educ

Virginia
Virginia Dept. of Education
Division of Teacher Education & Licensure
PO Box 2120
Richmond, VA 23218-2120
http://www.pen.k12.va.us/VDOE/newvdoe/teached.html

Washington
Washington State Board of Education
Professional Certification
Old Capitol Building
PO Box 47200
Olympia, WA 98504-7200
360-725-6400
FAX: 360-586-0145
E-mail: cert@ospi.wednet.edu
http://www.k.12.wa.us/cent

West Virginia
West Virginia Dept. of Education
Teacher Certification
1900 Kanawha Blvd.
East Charleston, WV 25305
800-982-2378
E-mail: mbowe@access.k12.wv.us
http://wvde.state.wv.us/certification

Wisconsin
Wisconsin Dept. of Public Instruction
Teacher Education and Licensing
Box 7841
Madison, WI 53707-7841
608-266-1027
FAX: 608-264-9558
http://www.dpi.state.wi.us

Wyoming
Wyoming Dept. of Education
Professional Teaching Standards Board
2300 Capitol Ave.
Hathaway Building, 2nd Floor
Cheyenne, WY 82002
307-777-6248
800-675-6893
FAX: 307-777-6234
E-mail: bmart@educ.state.wy.us
http://www.k12.wy.us

Index